STUDENTS, INVESTORS, BUSINESS PEOPLE, VIDEO GAME ENTHUSIASTS, COMPUTER HACKERS, CONSUMERS, TRAVELERS, RESEARCHERS . . .

Expand your personal computer to the limit of its power and potential by going online to computers and people all over the country.

Tap into the resources of hundreds of computer networks, many with useful free programs.

All the information you need to access the information you want is in

THE COMPUTER PHONE BOOK™ Guide to Using Online Systems

MIKE CANE has worked for a leading new electronic media market research firm and has also consulted on personal computers, data communications, and online database systems. He is the author of the companion volume to this book, *The Computer Phone Book™: Directory of Online Systems* (also available in a Plume edition).

THE COMPUTER PHONE BOOK™

Guide to Using Online Systems

by Mike Cane

A PLUME BOOK
NEW AMERICAN LIBRARY
NEW YORK AND SCARBOROUGH, ONTARIO

NAL BOOKS ARE AVAILABLE AT QUANTITY DISCOUNTS WHEN USED TO PROMOTE PRODUCTS OR SERVICES. FOR INFORMATION PLEASE WRITE TO PREMIUM MARKETING DIVISION, NEW AMERICAN LIBRARY, 1633 BROADWAY, NEW YORK, NEW YORK 10019

The Computer Phone Book™: *Guide to Using Online Systems* is the first of a two-volume, revised and expanded edition of *The Computer Phone Book*™. The second volume is *The Computer Phone Book*™: *Directory of Online Systems*.

Contacting the Author: The author of this book may be reached by conventional hardcopy mail only. Electronic mail is no longer being accepted. Mike Cane, 175 Fifth Avenue, Suite 3371, New York, New York, 10010. *Note*: Although all mail is read, I do not guarantee a reply. Remember, there is only one of me and thousands of you.

Equipment. This book was written and compiled with the following equipment: Commodore-64 computer, 1541 disk drive, VICModem, EasyScript word processing program, Vidtex-64 (version 4.0C), Card-A CardCo printer interface, Zenith amber monitor, and a Silver Reed EXP550 daisywheel printer.

SYSTEM REPRINTS AND ACKNOWLEDGMENTS.

The following individuals and companies have granted permission to reproduce their copyrighted online menus, prompts, illustrations, and help files: Bibliographic Retrieval Service, Inc.; Bill Blue; Business Computer Network, Inc.; Capital Cities Communications, Inc.; Ward Christensen & Randy Seuss; Collector's Data Service; The CommuniTree Group; CompuServe Information Service, Inc.; Dialog Information Services, Inc.; Dow Jones & Company, Inc.; GameMaster Corporation; General Videotex Corporation; Matchmaker Enterprises; MCI Communications Corporation; NewsNet, Inc.; PlayNet, Inc.; Steve Punter; Joe Simon/Bullett-80; Craig Vaughan/Software Sorcery, Inc; Source Tele Computing, Inc.; Taylor Electronics, Inc.; Western Union, Inc.

(The following page constitutes an extension of this copyright page.)

Bounce Back, Feedback, Forum, Online Today, Vidtex; Control Video Corporation: GameLine, MasterLine, Master Module; Dialog Information Services, Inc.: Knowledge Index; Digital Research, Inc: CP/M, DRI, GEM; Dow Jones & Company, Inc.: Barron's, Corporate Earnings Estimator, Dow Jones News/Retrieval Service, Dow Jones News Service, Dow Jones Quotes, News/Retrieval Sports Report, News/Retrieval Weather Report, The Wall Street Journal, The Wall Street Journal Highlights Online, Wall Street Week Online, Weekly Economic Survey, Weekly Economic Update; GameMaster Corporation: Cosmic Cartels, GameMaster; General Videotex Corporation: Delphi, Grouplink; International Business Machines, Inc: IBM, IBM PC, PC, Personal Computer, PCjr; Matchmaker Enterprises: Dial-Your-Match, DYM; MCI Communications Corporation: MCI Mail; NewsNet, Inc.: NewsNet; PARTICIPATE Systems, Inc: PARTICIPATE; PlayNet, Inc.: PlayNet, Quad-64, Sea Strike; Steve Punter: CBMBBS; Joe Simon/Bullet-80: Bullet-80; Craig Vaughan/Software Sorcery, Inc: ABBS, Apple Bulletin-Board System; Source Tele Computing, Inc.: THE SOURCE, SMail, SourceMail, SourceNet; Tandy Corp.: Color Computer, Tandy, TRS-80; Taylor Electronics, Inc.: MicroShare; United States Postal Service: E-COM, Electronic-Computer Originated Mail; Western Union, Inc.: EasyLink, Mailgram, Telex.

PERSONAL ACKNOWLEDGMENTS

The author would like to thank the following people who gave so graciously and generously of their time: Dave Panzl of PlayNET; Cathy Anderson of PlayNET; Nancy Beckman of THE SOURCE and her crack assistant, JoAnna Montgomery; Harlow Stevens of GameMaster; Bill Stern of MCI Mail; Andrea Krupa, Mel Howard, and Don Steinberg of Miller Communications; Robbie Kolman and Debra Miranda of BRS; Bobbie Massey of BCN; Marilyn Watson of Dow Jones; Gary Reibsamen of NewsNet; John Taylor of MicroShare; Gerry Barker of Startext; Wes Kussmaul of Delphi, and others too numerous to mention.

Library of Congress Cataloging in Publication Data

Cane, Mike.
The computer phone book.

On t.p. the registered trademark symbol "[tm]" is superscript following thc book in thc title.
Rev. and expanded ed. of: The computer phone book. 1983.
To be published in two volumes.
Contents: v. 1. Guide to using online systems.
1. On-line data processing—Directories. 2. Information storage and retrieval systems— Directories. 3. Data libraries—Directories.
4. Computer networks—Directories. I. Title.

QA76.55.C36 1985 004.6'16 85-15233
ISBN 0-452-25652-6 (v. 1)

PLUME TRADEMARK REG. U. S. PAT. OFF. AND FOREIGN COUNTRIES
REG. TRADEMARK—MARCA REGISTRADA
HECHO EN HARRISONBURG, VA., U. S.A.

SIGNET, SIGNET CLASSIC, MENTOR, PLUME, MERIDIAN and NAL BOOKS are published *in the United States* by New American Library, 1633 Broadway, New York, New York 10019, *in Canada* by The New American Library of Canada Limited, 81 Mack Avenue, Scarborough Ontario M1L 1M8

First Printing, June, 1986

1 2 3 4 5 6 7 8 9

PRINTED IN THE UNITED STATES OF AMERICA

In Memory
of my most precious
most beloved
cat

Backspace

September 15, 1985

ATTENTION!

This year I finally just might get around to publishing the long-awaited newsletter update of this book.

Send no money!

To get on the mailing list for a *free* copy of *The Computer Phone Book* newsletter (when it is published), just send your name and address to

CPB: The Computer Phone Book Update
175 Fifth Avenue, Suite 3371
New York, New York, 10010, USA

Do *not* send any money with your request. When the newsletter is finally published, you'll get a free copy, details about how to subscribe to it, and other really neat information. Send in your name *today* so you won't miss out.

Contents

Introduction: The Siamese twin syndrome

This is the first volume of the second edition of *The Computer Phone Book*™. In other words, you're holding just *half* of the second edition of *The Computer Phone Book*.

Let me explain.

The first edition, published in November 1983, contained the following:

- Descriptions of how to use 6 National Systems
- Listings of 15 National Systems
- Listings of 14 Local Systems
- Listings of 381 Bulletin-Board Systems (BBSs)

The manuscript was a little over 650 pages long.

By the time my publisher started talking about doing a second edition, National Systems started to pop up right and left, more Local Systems came online, and the number of new BBSs outpaced any baby boom.

When my research for a second edition was finished, I estimated a manuscript length of about 2400 pages.

After my editor was revived with some potent smelling salts, he came up with the idea of cutting the manuscript length in half and then splitting the book into two volumes:

- The first, which you hold in your hands, would cover the how-to-use aspects of online systems.
- The second, which I hope you will also buy, is the directory of online systems, *The Computer Phone Book*™: *Directory of Online Systems*.

Let me describe what you'll find in this half of the second edition of *The Computer Phone Book*:

- A clear explanation of the jargon you'll come across in computer communications
- Some sobering advice on the solemn and very serious task of buying a terminal program for your computer
- Descriptions of how to use 12 National Systems
- Descriptions of how 3 Local Systems work
- Descriptions of how to use the 5 most popular types of Bulletin-Board Systems
- Several appendixes filled with details about how to use 6 different types of BBSs

In between all of this material you'll find

- A cram course in how to use *any* online system
- Never-before-told tips on how to judge the design of any online system so you'll know if you're getting your money's worth or just a fast trip to the poorhouse
- And a closing chapter that, I promise, is *alone* worth the price of this book

As Lloyd Dobyns and Linda Ellerbee would say, "And so it goes."

—Mike Cane
1985

1 How to use this book

This book was written with these purposes in mind:

- To teach you how to use online systems
- To show you the majority of types of online systems that are available
- To provide you with a single volume of reference material about most online systems
- To expand your knowledge of online systems so you can develop a critical faculty in deciding which are the best and which are the best for you

Let's look at each of these.

To teach you how to use online systems. Even if you're currently a subscriber to an online system or a caller to a Bulletin-Board System (BBS), there are probably still some aspects of the system that you haven't mastered or that you thought were too complicated for you to understand and tackle. In this book, I explain the most complex aspects of the systems described, showing you step-by-step how to use them, with illustrations of the screens you'll see when you're actually online. With this book, you'll gain enough confidence to venture into parts of online systems you previously thought were over your head or too obscure to learn.

To show you the majority of types of online systems that are available. You won't find every online system represented here. Only most *types* of online systems. If every online system were represented in this book, it would never be published because it would forever be in the process of being written. Even if it were possible to get every system between the covers of one book, its cover price would be astronomical. Still, in this book you'll see a wider selection of online systems than ever before published in one book. This selection will be enough to provide you with the knowledge you'll need to get online with virtually any system that's not illustrated in this book. All systems operate on the same principle: to try to give you what you want. Online systems operate in only a few different ways. They look more different than they operate. Every way that a system can operate is in this book.

To provide you with a single volume of reference material about most online systems. If you plan to travel and still access the online systems that you subscribe to, you'll be better off if you leave the 10 pounds of system instruction manuals at home. Take this book with you, instead. If you're a subscriber of the Business Computer Network (BCN), you'll find this book very helpful in using some of the online systems available through BCN. If you use an online system at work that's presented in this book, you won't have to keep bringing home the system's manual. You can keep this book at home and use it instead. Even if you're already subscribing to an online system that you're satisfied with, this book can help you to appreciate it even more—or show you what you're missing.

To expand your knowledge of online systems so you can develop a critical faculty in deciding which ones are the best and the best for you. It's getting crowded in the online world. More systems are debuting today than ever before. Their features and virtues are being proclaimed in glossy color ads in many magazines. Unfortunately, some of these new systems are lacking in the features department, and others have no virtue. You need to be more discriminating before you sign a contract with an online system. No one (not even I) can afford to subscribe to every system. Plus, there are only so many people willing to pay for online entertainment or information for any length of time. Even the established online systems tend to have an astonishing turnover rate of subscribers. This means that not every new system that's launched will survive. Some of these new systems might not have what you're looking for. Some online companies may be underfinanced and will disappear into Chapter 11. Read this book carefully and look beyond the illustrations that I present to the principles that are at work on each system. This book will help you to see what qualities and services each system has to offer and help you to formulate a better idea of what you want an online system to do for you.

Ideally, you should read this book in this manner:

- Start at the front and read all the way to the back without skipping any pages.

- Reread the chapters about the systems that you're online to or are about to subscribe to.
- Skim the book from front to back again.
- Skim the book as necessary.

These instructions are not meant to be facetious. This book was designed to be read in this manner.

This book is in a narrative form. It starts out introducing fundamental concepts that pertain to all online systems and then cross-references and alludes to these concepts in the rest of the book.

For instance, you'll learn what a menu is in Chapter 2. You'll then see your first menu in Chapter 4. If you've never been online before and you start reading this book at the last chapter, you won't find an explanation there of what a menu is because it was already explained at the front of the book. I don't repeat the concepts and explanations in each chapter. The more toward the end of the book you get, the fewer explanations there are. That's because I'm assuming that you took my advice and started at the front of the book and learned all of that stuff *there*, where I put it to be read *first*.

In each chapter or description of a system, I'll also make cross-references to other systems or descriptions that have been previously presented. I'll contrast the operations of systems, as well as point out their similarities. I'll also let you know when you should pay particular attention to an aspect of a system because you'll see something like it in an upcoming part of the book. All of this is to help you build a solid foundation of knowledge about the ways systems operate. Instead of stumbling upon these insights on your own through painful and expensive experience, this book will provide a very quick, yet very broad, shortcut for you.

Once you've read the whole book, you can start concentrating on the chapters that deal with the specific online systems that you use. Now and again, you should skim from front to back to reacquaint yourself with the concepts and explanations that are scattered throughout this book. After that, you're on your own to reread this book or just skim it—or not—as you wish.

Have fun!

2 Beginners start here

When you use the telephone, you don't think about all of the technology that resides between your phone line and the one of the person you're calling. It doesn't matter to you what frequency is put out by each individual button on your phone or whether or not your call is careening across the country via land line or being bounced off satellite dishes. These things don't matter to you. They aren't important to know. All that concerns you is that a dial tone is present when you lift the receiver and that a (good) connection is made with the party you're calling. This is as it should be.

Unfortunately, the state of computer communications has not reached the level of simplicity that the phone network possesses. Despite the great advances that have been made since the publication of the first edition of *The Computer Phone Book*, computer communications still reside in a level of complexity, not simplicity. This is not as it should be. It's my contention that communicating by computer should not be any more difficult than communicating by telephone. That said, you will understand why my explanation of the various terms and equipment used in computer communications is relatively brief. You shouldn't have to learn any of this stuff. You shouldn't *have* to—but you must. Computer communications isn't simple yet, but my explanation is. Anyone interested in terms that only a technician can understand are hereby given notice to read another book. This book is for people who want to use their computers to communicate with other people—not for people who want to communicate with computer technicians.

As simple as I'd like to make your introduction to computer communications, there are still some terms and concepts that you need to understand before you can use any microcomputer as a communications device. This information applies to any computer you may own or use, no matter what its particular brand name.

As you know, all computers are digital devices. That is, they operate by using a series of off and on switches. These switches, at the most basic level a human can understand, are represented as a zero (0) and a one (1). These are the smallest units of information that may be handled by a computer and their proper name is the first term you must know.

Bit. This is an abbreviation of *binary digit*. It's the smallest amount of information that can be processed by a computer. A computer is basically a series of switches. Each switch can only be on or off. The off state is represented by a zero (Ø), and the on state is represented as a one (1) for the purposes of programming the machine. Although a computer can get along with just two symbols in its vocabulary, zero and one, human beings need more symbols. We have our own alphabetic (A–Z) and numeric (Ø–9) codes. So, a way was devised to translate our symbols into ones the computer could understand.

Byte. This is the first step in the translation process. Each of the alphabetic and numeric symbols we use is represented as a unique series of eight zeros and ones. In other words, one byte equals one character on your keyboard. When you press the "A" key on your computer, the computer is actually receiving a series of zeroes and ones to process (in the form of its switches being turned on and/or off). This is fine. The computer can now understand our symbols. But it would be nice if every computer used the same method of translating our symbols into its symbols.

ASCII. This is the next step in the translation process. ASCII is the standard code that was agreed upon for most computer keyboards. When you press the "A" key on your computer, you're sending the same sequence of zeros and ones as most people do when they press the "A" key on their computers. ASCII stands for the American Standard Code for Information Interchange and is pronounced "ask-ee."

Online. This is the process of using your computer to communicate with another computer. Computer-to-computer communications is usually, though not exclusively, accomplished over the telephone lines. This book, however, is solely concerned with computer communications that take place over conventional telephone lines.

Modem. This is a device that connects to a computer and enables it to use a telephone. The word "modem" is a truncation of *mo*dulator-*dem*odulator and is pronounced "*moe*-dem." This device is needed because the existing telephone system cannot, at least not yet, directly accept the zeros and ones used by computers. The existing telephone system can only handle a modulating signal, that is, sound. To get a computer to talk over the telephone, it must transmit sound. This is where a modem fits in. It translates the zeros and ones that a computer uses into an audio signal that can be transmitted by any telephone. The computer at the other end of the line will also be equipped with a modem, which will translate the audio signal it receives back into digital form. One modem takes its digital signal and modulates it into sound, while a second modem receives the audio signal and demodulates it back into its original digital form. If you were to listen in on the telephone when calling another computer, you would hear a high-pitched sound.

Carrier signal. This is what the high-pitched sound is called. It's a ready and waiting signal that lets you know that computer communications may proceed.

Modems come in three different types:

Acoustic coupled modem. This is a unit that attaches to the computer from the outside. It features two hard plastic or rubber cups. The cups are round and are meant to wrap around a conventional telephone handset (the type with round mouth- and earpieces). The handset is placed in the cups, and the circuitry in the handset is used to transmit and receive the sound signal. Acoustic coupled modems aren't used much nowadays.

Standalone modem. This is a self-contained unit that is attached to the computer by an external connection and sits outside of the machine. A wire leading from the modem is plugged directly into the base or wall jack of the telephone.

Onboard modem. This is a collection of chips on a printed circuit board that fits inside the computer itself in a slot. It also has a wire that plugs into the base or wall jack of the telephone. Although onboard modems can be purchased separately, some manufacturers are building them into computers.

The kind of modem you buy will depend on your brand and model of computer. Any kind will work fine, although one that plugs directly into the telephone or wall jack will work better. This is because the connection will be more secure. You should make certain that you have RJ11 modular plugs on your phone or your wall jack for this type of modem.

Bits per second. Also known as *bps*, this is how the rate of speed of computer communications is measured. You may have also heard this rate of speed described as baud or the baud rate. These latter terms are not entirely accurate. It actually takes a mathematical formula to convert bits per second into baud. You don't need to know this formula or even care that it exists. All that you need to know is that bits per second is the precise term to use when describing the rate of speed of transmission and reception.

In general, any time that you come across the term baud, bits per second is probably what's meant.

300 bps and *1200 bps*. These are the two primary transmission speeds that you'll use when communicating between computers. The speeds 300 and 1200 bps are usually referred to by the modem frequency standards set for them by AT&T; that is, Bell 103 for 300 bps and Bell 212A for 1200 bps. When buying a modem, it would be best to ensure that it is a Bell 103 standard, Bell 212A standard, or a combination of the two (that is, one that can transmit at either 300 or 1200 bps). Although other standards exist, it would be best to stick with these standards to make sure that your equipment will be compatible both with the telephone system as it's upgraded and with most online computer systems. If you're new to computer communications, start with an inexpensive Bell 103 300-bps modem. Once you've become used to online communications, you'll want to switch to a Bell 212A 300/1200 bps modem so you can cut down on the time you actually spend online.

Duplex. All you need to know about duplex is that there are two types—full-duplex and half-duplex. Full-duplex allows your computer to talk at the same time as the computer you are calling. As you'll see in upcoming chapters, this feature is important because it'll allow you to interrupt the computer being called so you may issue a command. Half-duplex permits only one computer at a time to talk; this mode is usually used in business or when transmitting a large amount of information. It's doubtful that you will ever use it.

Echo. This is what is done by the computer you're calling when you're set in full-duplex. For example, if the computer being called asks you to type your name, you'll see each letter of your name appear on your screen as you type it. Each letter typed was sent to and received by the other computer; then it was sent back to your computer, which displayed it on its screen. Echoing is a good way of seeing if what's being sent is getting through to the other computer. For instance, if you were to type in your name, say, "John," but saw "$@*%" on your screen, you'd know right away that something was awry. Generally, this is a minor problem: It's noise on the telephone line or an incorrect communications protocol setting. In half-duplex, the receiving computer doesn't echo what you send it, so what you type will not appear on your screen. If you were to have your modem accidentally set to half-duplex when calling a system designed for full-duplex operation, you'll know right away. "John" would become "JJoohhnn." Each letter is being echoed twice. This is an annoyance and should convince you to set your modem correctly to full-duplex.

Originate/Answer. Lastly, you need to know that a modem has a switch that is labeled "Originate/Answer" (or simply "O/A"). The setting for this switch is determined by which computer is calling which. Since you'll be making most of the calls to other computers—originating the contact—the switch should be set to originate. The answer setting is used when your computer is being called by another computer. You might like to try to have your friend call your computer to try it out. Don't be surprised if you spend more time on the phone talking with your friend directly than by computer. Sometimes it takes a while to get all of the settings just right.

Communications package. This is a piece of software used in communications. It is also known as a *terminal program* or *terminal emulator*. There are two types of terminal programs: dumb and smart.

Dumb terminal program. This simply converts a computer into a terminal much like those seen in airports and banks. The most it will allow is the information from an online system to be displayed on a TV screen or monitor. This type of program does not take advantage of a computer's available memory; it's not designed to "remember" what it receives from an online system. That's why it is called a "dumb" terminal program.

Smart terminal program. In contrast, the distinguishing characteristic of a smart terminal program is its ability to use the memory available in a computer to store what it receives from an online system. The program allocates a portion of available RAM into which the information that is received may be stored for later use.

Buffer. This is what the section of RAM that is partitioned for storage by a smart terminal program is called. The size of a buffer depends on the amount of available memory in a computer and the ingenuity of the program's author. On a computer with 64K of RAM, for instance, a buffer could range from a low of 8K to a high of 40K. The advantage of having a buffer is the ability to store and later manipulate information received from online systems.

Information. This is anything that can be recorded onto a floppy disk. It can be a simple text file (such as a memo), a program that can run on a computer, or even graphics—all of which can be filed on a cassette tape or a floppy disk. It can also be printed out, transferred to a word processor for editing, or even transferred online to another computer. One of the many things that may be done while online is the exchange of text and program files.

Uploading. This is when your computer is sending a file to another computer.

Downloading. This is when your computer is receiving a file from another computer.

Additional features available in smart terminal programs can be found in Chapter 3 (cleverly titled "Choosing a Terminal Program").

Communications protocol. This is what an online system expects to receive in terms of bits. The protocol is in three parts:

Word length. This is the first part of the protocol. The term itself is misleading, since it doesn't mean the size of actual words but the number of bits that are used to form a single character. There are one of two settings you'll use the most: 7 or 8.

Stop bits. This is the second part of the protocol. A stop bit follows the 7 or 8 bits that comprise a single character. A stop bit informs the receiving computer that it has just received all of the bits that are required to form a single character. More than one stop bit may be necessary in some online applications.

Parity. This is the third part of the protocol. There are up to five possible choices: Even, Odd, Mark, Space, or None. Parity is used in situations in which error-checking is necessary, such as the transfer of programs between computers. Most systems use either even parity or none.

Serial Port. Even with a modem and a terminal program, you may not have everything that is needed to go online. A modem is attached to most computers through a serial port. Some computers have serial ports built into them. Some don't. Some computers need a serial port; for instance, some early models of Apple computers. Some computers don't; for instance, Commodore VICs and 64s. If your computer doesn't have a serial port, you may have to buy one. Check with your dealer. This is the extent of my explaining serial ports. The technicians are invited to take over from here on the subject.

When you're finally ready to go online, your modem should be set at

- Speed: 300 bps
- Duplex: Full
- Mode: Originate

Your terminal program should be set at

- Word length: 8
- Stop bits: 1
- Parity: None

These settings may be changed at any time when needed for individual situations. *The Computer Phone Book: Directory of Online Systems* provides complete information about the communication protocols needed to go online with each system.

After you've purchased and installed a modem and terminal program, your next step will be to find a system on which to use them. There are three types of online systems:

- *National Systems*
- *Local Systems*
- *Bulletin-Board Systems* (commonly referred to as *BBSs*)

Of course, this means even more terminology you'll have to learn. Here are those terms.

Database. A database is simply a collection of information in electronic form. For example, a collection of information would be your computer's owner's manual; it would become a database once it has been put into electronic form.

Network. In telecommunications, a network can consist simply of the existing telephone network maintained by AT&T or a series of microwave towers and relays such as those provided by MCI, Sprint, ITT, and Western Union.

Value-Added Network. This is also known as a *packet-switched network* This is a telephone network that is specially designed to handle data communications, in other words, communications between different types, sizes, and brands of computers. It's used when subscribing to a National System. This type of telephone network enables the computers of a National System to be dialed-up for the price of a local phone call, even though the system's computers may reside in another state. When you're a subscriber of a National System, you will be given a local phone number of a packet-switched network to call. This is called a local *node*. A value-added network is less expensive and more reliable than making a long-distance call.

Information Utility. This is the actual collection of computers that make available the various services on a National System. The individual computers themselves are called *mainframes*, and because they are providing the service, they are also known as the *host* computers.

Connect-time. This describes the fee most National Systems charge for use. Connect-time is described as a per-hour fee because that gives a clearer idea of how much the system will cost. It does not mean a system will charge for an hour's worth of time if it is only used for a few minutes. Most systems bill you to the nearest minute, just like most long-distance voice phone companies.

National System. As its title implies, a National System is available nationwide (and even worldwide) by the above-defined packet-switched network. When you subscribe to one, you'll be given a phone number for a local node to connect with a packet-switched network that ties into the system. Sometimes there will be an additional charge for using a packet-switched network above the cost of a system's connect-time rates. Sometimes there isn't an additional charge. It depends on the system. Connect-time rates for National Systems are generally divided into two categories: prime time and non-prime time (sometimes called office and home time).

Prime time. This is generally from 8AM to 6PM local time (that is, your time) weekdays.

Non-prime time. This is generally from 6PM to 8AM local time (again, your time) weekdays and includes weekends and most holidays. Non-prime time is generally used by most computer owners since it is less expensive.

Local Systems. Local Systems have a different pricing structure. Most, but not all, charge a flat monthly subscription fee for unlimited access to the system. There are no hourly connect-time charges, and subscriptions can be for as short as 1 month to as long as 1 year. Of course, you must live in the area in which the service is located or pay for a long-distance phone call since Local Systems are not accessible through packet-switched networks.

Bulletin-Board Systems (BBSs). In most cases, BBSs are free. Mostly, they are operated by individual computer hobbyists and can only handle one caller at a time. This is because the system is running on a microcomputer such as an Apple, TRS-80, PET or Commodore-64. Since a BBS can only accommodate one caller at a time, when the system is in use its phone line will respond to other callers with a busy signal. To give as many callers as possible a chance to use the system, some BBSs have instituted time limits. The time limit can range anywhere from 10 to 30 minutes per day. More people are calling BBSs all of the time and some systems seem as if they're always busy. There'd be room for more callers if most people started to use 1200 bps modems to reduce their online time. This is another reason why you should think about getting a 1200 bps modem. Some BBSs ask for monetary contributions to help maintain the system. This is not an unreasonable request, since the equipment running the system is subjected to constant, daily use and requires repairs more frequently than a home computer that is used just a few hours a day.

System operator. This is the person who runs the BBS.

Sysops. This is the common abbreviation for system operator. It is pronounced "sis-op" not "cy-sop."

There are three ways of moving through each of the online systems just described:

Menu. This is the first method of moving through an online system. A menu is simply a list of available choices. The list may be numbered, in which case you just type the appropriate number key on your computer's keyboard. If a menu is not numbered, the first letter or letters of a desired selection must be typed, depending on its uniqueness within the list. For example, in a menu in which both *Banking* and *Bulletins* are presented, **Ba** or **Bu** must be typed, not just the letter "B," since both would answer to that letter.

Keyword. This is in the second method of moving through an online system. A keyword is simply a unique group of letters or words that corresponds to a title under which the information or service is classified. In most cases, this can be thought of as retrieving a folder from a file cabinet. The keyword is the name of the folder being sought.

Direct command. This is the third way of moving through an online system. A direct command may be similar to a keyword but in most instances it is preceded by a verb, which tells the system to take a specific action.

These three ways of moving through online systems describe the manner in which online systems are *driven*; that is, the way to move through them. The phrases, *menu-driven*, *keyword-driven*, and *command-driven* are used to describe these methods. Don't worry if you are still a bit confused at this point. Examples of each method will be shown in later chapters.

To review quickly, there are three types of online systems and they generally have the following attributes:

- *National Systems*
  Prime time and non-prime time rates
  Hourly connect-time charge
  Accessed by a local call through a packet-switched network

- *Local Systems*
  Monthly subscription fee
  Unlimited connect-time with no additional charge
  Accessed by a local or long-distance call

- A *Bulletin-Board Systems*
  Possible daily time limit
  Generally free of charge to use
  Accessed by a local or long-distance call

Information and services on these systems can be found by one or more of these methods:

- Menus
- Keywords
- Direct commands

Another type of system that has not yet been covered and that combines some of the elements of the above systems with some unique features of its own is still in its development stage. It is a videotex system.

Videotex is generally used to describe a system that relies heavily upon graphics as part of the information and services it offers. In the strictest sense, a videotex system is one that uses a *non-ASCII* coding format to transmit and display text and graphics. The major coding standards currently in use are Prestel (the first one devised; it originated in Great Britain), Telidon (from Canada), and NAPLPS (North American Presentation-Level Protocol Standard; developed by AT&T in the United States). All of these standards were primarily meant to be used with specially designed terminals or decoder boxes that can accept and display the encoded color graphics on a monitor or TV screen. Videotex is usually transmitted over telephone lines, just like systems designed to be used with personal computers, although there have been tests of delivering it over cable TV. The transmission speed of videotex is usually 1200 bps from the host and 75 bps to the host. This is quite different from the 300/300 and 1200/1200 bps speeds used by personal computers in online communications.

Videotex systems are menu-driven and are primarily offered on a flat monthly subscription basis, although there may be additional charges for special information or transaction services. Videotex systems, at least those based in the United States, are designed to serve a local area and may not be accessed through a national packet-switched network.

Videotex may be the wave of the future, if the technology ever stops bankrupting those who invest in it. Some of the ASCII-based commercial systems covered in this book eventually plan to offer NAPLPS graphics on their systems. Some of the ASCII-based online systems covered in this book insist on calling themselves "videotex systems." For the record, *The Computer Phone Book* only recognizes non-ASCII, graphic-enhanced online systems as being true videotex. This book cannot answer the question as to why ASCII online services insist on confusing the general public by using the term videotex so cavalierly. Nor can I say why ASCII services would want to be considered the same as a technology—videotex—that has so far gone nowhere in 10 years.

Until videotex takes over the online world, you'll need to know the various special commands available to you on conventional ASCII-based online systems.

When you LIST a program on your computer, the text moves from the bottom of the screen to the top. This is known as *scrolling*. Text sent to a computer from an online system will scroll in a similar, though not identical, manner. When online, this scrolling can be stopped and restarted by using a *Control function*. On most computers, Control functions are executed by using two keys. One is marked *Control*, *CTRL*, or *CTL*. This key, when pressed in conjunction with one of several letter keys, sends a command to the online system, telling it to perform one of several functions. Online systems generally accept these commonly used Control functions:

Control-C. This interrupts the current command the system is executing and returns it to a state of readiness for the entry of a new command or selection.

Control-G. This sounds a bell. Not all systems permit this and filter it out, although the system itself may send it to get your attention.

Control-H. This moves the screen cursor back one space to erase a letter so it may be replaced with a new one. Note that this is used by some systems only as a simple *backspace* command as opposed to a *destructive backspace* command; that is, the cursor may move back one space and then type over the character, but when printed out the effect is of two letters occupying the same space. This makes messy printouts.

Control-O. This tells the system to skip through the text it is sending. The end result may be a system prompt to enter a new command, or the next block of text in sequence will be sent.

Control-P. This function is similar to Control-C. Some systems use both, whereas some only accept Control-P.

Control-Q. This will resume output, restarting the scrolling of paused text. This is issued after pausing with a Control-S.

Control-R. On some systems, this function redisplays the line of text that has been typed, before the Return key has been pressed. On a printing terminal, this command is handy if text has been overwritten by overusing Control-H and the line must be seen clearly. This function also comes in handy on video terminals on which telephone line noise has interfered with the display of inputted characters.

Control-S. This causes a pause in system output, stopping the scrolling of text. The scroll is resumed by issuing a Control-Q.

Control-U. This erases the entire line that has been typed into the system, if the Return key has not been pressed, and allows a new line to be typed.

Control-V. This function is similar to Control-R. Some systems use this instead of Control-R.

Control-Z. On some systems, this function indicates *end of file*, a command that is used to tell the system that a file that has been typed or uploaded is completed and should be stored. This function may also be used on some systems to return to a prior system prompt.

All of the above commands are normally executed by pressing the

Control key and the appropriate letter *at the same time*. The Hyphen (-) key is not pressed. Imagine the Control key as a Shift key. When a capital letter is needed, the Shift key and a letter key are pressed simultaneously. The same method is normally used in executing a Control function.

All of these commands, when available, place an online system at your beck and call. The system is working for you, not the other way around. When using an online system, if it seems to be acting strangely or malfunctioning outright, blame the system or the telephone connection or even the modem, not yourself. This rule is especially true if you check the modem on another system, have no trouble with the telephone, and find that communication protocols were properly set in the first place. Hundreds of thousands of other computer owners have already used the online systems listed in this book. If the systems were prone to fail at the slightest touch of the wrong key, this book would not have been possible. Don't worry: *There is nothing you can do to accidentally break a system.*

This completes your introduction to microcomputer telecommunications. If you don't already own a terminal program, read the next chapter to learn the guidelines you should use in selecting one. If you already own a terminal program that you're satisfied with, you may turn directly to Chapter 4 to begin reading about how each online system operates.

3 Choosing a terminal program

Shopping for a terminal program can be just as confusing—and trying—as shopping for a word processing or database program. Just as there is no shortage of poor word processing and database programs, there is no shortage of poorly thought out terminal programs. The phrase *caveat emptor* takes on a whole new dimension when you're sitting at your computer and you discover that the program you bought can't do what the computer store salesmen said it could, or that it isn't as good as the reviews made it out to be, or that it uses a sequence of keyboard commands that requires you to grow another hand.

Why is this so?

Let me give you the answer in the form of a question. Have you ever been in a situation—whether in business, school, or just life—in which the rules under which you were expected to perform were illogical, muddy, contradictory, unnecessarily time consuming and just plain stupid? Further, have you found that when you've tried to find out *why* things are done the way they are, you've only been told, "That's the way things are," as if that's the final word on the subject? Most of us, unfortunately, have been in such situations at one time or another. Once exposed, we try to avoid similar situations as if they were a plague. What does this have to do with terminal programs? It's simple.

When you sit down at your computer ready to use a program, you are telling your machine to carry out a series of instructions that someone else thinks your machine should do. Unfortunately that "someone else" may not have tried to put himself in your position, and this explains why some programs may require you to press the ALT, CTL, @ and / keys simultaneously. It's because that's the way some programmer designed it.

Programs are nothing more than a series of instructions for a computer to follow. The instructions are thought up by a person, called a programmer. The programmer may know all there is to know about coding in machine language, Pascal, C, or FRED, but when it comes to arranging things in a logical and simple order, he has to call in a battery of consultants to help straighten out his file cabinets and tax records. Of course, not all programmers are like that. But too many are—and *that's* why shopping for a terminal program can be a very trying experience.

It's not fun to sit down with a newly purchased terminal program only to find its instruction manual was written by someone who has ignored the English language and that the software's advanced features require you to disregard your knowledge of the English language by making you type things like "%ml:c@@[password]@@*2+%$."

Unfortunately, I can't help you avoid incomprehensible manuals or software commands that look like ancient sanscrit. The extent of the help I can give is to let you know that such horrors exist and that you should be on the lookout for them. When you run into them, flee. Don't get caught with a terminal program that won't let you do what you want to do because "that's the way things are."

Here are some of the features that you should look for in a terminal program. They are not listed in any specific order, and you may not need every one of them. That's fine. On the other hand, you *may* need every feature that is listed, in which case you would be in trouble from the start. I have yet to find one program that contains every one of these features. But that's OK. As I write this, I'm sure some terminal programs are under development that will incorporate some features I have never thought of. Eventually, most terminal programs will have to incorporate all of the features listed below. No software publisher can afford to be negligent in improving its product. The marketplace is unforgiving to such publishers, sending them into Chapter 11 and deserved obscurity.

Here is the list:

Auto dial. This is combined with a built-in phone directory and the program's ability to issue commands to an intelligent modem. The program will dial the system telephone number for you. If you call several online systems, you needn't carry all of the phone numbers on a scrap of paper or in your memory—let the program and computer remember for you.

Auto answer. This is the ability to interact with another computer calling in. This would enable you, say, to upload files from your computer at work to your computer at home or to call up a file frm your home computer's disk drive and download it to your computer at work. (Of course, your home computer must be turned on and the modem plugged into the phone.)

Auto logon. With this, the program will "type" (transmit) your User ID and password, automatically logging you on to an online system. You just press one button and the terminal program does the rest.

Auto commands. This is similar to auto logon. Some terminal programs offer this feature, which is sometimes called *macros*. You can tell the terminal program to issue a sequence of commands automatically in response to prompts sent by the online system you are on. Ideally, the three features—auto dial, auto logon, and auto commands—can be used in an uninterrupted sequence and will allow your computer to access online systems unattended. There are problems, however, with some of the programs that offer an auto command feature. Some programs require you to type a nonsensical collection of characters in order to get the program to carry out a simple task. Investigate programs that offer this feature carefully. You shouldn't have to learn a whole new language just to use one program.

Customized function keys. Most terminal programs offer this feature, which is also known as *user-definable* (a wretched phrase) function keys. You just assign each function key on your computer the commands you use most frequently (or dread typing) and let the terminal program send them to the online system at the press of a single key.

Built-in word processing. It is a constant wonder to me why more terminal programs do not offer this feature. The most popular use of micro telecommunications is messaging—the use of bulletin boards and electronic mail. Being able to exit the terminal program temporarily, while online, to compose a short message for instant uploading seems only natural. Online text editors are cumbersome, even to expert users. Having access to a word processor—even one with a very few features—while online would help immeasurably.

Manual/automatic timer. Although plenty of programs offer an online timer, all of them begin ticking away a few seconds after the program has started to run. By the time an online system has been called, several minutes have gone by, effectively making the timer useless for measuring connect-time. I'd like to see one that would start timing at the reception of a carrier signal. There should also be an option for the user to restart the clock at any time. An alarm feature, which would notify you after a specified period of time had elapsed, would also be welcome. Ideally, there would be two timers. One that shows the current "real time" (i.e., 7 PM), the second one showing elapsed time online (i.e., 34 minutes). Neither clock should be in military time (i.e., 18:00). Another feature I would like to see is something I call a "connect-timer" or a meter. It would be tied to the timer and would let you know how much money you've spent online. Ideally, it'd be able to tabulate either system connect-time or long-distance phone charges—in real-time—while you are online. You would simply input the connect-time or long-distance per-minute charge into the program, and it would do the rest for you. No terminal program currently offers a "connect-timer," although some have a feature that gives an estimated cost total once you're offline.

Word wrap. This is a feature that is more important for machines with 40-column screens. Like word wrap in a word processing program, this feature would make sure that the words on your screen are not split onto two lines. This would allow you to set the system line length for a full 80-columns for printing while letting you see a comfortable 40-columns on the screen.

Pull-down menu(s) without screen blanking. Although several programs allow access to a menu or help screen, most programs wipe out the previous screen. If you are online with a full screen of data and then access the help/menu screen, when you exit the help/menu screen, you find that your screenful of data from the online system has been wiped out. This is a serious flaw and often frustrates both new and experienced users.

Exit to DOS while online. This is a must. I am amazed to find disk-based terminal programs on the market that do not allow a user to access Disk Operating System commands. Access to DOS is an absolute for uploading and downloading; it cannot be considered an option or a frill. It is a necessity. You will need to see how much free space is left on your disk, which filenames have been used, which files have to be uploaded, and how much space a downloaded file has taken. Any terminal program that does not allow easy access to at least most, if not all, available DOS commands is not worth buying.

Protocol download and upload. This is required for the error-free transmission and reception of files and programs. A terminal program should feature at least one protocol—preferably XMODEM. That's at the very least. Don't, however, buy any terminal program if it *only* offers a proprietary protocol *unless* you intend to use it to communicate with other computers (micro, mini, or mainframe) that use the *same* protocol. You will not be able to use a terminal program that has a proprietary protocol for file transfer except with another computer that is using the same proprietary protocol. There are two micro telecommunication protocols that are in wide use: X/On-X/Off (also known as MODEM, XMODEM, and the "Christensen Protocol"), and the "Punter" protocol (mainly used on Commodore-based BBSs). If you intend to communicate with a wide variety of computer types (eventually you will, even if you don't plan to at the start), make certain that your terminal program contains XMODEM protocol ability. If you own a Commodore-64, look for "Punter" protocol capability. There are low-cost terminal programs that are available in the public domain that feature each of these protocols. So why should you pay for them in an expensive terminal program? For one, a public domain program will rarely contain all of the features that you will need. Second, it may require some knowledge of programming on your part. Third, you won't be automatically notified of improvements to the program by its publisher. Fourth, when you have a problem with the program, you can't pick up a telephone and call the publisher for assistance—because there is no publisher, just a wide assortment of distributors. Public domain programs are more of a mixed bag than professionally published programs. Wait until you have purchased a good professional program and have been online a while; then you can afford the luxury of experimenting with public domain terminal programs.

Setting bps, word length, stop bits, parity, and duplex while online. Many programs only allow you to set these parameters before you go online. Then, once you are online, you are stuck with them. The option of changing them while online is needed, sometimes, for applications such as downloading (for instance, going from full- to half-duplex). Also, sometimes you may call an online system and forget to make the correct settings. It's better to be able to make an adjustment while you're still online rather than having to hang up, reload the software, change the settings, and call the system again.

Modem commands. The trend in modems is toward intelligence: built-in microprocessors that make the modem a sort of computer in itself. To take advantage of features such as auto dialing, you'll have to make sure that your terminal program can "talk" to your modem and that your modem will recognize the commands that the software is giving it.

Phone directory. Some programs have this, some don't. More should, and all eventually must. As micro telecommunications grow both in popularity and usefulness, people will have more and more system phone numbers to call. Even with the best filing procedures, numbers get lost. It'd be nice to be able to file them in the terminal program, where they can be selected and automatically dialed by the computer.

Large customized buffer. The larger the buffer, the better. How large a buffer you will be able to get depends on your computer and the terminal program. For instance, if you have a Commodore-64, you can't reasonably expect to find a buffer larger than 40K; and that's pushing it. If you have an IBM PC stuffed wiht RAM, you'll have to make sure that the terminal program can take advantage of your PC's extra memory. Very few terminal programs currently offer the capability of setting the size of the buffer.

Setting the buffer size is important if you intend to capture plenty of text. Sure, a 40K text file is fine on disk . . . until you later find out you can only load about 30K of it into your word processing program, leaving you with an unaccessible 10K of data stuck on the disk. Be forewarned.

Virtual memory option. Some terminal programs offer a primitive form of virtual memory, automatically writing to disk when the buffer gets filled and keeping the file open to append new data. This feature would be tied to the one allowing the setting of the buffer's size. The appending of new material to a disk file would also be user selectable.

Buffer review online and offline. Sometimes it is necessary to quickly review what you've captured in your buffer, like a menu to an online system you're trying out for the first time, or to reread the electronic mail you're replying to. The program should be able to display the buffer contents quickly and allow you to pause the output, all without blanking the current screen display from the online system. This feature should also allow you to load a downloaded disk file into the buffer for review when you're offline. The size of the disk file should not matter, since the program should offer virtual memory retrieval.

Program status line(s). At the top (*not* the bottom) of the screen, one or two lines should be dedicated to presenting information about the functioning of the program. This information should include some of the following: whether the buffer is open or closed; how much space is left in the buffer (in terms of characters and expressed as a number); the current bps, word length, stop bit, parity, and duplex settings; the timer (showing elapsed time and current time); the "connect-timer," showing how much money you've spent so far online; the phone number that is being called (although this feature can be blanked by the user for security situations); protocol being used while transferring files; and the status of files being downloaded or uploaded (whether any errors are being encountered plus how much has been received or how much remains to be sent).

Customized color. This should include cursor, text, background, and border colors. Some terminal programs designed expressly to be used with online search services also highlight keywords in a specific color; this is a wonderful application of color. I'd also like to see online system output highlighted by a color and user input highlighted by a separate color.

Terminal emulation. This is necessary if you plan to communicate with mainframes. The most popular emulations are VT52, VT100, and IBM 3270. Ideally, the program should allow you to integrate a custom-written terminal emulator program.

Screen dump to printer. This allows you immediately to send to the printer the data that is currently on your screen. If you don't want to save data to disk, you should be able to get an immediate hardcopy by a screen dump.

Upload with customized prompt. Most terminal programs offer this. Some online systems cannot handle a continuous stream transmission when you are uploading a file. Instead, they let you know when it is OK to continue transmission by sending a prompt. Since prompts differ on each online system, the terminal program should allow you to tell it what to look for as a prompt from the system.

Use your printer online. This is also known as *streaming*, and your printer should be fast enough to handle it. If your printer is slow, the terminal program should be able to send a Control-S (X-Off) to the online system to halt transmission temporarily and then a Control-Q (X-On) to resume. I don't advise that you use streaming with a daisywheel printer; it'll just run up your telephone or system connect-time bill. Make sure that you have a dot matrix printer that can keep up with an online system's output.

Remember: No terminal program currently on the market offers *all* of these features. Further, if your computer has a 64K memory limit, you can virtually forget about ever having all of these features in a terminal program for your computer. (Of course, I'd like to be proven wrong about this last sentence.) Carefully examine what you want to accomplish online and set out to examine the terminal programs that will best help you to do what you want.

Here are four things you can try to do before you purchase any terminal program:

1. Seek out published reviews of the product. Never regard these as the final word about any software product, though. Use them as a guideline and as a starting point, no matter how much they may gush about the product.
2. Go to your local computer dealer and see if you can witness a demonstration of the program. Make sure that your local dealer is someone you have actually bought equipment or supplies from.
3. Call the company that publishes the program and ask if it is possible to buy a copy of the instruction manual *before* you have to shell out \$50–\$250 for the program itself. If you can buy the manual separately, make sure that you can deduct the price from the software, if you decide to buy it.
4. Join a local computer user group. They are virtually everywhere.

Plenty of magazines publish lists of them. There are even books out with user group lists in them (this isn't one of them, though). User groups are filled with people who will be glad to give you a helping hand. They've already been through the mill with bad products and are always willing to keep others from having to go through the same ordeal. They'll be able to tell you if the reviews you've dug up are on target, if your local dealer has told you everything about a particular program, and if the manual you purchased really tells the whole story.

If you go through these four steps, you will appreciably reduce the risk of getting a terminal program that won't do—or can't do—all that you need it to do.

Starting with the next chapter, you will see the different online systems on which you can put your computer, modem, and terminal program to use.

4 Using BRS after dark

Control characters used on this system: Control-H, destructive backspace; Control-P, system interrupt (on Telenet only); Control-Q (XON), resume output; Control-S (XOFF), pause output; and Break, system interrupt.

BRS After Dark (CPB100040) is from Bibliographic Retrieval Service (BRS), a company that has primarily provided online databases to businesses, universities, and libraries. In late 1982, BRS introduced its After Dark service, offering several of its online databases to the general public at a fraction of the cost its professional clients pay. The online databases made available through the After Dark service are exactly the same in content as those offered during business hours. In other words, the ABI/Inform database that BRS's professional clients pay over $100 per connect hour for during the day can be accessed by you for only $12 per connect hour. You can also pay as little as $6 per connect hour for some databases. What's the catch? First, you can only access the system after 6 PM your local time. Second, the command structure that you'll use is not as powerful as that used by BRS's corporate clients. These are minor inconveniences compared to the breadth of information that is housed in the system. Plus, the fact is you probably won't require the complex command structure that's frequently used by librarians and professional researchers. The bottom line is that BRS After Dark is a tremendous bargain.

It costs $75 to subscribe to BRS After Dark, and billing is to your credit card. A direct-billing account can also be set up for a one-time $250 charge, which is deducted from your connect-time charges. There is also a $12 monthly minimum.

When you subscribe, you'll get a User ID and a password, along with a list of phone numbers that are available to access the system via one of three packet-switched networks (DataPac, Telenet, and Uninet). You'll also get a user's manual that is filled with descriptions and prices of each online database, their content format, the commands that you may use, and sample search sessions.

This is what it looks like to use BRS After Dark. Once you've called the system and finished entering your User ID and password, you'll see

```
*SIGN-ON      20.02.59            9/14/85:

WELCOME TO BRS AFTER DARK

PLEASE TYPE IN SCREEN LINE LENGTH (20, 40, OR 80)
```

This should be obvious. It means to type in the width of your computer's screen; that is, how many characters can fit across your screen. Once you've done that, you'll be asked to

```
PLEASE TYPE IN THE NUMBER OF LINES ON YOUR
SCREEN (20,21,22, ETC.)
```

of course, this means how many lines of text can fit on your screen from top to bottom. (Note that you may just press Return if you are using a printing terminal.)

You have just encountered two prompts. A *prompt* is a request from a system to enter information or a notification from the system that it's your turn to do something. Prompts come in various forms, as you will see.

Once you have specified your screen dimensions, this will appear:

```
    CHECK MENU ITEM 6 FOR INFORMATION ON NEW
    AFTER DARK DATABASES AND SYSTEM ENHANCEMENTS.

TONIGHT'S MENU IS:

NUMBER    ITEM
   1      LOOKING FOR INFORMATION?. . .SEARCH SERVICE
   2      WANT TO HEAR THE LATEST?. . .NEWSLETTER SERVICE
   4      KEEP IN TOUCH!. . .ELECTRONIC MAIL SERVICE
   6      WHAT'S NEW?. . .NEW SYSTEM FEATURES
   7      WANT TO CHANGE YOUR SECURITY PASSWORD?. . .
          SECURITY

TYPE IN MENU ITEM NUMBER THEN HIT ENTER KEY FOR DESIRED SELECTION
```

Let me back up a bit. The above is what will appear on your screen, although it may not look exactly as shown here. There are two reasons for this. The first one was mentioned earlier: The online world moves so fast that it often outdates material in books, such as this one, that attempt to cover it. BRS may add an item or two to this menu (notice that choices 3 and 5 are *missing.*) The second reason why this may look different has to do with format. Your replies to the two questions that are always asked at signon will determine how BRS formats itself for your screen. This is so your screen display will not look cluttered. For example, if you had replied with **20** to the screen width question, it would look like this:

```
TONIGHT'S    MENU    IS..
                        .
NUMBER    ITEM          .
   1      LOOKING FOR
          INFORMATION
          . . . . .SEARCH
          SERVICE       .
                        .
   2      WANT TO       .
          HEAR THE      .
          LATEST?. . . .
          NEWSLETTER.
          SERVICE       .
```

and so on. (By the way, I doubt that BRS will offer this narrow width much longer. The only computer with such a narrow screen is the Commodore VIC-20, which is no longer being manufactured. Also, I doubt that anyone with a $60 VIC would subscribe to a service such as BRS After Dark, since the connect-time charges would easily surpass the price of the computer in the course of a year.) If you typed **40,** it would look like this:

```
TONIGHT'S MENU IS. . . . . . . . . . . . . . . . . . . . .
                                                          .
                                                          .
NUMBER    ITEM                                            .
                                                          .
   1      LOOKING  FOR  INFORMATION?. . . .
          SEARCH SERVICE                                  .
                                                          .
   2      WANT  TO  HEAR  THE  LATEST?. . . .
          NEWSLETTER SERVICE                              .
```

and so on. (I expect this screen option to remain available for some time yet, since there are still plenty of 40-column Apples in use, not to mention over 1 million Commodore 64s.) This is how it would appear on your screen—and also how it would appear when printed out on paper. I'm not sure that anyone would like to read such narrow text or waste paper in printing it out. Short of running the material through a word processing or file utility program for reformatting, these solutions are possible: First, you can make certain that your terminal program allows for word wrapping on its display. This is similar to word wrap in word processing: No split words are permitted on the screen. Some programs offer this feature as an option, whereas others don't have it at all. The second solution is for you to put up with split words on your screen. This is not as bad as it seems. When you consider that your printouts will look better and that you'll save paper when printing them, it's a small price to pay. Thus, the above, on a 20-column screen, would look like this:

```
TONIGHT'S MENU IS:

NUMBER          ITEM
   1           LOOKI
NG FOR INFORMATION?
. . .SEARCH SERVICE
   2            WANT
TO HEAR THE LATEST?
. . .NEWSLETTER SERVI
CE
```

On a 40-column screen, it would look like this:

```
TONIGHT'S MENU IS:

NUMBER     ITEM
   1       LOOKING FOR INFORMATION?..
.SEARCH SERVICE
   2       WANT TO HEAR THE LATEST?..
.NEWSLETTER SERVICE
```

The second question, regarding the number of lines your screen can display, tells the system when to pause its output. The pause is so you'll have a chance to read what's on the screen before the material continues to travel past the top of your screen. After the system has sent, say, 24 lines of text, it will stop and print

```
HIT ENTER FOR NEXT SCREEN
```

on the last line as a prompt. You will not get this prompt if you pressed Return in response to the second signon question. "Hit Enter" means to press your Enter key, which is labeled "Return" on most computers. Once that is done, the system will again transmit text.

The list you've been seeing, in various widths, is called a *menu*. Here it is again:

```
TONIGHT'S MENU IS:

NUMBER     ITEM
   1       LOOKING FOR INFORMATION?. . .SEARCH SERVICE
   2       WANT TO HEAR THE LATEST?. . .NEWSLETTER SERVICE
   4       KEEP IN TOUCH!. . .ELECTRONIC MAIL SERVICE
   6       WHAT'S NEW?. . .NEW SYSTEM FEATURES
   7       WANT TO CHANGE YOUR SECURITY PASSWORD?. . .
           SECURITY

TYPE IN MENU ITEM NUMBER THEN HIT ENTER KEY FOR DESIRED SELECTION
```

Each choice is numbered and, as the last line states, you only have to type the number that you want, press the Enter (Return) key, and you'll be ushered toward your goal. For instance, typing **1** and pressing **Return** will display this next menu:

```
YOU ARE NOW CONNECTED TO THE BRS AFTER DARK SEARCH SERVICE.
THE FOLLOWING CATEGORIES OF DATABASES ARE AVAILABLE FOR
SEARCHING.

CATEGORY     DESCRIPTION
    1        SCIENCE AND MEDICINE DATABASES
    2        BUSINESS AND FINANCIAL DATABASES
    3        REFERENCE DATABASES
    4        EDUCATION DATABASES
    5        SOCIAL SCIENCE AND HUMANITIES DATABASES

TYPE IN CATEGORY NUMBER THEN HIT ENTER KEY FOR
CATEGORY OF DATABASES DESIRED.
```

These are the five broad categories of databases carried on BRS After Dark. A complete list, along with each database's connect-time charge, can be found at the end of this chapter.

Let's look at what a sample search would be like. First, let's type **2**, for Business and Financial Databases. This will bring up

```
BUSINESS AND FINANCIAL DATABASES
*****************************************************

DATABASE NAME                                     LABEL
ABI/INFORM                                        INFO
HARVARD BUSINESS REVIEW                           HBRO
```

```
INTERNAL REVENUE SERVICE PUBLICATIONS     IRSP
MANAGEMENT CONTENTS                       MGMT
ONLINE MICRO-SOFTWARE DIRECTORY           SOFT
PATDATA                                   PATS

TYPE IN LABEL FOR DATABASE DESIRED:
```

These are the databases that cover business and financial topics.

You may find it odd that a directory for microcomputer software would be listed under this category, but there is a good reason. If you were looking for a software package such as a spreadsheet or a mailing list database, you'd be more likely to think of it in a financial or business context. Of course, since such information would reside in a directory, you could also think of looking under the category Reference Databases in the previous menu. Either way would be correct. The directory is found under both menus. This is an example of how BRS After Dark—and other search services—cross reference their databases.

Getting back to the matter at hand, notice that the selections on this menu are not numbered. Instead, you are asked to type in a "label" for a database. These unique combinations of four letters are called *keywords* on some systems. This is the first type of keyword that was mentioned in Chapter 1. Soon, you'll see the second type. Let's look at the ABI/Inform database by typing **INFO**.

```
TYPE IN LABEL FOR DATABASE DESIRED: INFO

WOULD YOU LIKE INSTRUCTIONAL PROMPTS? PLEASE TYPE
YES OR NO:
```

When using BRS After Dark for the first time, it's best to ask for the prompts. Once you've gained some mastery of the system, this option may be bypassed. In this example, I will show you what the instructional prompts look like in an actual search.

```
WOULD YOU LIKE INSTRUCTIONAL PROMPTS? PLEASE TYPE
YES OR NO: Y
```

Notice that I did not type either "Yes" or "No" as requested by the system. On most systems—but not all—commands may be abbreviated. This is a time saver. Next, the system asks

```
WOULD YOU LIKE A DESCRIPTION OF THE DATABASE? (YES OR NO)
```

I will not show a description of the database here. The user's manual as well as BRS After Dark advertising brochures adequately explain the contents of each database. I want you to note that the only time you should ask for a database description is when the system has added a new one. Each description is a paragraph long and contains the connect-time charge for using the individual database.

```
WOULD YOU LIKE A DESCRIPTION OF THE DATABASE? (YES OR NO) N

BRS/INFO/1971 - SEP 1984
TYPE IN SEARCH TERMS, OR ENTER COMMAND
        M TO RETURN TO MASTER MENU, D TO CHOOSE NEW DATABASE,
     OR O TO SIGN OFF.
S1 —>
```

These instructions are rather clear. You may enter one of three commands: M to have the main menu reappear, D to choose a different database, or O to terminate your online session. Your other option is to type a search term. That's the clear part. But what is a "search term" and what does the "S1 —>" mean?

A search term is what you'll use to locate the information you are interested in finding. A synonym of search term is *keyword.* This is the second type of keyword used by online systems, as mentioned in Chapter 1.

The "S1 —>" is simply a prompt. I told you that prompts come in various forms. This is one such form.

As an example of a search, let's say you were interested in finding any published reports about Apple Computer's estimates of how many Macintosh computers would have been sold in 1984. A place to start would be to find how many times the word "apple" appears in the database. To do this, you just type **apple**, like so:

```
S1 —> APPLE

A1      673 DOCUMENTS FOUND
TYPE IN SEARCH TERMS, OR ENTER COMMAND
        P TO PRINT DOCUMENTS FOUND, R TO REVIEW SEARCH QUESTIONS,
        M TO RETURN TO MASTER MENU, D TO CHOOSE NEW DATABASE,
     OR O TO SIGN OFF.
```

For now, let's ignore the new commands that are mentioned in the instructional prompt and concentrate on the search.

The word "apple" appears 673 times in this database. (This bears repeating: Remember that if you carry out these examples online, you will get different results since the databases are being added to regularly.) Is it possible that every mention of the word "apple" is about the computer company? There could be some instances in which "apple" refers not to a company or a computer, but to the actual fruit. The search has to be narrowed. This can be done by adding "computer" and "computers" to the list of keywords, as follows:

```
S2 —>    APPLE AND COMPUTER$

A2       572  DOCUMENTS FOUND
TYPE IN  SEARCH TERMS, OR ENTER COMMAND
         P TO PRINT DOCUMENTS FOUND, R TO REVIEW SEARCH QUESTIONS,
         M TO RETURN TO MASTER MENU, D TO CHOOSE NEW DATABASE,
OR       O TO SIGN OFF.
```

It worked. Out of 673 documents, only 572 are about the company or the computer. The search has been narrowed by 101 documents, a significant amount. But wait a minute. What does "COMPUTER$" mean? This is a way that you can truncate words on BRS After Dark. Instead of having to put the words "computer" and "computers" on the search line, you can tell the system to search for any words that contain the stem "computer." Thus, "computers" would also be found, as would "computerize," "computerphobia," "computerization," and so on. The dollar sign, $, is called a *wild card*. It represents all possible groups of letters that would be part of a word that starts with "computer." The group can be as short as one, as in "computer*s*," or as long as necessary, as in "computer*ization*." Let's narrow the search again, this time only looking for documents that contain the words "computer" and "computers" in them.

```
S3 —>    APPLE AND COMPUTER$1

A3       567 DOCUMENTS FOUND
TYPE IN  SEARCH TERMS, OR ENTER COMMAND
         P TO PRINT DOCUMENTS FOUND, R TO REVIEW SEARCH QUESTIONS,
         M TO RETURN TO MASTER MENU, D TO CHOOSE NEW DATABASE,
OR       O TO SIGN OFF.
```

Only five documents were excluded. Notice that the wild card can be delimited, or restricted, by specifying how many characters it should look for after the stem "computer." In this case, it was told to look only for words with "computer" and "computer-plus-one-letter" or "computer" and "computers."

It is time to narrow the search even more:

```
S4 —> APPLE COMPUTE$2

A4        284  DOCUMENTS FOUND
TYPE IN SEARCH TERMS, OR ENTER COMMAND
          P TO PRINT DOCUMENTS FOUND, R TO REVIEW SEARCH QUESTIONS,
          M TO RETURN TO MASTER MENU, D TO CHOOSE NEW DATABASE,
OR        O TO SIGN OFF
```

Bingo! Nearly half of the documents were excluded using this tactic.

Let's stop to review exactly what was done. First, notice that each prompt has a different number, corresponding to the number of searches done thus far, 1–4. In the four searches just completed, we narrowed "apple" to the words "apple" and "computer," then to "apple" and any word that started with "computer," and then to "apple" and any word that started with "computer" but contained no more than one additional letter. Finally, we told the database to look only for the phrase that contains the word "apple" and any word that begins with "compute" but has no more than 2 additional letters (or "computer" and "computers"). This is an example of *boolean logic*, a strategy that is used on search services such as BRS After Dark.

Boolean logic may be an intimidating term, but it's actually quite simple. It means that, when using more than one search term (or keyword), you can describe what you are looking for in a few simple ways. You can look for Keyword-A *and* Keyword-B; that is, all instances in which Keyword-A and Keyword-B are found in a document. You can look for Keyword-A *or* Keyword-B; that is, instances in which either Keyword-A or Keyword-B appear. You can look for Keyword-A Keyword-B; that is, instances in which Keyword-A appears next to Keyword-B. You can look for Keyword-A *not* Keyword-B; that is, instances in which Keyword-A appears but not Keyword-B. This may be a little confusing. I know it reminds me of several high school math classes I dreaded, so let me simplify it.

Remember that we looked for "apple" *and* "computer(s)." The database was searched for all documents that contain those words. The first sentence of the document may have read, "Apple Computer began shipping . . . .". or "The new Apple portable computer . . . .". The keywords "apple" and "computer(s)" do not have to be next to each other, or even in the same sentence, using this technique.

Remember that we then looked for "apple computer(s)." Using this technique, only one of the two sample sentences used above would be found—the one that reads, "Apple Computer began shipping . . .". This is because the two keywords must appear next to each other in a document.

Using *not* would have only come into play if we were interested in apple as a fruit not as a computer manufacturer. Then the search term would have been "apple not computer." Using *or* would have come in if we had been using two terms that could be considered synonymous, such as "automobile" and "car." Then the search term would have been "automobile or car" to find all documents that contained those words. The only time to use "or" is when the search terms are different yet may be attributed to the same concept.

Let's continue to narrow the search to give you a better idea of how to use Boolean logic.

```
S5 —> APPLE MACINTSOH

MACINTSOH                KEYWORD NOT IN DICTIONARY
NO DOCUMENTS FOUND
TYPE IN SEARCH TERMS, OR ENTER COMMAND
        P TO PRINT DOCUMENTS FOUND, R TO REVIEW SEARCH QUESTIONS,
        M TO RETURN TO MASTER MENU, D TO CHOOSE NEW DATABASE,
OR      O TO SIGN OFF.
```

No documents were found. This will happen to you only one of two times. The first, obviously, if there are no documents that contain your keywords. The second time is if one of the keywords does not appear in the database dictionary (this will happen if, like above, you misspell your keyword). What is a database dictionary? It is a list of keywords that appear in the database. When you enter a keyword to start a search, the system first goes to the dictionary to see if the keyword is present. If the keyword is present, the dictionary tells the system where to find all instances of the keyword. If the keyword is not present, the search is stopped. Let's type it right this time:

```
S6 —> APPLE MACINTOSH

A6      6  DOCUMENTS FOUND TYPE IN SEARCH TERMS, OR ENTER COM-
MAND
        P TO PRINT DOCUMENTS FOUND, R TO REVIEW SEARCH QUESTIONS,
        M TO RETURN TO MASTER MENU, D TO CHOOSE NEW DATABASE,
OR      O TO SIGN OFF
```

Since there are only six documents, the search has probably been narrowed too soon. Let's expand it a bit:

```
S7 —> APPLE AND MACINTOSH

A7      55  DOCUMENTS FOUND
TYPE IN SEARCH TERMS, OR ENTER COMMAND
```

P TO PRINT DOCUMENTS FOUND, R TO REVIEW SEARCH QUESTIONS,
M TO RETURN TO MASTER MENU, D TO CHOOSE NEW DATABASE,
OR O TO SIGN OFF.

That's more like it. Now let's move in for the kill:

S8 —> **APPLE AND MACINTOSH AND SALE$1**

A8 13 DOCUMENTS FOUND
TYPE IN SEARCH TERMS, OR ENTER COMMAND
P TO PRINT DOCUMENTS FOUND, R TO REVIEW SEARCH QUESTIONS,
M TO RETURN TO MASTER MENU, D TO CHOOSE NEW DATABASE,
OR O TO SIGN OFF.

Only 13 documents were found after starting out with 673. That's quite a feat. Imagine being given over 600 pages of typewritten text and having to go through them to find the 13 that meet your needs. It would take you hours to read. Here, using an online search service, it was done in a few moments. Let's take a peek to see if this is, indeed, the material we've been looking for. We'll issue the print command, **P**, like so:

S9 —> **P**

ENTER A SEARCH QUESTION TO PRINT FROM (E.G. 1 OR 2, ETC.)

Remember that each prompt in the database labels your search with a number. Since the last query is what we want to print from, we type in its number, **8**.

ENTER A SEARCH QUESTION TO PRINT FROM (E.G. 1 OR 2, ETC.) **8**

ENTER S FOR SHORT PRINT FORM, M FOR MEDIUM PRINT FORM,
OR HIT ENTER FOR LONG PRINT FORM.

There are three formats in which the documents that have been found can be printed. As listed above, they are short, medium, and long. It's always best to print out a few in short form, first, to see if you are given any indication that your search is, indeed, a success.

ENTER S FOR SHORT PRINT FORM, M FOR MEDIUM PRINT FORM,
OR HIT ENTER FOR LONG PRINT FORM. **S**

ENTER DOCUMENT NUMBER(S) TO BE PRINTED. USE
A HYPHEN FOR SEQUENTIAL DOCUMENTS (X-X),
COMMAS FOR NON-SEQUENTIAL DOCUMENTS (X,X,X),

OR ENTER INDIVIDUAL NUMBER (X). TYPE ALL TO
PRINT ALL DOCUMENTS OR HIT ENTER TO PRINT FIRST
DOCUMENT.

This may be confusing if you've never had to deal with instructions like these before. Let's take them one by one. If you want to print a series of documents, say, number 1 through number 4, you would type the first and last numbers, separated by a hyphen, like so: 1–4. If you want to print two or more documents that are out of sequence, say number 3 and number 7, or vice versa, you would type them, separated by a comma, like so: 3,7 or 7,3. If you just want one document, you just type its number, like so: 3. If you want the whole collection, you would just type: all. If you just want to peek at the first one, you just press Return, as I will do in this example.

```
ENTER DOCUMENT NUMBER(S) TO BE PRINTED. USE
A HYPHEN FOR SEQUENTIAL DOCUMENT (X-X),
COMMAS FOR NON-SEQUENTIAL DOCUMENTS (X,X,X),
OR ENTER INDIVIDUAL NUMBER (X). TYPE ALL TO
PRINT ALL DOCUMENTS OR HIT ENTER TO PRINT FIRST
DOCUMENT. [RETURN]

  1
AU      Anonymous.
TI      Macintosh: What Apple Needs to Start the Juices Flowing Again.
SO      Business Week. VOL: n2833 (Industrial/Technology Edition). PAG:
        68
        B,D, 2 pages. Mar 19, 1984.
END OF DOCUMENTS IN LIST.
TYPE ANOTHER DOCUMENT NUMBER, OR
TYPE S TO CONTINUE SEARCHING, P TO PRINT DOCUMENTS FOUND,
R TO REVIEW SEARCH QUESTIONS, M TO RETURN TO MASTER
MENU, D TO CHOOSE NEW DATABASE, OR O TO SIGN OFF.
```

That looks very promising. After all, it's from *Business Week.* Let's print it all out:

```
END OF DOCUMENTS IN LIST.
TYPE ANOTHER DOCUMENT NUMBER, OR
TYPE S TO CONTINUE SEARCHING, P TO PRINT DOCUMENTS FOUND,
R TO REVIEW SEARCH QUESTIONS, M TO RETURN TO MASTER
MENU, D TO CHOOSE NEW DATABASE, OR O TO SIGN OFF. P;8;L;1

  2
AN      84-11492. 8405.
AU      Anonymous.
TI      Macintosh: What Apple Needs to Start the Juices Flowing Again.
```

SO Business Week. VOL: n2833 (Industrial/Technology Edition). PAG: 68
B,D, 2 pages. Mar 19, 1984.
CC 5230 8651 9110.
DE Microcomputers. Apple-Computer-Cupertino-Calif.
Production-capacity. Software-packages. Case- studies.
AV ABI/INFORM.
AB The Macintosh personal computer, manufactured by Apple Computer Inc. (Cupertino, California), appears to be a runaway success. The first 2 months' shipments were sold in the first week....

Of course, the document is longer than shown here. And it does contain an estimate of Apple's 1984 sales for the Macintosh. Our mission has been accomplished.

You'll notice that the document has a specific format. There are two-letter codes in uppercase next to some lines. These codes are the names of the *fields* within the document. The BRS After Dark user's manual contains the translations for these field codes, as well as the document format that is used by each database. Some of the field codes that are shown above are self-explanatory if you think about them for a few moments. AU means author, TI means title, SO means source, AB means abstract. Similarly, their use is simple to discern. Whatever text follows the AU field code will be an author's name (or "anonymous" if there isn't a bylined author in the original document). Likewise, whatever follows the TI field code will be the title of the article (or the title of a book in some databases). This is a standardized way of arranging the information in the documents stored online. Later, you'll be shown how these codes can be very useful to you in searching.

Let's go on to some advanced material. First, let's take a look at the last command I used to print the document. I typed P;8;L;1. I truncated four steps into one, which is another time-saver. Instead of going through a series of four prompts, I bypassed three of them by entering all of my commands at the first prompt. This is known as *command stringing.* Not every online system offers this feature, however. On the ones that do, such as BRS After Dark, you can save time by jumping over prompts. Go back to look at the three prompts I passed. The three prompts asked for the number of the query to print from, the format of the document, and the document number. By typing **P;8;L;1,** I told the system to *P*rint from query *8* in the *L*ong format the document numbered *1*. Each command is separated by a semicolon (;) so the system understands each one is an individual step.

Another advanced feature is the ability to review the keywords, and their arrangements, you've used in the course of a search. After the above document was printed, this prompt appeared:

```
END OF DOCUMENTS IN LIST.
TYPE ANOTHER DOCUMENT NUMBER, OR
TYPE S TO CONTINUE SEARCHING, P TO PRINT DOCUMENTS FOUND,
R TO REVIEW SEARCH QUESTIONS, M TO RETURN TO MASTER
MENU, D TO CHOOSE NEW DATABASE, OR O TO SIGN OFF.
```

Notice the prompt for the new command: R to review search questions. Typing it will display the following:

```
END OF DOCUMENTS IN LIST.
TYPE ANOTHER DOCUMENT NUMBER, OR
TYPE S TO CONTINUE SEARCHING, P TO PRINT DOCUMENTS FOUND,
R TO REVIEW SEARCH QUESTIONS, M TO RETURN TO MASTER
MENU, D TO CHOOSE NEW DATABASE, OR O TO SIGN OFF. R

BRS/INFO/1971 - SEP 1984
1 (APPLE)
        RESULT         673
2 (APPLE AND COMPUTER$)
        RESULT         572
3 (APPLE AND COMPUTER$1)
        RESULT         567
4 (APPLE ADJ COMPUTER$2)
        RESULT         284
5 (APPLE ADJ MACINTOSH)
        RESULT           Ø
6 (APPLE ADJ MACINTOSH)
        RESULT           6
7 (APPLE AND MACINTOSH)
        RESULT          55
8 (APPLE AND MACINTOSH AND SALE$1)
        RESULT          13
```

Not only are the keywords displayed but so are the results of each search. You can see how your search has gotten to the point it has and also look for any areas you may have missed. Notice that query number 6, where the keywords were "Apple Macintosh" is displayed "Apple adj Macintosh." This means the keyword "Apple" *adjacent* to the keyword "Macintosh" or just "Apple Macintosh," treated as a single phrase.

No doubt you've looked at this example as a fairly inefficient use of a search service. You're right. I did it on purpose. The point was to show you how BRS After Dark looks with all of its lengthy prompts, to show you what happens if you input a misspelled keyword, and to give you an idea of how a search evolves.

The best way to use BRS After Dark—and any search service—is to prepare offline *first, before* you've spent any money. Search services are designed to save you time. Search services also collect a fee for the amount of time that you use them. The old saw, time is money, takes on a double meaning here: the amount of time it would spend you to do research the old fashioned way in a library is translated into the amount of money you would spend online with a search service and the amount of time you would save using a search service is translated back into both money and time saved. As an equation, it would look like this:

(Library + Time) − (Search Service + Money) = (Time + Money)

The point is that the more time you spend offline planning a search, the less time you'll spend online, the more time *and* money you'll save, and the more likely you'll be to retrieve the information you require. For instance, the sample search shown here could have been planned offline first. By going through the BRS After Dark user's manual, you could have read the database descriptions, made a list of the ones that were likely to contain information about Apple Macintosh sales projections, and then created a list of keywords for yourself that would help you narrow the search *before* you signed on. This is not to disregard the spontaneity factor. You may find that once you are online, you'll think of a new keyword after retrieving a few documents. That is fine. Just don't get carried away or you'll defeat the whole purpose of your offline planning and run up a bigger connect-time bill than you had wanted.

Let's take a look at how the sample search could be done in the least amount of time. Once you've earned your wings online, you'll be able to carry out a search like an expert, like so:

```
TONIGHT'S MENU IS:

NUMBER    ITEM
     1    LOOKING FOR INFORMATION?...SEARCH SERVICE
     2    WANT TO HE(-break-)
1;2;INFO
```

First, you interrupt the system by pressing your Break key. If you are accessing BRS After Dark through Telenet, you may use Control-P. This will gain the system's attention for you to input a command. By using command stringing, you type **1;2;INFO**. This means you're selecting main menu item *1* (the search service) then item *2* (business and financial) from the database menu and then *INFO* (ABI/Inform) from the list of business and financial databases. You've bypassed most of the menus and get

```
WOULD YOU LIKE INSTRUCTIONAL PROMPTS? PLEASE TYPE
YES OR NO: N
```

You know the search service commands and you know how long and time consuming the instructional prompts are, so you decide to suppress the prompts. Then you see

```
WOULD YOU LIKE A DESCRIPTION OF THE DATABASE? (YES OR NO) N
```

Since you planned your search offline, you already know which database you are accessing and what it contains. An online description would be redundant. Finally, you see

```
BRS/INFO/1971 - SEP 1984

TYPE IN SEARCH TERMS OR ENTER COMMAND
S1 —>
```

Offline, you decided to try three search phrases. You type them in like so:

```
S1—>     APPLE MACINTOSH

A1       6  DOCUMENTS FOUND
TYPE IN SEARCH TERMS OR ENTER COMMAND
S2—>     APPLE AND MACINTOSH

A2       55  DOCUMENTS FOUND
TYPE IN SEARCH TERMS OR ENTER COMMAND
S3—>     2 and SALE$1

A3       13  DOCUMENTS FOUND
TYPE IN SEARCH TERMS OR ENTER COMMAND
S4—>     P;3;S;1

 1
AU    Anonymous.
TI    Macintosh: What Apple Needs to Start the Juices Flowing Again.
SO    Business Week. VOL: n2833 (Industrial/Technology Edition). PAG: 68
      B,D, 2 pages. Mar 19, 1984.
END OF DOCUMENT. HIT ENTER TO SEE NEXT DOCUMENT, OR
TYPE ANOTHER DOCUMENT NUMBER, OR
ENTER COMMAND P;3;L;1

AN    84-11492. 84Ø5.
AU    Anonymous.
```

TI	Macintosh: What Apple Needs to Start the Juices Flowing Again.
SO	Business Week. VOL: n2833(Industrial/Technology Edition). PAG: 68 B,D, 2 pages. Mar 19, 1984.
CC	523Ø 8651 911Ø.
DE	Microcomputers. Apple-Computer-Cupertino-Calif. Production-capacity. Software-packages. Case-studies.
AV	ABI/INFORM.
AB	The Macintosh personal computer, manufactured by Apple Computer Inc. (Cupertino, California), appears to be a runaway success. The first 2 months' shipments were sold in the first week....

In just a few short steps, you've located the information you needed. No library can match that. No amount of digging through your own collection of magazines and newspapers could match that speed.

Notice that in query 3 I used another shortcut. I typed **2 AND SALE$1.** You should be able to deduce that I told the system to use the keywords from query 2 along with the new keyword in query 3, SALE$1. The effect is the same as having typed "APPLE AND MACINTOSH AND SALE$1" except I didn't have to type that. The system is able to remember the keywords that are used. You only have to refer to them by the query number. This is another time-saver.

Let's move onto some final points about searching on BRS After Dark. These have to do with boolean logic again, specifically, the use of *nested logic*. This is a very advanced command structure and should not be used until you've mastered simple boolean logic (the use of "and," "or," and "not" in search statements).

Nested logic is used when you want to search with several keywords at once, using a logical search structure. For instance, if you were interested in finding documents about car accidents in which the braking or steering mechanisms were at fault, you might use a search line such as this:

S1—> **(AUTOMOBILE$2 OR CAR$2) AND (ACCIDENT$2 OR MISHAP$2) AND (BRAK$3 OR STEER$3)**

In English, that line tells the system to look for all instances in which the following words appear: automobile, automobiles, automobile's, car, cars, car's, accident, accidents, accident's, mishap, mishaps, mishap's, brake, braked, brakes, brake's, braking, steer, steers, steered, steering. It will also pick up a few other words, for example, care, cares, and cared. Still, this sentence is restrictive enough that you are bound to locate the information you're looking for—in the fastest possible manner. The only limitation in using this technique is that your search line cannot exceed 234 characters. After you've done some elementary searches on BRS After Dark with boolean logic, prepare some samples of search queries using nested logic. In fact, you may want to conduct a search using boolean logic and then try it using nested logic. Compare the results and see what happens. If you've done everything correctly and your nested logic is, in fact, logical, you should have the same number of documents from both search techniques.

Another helpful searching technique you should know about is the ability to search on just one field within a database. Earlier, I briefly discussed the two-letter codes that appear in a document that has been retrieved from a database. These are field codes. When you use keywords to search a database on BRS After Dark, the system looks for your keywords in every part of a document. In the sample search, the keywords "Apple Macintosh" could be present anywhere within the document. If you wanted to narrow your search, you could search just on specific fields of a document. A good example would be the TI (title) field. If your were only looking for articles that contained both "Apple" and "Macintosh" in the title, you would type the keywords thusly:

S1—> **APPLE AND MACINTOSH.TI.**

The period-TI-period (.TI.) at the end tells the system to restrict its search to the title fields of documents. Why would you wish to search for articles that only contain keywords in the title field? Let's say that you are a college student and part of your term project is to determine the amount of publicity the introduction of the Macintosh computer received. A sure way of doing this is just to find articles with the machine's name in the title. This would assure you that the articles were strictly about the Macintosh. You can search on any field within any database just by appending the field code to the search statement inbetween two periods. The field code must always appear between two periods. If you wish to search on more than one field code, you can separate the codes by commas, but they must all be between two periods, like so:

S1—> **APPLE AND MACINTOSH.TI,AB,DE.**

This would search the title (TI) field, the abstract (AB) field, and the descriptor (DE) field. Again, notice that each is separated by a comma and that all three are surrounded by periods.

You can also restrict your search to specific fields *after* you've started a search with keywords. It would look like this:

```
S1—>      APPLE MACINTOSH

A6        6  DOCUMENTS FOUND
TYPE IN   SEARCH TERMS OR ENTER COMMAND
S2—>      1;.TI.
```

Note, however, that you cannot restrict a search to one field if you've used "and" in your search statement. So, although you can restrict the query "Apple Macintosh," you *cannot* do the same to "Apple and Macintosh."

In restricting searches to one field of a document, it doesn't matter if the word is typed fully or is truncated; that is, both "CARS" and "CAR$1" are acceptable in a search statement. So, you can type:

```
S1—> CARS.TI.
```

or

```
S1—> CAR$.TI
```

and achieve the same result.

Here is a final example of the search service, incorporating all of the techniques described:

```
TONIGHT'S MENU IS:

NUMBER     ITEM
   1       LOOKING FOR INFORMATION?...SEARCH SERVICE
   2       WANT TO HEAR THE LATEST?...NEWSLET (-BREAK-)
1;3;A4ØØ;N;APPLE MACINTOSH OR APPLE AND MACINTOSH.TI.;P;1;S;1
A1          6  DOCUMENTS FOUND
 1
AU       AUTHOR/S: Sandberg-Diment, Erik.
TI       TITLE: Macintosh: easy as apple pie?.
SO       SOURCE: Science Digest. v92. June, 1984. p82(2).
YR       YEAR: 1984.
END OF DOCUMENT. HIT ENTER TO SEE NEXT DOCUMENT, OR
TYPE ANOTHER DOCUMENT NUMBER, OR
ENTER COMMAND
```

As soon as the Main Menu started to appear, the Break key (if you call through Telenet, you may use Control-P) was pressed to call the system to attention. The one long command string was given: **1;3;A4ØØ;APPLE MACINTOSH OR APPLE AND MACINTOSH;P;1;S;1.** Translated, this command means

1–Select the BRS Search Service

3–Choose 3 from the Search Service menu, which is Reference Databases

A4ØØ–Select the database labeled A400 from the menu of Reference Databases, which is Abtrax 400

N–An explanation of the database is not required nor are long prompts

APPLE MACINTOSH OR APPLE AND MACINTOSH–Search for all instances of the phrase "Apple Macintosh" or the words "apple" and "macintosh"

P–Issue the Print command

1–Print from this query number

S–Print documents in short form

1–Print just the first document

In just one step, you are able to conduct a search and take a peek at the first result to see if you are on the right track. Of course, you can also delimit searches to one field. Remember, though, that this cannot be done if "and" is used in the query (such as in the example above).

There are two more things you should know about the Search Service portion of BRS After Dark: factboxes and full-text scrolling.

The Academic American Encyclopedia database contains the full text of this publication. Part of the text online, as in the printed version, is made of factboxes. This is information that is surrounded by a box that highlights it from the remaining text in the printed edition. Usually, the type used is smaller than that in the body of the article. A factbox contains the vital statistics associated with the article. For example, if you wanted to get a quick overview, say, of Great Britain, read the factbox in the Academic American Encyclopedia database. It would give facts such as the country's population, principal industries, and current political leadership. To call up a factbox, you must structure the query as if you were just scanning a document field. The field code is FB. So, the search for an overview on Great Britain would look like this:

S1—> **GREAT BRITAIN.FB.**

Don't forget to surround the field code, FB, with periods. Try this when you are online. It will come in very handy when you need a broad overview on a subject. It opens up a whole new horizon in doing school reports at the last minute.

The second feature, full-text searching, is only used in certain databases. Up to now, you've seen examples of databases that only give bibliographic citations: a brief synopsis with pertinent source information. In contrast, a full-text database contains the entire article online, not just a synopsis. I will only give enough of an example to let you try the feature. Consult the BRS After Dark user's manual for more details. A sample search output would look something like this on your screen:

```
TX 10 OF 36.

     [TEXT]

ENTER +, −, PARAGRAPH NUMBER, ENTER, OR COMMAND.
```

[TEXT] is where a screenful of text from an article would appear. The first paragraph that would be displayed from a full-text search would contain the keyword(s) from your search query. There may also be other paragraphs that contain your keyword(s). Keep this in mind for the moment, and also notice the top line and the prompt at the bottom. The top line reads TX 10 OF 36. This means you are currently seeing paragraph 10 out of a total of 36 for that article. Now look at the prompt. Aside from the options to press Return or enter a new command, you are allowed to type a plus sign (+), a minus sign (−), or a paragraph number. You may have already caught on to what this means. First, pressing Return will show you the next paragraph (or paragraphs) that contain your keyword(s). Typing a plus sign (+) will let you see the next paragraph, that is, number 11. Typing a minus sign will take you back one paragraph, to number 9. If you want to jump to the final paragraph to get a summary, type 36. You are allowed to roam throughout the article at will, reading it in any order that you desire. This is full-text searching. This is also the end of my coverage of the BRS After Dark Search Service.

Next, we will see the Main Menu again:

```
TONIGHT'S MENU IS:

NUMBER     ITEM
   1       LOOKING FOR INFORMATION/. . .SEARCH SERVICE
   2       WANT TO HEAR THE LATEST?. . .NEWSLETTER SERVICE
   4       KEEP IN TOUCH!. . .ELECTRONIC MAIL SERVICE
   6       WHAT'S NEW?. . .NEW SYSTEM FEATURES
   7       WANT TO CHANGE YOUR SECURITY PASSWORD?. . .
           SECURITY

TYPE IN MENU ITEM NUMBER THEN HIT ENTER KEY FOR DESIRED SELECTION
```

Notice again that choices 3 and 5 are absent from the Main Menu. BRS After Dark might, sometime in 1985, inaugurate a software downloading service and/or a type of user bulletin-board service. From the start, both of these services were planned to be on the system, but neither has made it as this book goes to press. This gives you something to look forward to should you subscribe to BRS After Dark.

Choice 4, the Electronic Mail Service, is a connection to the MCI Mail service. (Note: BRS After Dark will no longer offer MCI Mail, but at press time they did.) I won't go into MCI Mail here, since it's covered as a system unto itself in Chapter 12. MCI Mail works the same way no matter which system it's accessed through.

Choice 6, New System Features, is a short text bulletin that describes the additions to the system and software improvements. Usually, a signon bulletin will alert you to check into here for new developments.

Choice 7, Security, is a program for changing your password. Never share your password with another person, since you are held liable for all connect-time that is billed to you. If you think your password may have gotten into someone else's hands, use this facility to change your password before any damage is done. Then write your password down and hide it in a safe place.

The final item from the Main Menu that I'll give you a glimpse of is choice 2, the Newsletter Service. I like to save some of the best for last, so excuse me for presenting this out of numerical order. Typing **2** will show you a table of contents, like this one for a back issue:

```
                     1 AFTER DARK DATALINES

VOLUME 1, NUMBER 2                    NOVEMBER-DECEMBER 1983

TABLE OF CONTENTS                          DOCUMENT NUMBER

FEATURE
  MCI Mail: Expressly For Your Communication Needs        2

TECHNICALITIES
  The Long and Short of It: BIOL Adds Abstracts           3
  Electronic Text Comes to AFTER DARK                     4
  Nested Logic                                            5
  Truncation As You Like It                               6
  Searches That Qualify                                   7

WHAT'S IN IT FOR ME
  It's in the Encyclopedia                                8
  The Harvard Business Review                             9
  AFTER DARK Expands Social Science Coverage
      with Social SciSearch and Religion Index           10
  Canines, Felines and Bovines. . .All in MEDLINE        11

THE LOGICAL OWL
  The Compleat Strategist                                12

READOUT
  Decoding Those Cryptic References: AAED                13
```

IN THE AFTER DARKROOM 14

CONNECTIONS
  Gimme a Break 15

****

ENTER DOCUMENT NUMBER, DOCUMENT RANGE, ALL, OR ENTER M TO RETURN TO MASTER MENU, OR O TO SIGN OFF.

Although this looks like a conventional magazine or newsletter contents page, it's still a menu (albeit quite a lengthy one). You just type the number for the selection you wish to read. After Dark Datalines is quite a good newsletter, filled with advice on how to get the most out of the system. My favorite parts of this issue include the headline, "After Dark Gets Religion," for an article that explains how to use the Religion Index database to find documents on such diverse topics as architecture, film criticism, mythology, bioethics, and genetic engineering. My favorite sentence in the entire issue was this beauty: "Many other beastly animal questions can be successfully answered using MEDLINE. . .," which appeared in an article about using the MEDLINE database to research animal diseases. This newsletter singlehandedly proves that using a search service doesn't have to be a humorless event. The After Dark Datalines editors are having a fun time. So should you.

Additional Information

CONTACT

BRS, 1700 Route 7, Latham, NY, 12110. (518) 783-1161 or 1-(800)345-4BRS.

DATABASES (LABELS)

Science and Medicine. Abledata (ABLE); Agricola (CAIN); American Chemical Society Primary Journals (CFTX); Biosis Previews (BIOL, BIOB); Chemical Abstracts (CHEM, CHEB); Disc (DISC); Health Planning and Administration (HLTH); Inspec (INSP); International Pharmaceutical Abstracts (IPAB); IRCS Medical Science Database (IRCS); Kirk-Othmer Encyclopedia of Chemical Technology (KIRK); Mathematical Reviews (Math); Medlars (MESH, MS78, MS74, MS70); NTIS (NTIS); Pre-Med (PREM); Robotics (RBOT).

Business/Financial. ABI/Inform (INFO); Harvard Business Review Online (HBRO); Internal Revenue Service Publications (IRSP); Management Contents (MGMT/$14); Patdata (PATS).

Reference. Abtrax (A400); Academic American Encyclopedia (AAED); Books in Print (BBIP); National College Databank(tm) (PETE); Online Micro-Software Directory (SOFT).

Education. Bilingual Education Bibliographic Abstracts (BEBA); ERIC–Education Resource Information Center (ERIC); Exceptional Child Education Resources (ECER); Ontario Education Resources Information Database (ONED); Texas Education Cooperative Database (TECC); School Practices Information File (SPIF); Resources in Computer Education (RICE).

Social Science/Humanities. Family Resources (NCFR); Mental Measurements Yearbook (MMYD); National Rehabilitation Information Center (NRIC); PAIS (PAIS); PsycINFO (PSYC); Religion Index (RELI); Social Science Citation Index (SSCI, SSCB); Sociological Abstracts (SOCA).

Note. As this book went to press, BRS announced a new online system called BRKTHRU (pronounced "Breakthrough"). It's somewhat like BRS After Dark but is available during Prime Time hours and has different connect-time rates. BRS states that BRKTHRU is aimed at business users rather than the general public. For more information about BRKTHRU, contact BRS at the above address.

5 A brief look at the Business Computer Network

Control characters used in this system: Special terminal program key sequences (see text).

The Business Computer Network (BCN) (CPB100042) started operation in 1983. BCN is unlike other online systems listed in this book: It really isn't a system but a way of gaining access to several other online systems without having to pay the subscription costs or monthly minimum fees associated with each system. BCN is, in effect, a wholesaler of online systems. I wouldn't be at all surprised if this explanation confuses you. Until I saw BCN for myself, I was confused by the whole idea, too. Now, though, I can see how it works and I'll pass my knowledge on to you.

At press time, BCN was changing its prices (see end of this chapter for details). Previously, you could join BCN for free, just by requesting a copy of their free terminal program called SuperScout. But by the time you read this, you'll be required to pay an up-front registration fee plus a $10 a month subscription fee. BCN's SuperScout terminal program is only available for the IBM PC, some PC compatibles, Kaypro computers, the DEC Rainbow, and the Apple Macintosh. BCN may develop versions of SuperScout for other computers, so check with BCN to see if SuperScout is available for your computer.

To use SuperScout, you must have a modem with autodial capability; auto-answer is also valuable. Check with BCN to see if your modem will work with SuperScout.

After you load SuperScout, you have to go through an installation procedure. This is a series of questions about the type of computer, modem, and printer you're using. This information is needed by the program so it will work properly with your equipment.

Next, you have to fill in an online form that will appear on your screen. You will be asked to type your name, address, phone number, and a credit card number. This information is required so BCN can charge your connect-time to your credit card and send your monthly bill to your address. The SuperScout program cannot be used as a terminal program until this information has been provided.

After you've filled in the form, the SuperScout program will automatically dial a toll-free number for the BCN host computer and transmit your information. The BCN host computer will unlock the SuperScout program so you can use it as a terminal program. BCN will also poll your SuperScout program to see if you're using the most current version. If a new version of SuperScout is available, BCN will automatically download it to your computer. Once the BCN host has disconnected, you will see the main menu of the SuperScout terminal program. It will look like this:

```
*****************************************************************************
*                                                                           *
*              Welcome to the Exciting World of Networking                  *
*                                                                           *
*           Copyright 1985–Business Computer Network, Inc.                  *
*                                                                           *
*****************************************************************************

Select the database you desire:

Ø. OFF-LINE MENU                    5. CIS Executive
1. EasyLink by Western Union        6. Dialog
2. FYI News Svc From WU             7. BRS
3. General Electric Info Svcs       8. NewsNet
4. CompuServe Info Service          9. More Database Choices!

Your Choice?__
```

If you're using an Apple Macintosh, this screen will probably look different because SuperScout will use the Mac's pull-down menu user interface.

Typing **9** at the above menu displays the other databases that BCN makes available.

```
*******************************************************************************
*                                                                             *
*            Welcome to the Exciting World of Networking                      *
*                                                                             *
*          Copyright 1985–Business Computer Network, Inc.                     *
*                                                                             *
*******************************************************************************
```

Select the data base you desire:

```
Ø. OFF-LINE MENU               5. Billboard
1. VU/Text                     6. SDC Orbit
2. I.P. Sharp                  7. Weather and Sports by WSI
3. MJK Commodities             8. Agnet
4. Securities Data Services    9. More Database Choices!

Your Choice?__
```

These menus will have more online systems on them by the time you read this. BCN is always scouting for new systems, and negotiations with several online systems were underway as this book went to press.

When you want to connect with one of these systems, just type the appropriate number. Then the SuperScout program will call the BCN computer automatically. The BCN computer will poll your copy of SuperScout to get your credit information again, check to see if you have the latest version of SuperScout, and see which online system you want to log onto. The BCN computer will then download a User ID and password into your SuperScout program and hang up. Next, your SuperScout program will automatically call the online system that you've chosen and log it on. If you had chosen to log onto CompuServe, for example, the whole procedure will look like this on your screen:

```
Standby Please...

[Verifying network routing and procedure status]
[Allow 35 seconds -- otherwise program will be updated -- Thank you!]

Network logon in progress for CompuServe
Standby Please...

Logon procedure can be aborted by striking
the X key at any time during the procedure.
4
3
2
1
```

The next thing that would appear on your screen is the top menu for CompuServe.

Access to the systems that BCN carries is through Tymnet or Telenet. The SuperScout program is given the local phone number to call, according to one of the questions that you fill out in the credit application.

Remember that BCN itself costs $10 per month. There may also be additional charges for logging onto other systems through BCN. Previously, BCN was only $5 a month, and this included the cost of 20 online sessions (in other words, logging onto systems via BCN 20 times). Each additional session used to cost 25¢. This cost was for BCN downloading the User ID and password to your SuperScout program. You will have to check with BCN for their latest prices, since they were being revised at press time. Remember that these charges do not include connect-time to the various online systems. Each online system has its own connect-time rates. None of the systems is less expensive to use through BCN. If a system is $6 an hour, you will be charged that rate by BCN plus any additional fee BCN may charge you for downloading a User ID to your computer. No matter how many different systems you access, you will only get a single bill in the mail from BCN. You won't get separate bills from each system.

Once you've subscribed to BCN, you can use SuperScout as a conventional terminal program to call BBSs or other online systems. The program allows for uploading and downloading of text and binary files, data capture to disk (with automatic saving to disk, so you can store more data than the program's buffer can hold), autodialing, the ability to create a message for uploading (using rudimentary word processing), and a personal phone book, among other features. The program is comparable to others sold for several hundred dollars.

The SuperScout program uses its own scheme for Control functions. On the IBM PC and Kaypro versions, the ESCape key is used in combination with a letter key to generate a Control function. For instance, ESCape-N generates Control-S, and a second ESCape-N generates a Control-Q. Some of the ESCape sequences are for local control, such as turning a printer on and off.

An advantage of subscribing to BCN includes having access to several online systems without having to pay their up-front membership fees or any monthly minimum charges they may have. At the time this book was being written, this meant a subscriber would save over $3,000 in the course of a year. As BCN adds online systems, this yearly savings will increase dramatically. Each BCN subscriber is also given a mailbox on the Western Union EasyLink system, allowing access to the worldwide telex network for sending messages (see Chapter 10, "Using EasyLink," for more information).

There are some disadvantages, though. First, BCN's instruction manual for the online systems it carries is inadequate. It's confusing and incomplete. This is true at the time this book is being written. Like anything, this can change and possibly will. BCN sells manuals that are published by each system, however, so you can order those in a clinch. The cost would be minimal when compared to the money you save by using BCN.

The second disadvantage to using BCN is not BCN's fault. It's the fault of some of the systems BCN carries. When you get on CompuServe, for instance, you won't have your own electronic mailbox (see Chapter 7, "Using the CompuServe Consumer Information Service," for more information). You will be sharing one with other BCN subscribers. Since BCN uses several CompuServe IDs, you won't even be assured that you will get the same one so you can read any mail that's waiting for you on CompuServe. Effectively, this means that you don't have the ability to receive electronic mail on CompuServe. Remember, though, that this is offset—to some extent—by having an EasyLink mailbox. If you can live without electronic mail on CompuServe (and many people can), this will not be a liability for you. However, not having an individual CompuServe ID will also have an effect on your ability to use CB and the Forums on CompuServe (again, see Chapter 7). You can bypass these problems by subscribing to CompuServe on your own and only using BCN to access other online systems. It's a small expense.

This problem is not caused by BCN, but by the individual online system. BCN buys bulk connect-time on online systems. Sometimes an online system will provide individual account numbers to BCN for each of BCN's subscribers. Other times, an online system cannot do this for various reasons. Overall, this is a minor point. Check with BCN before you subscribe to see if any of this has changed. Hardly anything is written in stone in the online world.

Despite some minor disadvantages (which may all be fixed by the time you read this), the Business Computer Network offers its subscribers an ever-increasing number of online systems at a savings that can only be called incredible. BCN is especially useful if you only need irregular access to some online systems, since you won't have to worry about paying monthly minimum charges for each system. For researchers and the budget conscious, BCN can't be beat and is hard to resist.

UPDATE

At press time, BCN announced several new products and additions to its service.

BCN is now selling a new terminal program called Telpath, which costs $139.95 from dealers or directly from BCN. Telpath will run on the IBM

PC and True Compatibles, and requires 128K RAM. A version is also available for the Kaypro II and 10, requiring only 64K RAM. A Macintosh version is expected by the time this book is in stores.

Telpath is a standalone terminal program, although to use it, one must first call BCN's host to register the program. Each disk is serialized for copy-protection. Telpath cannot be used by itself to access the many other online systems BCN offers.

Telgate is the enhancement to Telpath that allows full access to the services BCN offers. It costs an additional $39.95 and can only be purchased from BCN. If you buy Telpath (the first program) from a dealer, you can purchase online and download the Telgate module directly from BCN. The new Telgate program is designed to replace the old SuperScout program, previously illustrated.

Telmail, priced at $69.95, is the last link in the chain. It requires that you have Telgate (the BCN module). Like Telgate, it can also be purchased online and downloaded. At press time, it has still not been made clear to me just what Telmail is or will be. BCN asserts that it will be a way for people who have many electronic mailboxes to consolidate their mail. In other words, if you have electronic mailboxes on 5 systems, you'll be able to call BCN to collect all of your mail. One call to BCN instead of 5 calls to 5 systems. This is, at least, the principle. The actual practice has yet to be realized.

Lastly, BCN has raised its monthly subscription fee from $5 per month to $10 per month. This is offset, though, by the fact that this new fee includes an unlimited number of logins each month, as opposed to the previous 20 logins per month.

As with any system in this book, however, please check with BCN for current prices.

* * *

Additional information

CONTACT:

Business Computer Network (BCN), 1046 Central Pkwy South, San Antonio, TX, 78232, 1 (800) 446-6255; in Texas, (512)491-9441.

6 Using Collector's Data Service

Control characters used on this system: Control-H, destructive backspace. XON/XOFF (Control-Q/Control-S) is not available.

Note. As this book went to press, Collector's Data Service went offline to enhance their software. Although the system is not expected to look much different than shown here, new features will be added. These features will be discussed at the end of this chapter. Rather than pull this chapter from the book, I've decided to keep it because this system illustrates key points and concepts that have value beyond CDS's own operations.

Collector's Data Service (CDS) (CPB100043) went online in October 1984. Its purpose is to provide a communications medium for those who wish to buy or sell collectibles and other items.

Collector's Data Service allows you access to the system in two ways. The first is without a membership fee, a monthly charge, or a monthly minimum. Connect-time charges are all that you pay when you read the listings on the system. The second way is a regular subscription, the advantage of which is a discount on connect-time rates. The connect-time rates, as shown on the following signon screen, come to $16.80 an hour from 7 AM to 6 PM and $8.50 an hour after 6 PM. All stated hours are based on your local time. Note that these rates will differ by the time this book is published due to CDS system enhancements. If you decide to post a listing on the system, to offer something to sell, or to ask for an item you're looking to purchase, you'll be charged 1¢ a line a day. A line of text is 40 characters long, and you can remove the listing, on your own, any time you wish. Posting a listing on the system will be explained later. There are some charges for special offline services, too, and these charges can be found at the end of this chapter. Remember, though, that the system enhancements mean that all charges listed in this chapter will probably be different than the actual ones CDS will quote to you when you contact them.

Collector's Data Service is menu-driven, easy to use, and, most importantly, clearly thought out. The system is formatted for 40 columns. This allows virtually all brands of personal computers to get a good screen display. Signing onto the system, which is available via Tymnet, looks like this:

```
          COLLECTOR'S DATA SERVICE
      HOURS: 4am to 11pm Pacific Time

      Enter a Carriage Return [RETURN]
              after every Input

        We accept Visa, MC, and AmEx.

             Connect Time Rates
  28 cents/min 7am-6pm M-F Local Time
        14 cents/min All Other Times

ENTER CREDIT-CARD (Number Only)
or [RETURN] to Exit:
```

The connect-time rates shown in the above signon screen will have changed since this book went to press, so check with CDS for the current ones. This, by the way, is a rule that holds true of any online system mentioned in this book.

There are two ways in which the service can be entered from this screen. The first way is by entering your credit card number, so CDS may bill you for your incurred charges. If you are a first-time user, this will be the only way you can enter the system. Once your credit card number has been typed, it will be instantly verified. The second way of entering the system is by typing in your Message Service number. The only way you can get a Message Service number is while you're on the system, and this will be illustrated later.

Once you've signed on, a brief announcement, somewhat like this one, will appear.

```
          *BILLING BEGINS*
```

CDS does not warrant the accuracy of any
listings and is not liable for damage
from database use. See "News + Info" [3]

ENTER [RETURN] to Continue:

Pressing your **Return** key will display this:

The following system commands are
effective after the Main Menu.

BASIC COMMANDS
Enter [RETURN] after every selection.

/H = Help
/M = Main Menu
/O = Options Menu of Current Category
/ = Previous Menu
/X = Exit Collector's Data Service

ENTER [RETURN] to Continue:

These are some of the navigational commands that are used to move around the system. The backslash (/) is part of the command and must be typed. The backslash, by itself, is also a command. It's used to go back to a previous menu. Pressing **Return** at this screen brings up the system's Main Menu:

All contents copyright
Collector's Data Service Ltd. 1984

MAIN MENU
/H = Help,/M = Main,/O = Optns,/ = Prev,/X = Exit

1. Listings - Category Menu
2. News and Information
3. Enter or Remove a Listing
4. Read Flagged Listings
5. Review Usage of a Listing
6. Leave a Message for Collector's Data
7. Help

SELECT NUMBER:1

If, as I suggested in Chapter 1, you are reading this book in sequential order from front to back, you'll already know that the above list is a menu and you'll know how it works. That's right: you just type the number of the selection you want and press your Return key. It's easy. Collector's Data Service goes one step further and tries to make things foolproof by adding a line that shows the system's navigational commands. This is a nice touch that has been in use on some types of BBSs for years. It's very helpful for new and infrequent users.

Before we go any further, I want you particularly to notice item 4, Read Flagged Listings. I'll refer to it later in this illustration. For now, type **1** and press **Return** to see what categories of listings are available:

```
                    MAIN CATEGORIES
  /H=Help,/M=Main,/O=Optns,/=Prev,/X=Exit

  A. Aircraft                 M. Purebred Pets
  B. Antiques                 N. Books/Manuscripts
  C. Arms/Armor               O. Rugs/Tapestries
  D. Art                      P. Stamps
  E. Photography              Q. Yachts
  F. Class. Vehicles
  G. Clocks/Watches           S. Gen. Collectibles
  H. Coins                    T. Whole Collections
  I. Exotic R.Estate          U. Extremely Rare
  J. Gems/Jewelry             V. King's Fire Sale
  K. Horses
  L. Musical Instrs.

     SELECT LETTER:
```

I doubt that any of this needs explaining. You can see for yourself the wide selection of categories that CDS offers. If you don't think this is a wide selection, be patient. You'll see. Being a writer, I have a special interest in books, so follow me as I explore that category by typing **N** and pressing **Return:**

```
  N          BOOKS/MSS - OPTIONS
  /H=Help,/M=Main,/O=Optns,/=Prev,/X=Exit

  A.    Item Listings
  B.    Wanted to Purchase
  C.    Services Offered
  D.    Announcements Events and Assns
  E.    Newsletter
  F.    Identity Puzzles
  G.    Stolen Items
  H.    Current Books and Catalogs
  I.    Auction Notices
  Y.    Glossary

        SELECT LETTER:
```

With this menu, you get a hint as to how broad the system is. Look at the top line of the menu. It has a title: Books/MSs–Options. This is an Option Menu. Using the navigational command /O will return you to this menu from any place within the Books category. This menu also has an N at the top left corner. That letter is there for a purpose, as you'll see later. For now, let me give you some information about some of the above selections.

Although some of the selections may seem self-explanatory, some can be taken in two ways. For instance, item E, Newsletter, is not where you'll find for-sale listings for newsletter collectors. Item E is an online newsletter for book collectors. Item F, Identity Puzzles, is not a game. It is where you'll find listings from people asking for identification of an item they own. For instance, someone may post a listing asking if the book in their possession is really a true first edition or only a first reprinting. Item G, Stolen Items, is where you can post a listing telling the system users that someone purloined your mint-condition set of Balzac's *The Human Comedy*. You can let everyone know that if they are approached by someone with such a collection for sale, they should notify the authorities and yourself. It's like putting out your own All Points Bulletin to the world of collectors. Item Y, Glossary, is a glossary of terms used in the field of book and magazine collecting. At the time this book went to press, the glossary had not yet been installed. When it is, it'll be a boon for amateur collectors. It'll help them use the same terms and condition grades as professionals.

Let's move further along into this search by typing **A** for Item Listings:

```
NA              LISTINGS - TYPES
 /H=Help,/M=Main,/O=Optns,/=Prev,/X=Exit

   A.     Books and Printed Materials
   B.     Manuscripts/Letters/Documents
   C.     Autographs
   D.     Maps
  +E.     Signed Photographs (Go to Photog.)

          SELECT LETTER:
```

Again, notice that this menu has its own title, Listings–TYPES and that the top left corner now has NA there. All of the menu selections are self-explanatory, except for +E. That's *plus* E. This is a cross-reference to another category. The cross-reference is given: Photography. If you were to select the cross-reference, you would move from the Books category to the Photography category. For now, let's continue looking for books by typing **A** once more:

```
NAA          PRINTED MATERIALS          116

 /H=Help,/M=Main,/O=Optns,/=Prev,/X=Exit

A.     Books
B.     Periodicals
C.     Ephemera
D.     Scores and Sheet Music
E.     Comic Strips and Books

       SELECT LETTER:
```

This menu's title is Printed Materials. Now there is NAA in the top left corner. Let's go on to Books by typing **A:**

```
NAAA              BOOK - TYPE           101
 /H=Help,/M=Main,/O=Optns,/=Prev,/X=Exit

A.     Fiction
B.     Non-Fiction
C.     Drama
D.     Poetry
E.     Children's Books
****************************************
F.     Fine Bindings
G.     Publishers
H.     Rare and First Editions

       SELECT LETTER:
```

New menu, new title. This time, Book–Type. NAA has now become NAAA in the top left corner. Don't ignore that top left corner. It's very useful, as you'll see later. For now, to go to Fiction, type **A** again:

```
NAAAA             FICTION - TYPE          2
 /H=Help,/M=Main,/O=Optns,/=Prev,/X=Exit

A.     No Preference
B.     Go Directly to Listings
C.     Novel
D.     Dime Novel
E.     Mystery, Detective and Crime
F.     Science Fiction and Fantasy
```

G. Westerns
H. Romance
I. Humor
J. Short Story
Z. Other

SELECT LETTER:

Menu title: Fiction–Type. Top left corner: NAAAA. The menu choices are the broad genres of fiction. Item Z is a catchall for hard-to-classify material. Item A tells the system that all genres are eligible for your search. Item B is for those who may be impatient by this point and just want to read *any* listing after going through these menus. We won't use item B yet. In fact it's time to type **A** again:

```
NAAAAA                          COUNTRY
 /H=Help,/M=Main,/O=Optns,/=Prev,/X=Exit

A.    No Preference
B.    Go Directly to Listings
C.    American
D.    English
E.    Continental
Z.    Other

      SELECT LETTER:
```

This menu doesn't need an explanation. Another typed **A** is needed, though:

```
NAAAAAA                              AGE
 /H=Help,/M=Main,/O=Optns,/=Prev,/X=Exit

A.    No Preference
B.    Go Directly to Listings
C.    Pre 1700
D.    1700 to 1800
E.    1800 to 1900
F.    1900 to the Present

      SELECT LETTER:
```

This menu, too, explains itself. I hope you've been looking at the menu titles and the metamorphosis in the top left corner letters. Once again, type **A:**

```
NAAAAAAA                          AUTHOR
 /H=Help,/M=Main,/O=Optns,/=Prev,/X=Exit

A.      No Preference
B.      Go Directly to Listings
C.          A - B - C - D
D.          E - F - G - H
E.          I - J - K - L
F.          M - N - O - P
G.          Q - R - S - T
H.          U - V - W - X - Y - Z

        SELECT LETTER:
```

Again, let's type **A:**

```
NAAAAAAAA                          PRICE
 /H=Help,/M=Main,/O=Optns,/=Prev,/X=Exit

A.      No Preference
C.      Under $5ØØ
D.      Under $1ØØØ
E.      Under $5ØØØ
F.      Over $5ØØØ

        SELECT LETTER:
```

An **A** is typed for the last time, and we see:

```
            LISTINGS - HEADLINES
A FLAG marks a Headline to read later
                 - ENTER -
              F(Flag) to Flag
       [RETURN] to continue (no flag)
       R(Read) to Read flagged listings

COMPLETE WORKS OF EDGAR ALLEN POE

- - Flag? (F or [RETURN]):
```

As explained in this last screen, typing an F will store a listing for later reading. This is the best method for going through the system. It has a limit, though. You can only flag 50 listing at a time. Alternately, you could choose to read a listing immediately after seeing its headline, just by typing R. This method is slow and can get slower if you happen to hit a streak of lengthy listings.

Remember that your aim on any online system is to use the least amount of connect-time. To get in, do what you need to do, and then get out. This will save you money. The arrival in the mail of one big system bill will immediately bring home this point. It's always best to avoid that day of reckoning, so plan accordingly. On CDS, you can do this by using the Flag command.

Typing F will store a listing. You will not get a notice from the system to verify the flag, however. This is not really necessary, since CDS will only accept an F or an R at this prompt. Pressing Return will just make the system repeat the prompt. Since all navigational commands begin with a backslash, it's unlikely that you can make a mistake in this area of the system. Since this is so, a flag verification is not necessary.

```
COMPLETE WORKS OF EDGAR ALLEN POE

- - Flag? (F or [RETURN]) :F

     END OF - LISTINGS THIS CATEGORY

ENTER R to Read Flagged Listings or
Enter [RETURN] for Options Menu:
```

Let's press **Return** here to see the result:

```
N                   BOOKS/MSS - OPTIONS
 /H=Help,/M=Main,/O=Optns,/=Prev,/X=Exit

A.     Item Listings
B.     Wanted to Purchase
C.     Services Offered
D.     Announcements, Events and Assns
E.     Newsletter
F.     Identity Puzzles
G.     Stolen Items
H.     Current Books and Catalogs
I.     Auction Notices
Y.     Glossary

       SELECT LETTER:
```

We're sent back at the top level menu in the Books category—the Options Menu. You see this immediately by looking at the top left corner.

A single N is there. N is the letter used in the Category Menu for the Books category. The top left corner plays a strategic role on CDS. You'll learn about it soon. In the meantime, let's take one more run through the Books category and widen the search this time. First, type an **A** at the above menu:

```
NA                    LISTINGS - TYPES
 /H=Help,/M=Main,/O=Optns,/=Prev,/X=Exit

   A.     Books and Printed Materials
   B.     Manuscripts/Letters/Documents
   C.     Autographs
   D.     Maps
  +E.     Signed Photographs (Go to Photog.)

          SELECT LETTER:
```

Another **A** is typed:

```
NAA          PRINTED MATERIALS          116
 /H=Help,/M=Main,/O=Optns,/=Prev,/X=Exit

A.     Books
B.     Periodicals
C.     Ephemera
D.     Scores and Sheet Music
E.     Comic Strips and Books

       SELECT LETTER:
```

This time, type **B,** for Periodicals:

```
NAAB               PERIODICALS            7
 /H=Help,/M=Main,/O=Optns,/=Prev,/X=Exit

   A.     No Preference
   B.     Go Directly to Listings
   C.     Magazines
   D.     Newspapers
   E.     Pamphlets
  +F.     Fanzines (Goto G.Coll-Perf.Arts Mem)
   Z.     Other

          SELECT LETTER:
```

This menu has a cross-reference on it: +F, Fanzines. The cross-reference is to General Collectibles–Performing Arts Memorabilia. Rather than go through some more menus, which will restrict the price, age, and country of origin, I'll type **B** to go straight to the listings. You'll see which headlines I flag for later reading:

```
                LISTINGS - HEADLINES
         A FLAG marks a Headline to read later
                     - ENTER -
                   F(Flag) to Flag
            [RETURN] to continue (no flag)
           R(Read) to Read flagged listings

E.A.COX, Illustrator

- - Flag? (F or [RETURN]) :F

              ***ART PERIODICALS***
- - Flag? (F or [RETURN]) :[RETURN]

               A COMPLETE RUN !!!
- - Flag? (F or [RETURN]) :F

             DILLUSION PERIODICALLY
- - Flag? (F or [RETURN]) :[RETURN]

**THE AURORA GENERAL ADVERTISER**
- - Flag? (F or [RETURN]) :F

NEWSPAPERS ISSUED ON HISTORIC DATES
- - Flag? (F or [RETURN]) :[RETURN]

THE LONDON GAZETTE
- - Flag? (F or [RETURN]) :F

**NEW YORK TRIBUNE**
- - Flag? (F or [RETURN]) :F

      END OF - LISTINGS THIS CATEGORY

ENTER R to Read Flagged Listings or
ENTER [RETURN] for Options Menu: /M
```

Notice that I used one of the system's navigational commands, **/M,** to go immediately to the Main Menu:

```
                   MAIN MENU
 /H=Help,/M=Main,/O=Optns,/=Prev,/X=Exit
```

1. Listings - Category Menu
2. News and Information
3. Enter or Remove a Listing
4. Read Flagged Listings
5. Review Usage of a Listing
6. Leave a Message for Collector's Data
7. Help

SELECT NUMBER:

This is where item 4 comes in. By typing **4**, you can immediately see the flagged messages. They'll appear in the same order in which they were flagged:

```
                LISTINGS - TEXT
1,1                                   Ø2193
COMPLETE WORKS OF EDGAR ALLEN POE
    Edgar Allen Poe
1Ø vols. New York, 19Ø2.
Book-Lover's Eldorado Edition,
limited. ¾ Morocco and cloth.
Nice. $4ØØ.ØØ

DISPLAY SELLER? (Y/N):
```

This is what a listing looks like. It is an actual listing as it appears on CDS. At the top left corner are two numbers, separated by a comma. These are usage statistic numbers. The first number is how many times the listing was flagged during the current month. The second number is how many flags the listing has received since it was first posted on the system. At the top right corner is the Listing Number. This is the listing's identification number and its importance will be made clear later. Next comes the listing's headline. The headline can be from 1 to 3 lines long, depending on how the seller posted the listing on the system. The text of the listing is displayed next. Then, you're given the option of displaying the seller's contact information. Let's look at that by typing **Y:**

```
DISPLAY SELLER? (Y/N) :Y

Jim Crawford & Co.
31 Bookmark Lane, Suite 3
Cincinnati, OH 45201
513-555-5555

ENTER [RETURN] to Continue:
```

This particular seller has decided to post full information about his firm. You can see the company name, address, and phone number. Not every seller will give this much information. Some will just leave their name and phone number. Others will just leave a mailing address. Others will only leave a phone number. If the seller requires anonymity, he or she may just use the Message Service. You'll see an example of this shortly. By the way, although the ad is the same as it appeared on CDS, the seller's information has been changed beyond recognition, so don't write to the phony address shown.

Let's press **Return** to look at some more listings. This will allow you to see the variety of merchandise available in the Books category and help you to see what CDS can offer:

```
1,1                                                    02078
E.A.COX, Illustrator
Salaman & Absal, Leigh on Sea.
F.Lewis Pub, 1946. 1 of 1ØØØ copies on
handmade paper, fine in dustwrapper.
An Allegory translated from the Persian
of Jami by Edward Fitzgerald. $65.ØØ

DISPLAY SELLER? (Y/N): Y

Andy & Josie's Books
1083 Bindery St.
New York, NY 10019
212-555-5555

ENTER [RETURN] to Continue: [RETURN]

2,2                                                    02401
     A COMPLETE RUN!!!
TRANSACTIONS AND PROCEEDINGS OF THE
JAPAN SOCIETY. London.
A complete run of this important and
scholarly journal, from Vol. I, 1892,
through Vol. XXXVII, 1941. Articles on
all aspects of Japanese art, literature,
culture, history, etc., by the scholar-
diplomat circle and other experts. Uni-
formly bound in cloth.
The set: $5,000.

DISPLAY SELLER? (Y/N) :Y

Rarity Book Co.
415-555-5555
```

ENTER [RETURN] to Continue: **[RETURN]**

1,1 Ø1625
THE AURORA GENERAL ADVERTISER
Philadelphia 1795 Fine 18th Century
newspaper printed by Benjamin Franklin
Bache (as printed at the top), grandson
to Ben, and printed on a printing press
once owned by Benjamin Franklin!
Very nice shape and very early....$1Ø.

THE BOSTON CHRONICLE
1769 A colonial newspaper! Pro-British
sentiments forced this paper out of
business in 177Ø, after just 3 years of
publication. Various news of the day

ENTER [RETURN] to Continue: **[RETURN]**

from this colonial city. Nice ..$6Ø.

DISPLAY SELLER? (Y/N): N

1,1 Ø1621
THE LONDON GAZETTE
1674
This is the world's oldest continually
published newspaper. This issue is 31Ø
years old, in very nice condition.
Singlesheet printed on both sides.
Genuine and inexpensively priced..$16

DISPLAY SELLER? (Y/N): **N**

1,1 Ø1622
NEW YORK TRIBUNE
1864 Genuine and interesting Civil War
newspaper with frontpage reports on the
War. Quite fascinating & inexpensive.$5.

THE NATIONAL ERA
Washington,D.C. 1849 Famous because just
below the headline is printed:
"John G Whittier,Corresponding Editor".
Good...$4.

BODIE STANDARD NEWS
California 188Ø. A bonafide ghost town

ENTER [RETURN] to Continue: **[RETURN]**

newspaper! Bodie was at one time larger
than San Francisco but today is deserted
and stands as a state historical park.
Fascinating newspaper!...$12.

NATIONAL INTELLIGENCER
Washington,D.C. 1836 Popular paper
from our nation's capital which
contains at least one ad for a runaway
negro. Nice..$5.

LEAVE MESSAGE FOR SELLER? (Y/N):

This prompt is for contacting the seller immediately via the online Message Service. Typing Y will place you into text entry mode. You can then type a message up to six lines long. Each line is restricted to 40 columns in width. You will see how the text entry mode works later. When contacting a seller in this manner, you should include your name and phone number. The online Message Service is *one-way*. You may contact sellers with an online message, but they cannot contact you with an online message. I'll type **N** to the above prompt:

END OF - FLAGGED LISTINGS
ENTER [RETURN] for Options Menu:

This should give you a good idea of the format of the listings found on the system. As you can see, they vary in length and in content. Some listings have more than one item for sale. This is not the ideal way of doing things, but it's up to the individual seller as to how to post a listing. CDS suggests that when you have multiple items for sale, you should make a separate listing for each item. The costs will be about the same. A separate listing for each item also gives each item its own headline. This is very helpful for buyers looking for a particular piece of merchandise.

Let's see how a listing is placed on the system. Typing **/M** will return us to the Main Menu:

MAIN MENU
/H = Help,/M = Main,/O = Optns,/ = Prev,/X = Exit

1. Listings - Category Menu
2. News and Information

3. Enter or Remove a Listing
4. Read Flagged Listings
5. Review Usage of a Listing
6. Leave a Message for Collector's Data
7. Help

SELECT NUMBER:

After typing 3, for Enter or Remove a Listing, you'll be asked to type in your name, address, and phone number. This is what the electronic form looks like (it has not been filled out yet):

```
              LISTING ENTRY

 /H=Help,/M=Main,/O=Optns,/=Prev,/X=Exit
NAME:
ADDRESS-1:
ADDRESS-2:
ADDRESS-3:
ADDRESS-4:
PHONE NUMBER:
```

Each of these lines will appear on your screen one at a time, to be filled in by you. You are given four lines for an address. This should be adequate even if your address is outside of the United States. If you don't need all four lines, you can just press **Return** to pass the unneeded lines. Filled in, the form will look like this:

NAME: **MIKE CANE**
ADDRESS-1: **THE COMPUTER PHONE BOOK**
ADDRESS-2: **175 FIFTH AVE, STE 3371**
ADDRESS-3: **NEW YORK, NY, 1ØØ1Ø**
ADDRESS-4: **[RETURN]**
PHONE NUMBER: **212-555-5555**

After you've filled in the last line with your phone number, you'll be asked if you want your

ADDRESS LISTED ONLINE? (Y/N):

You may not wish to list your address. Perhaps you desire anonymity or you just don't want your home address to be made public. That's fine. Just type **N** to keep your address off of the system. You *must* type your address whether you wish it to appear online or not. CDS will not accept any listings without your address.

After you've answered the address question, you'll be asked if you want your

```
PHONE NO. LISTED ONLINE? (Y/N):
```

Again, you may choose to keep your phone number private. But you still must type it in online or CDS will not post the listing. Keep in mind that if you choose to keep both your address and phone number off of the system, you'll have to use the online Message Service, since it will be the only way that prospective customers will be able to contact you.

This is what the next question is all about:

```
Do you wish BUYERS to be able to contact
you via the MESSAGE SERVICE? (Y/N):
```

If you answer Y to this question, you'll be given a Message Service Number. This is the number that you can use to sign onto Collector's Data Service for as long as your listing is on the system. You won't have to sign on by typing in your credit card number. The online Message Service is free up to a point. You must sign onto CDS at least every 10 days to pick up any messages that may have been sent to you. After 10 days, you'll be billed for the storage of the messages waiting for you. This charge is 1¢ a line a day. Since a message to you can be a maximum of six lines long, this is a maximum charge of 6¢ a message a day. (Remember, these charges will be different when you call CDS for rate information due to the system enhancements.)

If you can't check in less than every 10 days, you may want to explore the optional service offered by this next question:

```
Do you want the Mail Message-Forwarding
Service? (Y/N):
```

CDS will mail your messages to you each week. The cost for this service is 25¢ a message and $1.00 a week in postage. (Again, this charge will probably be different when you call CDS.)

After answering this question, the following choices appear:

```
              Listing Duration
1. Run Listing until Removed
2. Enter Listing Duration

SELECT NUMBER:
```

You can choose 1, which will keep your listing present on the system until you sign on to delete it. Deleting a listing will be shown later.

If you choose 2, you'll be told to

```
ENTER LISTING DURATION (No. of Days):
```

Type in the number of days that you want your listing to run. If you plan on leaving it on for more than 30 days, it would be easier for you to remove it yourself. Don't type Ø. It'll only make the previous menu, Listing Duration, repeat itself.

Finally, when this is done, you'll be asked

```
ARE NAME AND OPTIONS CORRECT? (Y/N):
```

If anything is wrong or you change your mind, you have the opportunity to start over by typing **N.** If everything is just as you want it, type **Y.** This will bring up the Main Menu:

```
                MAIN CATEGORIES
 /H=Help,/M=Main,/O=Optns,/=Prev,/X=Exit

A. Aircraft              M. Purebred Pets
B. Antiques              N. Books/Manuscripts
C. Arms/Armor            O. Rugs/Tapestries
D. Art                   P. Stamps
E. Photography           Q. Yachts
F. Class. Vehicles
G. Clocks/Watches        S. Gen. Collectibles
H. Coins                 T. Whole Collections
I. Exotic R.Estate       U. Extremely Rare
J. Gems/Jewelry          V. King's Fire Sale
K. Horses
L. Musical Instrs.

   SELECT LETTER:
```

Now you must select a category for your listing. In this example, I'll type **H,** for Coins:

```
                COINS - OPTIONS
/H=Help,/M=Main,/O=Optns,/=Prev,/X=Exit

A.    Coin Listings
B.    Wanted to Purchase
C.    Numismatic Services Offered
D.    Shows/Exhibits/Events and Assns
E.    Newsletter
F.    Identity Puzzles
G.    Stolen Coins
H.    Books and Catalogs
I.    Auction Notices

      SELECT LETTER:
```

Since I have a coin to sell, it will go under choice A, Coin Listings. If I were a coin appraiser offering a service, I'd put the listing under choice C. The subcategories are broad enough to encompass virtually all situations that could arise. After typing **A**, this menu appears:

```
A                   TYPE
/H=Help,/M=Main,/O=Optns,/=Prev,/X=Exit

A.    Coins
B.    Paper Money
C.    Bullion

      SELECT LETTER:
```

Since I don't have a note or gold, **A** is the obvious choice here. This will lead to menu Coins, which further narrows the classification of the listing:

```
AA                  COINS
/H=Help,/M=Main,/O=Optns,/=Prev,/X=Exit

A.    Ancients - Pre 5th Century
B.    United States
C.    Other Countries

      SELECT LETTER:
```

My coin is a quarter from the United States, so I type **B:**

```
AAB              U.S. COIN - TYPES              5
 /H=Help,/M=Main,/O=Optns,/=Prev,/X=Exit

C.      Colonials - Pre 1793
D.      Specific Denominations
E.      Tokens
F.      Confederates
G.      Proof and Mint Sets
H.      Uncirculated Rolls
I.      Topicals
J.      Errors and Oddities
Z.      Other

        SELECT LETTER:
```

If you're not a coin collector, I bet you're surprised to learn how many different categories of coins there are. I have to confess that I'm not a coin collector, and just going through these menus is an education in itself. You can see how much thought went into the design of Collector's Data Service by looking at these menus.

Since my imaginary coin is an oddity, I'll now type **J:**

```
AABJ                              PRICE
 /H=Help,/M=Main,/O=Optns,/=Prev,/X=Exit

C.        Under $5Ø
D.       Under $1ØØ
E.       Under $5ØØ
F.      Under $1ØØØ
G.      Under $5ØØØ
H.       Over $5ØØØ

        SELECT LETTER:
```

Here is where my ignorance about coins will reveal itself. I don't know how much my imaginary coin is worth, so I'll be conservative. I'll type **D** for Under $100. If this were a real listing, I'm sure someone would be getting a bargain. Although it might have been best for me to place it under Identity Puzzles, I've decided to throw caution to the wind in this example. In reality, you should look into the value of anything you want to sell before you post a listing on Collector's Data Service. Then you'll be able to price it fairly, as well as prevent yourself from being taken advantage of.

```
            HEADLINES
Basic Commands (/H,/M,/O,/ ,/X,/*) not
available until Listing Entry complete

Buyers first see a 1-3 line Headline.

This is either:
     The first line of the listing or,
     A Custom Headline of 1,2, or 3 lines

Custom Headlines cost 10c/headline/day

CUSTOM HEADLINES? (Y/N):
```

If you choose a custom headline by typing **Y**, you'll be able to type one to three lines of text. Each line will be up to 40 characters long. This is what people will see when they do the sort of scanning of the databases that I've previously illustrated. It costs a bit extra, as the above screen explains, but it may be worth it in some cases. (Again, check with CDS for current rates.) If you decide not to have a custom headline, the system will create a single-line one using the first line of your posting. If you're pretty good at writing ads, you could wind up having your cake and eating it here. Instead of creating a custom headline, you could just make that the first line of your listing. The system will then use it as the listing's headline. You could end up getting what you want without paying extra for it. In this example, though, I'll pay extra for the headline so you can see what it's like to use this option:

```
              CUSTOM HEADLINES
Enter [RETURN] to end a line.
Enter [RETURN] at new line to end entry.

- - - - - - - - LINE LENGTH- - - - - - - - -

LINE 1 :
TWO-HEADED QUARTER!
line 2 :
[RETURN]

ARE HEADLINES CORRECT? (Y/N) : Y
```

I didn't need the second line, so I just pressed **Return** to skip it and end the procedure. If I had wanted a three-line headline made up of two lines separated by a blank one, I could have pressed the Space bar on the second line and then pressed Return. The single space on that second line would be counted as a character, even though it would look blank. Then I would have typed my second headline on the third line.

After assuring the system that everything is as I want it to be, text entry mode begins:

```
                 TEXT
Enter [RETURN] to end a line.
Enter [RETURN] at new line to end entry.

- - - - - - - - LINE LENGTH- - - - - - - - -

LINE 1 :
```
US 1976 quarter with Washington stamped

```
IS THIS LINE CORRECT? (Y/N):
```

While typing, you can use Control-H to backspace to correct any errors. As you can see, the system pauses after you've entered a line. It wants you to make sure that everything is OK. If you type **N**, you'll be able to start the line again. Typing **Y** will continue the process, like so:

LINE 2 :
on both front and back. RARE!
IS THIS LINE CORRECT? (Y/N) : **Y**
LINE 3 :
Best offer over $5Ø gets it.
IS THIS LINE CORRECT? (Y/N) : **Y**
LINE 4 :
[RETURN]
IS ENTRY COMPLETE? (Y/N) : **Y**

1. Listing OK - Enter to Database
2. Cancel Listing and Start Again
3. Cancel Listing and Return to Main Menu

SELECT NUMBER:

As you can see, even if you told the system that each line of the listing met your approval, you are still given a chance to change your mind and cancel the whole thing. It would be difficult for you to post a listing that wasn't what you wanted. Since everything is just the way I want it, I type 1 to post the listing. The system responds with

Thank you.
Your Listing Number is 28Ø6
Your Message Number is Ø264239

ENTER ANOTHER LISTING? (Y/N):

The system has assigned me two numbers. The first is the Listing Number, which number is used at the Main Menu. It will allow me to see how many times the listing has been flagged for reading. The second number is the Message Service number. Since I took the option of online messaging, I can now use this number, instead of my credit card number, to sign onto Collector's Data Service. It will enable me to read the messages that prospective customers have sent about my listing. If you decide to add another listing by typing Y, you won't have to type in your name, address, and phone number again. The system will remember it. You'll just have to go through the process of selecting a category for your listing. Then you'll be able to type it in.

I don't want to add another listing, so I'll type **N**. This will return me to the Main Menu:

```
                    MAIN MENU
/H=Help,/M=Main,/O=Optns,/=Prev,/X=Exit

1. Listings - Category Menu
2. News and Information
3. Enter or Remove a Listing
4. Read Flagged Listings
5. Review Usage of a Listing
6. Leave a Message for Collector's Data
7. Help
        * YOU HAVE NO MESSAGES *

   SELECT NUMBER:
```

You can now see one of the effects of choosing the Message Service. The Main Menu states whether there are any messages waiting to be read. When you sign on with a Message Service number, the Main Menu will expand to include an additional choice, 8. Choice 8 is what is used to read waiting messages.

While we're at the Main Menu, let's take a look at choice 2, News and Information.

```
Low cost terminals are available if you
do not have a computer. 8ØØ-435-Ø1ØØ.

                  NEWS and INFORMATION
/H=Help,/M=Main,/O=Optns,/=Prev,/X=Exit

1. What's New on Collector's Data
2. System Description
```

3. Disclaimer and Liability Notice
4. Charges, Billing, and Credit
5. Telecommunications Glossary
6. Free Listing Offer - Information
7. CDS Software - License Information
8. Return to Main Menu

SELECT NUMBER:

This menu will probably look different when you actually sign onto the system. For instance, choice 6, Free Listing Offer, may have expired. Nonetheless, this is where you can go to choice 1 to get the latest news about the system. All of the menu items are text files that you can read. Unlike the other glossaries on the system, Choice 5, Telecommunications Glossary, was fully implemented when I signed on.

Let's type / to get back to the Main Menu. Remember, the backslash command by itself will take you to the previous menu. Since the previous menu was the Main Menu, you don't have to type /M.

MAIN MENU
/H = Help,/M = Main,/O = Optns,/ = Prev,/X = Exit

1. Listings - Category Menu
2. News and Information
3. Enter or Remove a Listing
4. Read Flagged Listings
5. Review Usage of a Listing
6. Leave a Message for Collector's Data
7. Help

SELECT NUMBER:

You saw choice 3, Enter or Remove a Listing, when I illustrated how to post a listing. The reverse of that, removing a listing, requires that you have the individual Listing Number. In fact, to remove any listing, you must have the Listing Number. The Listing Number must be for a listing that you have posted since the system will not allow you to remove a listing that is not yours. Choice 5, Review Usage of a Listing, will let you see how many times your listings have been flagged. As previously explained, there are two numbers that are separated by a comma. The first number tells you how many flags the listing has during the current month. The second number is the total number of flags since the listing was posted.

Let's look at how a message is sent to Collector's Data Service by typing 7:

```
MESSAGES FOR COLLECTOR'S DATA SERVICE

Enter [RETURN] to end a line.
Enter [RETURN] at new line to end entry.

- - - - - - - - LINE LENGTH- - - - - - - - -

LINE 1 :
```
Hello, I was wondering if it is at all
```
LINE 2 :
```
possible to access Collector's Data Service
```
***LINE LENGTH EXCEEDED, REENTER LINE***
```

If your line is longer than 40 characters wide, the system will reject it and you'll have to type the line again. This is a design flaw that I hope will be corrected when CDS enhances the system. The system's software should be able to handle text reformatting in such an instance (this is a feature offered even by single-user BBSs). You can also see that this text entry mode does not have text confirmation. That is, the system does not ask you if each line is correct after you type it, although it does ask for confirmation when you're typing a listing. This may be changed, though, by the time this book is printed. This text entry mode is identical to the one that is used to send a message to a seller through the Message Service. Not having line confirmation in either of these text entry modes is a disconcerting inconsistency in an otherwise well-designed system.

To continue with the message.

```
LINE 2 :
```
possible to access Collector's Data
```
LINE 3 :
```
from outside the continental US?
```
LINE 4 :
```
[RETURN]

```
Thank you, Message received
```

The answer to the question, by the way, is yes. Collector's Data Service is available via Tymnet, which has nodes worldwide. You won't get a reply to any message you send to CDS unless you have a Message Service number. As you've already seen, CDS doesn't have two-way electronic mail, just one-way electronic messaging. This may change with the enhanced software. At the time I accessed CDS for this chapter, it seemed likely that any questions sent to CDS by its users would probably be answered under choice 2 from the Main Menu, News and Information.

After the message has been sent to CDS, the Main Menu reappears:

```
                MAIN MENU
/H=Help,/M=Main,/O=Optns,/=Prev,/X=Exit

1. Listings - Category Menu
2. News and Information
3. Enter or Remove a Listing
4. Read Flagged Listings
5. Review Usage of a Listing
6. Leave a Message for Collector's Data
7. Help

   SELECT NUMBER: 6
```

Lastly, let's take a look at some of the advanced commands available on the system. To understand how these commands work, you'll first have to look at the menus we passed by in the Books category. I'll reproduce the whole tour that was taken, starting from the Main Menu:

```
                MAIN MENU
/H=Help,/M=Main,/O=Optns,/=Prev,/X=Exit

1. Listings - Category Menu
2. News and Information
3. Enter or Remove a Listing
4. Read Flagged Listings
5. Review Usage of a Listing
6. Leave a Message for Collector's Data
7. Help

   SELECT NUMBER: 1

            MAIN CATEGORIES
/H=Help,/M=Main,/O=Optns,/=Prev,/X=Exit

A. Aircraft              M. Purebred Pets
B. Antiques              N. Books/Manuscripts
C. Arms/Armor            O. Rugs/Tapestries
D. Art                   P. Stamps
E. Photography           Q. Yachts
F. Class. Vehicles
G. Clocks/Watches        S. Gen. Collectibles
H. Coins                 T. Whole Collections
I. Gems/Jewelry          V. King's Fire Sale
K. Horses
L. Musical Instrs.
```

SELECT LETTER: **N**

N BOOKS/MSS - OPTIONS
/H = Help,/M = Main,/O = Optns,/ = Prev,/X = Exit

A. Item Listings
B. Wanted to Purchase
C. Services Offered
D. Announcements, Events and Assns
E. Newsletter
F. Identity Puzzles
G. Stolen Items
H. Current Books and Catalogs
I. Auction Notices
Y. Glossary

SELECT LETTER: **A**

NA LISTINGS - TYPES
/H = Help,/M = Main,/O = Optns,/ = Prev,/X = Exit

A. Books and Printed Materials
B. Manuscripts/Letters/Documents
C. Autographs
D. Maps
+E. Signed Photographs (Go to Photog.)

SELECT LETTER: **A**

NAA PRINTED MATERIALS 116

/H = Help,/M = Main,/O = Optns,/ = Prev,/X = Exit

A. Books
B. Periodicals
C. Ephemera
D. Scores and Sheet Music
E. Comic Strips and Books

SELECT LETTER: **A**

NAAA BOOK - TYPE 101
/H = Help,/M = Main,/O = Optns,/ = Prev,/X = Exit

A. Fiction
B. Non-Fiction
C. Drama

D. Poetry
E. Children's Books

****

F. Fine Bindings
G. Publishers
H. Rare and First Editions

SELECT LETTER: **A**

NAAAA FICTION - TYPE 2
/H = Help,/M = Main,/O = Optns,/ = Prev,/X = Exit

A. No Preference
B. Go Directly to Listings
C. Novel
D. Dime Novel
E. Mystery, Detective and Crime
F. Science Fiction and Fantasy
G. Westerns
H. Romance
I. Humor
J. Short Story
Z. Other

SELECT LETTER: **A**

NAAAAA COUNTRY
/H = Help,/M = Main,/O = Optns,/ = Prev,/X = Exit

A. No Preference
B. Go Directly to Listings
C. American
D. English
E. Continental
Z. Other

SELECT LETTER: **A**

NAAAAAA AGE
/H = Help,/M = Main,/O = Optns,/ = Prev,/X = Exit

A. No Preference
B. Go Directly to Listings
C. Pre 17ØØ
D. 17ØØ to 18ØØ
E. 18ØØ to 19ØØ
F. 19ØØ to the Present

SELECT LETTER: **A**

```
NAAAAAAA                          AUTHOR
 /H=Help,/M=Main,/O=Optns,/=Prev,/X=Exit

A.      No Preference
B.      Go Directly to Listings
C.         A - B - C - D
D.         E - F - G - H
E.         I - J - K - L
F.         M - N - O - P
G.         Q - R - S - T
H.         U - V - W - X - Y - Z
```

SELECT LETTER: **A**

```
NAAAAAAAA                         PRICE
 /H=Help,/M=Main,/O=Optns,/=Prev,/X=Exit

A.      No Preference
C.         Under $5ØØ
D.        Under $1ØØØ
E.        Under $5ØØØ
F.         Over $5ØØØ
```

SELECT LETTER: **A**

[Listings follow]

Now you can see more clearly the steps that were taken to move from the Main Menu to the one menu prior to the listings display. The complete sequence was like a search statement: Find all fiction books; genre, country of origin, age, author, and selling price do not matter.

CDS is not a search service in the traditional sense. It's menu-driven. Still, it would be nice to be able to simulate a search statement. If you plan to use CDS regularly to look under a certain category for the same thing, it could get tiresome to plow through the same menus over and over. You can skip the menus if you're always going to be looking for the same things when you sign on. For instance, if you were always going to search the Books category in the manner shown, you wouldn't have to go through the same 10 menus. You can skip them. This is an advanced feature of CDS, and this is where the codes in the top left corner of menus are useful.

Look at the menus once more. In the top left corner, we started with N. At that menu, we typed **A** as our selection. The next menu had the code NA in its top left corner. At this menu, we again typed **A.** The next menu had the code NAA in its top left corner. Every time you make a letter selection, that letter is added to the top left corner code. So, after choosing A eight times, we had the code NAAAAAAAA (N and eight As) in the top left corner. The final *A*, typed at the last menu, placed us at the qualified listings. The complete code was NAAAAAAAAA (N and nine As). This final code is the *path* that we took to get to the listings. So instead of moving through the same 10 menus each time, you can just type in the path name. Well, almost. Path commands are preceded by a backslash (/) and an asterisk (*). Thus, the path just taken could be followed instantly by just typing **/*NAAAAAAAAA**.

Let's see an example of how this would work by using the second Book category search that was illustrated. This is how it was done originally:

```
                    MAIN MENU
/H=Help,/M=Main,/O=Optns,/=Prev,/X=Exit

1.    Listings - Category Menu
2.    News and Information
3.    Enter or Remove a Listing
4.    Read Flagged Listings
5.    Review Usage of a Listing
6.    Leave a Message for Collector's Data
7.    Help

      SELECT NUMBER: N

N                     BOOKS/MSS - OPTIONS
/H=Help,/M=Main,/O=Optns,/=Prev,/X=Exit

A.    Item Listings
B.    Wanted to Purchase
C.    Services Offered
D.    Announcements, Events and Assns
E.    Newsletter
F.    Identity Puzzles
G.    Stolen Items
H.    Current Books and Catalogs
I.    Auction Notices
Y.    Glossary

      SELECT LETTER: A

NA                    LISTINGS - TYPES
/H=Help,/M=Main,/O=Optns,/=Prev,/X=Exit

  A.    Books and Printed Materials
  B.    Manuscripts/Letters/Documents
```

C. Autographs
D. Maps
+E. Signed Photographs (Go to Photog.)

SELECT LETTER: **A**

NAA PRINTED MATERIALS 116
/H = Help,/M = Main,/O = Optns,/ = Prev,/X = Exit

A. Books
B. Periodicals
C. Ephemera
D. Scores and Sheet Music
E. Comic Strips and Books

SELECT LETTER: **B**

NAAB PERIODICALS 7
/H = Help,/M = Main,/O = Optns,/ = Prev,/X = Exit

A. No Preference
B. Go Directly to Listings
C. Magazines
D. Newspapers
E. Pamphlets
+F. Fanzines (Goto G.Coll-Perf.Arts Mem)
Z. Other

SELECT LETTER: **B**
[Listings follow]

Now, this is how the whole sequence would look when using the path command /*NAAB to go directly to the same listings:

MAIN MENU
/H = Help,/M = Main,/O = Optns,/ = Prev,/X = Exit

1. Listings - Category Menu
2. News and Information
3. Enter or Remove a Listing
4. Read Flagged Listings
5. Review Usage of a Listing
6. Leave a Message for Collector's Data
7. Help

SELECT NUMBER: **/*NAAB**

[Listings follow]

See how much faster it is? If you have a particular collecting interest and find yourself always looking for the same item and using the same search criteria, make a note of the path you're taking online. Write it down and keep it handy for the next time you sign on. Then use it at the Main Menu to get to the listings immediately. It'll save you time; online, that means money. (To save its customers more money, one of the enhancements CDS is adding to the software is the ability to do keyword searching in certain parts of the system. This may or may not take the place of path commands.)

There is one more thing that you should know about paths. It has to do with the way Collector's Data Service was designed. Look at the following menus to see if you can spot what I'm about to point out:

```
A                    AIRCRAFT - OPTIONS
 /H=Help,/M=Main,/O=Optns,/=Prev,/X=Exit

A.   Aircraft Listings
B.   Wanted to Purchase
C.   Services Offered
D.   Shows, Races, Events and Associations
E.   Newsletter
G.   Stolen Aircraft
H.   Plans/Kits/Posters/Books
I.   Leases, Charters and Rentals
J.   Parts and other Equipment
Y.   Glossary

     SELECT LETTER:

B                         ANTIQUES - OPTIONS
 /H=Help,/M=Main,/O=Optns,/=Prev,/X=Exit

A.   Listings of Antiques
B.   Wanted to Purchase
C.   Services Offered
D.   Shows, Conventions, Events and Assns
E.   Newsletter
F.   Identity Puzzles
G.   Stolen Antiques

     SELECT LETTER:

E                    PHOTOGRAPHY - OPTIONS
 /H=Help,/M=Main,/O=Optns,/=Prev,/X=Exit

A.   Item Listings
```

B. Wanted to Purchase
C. Repair and other Technical Services
D. Shows/Conventions/Events and Assns
E. Newsletter
F. Identity Puzzles
G. Stolen Equipment
H. Manuals, Books and Catalogs
Y. Glossary

SELECT LETTER:

H COINS - OPTIONS
/H = Help,/M = Main,/O = Optns,/ = Prev,/X = Exit

A. Coin Listings
B. Wanted to Purchase
C. Numismatic Services Offered
D. Shows/Exhibits/Events and Assns
E. Newsletter
F. Identity Puzzles
G. Stolen Coins
H. Books and Catalogs
I. Auction Notices
Y. Glossary

SELECT LETTER:

I REAL ESTATE - OPTIONS
/H = Help,/M = Main,/O = Optns,/ = Prev,/X = Exit

A. Property Listings
includes Leases and Rentals
B. Wanted to Purchase
C. Services Offered
E. Newsletter
Y. Glossary

SELECT LETTER:

L MUSICAL - OPTIONS
/H = Help,/M = Main,/O = Optns,/ = Prev,/X = Exit

A. Instrument Listings
B. Wanted to Purchase
C. Lessons and Services Offered
D. Announcements/Events and Assns
E. Newsletter
F. Identity Puzzles

G. Stolen Instruments
H. Instrument Plans/Kits/Books
+I. Scores, etc.(Goto Books-Print.Mats.)
Y. Glossary

SELECT LETTER:

N BOOKS/MSS - OPTIONS
/H=Help,/M=Main,/O=Optns,/=Prev,/X=Exit

A. Item Listings
B. Wanted to Purchase
C. Services Offered
D. Announcements, Events and Assns
E. Newsletter
F. Identity Puzzles
G. Stolen Items
H. Current Books and Catalogs
I. Auction Notices
Y. Glossary

SELECT LETTER:

O RUGS - OPTIONS
/H=Help,/M=Main,/O=Optns,/=Prev,/X=Exit

A. Rug and Tapestry Listings
B. Wanted to Purchase
C. Repair and other Services
D. Exhibitions/Conventions/Events/Assns
E. Newsletter
F. Identity Puzzles
G. Stolen Rugs and Tapestries
I. Auction Notices
J. Reproductions
Y. Glossary

SELECT LETTER:

S GEN. COLL. - OPTIONS
/H=Help,/M=Main,/O=Optns,/=Prev,/X=Exit

A. Gen. Collectibles Category Menu
B. Wanted to Purchase
C. Services Offered
D. Shows, Events and Associations
E. Newsletter
F. Identity Puzzles

G. Stolen Items
H. Books, Catalogs, Manuals etc.
I. Auction Notices
Y. Glossary

SELECT LETTER:

Did you notice it? If you noticed that each menu shares a similar structure, you're close. If you noticed that they all have almost the same choices, you're even closer. If you noticed that each menu has its choices lettered the same as the others, you've hit the nail on the head.

Take another look at them. Choice A in nearly all of them leads to the first step in finding listings. The exception is the last menu, which leads to two submenus (not shown). Choice B is for Wanted listings, choice C for Services Offered, choice D is for Shows, Events, and Associations, choice E is for Newsletter, and so forth. The menus are *consistent.*

The system's structure also allows for expansion. You can see this by looking at the Rugs option menu and the General Collectibles option menu. The Rugs option menu features choice J, Reproductions. The General Collectibles option menu does not have a choice J. But if it did, its choice J would logically be Reproductions.

How does this logical design help you? It helps you to jump quickly from one part of the system to another, bypassing menus. This can get very complicated, so I'll just give you one short example since I don't want to spoil your fun in exploring the system and devising your own shortcuts.

If, for instance you wanted to read all of the newsletters that are available on the system, you could do it very easily by following logic. On each menu, choice E is for Newsletter. Each category is represented by a letter. So, it is only logical that if you combine the category letter with the choice letter (J), you'd be able to get to any newsletter quickly using the path command. Aircraft is category A. The Newsletter choice is always E. So, if you wanted to jump to the Aircraft newsletter, you would combine the two: **/*AE.** When you're through with the Newsletter, you can hop to the Books newsletter. Books is category N. The Newsletter choice is *always* E; thus you type **/*NE.** It's very easy. Don't be afraid to use path commands. If you hit a newsletter that isn't yet available on the system, all that you'll see is

```
EE                 NEWSLETTER
 /H=Help,/M=Main,/O=Optns,/=Prev,/X=Exit

        The newsletter for this category
              will be coming soon.
```

Similarly, don't be timid about typing a path command, even if you're only guessing. The worst thing that will happen is that the system will say:

```
***INVALID PATH***
```

Nothing serious will result nor will you be hurting the system by such an honest mistake. Just don't get carried away and try to play hacker on the system. That kind of malicious exploration can get you banned from any system. In the meantime, it would increase your connect-time bill. Playing with an Adventure game offline on your computer would be cheaper and more rewarding anyway.

Collector's Data Service is a unique online system. It can help you to locate, sell, or purchase virtually any type of rare or old item or even new or interesting item. If you have a special collecting passion, Collector's Data Service can help you fulfill it online—quickly, easily, and inexpensively.

Closing note. Some of the enhancements to CDS will include online auctions, an identification and appraisal service for buyers and sellers, a "want list" notification service (which should be wish fulfillment for collectors), more specialized information files, and more advanced commands that will help regular users move the system as quickly as possible. CDS stated it would try to keep connect-time rates for the basic service within 10 percent of the ones shown in this book. Again, check with CDS for the new rates and new services.

* * *

Additional Information

CONTACT:

Collector's Data Service, Ltd., 420 West Mercer, Seattle, WA, 98119; 1-(800)435-0100. In Washington state, call (206)281-7273.

HELP FILES

These are the help files that are on the Collector's Data Service online system. Although they will help you to use the system, also check the help files once you are on the system to get an update of new commands that have been added. Again, remember than any prices quoted here will have changed, so contact CDS directly for the latest rates.

BASIC COMMANDS

ENTER **[RETURN]** means pressing the carriage return key. This must be done after every selection or command. [RETURN] is often used to move from one place to the next in the database, and to continue from one screen to the next. In Headline, Text and Message entry [RETURN] is used to indicate the end of a line, or at the beginning of a new line to end the entry.

There are 5 commands that may be used whenever the computer is waiting for a response. These may be used anywhere, *except* while entering the actual words of a Headline, Text or Message. They must all be followed by [RETURN].

/H - will take you to Help.

/M - will take you to the Main Menu.

/O - will take you to the Options Menu of the Category you are in.

/ - will take you to the menu immediately above where you are.

/X - will Exit you from Collector's Data Service.

(Y/N) - after a question, indicates that a "Yes" or "No" answer is required. Enter a **Y** for Yes, or an **N** for No.

If you make an entry or selection that is not accepted by the computer, you have made an entry error. Try again.

The maximum length of a line is 40 characters. Some lines, such as name and address entries, are shorter. Spaces always count.

ADVANCED COMMANDS

The following commands offer ways to move more quickly around the database.

Direct access is available to any menu. Enter slash asterisk **/*** followed by the letter—called the Path—to the left of every menu name. For example, to go to menu ACFE, enter **/*ACFE.**

This Path is made up of the selections that would be required to proceed from the Category Menu to the level at which the path appears. It may be entered at any prompt. If you frequently access a particular sub-category or menu, make a note of its Path.

A plus sign preceding a menu selection, e.g. +H, indicates a cross reference. This is to remind you that entering this selection will take you out of the category you are in and to the category indicated after the selection. For a full explanation, see "How to Search the Listings."

Other Advanced Commands will be added in the future.

HOW TO SEARCH THE LISTINGS

Start by selecting the category you are interested in from the Category Menu. You will then be led through a series of menus that will allow you to reach the specific subcategory you wish to search.

You do not have to select all the sub-categories. The number to the right of the menu name indicates the number of listings at that level. This will help in deciding where to start your search.

Note: This number does not appear at every menu level.

There are two selections that appear on most sub-category menus. Selecting "No Preference" indicates that all of the choices of that menu will be included. Selecting "Go Directly To Listings" indicates that you wish to start looking at the listings immediately and no further menus or choices are required.

You can get to anywhere in the listings by following menu selections or using the Basic Commands. In addition, there are a number of more sophisticated ways to move, and these may be found under "Advanced Commands" (above).

Each listing is divided into three separate pieces of information for fast and easy searching.

1) The Headline
2) The Text
3) The Seller's information

A 1–3 line summary, called the Headline, is presented first. If the item is of interest, the full listing, called the Text, may then be displayed and read. If the item is still of interest, the Seller's contact information may then be displayed.

Headlines appear automatically after category selection is complete. They may also be reached at any time by selecting "Go Directly to Listings" from menus that have this option.

The newest item's Headlines are displayed first.

At each Headline there are 2 options:

1) Flag the headline—if you wish to read the full text of a listing. Enter an **F** to flag.

2) Enter **[RETURN]** to go directly to the next Headline, if you do not wish to read the full listing.

The most efficient procedure is to read and flag Headlines first, then read the listings you have flagged.

At any point you may leave Headlines and go to the listings you have flagged by entering an **R** (for Read). However, if you have not finished the Headlines in that category, you will have to start again at the top.

You may browse in different categories, flagging Headlines that interest. When you choose to read the listings whose Headlines you have flagged, they will be displayed in the order you flagged them.

Flagged listings may also be accessed at any time from Main Menu [4].

Up to 50 Headlines may be flagged at one time. The flag will be removed after the listing has been read.

Three numbers are displayed with the text of a listing. The two numbers to the left, separated by a comma, are Usage Statistics. The first indicates the number of times a listing has been read in the current month. The second the total number of times a listing has been read since it was entered.

The number to the right is the Listing Number. The same statistics may be reviewed from Main Menu [5].

These statistics provide a useful marketing tool, see Help [8].

After reading each listing Text, there is the option of displaying the Seller's contact information, or going directly to the next listing.

If the Seller has elected the Message Service option, a message of no more than 6 lines may be left. Include your name/address/phone if you wish the seller to be able to contact you.

Certain menu selections have a plus sign in front of the letter, e.g. +H. This indicates a Cross Reference. This is a reminder that entering this selection will take you out of the category you are in and to the category indicated after the selection. The listings you see will be the listings of the new category. For example in Musical Instrument-Types, you will find, "+J. Musical Toys—(Go to G.Coll-Toys)." Entering **+J** will take you directly to the Toys sub-category of General Collectibles. Entering a slash (**/** = Previous Menu), will take you back to where you were in Musical Instruments. If however you move within General Collectibles, it may take more than one slash (**/**), or other commands, to return you to Musical Instruments.

The same result may be achieved less efficiently by going back to the Category Menu and working through General Collectibles to Musical Toys.

"No Preference" should be selected when you are interested in all the items in a menu, or when you are uncertain as to which selection is appropriate.

General Collectibles has many categories within it. They are listed on 2 menus. If you do not find the item you are looking for, try "And Everything Else" on General Collectibles—Menu 2.

HOW TO ENTER A LISTING

General Listing Policy: All items of interest to collectors are welcome. However, to best serve our customers we reserve the right to refuse any item we feel inappropriate.

Business or Company names may not be listed on their own, without either a specific item or a service listing.

Listings may be entered in three ways:

1) Directly via any computer or terminal
2) By toll free number (800-435-0100)
3) By mail

Listings via the 800 number are limited to 10 lines, not including name and address.

To enter a listing from your computer, select Main Menu [3], and enter the information as prompted.

Your name and address will be shown online exactly as you enter it. If you choose not to list it online, it will be treated with complete confidence and will not be given out.

There are 2 options in regard to the listing Stop Date:

1) As you may remove a listing at any time, it may be left on until you decide to remove it.
2) You may enter the number of days you wish the listing to run and it will be automatically removed.

Category Selection: Items must be listed in the appropriate categories and sub-categories. After you select the Main Category for your listing, a series of menus will guide you through sub-category selections.

If a menu's selections do not include your item, select "Other." If the menu itself is not appropriate, or if you do not know which selection applies to your item, select "No Preference." The "No Preference" option is not offered in every menu.

If you do not see a suitable category in the Category Menu, try the "General Collectibles" categories.

If an item could list in two places, e.g. an antique rug could be either "Antiques" or "Rugs," it should list in the specific category, i.e. "Rugs."

"Extremely Rare." If your item is one of very few, this is the place for it. However, we suggest you list it in the specific category as well.

The "Kings Fire Sale" is for bargains; but please, collectible bargains only.

A 16 line/month free listing is offered to non-profit organizations under "Announcement And Events." These listings must be entered with a Stop Date.

If you have an item you need help identifying, or gathering information about, "Identity Puzzles" is the place. Select this option and enter the item as a regular listing.

"Stolen Property" allows you to list stolen items free. Entries are limited to 5 text lines per item. They should include the date and place stolen, and who to contact.

You have the option of including your Asking Price in the text of your listing, where it will be displayed online, or if you do not wish it displayed, of selecting the appropriate category in the price selection menu which will indicate the general price range. One or the other is required.

Headlines are used so a buyer may easily select the items that interest them, without having to read the full listings of all the items. As a Headline is what a buyer sees first, it is important and should be carefully worded. There are choices in regard to Headlines.

1) The Auto Headline is a Headline identical to the first line of your listing text. If you do not enter a Custom Headline, the Auto Headline will be generated automatically.
2) Custom Headlines may be used for added emphasis and attention. 1, 2, or 3 lines may be entered. Custom Headlines cost extra, see "Charges."

It is possible to list only Headlines. To do so, enter the Headlines, then enter **[RETURN]** at the beginning of the first text line. If you enter Headlines only, they must include your name and address or phone number as the usual display of these will not be available. You may not enter a business or company name only. A specific item or service must be included.

The Text of a listing is entered and corrected one line at a time. Within a line the "backspace" or "delete" keys will allow backing-up to correct errors. To get a blank line, enter a "**space**" and then **[RETURN]**. At the end of each line enter **[RETURN].** You will then be able to correct the entire line if necessary.

To end the entry, enter **[RETURN]** at the beginning of a new line. If you are not satisfied with the entry you will be given an opportunity to rewrite before it is entered into the database.

The Basic Commands are effective during listing entry prior to Headline entry. From Headlines on they are not available until the entry is complete.

You may lay out the text of a listing in any way you choose. For example:

```
              *** MAHARAJA'S THRONE ***

Rare, jewel encrusted, gold-leaf covered
throne. 30"×56"×36". Originally owned
by the Rajah of Jalapoor and brought to
England in 1850 by Sir Hubert Englebert.
     Offers over $300,000 considered.

          --------Museum Quality--------
```

or

```
*********************************************************
*            WHITEHALL PULLING BOAT                      *
*                                                        *
*                   14'X4'X18'                           *
*         Built Maine - 1932. Cedar on Oak               *
*               Immaculate Condition                     *
*                      $850                              *
*                                                        *
*       Call John Slocombe - (213) 555-1234              *
*********************************************************
```

There is no limit to the length of a listing. But remember that one listing, however long, can only have one Headline. If you have a number of items, it may be better to list them separately, with a Headline for each.

This need not be more expensive, as you only enter your name and address once, at the beginning of the listing entry. It will be displayed, when requested by a buyer, with each of your listings.

After entering a listing, you will be given 2 numbers. The Listing Number is the number of the particular listing and is public. If you lose your Listing Numbers you may retrieve them from Main Menu [5].

If you elect Message Service, you will be given a Message Service number. This number is used to retrieve messages and may also be used to enter the database instead of a credit card or account number. If entry is made with the Message number it will not have to be re-entered to retrieve messages.

The Message number is private. If you lose this number your only option is to contact Collector's Data. This is to ensure complete security for Message Service users.

Listings will be available online within 48 hours, from midnight of the day they are placed.

HOW TO REMOVE A LISTING

Listings may be removed by selecting Main Menu [3], and entering the listing number when prompted.

You may only remove listings associated with the account or credit card number you used to enter the database.

If the system responds with "Invalid Listing Number," you may check your listing number from "Listing Usage"—Main Menu selection [5].

After you "remove" a listing, it will continue to display until midnight on the day you placed the "remove" command. If it continues after that date, please contact Collector's Data Service.

HOW TO MESSAGE SERVICE

Two Message Service options are offered.

The online service for those with computers, and the "Mail Message Service" for those without.

The Message Services allow potential buyers to initiate contact immediately while their interest is fresh, and it is particularly useful where anonymity is required by the seller for reasons of privacy or security.

The buyer is given an opportunity to enter a message immediately after they have read the text of a listing. If this is not offered, the seller is not accessible via the Message Services.

Sellers who select a Message Service option, and who do not list their name and address online, may be assured that their personal information will remain strictly private. The computer keeps this information in a file inaccessible to other online customers. If you lose your Message Service number, contact Collector's Data and we will mail your number to the address on your listing form. We will not give the number out over the telephone, and will not mail the number to any other address.

A seller with online messages waiting will be advised of this when first entering the Main Menu. Messages may be retrieved by selecting Main Menu [8] and entering the Message Service number. This advice message will remain until midnight of the day the messages were flagged for removal.

The Message Service number may also be used to enter the system instead of a credit card or account number. If entry is made with the Message number it will not have to be re-entered to retrieve messages.

The option to remove an online message is offered immediately after the message has been read.

Sellers who select the Mail Message option, will have their messages forwarded once a week.

Messages are restricted to maximum of 6 lines and will be erased, read or unread, after 30 days.

Messages will be online within 48 hours, from midnight, of the day they are placed, and where possible, within 24 hours.

For charges connected with the Message Services, see "News and Information."

The Message Service is intended to facilitate contact between buyer and seller. Messages not containing name/address or telephone, or information relevant to the listing will not be accepted.

The Message Service works one-way only. The buyer may leave a message for the seller, but the seller may not leave a return message for the buyer.

MESSAGES FOR COLLECTOR'S DATA SERVICE

Messages may be left for Collector's Data Service. These may be entered from Main Menu [6]. If your message requires a response, please include name, address and telephone.

HOW TO LIST USAGE

Listing Usage provides a convenient way to keep track of the performance of a listing. A listing not eliciting responses may need a different Headline, a lower price, etc.

Listing Usage is expressed in terms of Flag Count. The Flag Count indicates the number of times the full text of a listing has been read.

Two numbers are given, separated by a comma. The first is the number of flags received in the current month, and the second the total number of flags received. These two numbers will be useful in determining market strategy.

Listers may review the usage of all their current listings by selecting Main Menu [5].

7 Using the CompuServe Information Service

Control characters used on this system: Control-C, system interrupt; Control-H, backspace; Control-O, skip text; Control-P, system interrupt; Control-Q (XON), resume output; Control-S (XOFF), pause output; Control-U, erase typed line; Control-V, redisplay typing; Control-Z, end of file.

It often amazes me when I find people who think the CompuServe Consumer Information Service (CPB100060) always existed in its present form. It did not. Let me give you a brief history of CIS.

CIS began as an outgrowth of CompuServe, Inc., which was (and still is) in the business or providing mainframe computing resources to corporate clients. CIS was known as MicroNET when it started operations in 1979. This makes it one of the oldest National Systems in the United States.

MicroNET was created in part because CompuServe's mainframe computers weren't being used very much during the evening and night. It was a test to see if CompuServe could generate some income from their idle computers. MicroNET was an online system for people interested in using mainframe computers for programming. It didn't look anything like the current service. The response to MicroNET was enough for CompuServe to continue testing.

In 1980, CompuServe wrapped an information service around MicroNET. The system then became the CompuServe Information Service. It was a way to get more subscribers: People who didn't want to program their computers. It was no longer MicroNET. For about 2 years, CompuServe experimented with different contents and different ways of arranging its contents. What worked was refined. What didn't work was left out. This is still true today. It's a continuing process, although the way the system is arranged now will probably stay the same.

In 1983, CompuServe introduced a second online system, called the CompuServe Executive Information Service, and renamed its first system the CompuServe Consumer Information Service. As this book went to press, both systems have been combined into the original name, the CompuServe Information Service. I'll refer to it as CIS throughout this chapter.

CIS is mostly menu-driven and offers the option of direct commands. Some parts of the system are a bit tricky to use. CompuServe recognizes this, and its programmers are always working to make things easier to use.

CIS is available via its own pack-switched network called ComLink. It can also be accessed via DataPac, Tymnet, and Telenet. Prime-time hours are weekdays from 8 AM to 6 PM, local time, at the rate of $12.50 per hour for 300 bps service and $15.00 per hour for 1200 bps service. Non-prime-time hours are weekdays from 6 PM to 5 AM, local time, at the rate of $6 per hour for 300 bps service and $12.50 per hour for 1200 bps service. Non-prime time includes all weekend and some holidays. There are additional communications charges if you aren't calling via ComLink. Plus, some databases cost more than the basic connect-time rates just quoted. The more expensive services will let you know this before you spend any money. CIS bills you by credit cards or directly to your checking account if your bank has electronic funds transfer.

There are various ways of subscribing to CIS. For instance, Commodore owners who buy a VICmodem or Automodem get a free hour of connect-time and usually subscribe once online. Anyone who subscribes to the Business Computer Network (BCN) has instant access to CIS, but this is not an individual account for each BCN subscriber (see Chapter 5, A Brief Look at the Business Computer Network). Most people subscribe to CIS by purchasing a CompuServe Starter Kit in a computer store or Radio Shack outlet. It costs $30 and includes a free hour of connect-time and a short user's manual.

Whichever way you choose to subscribe to CIS, you'll see the same thing as everyone else (except BCN subscribers) when you sign on for the first time. First, there will be a brief notice describing your current CompuServe terminal settings. Then you'll see a brief sales pitch for the service and be invited to subscribe. If you plan to subscribe, you should do so at this time, before going anywhere else on the system. The online procedure for subscribing is very straightforward so I won't illustrate it here. Just follow the instructions that appear on your screen. You're given as many chances as you need to enter the subscription information correctly. Don't worry about making a mistake. Remember that you can use Control-H to backspace to correct any typos. Any serious mistake (such as an incorrect address) can easily be rectified by calling CompuServe Customer Support after you've finished your first online session.

Note: The following chapter has been written for readers who intend to subscribe to CIS. If you aren't going to subscribe, read this chapter completely before you go online. Since you'll only be staying on CIS for 1 hour, you can then explore the parts of the system that are of immediate interest to you.

Once you have completed the CompuServe subscription application, you'll see the following screen. If you decided not to subscribe to CompuServe, you'll see this screen immediately.

```
CompuServe            Page CIS-1

CompuServe Information Service

1 Home Services
2 Business & Financial
3 Personal Computing
4 Services for Professionals
5 The Electronic Mall (tm)

6 User Information
7 Index

Enter your selection number.
or H for more information.

!
```

This is what a CIS menu looks like. They are in a page format for easy reference. This is the top page of CIS. You can see that it's labeled page CIS-1. All CIS pages contain a three-letter service code and a page number. Here, CIS is the three-letter code for "Consumer Information Service." All of the available choices on a CIS menu page are numbered. Like on any menu, you just press the appropriate number key on your computer keyboard to make a selection. At the bottom of the page is an exclamation point (!). It is used as a prompt throughout most of the page-structured portion of CIS. The page-structured portion of CIS is called the DISPLA (pronounced "display") area. CIS menu pages are formatted for a 32-column wide screen. This is a holdover from the days when the TRS Videotex terminal and TRS-80 Color Computer were the most popular computers for accessing CIS. This format still works for most screens.

There are several commands that are available to navigate through CIS. The first navigational command you should know is T. Typing T at any exclamation point prompt will return you directly to Page CIS-1. If you ever get "lost" on the system, you can always start again from the first page. If you type H, for Help, at any exclamation point prompt, you'll see this page.

```
CompuServe            Page CIS-162

     BRIEF COMMAND SUMMARY
T - TOP menu page
M - previous MENU
F - FORWARD a page
B - BACK a page
H - HELP
R - RESEND a page
S n - SCROLL from item "n"
G n - GO directly to page "n"
N - display NEXT menu item
P - display PREVIOUS menu item
OFF or BYE - logs you off

Key S or <ENTER> to continue
!
```

These are the navigational commands that may be used in the DISPLA area. A detailed explanation of each one will appear if you press Return at this page. You won't need to use every one of these commands when you're on CIS. I won't explain any of these now since you'll see some of them illustrated later. If you've actually gone to this page online, remember that you can get back to page CIS-1 just by typing T at the exclamation point prompt.

The first thing you should do when you get on CIS is set your terminal parameters to get the most out of the system. At CIS-1, type **6** and press **Return** for User Information:

```
CompuServe            Page CIS-4

USER INFORMATION
 1 What's New
 2 Command Summary & Usage Tips
```

```
 3 Feedback to CompuServe
 4 Order Products, Guides, etc.
 5 Change Terminal Settings
 6 Change Your Password
 7 Billing: Your Charges, Rates
       Options, Making Changes
 8 Logon Instructions & Numbers
 9 Online Today
10 Documentation

Last menu page. Key digit
or M for previous menu.
!
```

The last line of this menu page reads "Last menu page. Key digit or M for previous menu." You must either make a selection from this menu or move back to the previous one. There aren't any sub-menus beyond this point. Although the last line says that you should type M for the previous menu, you can get back to it faster by just pressing Return. You don't have to type M and then press Return.

Here is a brief explanation of what the above choices will allow you to do:

- *What's New.* Read about additions and changes to CompuServe.
- *Command Summary & Usage Tips.* Read a brief tutorial about the commands most frequently used in the DISPLA portion of CompuServe. You've already seen the first page of this tutorial.
- *Feedback to CompuServe.* Send an electronic text message to CompuServe Customer Support to report trouble using or accessing the system. You won't be charged for connect-time while using this, although you do have to pay for communications charges if you aren't calling via ComLink. This feature will be illustrated near the end of this chapter.
- *Order Products, Guides, etc.* Order CompuServe telecommunications software (Vidtex terminal programs) and other products. Again, there isn't a charge for connect-time while using this, although you do have to pay for communications charges if you aren't calling via ComLink. This will be illustrated soon.
- *Change Terminal Settings.* This is self-explanatory. You'll see how to do it after these explanations.
- *Change Your Password.* Enter a new password to ensure that your account is secure from use by others.
- *Billing: Your Charges, Rates, Options, Making Changes.* Review your connect-time charges on a per-week basis, look up the current con-

nect-time rates, or let CompuServe know that you want to change the manner in which you are being billed; for instance, have your time charged to a credit card instead of a checking account.

- *Logon Instructions & Numbers.* Read a list of all packet-switched nodes that lead to CompuServe. These numbers come in handy if you want to access the system while on vacation or a business trip.
- *Online Today.* This is the electronic version of CompuServe's *Online Today* magazine. The printed magazine is sent to CIS subscribers for free. You can contact companies that have advertised in the magazine by using the Electronic Bounce Back (EBB) feature available here. Don't be intimidated by the Electronic Bounce Back title. It just means sending an electronic text message.
- *Documentation.* Where you can order various manuals to help you use CIS and some individual databases.

Choice 4 on the above menu is the one to use to change your CompuServe terminal settings. Type **4** and press **Return:**

```
CompuServe            Page CIS-9

     Welcome to DEFALT

1 Instructions
2 Setting Your Terminal Type
3 Setting Your Logon Actions
4 Setting Delays for Printers
5 View or Change Current
      Terminal Parameters
6 Exit DEFALT

Last Menu Page. Key digit
or M for previous menu.
!
```

Don't be intimidated if any of the menus you'll see from this point on are slightly different when you actually sign onto CIS. More likely than not, everything will look pretty much the same and you'll still be able to follow these examples to carry out your own terminal settings.

When you're online, you may read selection 1, Instructions. I'll dispense with these and go ahead and show you what you need to do.

First, you have to consider what you want to do when you are on CompuServe. What do you want to get out of it? Do you plan to receive a lot of electronic test messages? Will you just be checking into a certain service? What type of terminal program are you currently using? Do you eventually plan to buy another? These are the questions you have to consider when you make any changes to your terminal settings. These changes won't be irreversible. You can reset them any time you wish or need to. But the settings you make should reflect the most effective way you can use the system. I won't be covering every combination of settings that could be used for your terminal. I'll show what most CIS subscribers use and discuss the options that are available to you along the way.

Type **2** and press **Return** for Setting Your Terminal Type.

```
Your Terminal Type:
OTHER
Baud Rate: 3ØØ

    Terminals we Support

1 VIDTEX software compatible
    ( Default 32 × 16 )
2 ANSI compatible (VT-1ØØ)
3 Teleray
4 Other

Choose terminal type
desired. <ENTER> keeps
current terminal type.
!
```

Most likely, you'll only be concerned with two of these selections: choices 1 and 4. Choice 1 is for those who use the CompuServe terminal program Vidtex. This program is used for downloading public-domain programs that are available on the system. You'll learn more about this later. This setting is necessary for Vidtex users because CIS does cursor addressing to the program. That's a technical way of saying it makes the display on your screen look nice. Also, when you download programs, the process is monitored for transmission errors using CompuServe's proprietary B protocol.

If you're using Vidtex on CompuServe, type **1**. If you're brand new to CIS, you probably won't be using Vidtex. In that case, just press **Return** to leave your terminal type specified as Other. If you eventually buy Vidtex to use it on CompuServe, come back here and type **1** so that you can take full advantage of either Vidtex or CompuServe. After we finish making the terminal settings, I'll show you how to order Vidtex online. By the way, don't worry if everything is in uppercase on your screen. You'll be able to change that soon. Once you've typed the appropriate choice, a notice will tell you that the change has been made. Then you'll see

```
        Welcome to DEFALT

1 Instructions
2 Setting Your Terminal Type
3 Setting Your Logon Actions
4 Setting Delays for Printers
5 View or Change Current
   Terminal Parameters
6 Exit DEFALT

Last Menu Page. Key digit
or M for previous menu.
!
```

Next, type **2**, for your logon actions:

```
Actions when logging on:

 1 If EMAIL waiting,              ANNOUNCE IT
 2 You now receive               FULL PROMPTS
 3 Automatically run               NO PROGRAM
 4 The first service is              VIDEOTEX
 5 Create/Edit your Personal Menu

Select item to be changed or
press <ENTER> for no change.
!
```

Things begin to get a bit tricky here, and it's important that you know what you want to do with CompuServe. Again, don't worry about changing your settings throughout any part of this procedure. Once you're familiar with CompuServe, you can always repeat this procedure to change anything you want. In a moment, I'll start taking you through each step of this process.

First, though, you have to know that EMail means electronic mail. You also have to know that as this book went to press, CIS changed both the name and the software of their electronic test message service. EMail is now EasyPlex. (The name EasyPlex is derived from CIS's business electronic text message software, which is called InfoPlex.) I expect you'll see EasyPlex instead of EMail in these menus. Since this change had not yet occurred at press time, I'll refer to EMail instead of EasyPlex.

Choice 1, for EMail, is set to tell you when you have an electronic text message waiting to be read. This will occur whenever you sign on the system.

This notice will appear:

```
You have EMAIL waiting
```

You must then go to Page EMA-1 to read your messages. EMail—rather, EasyPlex—will be illustrated later in this chapter. For most people, this signon notice is enough. But if you can't wait to see who has sent you a message, you can use this choice to make the system take you directly to Page EMA-1 (now just Page EASY, without a number) at signon so you can read your messages immediately. To do this, type **1** and press **Return**:

```
When logging on:

1 Go to EMAIL if messages are
  waiting
2 Notify only if messages are
  waiting

Current setting is 2
<ENTER> leaves it unchanged
Key choice:
```

Type **1** if you want to read your waiting messages at signon. If you've decided not to change the setting of 2, just press **Return**. If you've already typed 1, you can use Control-H to delete it if you haven't already pressed Return. (If you've already pressed Return, just repeat these steps to fix it.) Again, you'll see

```
Actions when logging on:

 1 If EMAIL waiting,              ANNOUNCE IT
 2 You now receive               FULL PROMPTS
 3 Automatically run               NO PROGRAM
 4 The first service is              VIDEOTEX
 5 Create/Edit your Personal Menu

Select item to be changed or
press <ENTER> for no change.
!
```

Of course, if your EMail (EasyPlex) setting has been changed, it'll now say

```
1 If EMAIL waiting,   GO TO EMAIL
```

Choice 2, for prompts, is currently set to give you full prompts throughout CompuServe. This can be an annoyance at times, especially after you've become used to the system and its commands. Whenever you use the DISPLA portion of CompuServe, though, you'll always get full menus. This setting doesn't shorten or modify DISPLA in any way. This setting will mostly have an effect when you use the various Forums on CIS. You'll learn about Forums later.

If you're a new CIS subscriber, it'd be a good idea to leave this setting alone until you know your way around the system. If you've been using CompuServe for a while and know the system pretty well, type **2** to change this setting. This is what you'll then see:

```
When using certain CIS
services,

1 Use expert mode, prompts will
  be shortened
2 Use novice mode, prompts will
  be full

Current setting is 2
<ENTER> leaves it unchanged
Key choice:
```

To change the current setting, type **1** and press **Return**. Again, you'll see:

```
Actions when logging on:

 1 If EMAIL waiting,              ANNOUNCE IT
 2 You now receive               FULL PROMPTS
 3 Automatically run               NO PROGRAM
 4 The first service is              VIDEOTEX
 5 Create/Edit your Personal Menu

Select item to be changed or
press <ENTER> for no change.
!
```

If you've changed choice 2, it'll now read:

```
 2 You now receive          SHORT PROMPTS
```

Choice 3 isn't going to be covered now. This is an advanced feature that I'll explain at the end of the chapter. For now, leave this setting as it is.

Choice 4, for system entry, is set at Videotex. Videotex is another word for DISPLA, the menu- and page-structured portion of CIS. Let's take a look at these options by typing **4** and pressing **Return**:

```
Set first service to:

  1 Videotex
  2 Personal File Area
  3 Personal Menu
  4 Selected Videotex top page

Current setting is 1
<ENTER> leaves it unchanged
Key choice:
```

Leave this as it is right now. At the end of this chapter, I'll explain how you may use this to your advantage. I just want you to know that these choices exist.

Press **Return** to continue. For the last time, you'll see

```
Actions when logging on:

  1 If EMAIL waiting,             ANNOUNCE IT
  2 You now receive              FULL PROMPTS
  3 Automatically run              NO PROGRAM
  4 The first service is             VIDEOTEX
  5 Create/Edit your Personal Menu

Select item to be changed or
press <ENTER> for no change.
!
```

Selection 5, Personal Menu, is an advanced feature of CIS. You'll learn about it at the end of this chapter. If you've made changes to choices 1 and 2, your screen will look like this:

```
Actions when logging on:

  1 If EMAIL waiting,             GO TO EMAIL
  2 You now receive             SHORT PROMPTS
  3 Automatically run              NO PROGRAM
  4 The first service is             VIDEOTEX
  5 Create/Edit your Personal Menu

Select item to be changed or
press <ENTER> for no change.
!
```

Before you go any further, make sure that your screen looks identical to either of the two screens shown above. If any corrections are necessary, make them before taking the next step. Once everything is OK, press **Return** to see

```
Welcome to DEFALT

1 Instructions
2 Setting Your Terminal Type
3 Setting Your Logon Actions
4 Setting Delays for Printers
5 View or Change Current
   Terminal Parameters
6 Exit DEFALT

Last Menu Page. Key digit
or M for previous menu.
!
```

The next setting is choice 4, printer delays. This one doesn't need changing if you're using a good terminal program. If your online screen display has been OK so far, your terminal program is probably fine. If you're using a terminal program that you typed from a listing in BASIC, you'll probably need to set printer delays, even if you aren't using a printer.

Printer delays are known as *nulls*. Nulls are blank spaces sent by an online system after it has transmitted a line of text. They are required by some printing terminals. A slow printing terminal will need a chance to move its printhead back to the left-hand side of its carriage so it can print the following line. If it isn't given this chance, it will lose characters at the beginning of the next line. The problem will get worse as it stays online because it just isn't fast enough to keep up. This is where nulls come in. They allow a slow printing terminal to catch up by sending it blank spaces after each line. Nulls are also handy if you're using a terminal program written in BASIC, since it may be too slow to accept even 300 bps output from an online system. A slow terminal program can begin to lose characters at the beginning of a line. Even worse, it may display nothing but garbage (garbled characters) on a screen. The solution is to throw in a few nulls. This is done by typing **4**.

```
Delays for printers

 1 Delay after carriage return      Ø
 2 Delay after line feed            Ø

Select item to be changed or
press <ENTER> for no change.
!
```

There isn't any formula for setting nulls. You'll have to experiment with them to see what works best for you. Once you're finished, press **Return** to see

```
    Welcome to DEFALT

1 Instructions
2 Setting Your Terminal Type
3 Setting Your Logon Actions
4 Setting Delays for Printers
5 View or Change Current
    Terminal Parameters
6 Exit DEFALT

Last Menu Page. Key digit
or M for previous menu.
!
```

Now type **5**.

```
Your terminal type:
OTHER
Baud rate: 3ØØ

Current terminal parameters:

 1 Terminal width           8Ø CHARACTERS
 2 Page size is now              Ø LINES
 3 Form feeds are              SIMULATED
 4 Horizontal tabs are         SIMULATED
 5 Terminal supports          UPPER CASE
 6 Caps lock is                       ON
 7 Line feeds are                   SENT
 8 Parity is                        EVEN
 9 Blank lines are                  SENT

Select item to be changed or
press <ENTER> for no change.
!
```

If you've never dealt with settings like these on an online system, you may be confused. Each setting will be explained, along with its available options. By the way, "parameters" is computerese for "settings." Don't be intimidated by the word.

Choice 1, for terminal width, is currently set for 80 characters. For the moment, don't worry if your screen shows another number. This setting is a bit misleading. I discussed why in Chapter 4, Using BRS After Dark. This setting affects you if you have a display less than 80 columns wide. Briefly, if you plan to print out anything from any online service, it's best to print it out as wide as your paper (or printer) can handle. You'll save paper, it'll be easier to read, and it'll look better that way. Of course, if you set the width to make your screen display look OK, you'll waste paper when printing. On the other hand, if you set the width to take advantage of printing on a standard 80-column sheet of paper, your screen display won't look too good. It's up to you to choose a setting. If you don't believe that you'll be doing much printing, set the width to correspond to your screen. If you plan to do a lot of printing, set the width to correspond to a standard sheet of paper. I do a lot or printing, so my width is set for 63 characters. This allows for 1-inch margins on paper.

No matter which width you choose, it's set by typing **1:**

```
Terminal width 8Ø CHARACTERS
<ENTER> leaves it unchanged

How many characters per line
for this terminal?
```

Type the width you want, **40** or **63,** or press **Return** to leave it as it is. If your terminal type was previously set as Vidtex, you'll automatically have 32-column lines. Even if you're set to Vidtex, you can still change the width to whatever you want. After that, you'll see

```
Your terminal type:
OTHER
Baud Rate: 3ØØ

Current Terminal parameters:

 1 Terminal width           8Ø CHARACTERS
 2 Page size is now              Ø LINES
 3 Form feeds are              SIMULATED
 4 Horizontal tabs are         SIMULATED
 5 Terminal supports          UPPER CASE
 6 Caps lock is                       ON
 7 Line feeds are                   SENT
 8 Parity is                        EVEN
 9 Blank lines are                  SENT

Select item to be changed or
press <ENTER> for no change.
!
```

Choice 1 will have been changed to reflect your own width. As changes are made to your settings, this screen will reappear to confirm the change (or to confirm that no change was made). In the interest of brevity, I'm not going to repeat this screen after each change.

Choice 2, for page size, also brings up the conflict of screen versus printer. If your width was set for your screen, leave this as it is, set to zero. If you've set your width to take advantage of printing, change this to standard page length, either 54 or 55. If your terminal type was previously set as Vidtex, this setting will show 16 lines for a page. You can change it to whatever you need.

Choice 3, for form feeds, is only used with printing terminals. On a video screen, a real form feed will clear the screen and HOME the cursor. Although this can be a nice effect to impress your friends, it can be very annoying. There's nothing as irritating as having a screen go blank before you're finished reading it. My advice is to leave this setting the way it is. If your terminal type was previously set to Vidtex, you should change this to simulated form feeds in order to lessen screen blanking.

Choice 4, for horizontal tabs, isn't something you're likely to need. Just leave it as it is. If your terminal type was previously set at Vidtex, you'll see this listed as simulated tabs.

Choice 5, the case setting, is of great importance. Unless you previously set your terminal type to Vidtex, it's a good bet that all of these screens appeared online in UPPERCASE. New CIS subscribers are often in ALL CAPS, since they lack the knowledge to change their terminal settings. Being able to change your terminal settings is almost a rite of passage on CIS. It distinguishes you from the CIS novices. Type **5:**

```
1 Terminal supports upper
  and lower case. CAPS LOCK
  IS ON.
2 Terminal supports upper
  and lower case. Caps lock
  is off.
3 Terminal supports upper
  case only.
4 Terminal supports lower
  case only.

Current setting is 1
<ENTER> leaves it unchanged
Key choice:
```

Type **2** and you'll see everything change to upper and lowercase. Now you can travel throughout CIS without overtly looking like a novice. Notice that changing item 5 also changed item 6.

We can now skip to item 7, the linefeed setting. On a typewriter, you know that the Return key must be pressed in order to start a new line. This is known as a carriage return. In computer communications something similar takes place with your screen cursor. It must move down to the next line in order to display it. So must the printhead of a printer, whenever it prints a line of text. This is where a *linefeed* comes in. It lets your computer know that it must move the cursor down one line. It lets a printer know it must advance the paper upward one line. If a linefeed wasn't sent, you'd only see one line on your screen. This one line would be constantly overwritten and replaced by a new line. The result on your printer would be a single line repeatedly overwritten, becoming a black stripe. This setting should be left as it is. If you previously set your terminal type to Vidtex, you'll still need linefeeds.

Choice 8, the parity setting, should generally be even. The available choices are zero, even, odd, or one. If you have it set as even, leave it. If your screen shows otherwise, change it to even. Selecting Vidtex as a terminal type automatically sets this to even.

Setting 9, the blank line setting, should be left alone. It's doubtful that you'd want to do without blank lines.

Finally, your terminal settings should look like one of the following choices:

Settings Favoring Printer

```
Your Terminal Type:
OTHER
Baud Rate: 300

Current Terminal Parameters:

 1 Terminal width          80 CHARACTERS
 2 Page size is now             55 LINES
 3 Form feeds are              SIMULATED
 4 Horizontal tabs are         SIMULATED
 5 Terminal supports         UPPER/LOWER
 6 Caps lock is                      OFF
 7 Line feeds are                   SENT
 8 Parity is                        EVEN
 9 Blank lines are                  SENT

Select item to be changed or
press <ENTER> for no change.
!
```

Settings Favoring 40-Column Screen

```
Your Terminal Type:
VIDTEX
Baud Rate: 3ØØ

Current Terminal Parameters:

 1 Terminal width           4Ø CHARACTERS
 2 Page size is now              16 LINES
 3 Form feeds are               SIMULATED
 4 Horizontal tabs are          SIMULATED
 5 Terminal supports          UPPER/LOWER
 6 Caps lock is                       OFF
 7 Line feeds are                    SENT
 8 Parity is                         EVEN
 9 Blank lines are                   SENT

Select item to be changed or
press <ENTER> for no change.
!
```

Of course, your own selections may be different. Regardless of what you've selected, you'll be glad to know that your computer is now set to use CompuServe. All you have to do is let CompuServe know that by pressing **Return.**

```
   Welcome to DEFALT

1 Instructions
2 Setting Your Terminal Type
3 Setting Your Logon Actions
4 Setting Delays for Printers
5 View or Change Current
   Terminal Parameters
6 Exit DEFALT

Last menu page. Key digit
or M for previous menu.
!
```

Type **6** to exit. This will store your terminal settings. At any time, you may go back and reset them. Now that this is over, Page CIS-4, the User Information menu, will reappear:

```
CompuServe        Page CIS-4

USER INFORMATION
 1 What's New
 2 Command Summary & Usage Tips
```

3 Feedback to CompuServe
4 Order Products, Guides, etc.
5 Change Terminal Settings
6 Change Your Password
7 Billing: Your Charges, Rates
   Options, Making Changes
8 Logon Instructions & Numbers
9 Online Today
10 Documentation

Last menu page. Key digit
or M for previous menu.
!

It would be a good idea to show how to order something from CompuServe, since you'll probably want to order a copy of CompuServe's Vidtex terminal software. So, type **4** to get

CompuServe Page CIS-54

Request Recorded,
One Moment, Please

Whenever you see this notice on CIS, it means that you're being switched from one CIS computer to another. After a moment or so, you'll see

Thank You for Waiting

COMPUSERVE PRODUCT ORDERING
You are not charged for connect
time while in this service (you
will be charged the applicable
network surcharge).

INSTRUCTIONS: Review the on-
line descriptions carefully.

All sales are FINAL.

Call Customer Service if you
need additional information
before ordering.

Key <ENTER> for next page: **[RETURN]**

After entering your on-line
order, a summary is displayed.

```
You must verify the summary
to place your order. Please
allow 4–6 weeks for de-
livery. (Allow ample time
for delivery before in-
quiring.)

NOTE: Do not use the Control-C
command while in this service.

Key <ENTER> for next page:
```

Keep in mind while you read this book that CompuServe, like all other online services, is hardly static. If you've come across pages that look a bit different from the ones I've shown, it just means that CompuServe has made changes to benefit its subscribers. All of the pages and screens I'm showing did look like this at one time. Pressing **Return** will reveal:

```
Ordering options:
1  User guides and manuals
2  Products (VIDTEX & other)

Last menu page, Key digit
or M for previous menu.       :
```

Let's type **2:**

```
  Please Note: CompuServe
strives to provide the highest
quality software possible to our
customers. Please read the de-
scriptions and select your soft-
ware carefully. All software
sales are final (except in case
of damaged software).
We are sorry, the CompuServe
Adventure T-shirt is no longer
available.

Key <ENTER> for next page. :[RETURN]
1  Adventure Products
2  MegaWars Products
3  Terminal Software-TRS8Ø
4  Terminal Software-COMMODORE
5  Terminal Software-ALL OTHERS
6  Executive Info Service
7  Additional Services Kit
```

```
8 Consumer Info Starter Kit
9 Miscellaneous

Last menu page, Key digit
or M for previous menu.      :
```

Let's type **5:**

```
1 Prof Con-IBM PC,XT,PCjr           $59.95
2 Kaypro II VIDTEX 3.Ø              $29.95
3 Osborne 1 VIDTEX 3.Ø              $29.95
4 Apple II 3.3 Dos VIDTEX           $39.95
5 CP/M Terminal Software            $19.95
6 IBM Color Weath Radar             $59.95

By selecting an item from this
menu, you can review that item's
description and then place an
order if desired.

Last menu page, Key digit
or M for previous menu.      :
```

It doesn't matter which number is typed here. CIS will ask

```
Do you want a description of
this item (Y/N) ?
```

As you've already seen in Chapter 6, a (Y/N) prompt means to type Y for Yes, and N for No. I'll skip the opportunity to give an advertisement for CompuServe's Vidtex. When you're online, you can read the information for the particular terminal program you're interested in. You can also get additional information about Vidtex by typing Go VID-1 at any "!" prompt. After you've read the brief description in Product Ordering, you'll be asked if you wish to order the program. If you reply Y, the process will be self-explanatory. A negative (N) response will have the system ask

```
Do you wish to review more
selections (Y/N) ?
```

The rest of the Product Ordering section is just as straightforward. Since it's free of connect-time charges, you might want to spend some time here to familiarize yourself with it. This is one place on CompuServe where you won't have to pay while you learn.

After exiting Product Ordering, we'll be back at page CIS-4, where we'll type **T** (or just press **Return**) to get the top page of CompuServe—Page CIS-1. There, I will show you another way to navigate through the system:

```
CompuServe          Page CIS-1

CompuServe Information Service

1 Home Services
2 Business & Financial
3 Personal & Computing
4 Services f^P

^P Interrupt
!
```

This is how you can cut through the CIS page structure. Just issue a Control-C or a Control-P. Of the two, Control-P is faster. Let's type **3** for Personal Computing:

```
CompuServe          Page PCS-1

PERSONAL COMPUTING SERVICES
1 News
2 Reference
3 Communications
4 Shop at Home
5 Communication Forums
6 Personal File Area

Last menu page. Key digit
of M for previous menu.
!
```

Here, let's type **3** for Communications:

```
CompuServe          Page PCS-30

COMMUNICATIONS
1 EasyPlex
  (replaces EMail)
2 CB Simulation
3 National Bulletin Board
  (public messages)
4 User Directory
5 Access (public file area)
```

```
Last menu page. Key digit
or M for previous menu.
!
```

This menu shows the communication services available on CIS. We'll take a look at each of them, starting with EasyPlex.

Let's type **1:**

```
Welcome to EasyPlex, the
replacement for Email.

In the future for quick access,
type:

        GO EASYPLEX

           or,

        GO EASY

Key <ENTER> to continue

! [RETURN]

EasyPlex Main Menu

   *** No mail waiting ***

2  COMPOSE a new message
3  UPLOAD a message
4  USE a file from PER area

5  ADDRESS book
6  SET options

Enter selection,
or H for information
!
```

This is the main menu for CIS's electronic text message service. Of these five choices, I'll explain numbers 2, 5, and 6. Choices 3 and 4 will be explained at the end of this chapter because they're advanced features and you'll have to learn some other things about CIS before you can use these.

Let's type **2** to write a new message:

```
EasyPlex Main Menu
```

```
*** No mail waiting ***

2 COMPOSE a new message
3 UPLOAD a message
4 USE a file from PER area

5 ADDRESS book
6 SET options

Enter selection,
or H for information
! 2

EasyPlex Compose

Enter message. (/EXIT when done)

1:
```

This is the start of the message writing process. It's similar to entering a message on a BBS (Bulletin-Board System). It's very easy. Type in your message, like this.

```
1: This is a test of the EasyPlex system for myselff.
2: It's very easy to use this!
3:
```

Two lines are enough to illustrate the use of EasyPlex. On the third line, let CIS know that you're finished writing a message by typing **/EX** and pressing **Return:**

```
1: This is a test of the EasyPlex system for myselff.
2: It's very easy to use this!
3: /EX
```

Then you'll get this menu:

```
EasyPlex Send Menu

For current message

1 SEND
2 EDIT
3 TYPE

Enter your selection number,
or H for more information!
```

These selections are self-explanatory. Let's look at the message one more time by typing **3:**

1: This is a test of the EasyPlex system for myselff.
2: It's very easy to use this!

Key S or <ENTER> to continue!

There's a mistake on line 1 that has to be corrected. After pressing **Return** at the prompt, you'll see this menu again:

EasyPlex Send Menu

For current message

1 SEND
2 EDIT
3 TYPE

Enter your selection number,
or H for more information!

Typing **2,** for EDIT, will display this:

CompuServe EDIT

1 CHANGE characters in line
2 REPLACE line
3 DELETE line
4 INSERT line
5 TYPE all lines
0 SEND message

Last Menu page. Key digit
or M for previous menu!

If your message is long, you might want to type 5 to display all of the lines again. Since this is a short message, that won't be necessary. You already know that the mistake is on line 1. That mistake has to be corrected by typing **1,** for CHANGE characters:

Which line #:

This is simple. Just type **1:**

Which line #: **1**

Current line:
  1: This is a test of the EasyPlex system for myselff.

Text to replace:

Type the word or letters that have to be corrected. In this example, it's the word "myselff."

Text to replace:**myselff**
Replacement text:

This means to type in the correction:

Text to replace: myselff
Replacement text: **myself**
New line:
  1: This is a test of the EasyPlex system for myself.

Key S or <ENTER> to continue!

CIS then displays the line with the correction. It would be very hard not to get everything right with this system. This editing process is very similar to what you'll see later in this book when I illustrate the use of MCI Mail and BBSs.

Pressing **Return** at the prompt will redisplay the EDIT menu:

CompuServe EDIT

1 CHANGE characters in line
2 REPLACE line
3 DELETE line
4 INSERT new line(s)
5 TYPE all lines
Ø SEND message

Last Menu page. Key digit
or M for previous menu!

When you type **0** to send the message, you'll be given this address form to fill out:

EasyPlex

Send to (Name or User ID):
Subject:
Your name:

Notice that the first thing you have to fill out in the address form is "Send to" and that it says you can type either a name or a User ID. You won't be able to type a name this time. You'll have to type a User ID. Later in this illustration, you'll see how you can send people EasyPlex messages by using their names, rather than their User IDs. This is a feature that's rarely found on online systems.

In this example, I'll fill out the address form using a fictitious name and User ID. When you're composing a sample EasyPlex message to try the system, type your own name and User ID in the appropriate places.

```
EasyPlex

Send to (Name or User ID): 79736,1984
Subject: EasyPlex test
Your name: Winston Smith
Would you like to save this name
as your EasyPlex name so you do not
have to type it in the future?

(Yes or No):
```

In this example, I'll type **N** to the above prompt. If you've typed your name the way you want other people to see it when they get an EasyPlex message from you, type Y at this prompt. I'm typing N here because I want to show you how you can enter your name later or change it after you've already entered it.

Next, you'll see this:

```
To:       79736,1984
From:     Winston Smith
Subj:     EasyPlex test
Is this correct (Y or N)?
```

Your name and User ID, not the one above, will be shown. If everything is OK, type Y to send the message. If something is incorrect, type N and fill out the form again. After typing **Y**, you'll see:

```
Message sent to 79736,1984

Key S or <ENTER> to continue!
```

The message won't be in your mailbox for about 15–20 minutes. This delay is caused by the way EasyPlex is routed through CIS's many computers. You don't need to know anything about this routing, except that it exists and that it accounts for the delay. I won't show you how to read the sample message you've just sent until near the end of this chapter. There are other things about CIS you'll need to learn before you try to read EasyPlex messages.

Pressing **Return** at the above prompt will redisplay the EasyPlex main menu:

```
EasyPlex Main Menu

  *** No mail waiting ***

2 COMPOSE a new message
3 UPLOAD a message
4 USE a file from PER area

5 ADDRESS book
6 SET options

7 SEND last message
8 EDIT last message

Enter selection,
or H for information
!
```

As you can see, there are two additional choices on the menu: 7 and 8. By typing 7, you'll be brought back to the form you've just filled out. This will allow you to send the message you've just typed to someone else. This is a handy feature if you're corresponding with several other CIS subscribers and want to tell them all the same thing. You don't have to type the message again to send it to each person. Choice 8 will allow you to edit the message if you want to change something before sending it out again.

When you're corresponding with several other CIS subscribers, it would be easier to keep track of each person by his or her name not User ID. Remembering User IDs is difficult, at best. There's nothing quite as frustrating as writing someone an EMail message and discovering that you can't find that person's User ID. Without the User ID, the message can't be sent. This is where the Address Book can make your online life on CIS a lot easier.

Let's take a look at the Address Book selection by typing **4**:

```
EasyPlex Address Book

1 INSERT an entry
2 CHANGE an entry
```

3 DELETE an entry
4 LIST Address Book
5 Enter/Change your NAME

Last Menu page. Key digit
or M for previous menu!

These choices are self-explanatory. Let's take a look at how a few of them work, starting with the first one. Type **1**:

Your EasyPlex address book is a
list of names and User IDs and
can be used to easlly send mail
to your friends. It may contain
up to 5Ø entries. If you enter a
name at the Send to prompt, the
directory will be searched and
all matches will be displayed.

Press <ENTER> at the name
prompt when done.

Address 1

Name:

Before you use your Address Book, have ready the names and User IDs of the people you correspond with. The above prompt is clear: Just type in the name of one of your correspondents. The order in which you enter names doesn't matter; that is, they don't have to be in alphabetical order or anything like that. The only thing you must do is type the name exactly as you'll use it when sending an EasyPlex message. For instance,

Name: **Winston Smith**
Winston Smith's User ID:

Now type that person's User ID. For instance,

Winston Smith's User ID: **79736,1984**
Address 2

Name: **[RETURN]**

Pressing **Return** at the second Name prompt ends the process:

EasyPlex Address Book

1 INSERT an entry
2 CHANGE an entry

3 DELETE an entry
4 LIST Address Book
5 Enter/Change your NAME

Last Menu page. Key digit
or M for previous menu!

Now let's look at the Address Book by typing **4:**

EasyPlex

1 Winston Smith 79736,1984

Key S or <ENTER> to continue!

With this entry in you Address Book, you don't have to remember that person's User ID in order to send him an EasyPlex message. After you've written a message and get the address form to fill out, you could type Winston Smith at the "Send to" prompt instead of his User ID, 79736,1984. CIS looks in your address book and fills in the correct User ID address for you. Pressing **Return** at the above prompt returns us to the Address Book menu:

EasyPlex Address Book

1 INSERT an entry
2 CHANGE an entry
3 DELETE an entry
4 LIST Address Book
5 Enter/Change your NAME

Last Menu page. Key digit
or M for previous menu!

Let's place your name in EasyPlex so you won't always have to fill out the "From" field in the address form. Type **5:**

Enter the name you wish to use
as your EasyPlex name. This name
will be used when sending mail.

Your EasyPlex name:

If you typed N at the name prompt when you sent a test EasyPlex message earlier, this is what the process for entering your name will look like:

Your EasyPlex name: **Your Name**

If you typed Y at the name prompt earlier and want to change your name, this is what the process will look like:

```
Enter the name you wish to use
as your EasyPlex name. This name
will be used when sending mail.

Enter a period to erase this
name, or <ENTER> to leave it
unchanged.

Your EasyPlex name
  Old: Your Name
  New: Your Newname

EasyPlex Address Book

1 INSERT an entry
2 CHANGE an entry
3 DELETE an entry
4 LIST Address Book
5 Enter/Change your NAME

Last Menu page. Key digit
or M for previous menu! [RETURN]

EasyPlex Main Menu

  *** No mail waiting ***

2 COMPOSE a new message
3 UPLOAD a message
4 USE a file from PER area

5 ADDRESS book
6 SET options

7 SEND last message
8 EDIT last message

Enter selection,
or H for information
!
```

That's how CIS EasyPlex works. As you've seen in this illustration, it's very easy to use and allows you to send electronic text messages to other subscribers just by remembering their names, not their User IDs. In my book, a name is always better than a number.

Let's take a shortcut so I can introduce you to a way of moving through CIS without having to read menus. There's a direct command that you can use in DISPLA at any ! prompt. The direct command is GO. GO may be abbreviated as G. To use the GO command, you have to include a page number. For instance, GO CIS-1 or GO PCS-30. These can also be typed as G CIS1 or G PCS30. You can leave out the hyphen in the page number. Type **GO PCS-30** so we'll be taken back to the primary Communications menu:

```
CompuServe            Page PCS-3Ø

COMMUNICATIONS
1 EasyPlex
  (replaces EMail)
2 CB Simulation
3 National Bulletin Board
  (public messages)
4 User Directory
5 Access (public file area)

Last menu page. Key digit
or M for previous menu.
!
```

The next communication service available on CIS is the CB Simulator. This is real-time multi-user conferencing. It's like CB radio, only you're using a computer instead of a radio. Type **2** to get to it:

```
CB Information          Page CB-1Ø

CITIZENS BAND SIMULATOR

 1 Instructions
 2 CB Etiquette
 3 CB Band A (Mainframe A)
 4 CB Band B (Mainframe B)

 5 CBIG Special Interest Group
 6 CB Society: Cupcake's Column
 7 Computing Across America
 8 CB Simulator Special
   Late-Night Rates

Last menu page. Key digit
or M for previous menu.
!
```

When you're online, you may want to choose 1 to read the CB Instructions and 2 to read about how you should conduct yourself on CB. Choice 5 is a Forum for CB users. You'll see what a Forum is like later. Choice 6 is a column that profiles CB users. Choice 7 may not be available when this book is in stores. It's an ongoing journal of a fellow who is riding a bicycle across America and sends in online dispatches of his adventures. Choice 8 will probably be gone, too. It's a special offer of reduced connect-time that CIS introduced to stem its subscribers moving to a lower-cost competitor. Choices 3 and 4 are the entries to the CB Simulator. Choice 3, Band A, is the most popular and that's what we'll take a look at. Type **3:**

```
CB Information          Page CB-41

CAUTION! Under no circumstances
should you enter your password
while in CB or TALK.

The use of obscene language, or
other behavior that disrupts CB
conversations, may result in the
immediate suspension of service
with a $1Ø charge for account
reactivation.

Key S or <ENTER> to continue
!
```

Takc thcsc words to hcart. As much as cvcryonc likcs to think of computer owners as just one big happy family, the family has its share of black sheep. Never give out your password to *anyone.* This includes any other online passwords you may have, not just your CIS one. When you're using CB, conduct yourself in a courteous manner.

After pressing **Return** at this screen, you'll see

```
CB Information          Page CB-1

Request Recorded,
One Moment, Please
Thank you for Waiting
CB Simulator v3(7Ø)   Band A

What's your handle?
```

The system is asking you type a name that you'd like to be known as when using CB. This name won't be permanent, and you can change it later when you're using CB. No one uses his or her real name in CB. Think of a handle that's descriptive but not obscene. If you choose a handle that someone else uses, you'll know once you're in CB and start to get mistaken for that person. If that happens, change your handle. You'll see how to do that later in this illustration. It's also not polite to use someone else's handle.

In this example, I'll use **BROOKLYN** as a handle:

```
What's your handle?BROOKLYN

(Channel) users tuned in
(1)11,(3)1,(17)9,(33)4
Select a channel or key <ENTER>
for information:
```

These are the channels in CB that are currently occupied. Each channel number is in parentheses, followed by the number of people currently talking in the open on that channel. For example, (1)11 means that channel 1 currently has 11 people on it talking in the open. You don't have to choose one of these channels, by the way. There are 36 channels in CB. You can see a list of them by pressing **Return** here, like so:

```
? CBXNCN - No channel number
     1 through 36 are valid

Channels generally are un-
restricted. These guidelines,
however, do apply:

 1  Adult Meeting Channel
17  Teen Meeting Channel
33  Alternative Life Styles

Note: Disruptive or obscene
behavior or handles on ANY open
channel, including those above,
may result in the immediate
suspension of service.

Please enter a channel number
(1 through 36 are valid):
```

Of the 36 free channels, the three mentioned, 1, 17, 33, have been designated for recommended purposes and you'd do well to heed these suggestions. You'll find out why later in this chapter. Right now, we'll pop into an unoccupied channel to explore the system; type **7:**

```
Which channel: 7
(A7,COMAL Master) I don't think so.
```

It may look like channel 7 has someone else on it besides us, but that's not so. Sometimes CB shows a sentence from a prior user of that channel. Although it's confusing at first to see a phantom sentence, it does help you to know that you've made it to your selected channel. This sample sentence also shows what you'll see in CB. This is the standard format of a sentence typed by another person. In parentheses you see the CB Band letter, the CB channel number, and the person's handle: Band A, channel 7, handle "COMAL Master." Outside of the parentheses is the sentence that this person has typed.

Let's take a look at the CB commands. Type **/HEL,** for Help, and you'll see this list:

```
/HEL

Prefix commands with a "/"

/TUNE #        Tunes channel # (1-36)
/TALK #        Private talk w/ job #
/MON 1,4       Monitor extra chnls
/UNM 7,3       Unmonitor channels
/STATUS        Type channel status
/DAY           Type time, day, & date
/USERS         List on-line users
/USERS #       Users on channel #
/EXIT          Exit CB
/OFF           Exit CB and log off
/WHO           Last talker's User ID
/HANDLE        Change handle
/SCR xyz       Scramble on key "xyz"
/SMC xyz       Scr & Monitor Clear
/XCL xyz       Xmt CLear; unscr recv
/UNS           Unscramble (both clr)
/SQU abc       Squelch handle "abc"
/SBU #,#       Squelch by User ID
/JOB           Type your job #
/UID           User IDs w/ messages
/NOUID         Turn off /UID
/BAND x        Switch to Band "x"
/GO mm-n       Go to page "mm-n"
```

That's quite a list. Each command is typed with a slash (/) as the first character. You must also type the command by itself, with the slash as the first character. If you happen to put a space before the slash, the CB Simulator won't know that you're giving it a command. Each of these commands will be explained in the course of this illustration.

We'll begin with /USERS, which can also be typed /USE. When it's typed by itself, the system will display a list of everyone, on every channel, who is currently using CB. If /USE is typed with a channel number, the system will only show who is currently on that channel. Let's take a look at this by typing **/UST E**:

/UST E

Job	User ID	Nod	Ch	Tlk	Handle
-----	-------------	-----	----	---	---------------
35	79736,1984	NYC	7		BROOKLYN

The USERS list is divided into columns. The first is the Job number. This is a number that has a specific purpose that you will see later. All USERS lists are arranged in Job number order, from the lowest to the highest. Next is the User ID of the person. This is the address that's used for EasyPlex messages on CIS. Next is Nod, which means Node. It's a three-letter code that usually stands for the city that the subscriber is calling from. NYC means New York City. Not all Node codes are that obvious. Some codes that begin with a Q mean that the person is calling CIS via Tymnet or Telenet. The next column shows the channel number that the person is on. If you're only showing the users on your channel, this column is superfluous. But if you're listing everyone using CB, you'll be able to see who is on which channel. Next is the column Tlk, which means Talk. If the person is in talk mode, there will be an asterisk (*) here. You'll learn about talk soon. The last column shows the person's handle.

Let's take another look at the channels that are occupied in CB. This is done by typing /STA, for /STATUS:

/STA
(1)11,(7)1#,(1Ø)4,(33)4

The # symbol indicates the channel you're currently on. You can see yourself listed as being on channel 7.

Now we'll look at some of the types of conversations that take place on CB. We'll do this by eavesdropping, which is OK on CB. What we'll be doing isn't unethical in any way. There is a command for it, and everyone knows about it. The command is /MON and is used with a channel number. Let's look in on channel 10 by typing **/MON 1Ø:**

```
(A1Ø,Jackrabbit) ABC--> M or F?
(A1Ø,***ABC***) HE'S NOT LISTENING TO ME **SNIFF!**
(A1Ø,-QUERY-) WELL IF U PEOPLE R SO SMART, Y R U ALL
HERE???
(A1Ø,V*A*M*P*I*R*E!) Ixnay the rcank stuff, Query.
(A1Ø,V*A*M*P*I*R*E!) rcank = crank.
(A1Ø,***ABC***) RABBIT--> F. U?
(A1Ø,-QUERY-) U HAVE VERY BIG TEETH VAMPIRE.
(A1Ø,Jackrabbit) ABC--> M! Wanna /talk? /Job 15 here.
(A1Ø,V*A*M*P*I*R*E!) And u'll get a bite if u don't
behave, Query!
(A1Ø,***ABC***) ***gone to talk***
```

The /MON command will allow you to listen to two additional channels. Including the channel you're on, that means you can listen to three channels at once. You'll only be able to talk to those who are on your own channel, though.

The representative sample of chatter above has several of the conversational conventions that are used in CB. The first one is "M or F?" This is CB shorthand for "Are you a male or a female"? Next, you can see that "u" is short for "you," "r" is short for "are," and "y" is short for "why." When someone makes a typo, it's permissable to acknowledge it with a follow-up line; for example, the typo "rcank," is acknowledged with "rcank = crank." That's shorthand for, " 'rcank' should have been 'crank' back there." It's not only permissable to do this, it is sometimes a necessity if you want to get your message across. It also lets others know that you aren't a poor or sloppy typist. You can also see that arrows (-->) are used. These are typed with two hyphens (--) and a greater-than sign (>). This lets the person you're talking to know that he or she is the one being addressed. You can also see mention of /JOB and /TALK. These are the next two commands you'll learn.

First, though, let's take a look at our status, by typing **/STA.**

```
/STA
(1)11,(7)1#,(1Ø)4*,(33)4
```

Next to channel 10, there's an asterisk (*). This indicates that you're currently monitoring that channel. This may seem redundant, but it isn't. Sometimes a channel you've been monitoring can become barren. Having that asterisk appear when you look at your status will remind you to turn off the monitoring command. You'll see how to do that right now.

Type **/UNM 1Ø**. This is necessary to get your screen uncluttered so you can try out the /JOB and /TALK commands. Now, type **/JOB**:

```
/Job
35
```

CB displays a number in response to the command. That number probably looks familiar to you, so let's take a look at where you saw it the first time by typing **/UST E**:

```
/UST E
   Job      User ID      Nod    Ch   Tlk  Handle
   -----    ----------   ------ ---- ---- ---------------
   35       79736,1984   NYC    7         BROOKLYN
```

There it is, under the first column, labeled Job. This is your Job number. It is a number assigned to you by CIS. When you're on CIS, you actually have two numbers. The first is your User ID, which is your permanent identification and EMail address. The second one is your Job number. The Job number is different each time you sign onto CIS. It's automatically assigned to you out of the available pool of numbers. You don't need to know what a Job number is used for except for its purpose in CB. That's the only place on CIS where it has a useful purpose for you. The Job number ties in with the /TALK command. Talk is a way for two people to speak in CB without others being able to listen in. It's private. Just as the CB Simulator can be thought of as CB radio, Talk can be thought of as a telephone conversation between two people.

There are two ways of using the /TALK command. The first way is just to type /TALK. CB will then ask you for the Job number of the person you wish to talk with. That's your cue to type it. This method also allows you the option of trying to talk to anybody just by pressing Return instead of typing a Job number. I don't recommend doing this, though. The CB program just randomly grabs some poor soul and tells him or her that you wish to talk. This is an interruption that is not welcome at all times. It's best to have a specific person in mind when you want to talk and to have that person's Job number—as well as his or her permission to talk. The second way of using the /TALK command is to follow it with a Job number, for instance, /TALK 35 in this example. When you're online in CB trying this, make sure that you type your own Job number. Don't use 35 unless it actually is your Job number. Typing your own Job number will let you try out talking to yourself. It'll give you an idea of how the feature works.

```
/TALK 35

Job 35 [79736,1984] BROOKLYN is now in contact
(Use ^P to break contact)
```

>**TESTING**
>
<Testing
>**This is a test of talk in CB!**
>
<This is a test of talk in CB!
>**I type something...**
>
<I type something...
>**...and you type something!**
>
<...and you type something!
>**See how easy it is???**
>
<See how easy it is???
>**^P**

Contact broken

Type the boldfaced lines above to try out talking. You'll know when CB is ready for you to type something when you see the greater-than sign (>) prompt. All sentences from the person you're talking to will be preceded by a less-than (<) sign. To exit from talk mode, issue a Control-P.

When you've actually issued the /TALK command with a Job number to summon another person, you'll see a line like this on your screen:

Job 1ØØ [77777,68] Jackrabbit has been notified.
Please wait. (Use ^P to stop waiting)

Of course, the actual Job number, User ID, and handle will be different from the one I've shown.

When someone calls you to talk, you'll see a line like this:

***Please /TALK with Job 1ØØ [77777,68] Jackrabbit

In response, you'd type **/TALK 1ØØ** to make a talk connection. 100 is Jackrabbit's Job number in this example. When you're actually being called to Talk online, you'd type that person's Job number, not 100 as shown here.

A variation of Talk is Scramble. Its command is /SCR. This will allow more than two people to talk without others listening in. The conversation is scrambled and is also invisible to other people who may be on the same channel. The /SCR command is used with a code. The code can be any short word that you can dream up. Everyone has to use the same code in order to receive the scrambled messages in readable form. The best way to distribute the code to everyone who is going to be in a scrambled conversation is through Talk. If you're using the code word "action," for example, you'd type **/SCR ACTION.** Try it:

/SCR ACTION
** SCRAMBLE is ON **
This is a test

You won't notice anything different. But if someone mistyped the code word—say "acton" instead of "action"—they would see you typing something like this:

(A7,BROOKLYN) @*'8 [: (5$#"

It's a very effective way of preventing eavesdropping by others. It's also a good way to prevent being disturbed by others who wouldn't be interested in maintaining a serious conversation.

To get out of scrambled mode, just type **/SCR** without the code or use the command **/UNS.** You then see

/SCR
** SCRAMBLE is OFF **

When you're in Scramble, you won't see the conversations occurring on your channel among those who aren't in Scramble. If you wanted to see both your scrambled conversation and the unscrambled chatter of others, use the **/SMC** command which stands for Scramble but Monitor Clear. /SMC, like /SCR, is used with a code. You'll be able to see all of the conversations taking place, but you won't be able to talk to people who aren't scrambled. You can get out of this mode by typing /SMC again or by typing /UNS:

/SMC ACTION
** SCRAMBLE is ON **
** Rcving both clear and scr **
/SMC
** SCRAMBLE is OFF **

There are two more commands you should know about before you go to a channel with other people on it. These commands are /DAY and /HANDLE. /DAY will give you the current date and your current local time. This is handy if you don't have a clock or watch nearby. /HANDLE, which can by typed /HAN, will let you change your handle. It's used like this:

/HAN
What's your handle?

Just type your new handle. Then use the /USERS command for your channel to make sure that your new handle is correct. Never use this command to change your handle to someone else's intentionally. This is called handle stealing, and it's not something that'll make you popular or welcome in CB. No matter what your handle is, people can still get your User ID by typing /USERS for your channel and will report you to CIS for disruptive behavior. Handle stealing is not a prank. It is tantamount to impersonation. Don't do it.

Now that you've seen all of the commands that you can try out on your own, it's time to check into an actual channel to try CB. Let's use channel 10, the one that was monitored earlier. You'll have to move from channel 7 to 10. This is done by using the /TUNE command, which can by typed /TUN. To use it, you have to include a channel number. Type **/TUN 10:**

/TUN 1Ø
(A1Ø,***ABC***) ***back from talk***

Usually, the first indication that you'll get about the channel change will be a sentence from someone already on that channel. You could, however, pop in during a lull in the conversation.

To make sure that you've made the change, type **/STA** for Status:

/STA
(1)11,(1Ø)5#,(33)4

Channel 7 is gone. Channel 10 now has five people on it. Next to it is the # symbol, indicating that you're now on that channel. Now you're almost ready to join in CB conversation. Before you type something, you must know two things: First, you don't have to type your Band letter, channel number, or handle. The CB Simulator does that for you automatically. Second, anything you type must be less than 79 characters long. Any sentences past that length will be rejected by CB, and you'll be told to type the sentence again.

Let's type, **Hello, everyone!**

Hell(A1Ø,V*A*M*P*I*R*E!) Welcome back ABC.
(A1Ø,-QUERY-)**o, every** Hi again ABC

(A1Ø,Jackrabbit) Back again **one!**4 me 2.
(A1Ø,***ABC***) Thx, V.

This is what happens in CB. When you type a message, you're interrupted by the others who are talking. This also happens when you're in Scramble or Talk. These interruptions, however, do not have any effect on your message. On your screen, you would see something like the above. Everyone else's screen would look like this:

(A1Ø,V*A*M*P*I*R*E!) Welcome back ABC.
(A1Ø,-QUERY-)Hi again ABC
(A1Ø,Jackrabbit) Back again 4 me 2.
(A1Ø,***ABC***) Thx, V.
(A1Ø,BROOKLYN) Hello, everyone!

Actually, the other users wouldn't see something as neat looking as that, because what each one of them is typing is also being interrupted by others. A screen as neat as this one would only be seen by someone else on the channel who hasn't been typing messages.

Your screen will get very messy when you use CB. If there are many people on your channel, it'll be difficult to keep track of what you've typed. There are two commands that come in handy in this situation. They are two Control functions—Control-V and Control-U. Each one is used before you press Return to transmit a sentence. Let's use the first screen as an example to see how one of these two commands work:

Hell(A1Ø,V*A*M*P*I*R*E!) Welcome back ABC.
(A1Ø,-QUERY-)**o, every** Hi again ABC
(A1Ø,Jackrabbit) Back again **one!**4 me 2.
(A1Ø,***ABC***) Thx, V.
^V
Hello, everyone!
(A1Ø,***ABC***) Hi again, Jrabbit.

Typing Control-V will display the line you've typed. You must use this before pressing Return to send the line. Also, Control-V must be issued in between the chatter or the system won't acknowledge it. (If that happens, just issue Control-V again until the system recognizes it.) The other command, Control-U, will erase the message you've typed. Like Control-V, it has to be used before the Return key has been pressed. Think of these commands as Control-View and Control-Undo. That'll make them easier to remember.

Once you're in CB and chatting away, you may want to get someone's User ID so you can send him or her an EasyPlex message later. Instead of having to ask that person for the User ID or wading through a /USERS list for your channel, you can just type /WHO. /WHO will print the User ID of the person who transmitted the previous sentence.

Let's say you wanted Jackrabbit's ID, for example. Once a sentence from Jackrabbit has appeared on your screen, type /WHO to display his User ID, like so:

```
(A1Ø,Jackrabbit) Yeah, I love COMAL!
/WHO
Jackrabbit = 77777,68
```

If someone else's sentence is displayed on your screen before you've had a chance to type /WHO, you'll get that person's User ID, not Jackrabbit's. Sometimes you have to be quick on the draw, to execute this command successfully.

An easier way to display someone's ID is by typing /UID. This will display everyone's user ID, like this:

```
(A1Ø,V*A*M*P*I*R*E!) [77777,19] COMAL is great! Have u
tried PROMAL?
(A1Ø,-QUERY-) [77777,9ØØ] Has anyone tried ACTION?
(A1Ø,Jackrabbit) [77777,68] Yeah, I have PROMAL, 2.
(A1Ø,***ABC***) [77777,85] Doesn't any1 use BASIC
anymore?
(A1Ø,V*A*M*P*I*R*E!) [77777,19] ABC--> Why would anyone
want to???
```

Typing /NOUID will stop the display of User IDs.

Aside from getting one person's User ID to send an EasyPlex message, there's another reason why you may want to display everyone's User IDs. Earlier, I advised you not to use someone else's CB handle intentionally. Not everyone will be as wise as you and follow this advice. As in any group of people, there are bound to be some who will be pests, or worse, blatantly malicious. Their idea of a good time is to change their handle to someone else's. Then they'll type things the person they're impersonating would never type. Who gets the blame? The innocent person being impersonated does. Whose CB friendships are damaged? The innocent person being impersonated does. It's always best to note the User IDs of people you're talking with on CB. This way, you'll be able to tell when someone's handle doesn't match the User ID you're used to seeing. You can make a note of the offender's User ID and let CIS Customer Service know of the deception. Helping to keep CB free of handle stealers isn't finking. It's almost considered a duty by veteran CB users.

There are two commands you can use to block out transmissions from abusive CB users. They are /SQU and /SBU. /SQU means Squelch. /SBU means Squelch by User ID. Let's say that Jackrabbit has gotten particularly evangelistic in his enthusiasm for the COMAL programming language. In his enthusiasm for COMAL, he loses sight of his manners and begins to ridicule you for favoring BASIC. Instead of putting up with his abuse, you can stop the display of his invective by typing /SQU with his handle, like so:

```
/SQU JACKRABBIT
>Squelching 77777,68
>Type /SQU (no handle) to clear
```

Jackrabbit's comments will no longer appear on your screen. Everyone else will see what he types except you. If Jackrabbit were to change his handle, you'd see his transmissions again. To block him out once and for all, type /SBU with his handle, like this:

```
/SBU 77777,68
>Squelching 77777,68
>Type /SQU (no handle) to clear
```

Jackrabbit could change his handle all he wants, but his transmissions would not appear on your screen. Everyone else would still see them, though. /SQU and /SBU are only totally effective if everyone uses them to shut out an offender.

To reverse the squelch command, type /SQU, like so:

```
/SQU
>SQUELCH is now OFF
```

The last CB command is /BAN, which means Band. It allows you to switch from one CB mainframe to another. Currently, CIS offers CB Bands A and B. Most people use Band A. Band B is preferred when Band A has become too crowded and the CB program is beginning to slow down or lose sentences people have typed. I've never seen both Band A and Band B both used to capacity. It'll be a while before CIS offers a Band C, I think. This is what using the /BAN command looks like:

```
/BAN B

Request Recorded,
One Moment, Please
```

```
Thank you for Waiting
CB Simulator v3(7Ø) Band B

(Channel) users tuned in
(18)7,(33)2
Which channel:
```

Since you already gave the CB program your handle when you were on Band A, you're not asked for one when entering Band B. All of the CB commands that I've illustrated on Band A are available on Band B and work identically. You can move back to Band A anytime you wish by typing /BAN A.

Before I show you how to exit CB, there's something else you should know. It's about the way some people use CB.

If you've read any articles about CB in the past 2 years, you've probably come across the phrase "CompuSex." CompuSex is when two people go into Talk and then imagine themselves having a sexual liaison with one another. I don't know who started it or why or why it has caught on to the extent it has. Actually, I don't want to know, either. CompuSex is not something that *The Computer Phone Book* considers to be a high point in the use of online systems. If you want to know what CompuSex is like, invite someone to participate in it or take someone up on his or her invitation. That will tell you more than any description here could.

Before the advent of CompuSex, a certain faction of CB users picked a channel to call its own. Channel 33 is considered the domain of gay CB users. This is one of the channel designations you've seen earlier, called "Alternative Lifestyles." Don't step into 33 if you're antigay and intend to make that point known. Not only won't the channel 33 users appreciate it, hardly anyone else on CB will think highly of you, either. If the subject matter of 33 suits you, fine. If it doesn't, you now know that it exists and that you can avoid it. There are still 64 other channels, on two Bands, that you can freely roam through.

When you're finished using CB, you can leave by one of three ways. One way is by typing /OFF. This will enable you to exit CB and sign you off CIS. The second way is /EX, which will take you to page CB-10. The third way is by typing /GO and a CIS page number, which I'll illustrate here by typing **/GO PCS30:**

```
/GO PCS3Ø

Request Recorded

One Moment, Please
Thank You for Waiting
```

```
CompuServe          Page PCS-30

COMMUNICATIONS
1 EasyPlex
  (replaces EMail)
2 CB Simulation
3 National Bulletin Board
  (public messages)
4 User Directory
5 Access (public file area)

Last menu page. Key digit
or M for previous menu.
!
```

We'll type **3** here to look at CIS's bulletin board system. It's listed on the menu as the National Bulletin Board. To most CIS users, it's simply called Bullet. This is what will appear on your screen for this selection:

```
CompuServe          Page HOM-23

     National Bulletin Board

CompuServe's National Bulletin
Board (BULLET) allows you to
post messages that can be read
by thousands of subscribers in
the United States and Canada.

BULLET uses unique commands.
These will be listed for you
if you type HELP at the
asterisk (*) prompt.

Key S or <ENTER> to continue
![RETURN]

CompuServe          Page HOM-24

Request Recorded,
One Moment, Please

Thank you for Waiting

Notice: CompuServe reserves the right to review all publicly
posted information and to delete any which, in its sole
judgment, is inappropriate or offensive. CompuServe will be
```

```
indemnified against any loss or expense arising out of the
publication of advertisements, including those resulting from
claims or suits for libel, violation or right of privacy, or
publicity, plagiarism or copyright infringement. CompuServe
will not be responsible for any loss or expense arising from
customer's use of posted information, without limitation.
CompuServe makes no warranties, expressed or implied.

Please enter HELP if you
need instructions.

*
```

This disclaimer will always appear when you enter Bullet. You can skip it by issuing a Control-O or a Control-P. Don't use a Control-C or you'll exit Bullet. The actual width of the disclaimer will depend on the screen width setting you selected earlier in Defalt. In this area of CIS, an asterisk (*) acts as a prompt. To see all of the Bullet commands, let's type **HELP:**

```
*HELP
The CompuServe Information Service National
Bulletin Board is an information exchange
medium.
The following commands are implemented:
   SCAN        READ     INDEX    VIEW
   COMPOSE     POST     EDIT     ERASE
   CHECK       EXIT     AGE      OFF
Commands may be abbreviated to the first 3 letters.
For additional information about a command, type:
HELP command
For example: HELP SCAN

*
```

In case those instructions aren't clear, I'll put them in different words. You can see the list of commands that can be used in Bullet. If you want to know how to use one of them, type HELP and the command. For instance, if you wanted to know how to use the Scan command, you'd type HELP SCAN. All of the commands longer than three letters may be typed as three-letter abbreviations. Thus, SCAN would become SCA.

Bullet is divided into three sections: Sale, Wanted, and Notice. Although other online systems may offer bulletin boards for specific brands of computers or individual topics, CIS doesn't need to. CIS's Forums fulfill that purpose. (You'll learn about the Forums later in this chapter.) The three sections of Bullet are broad enough to cover virtually any kind of message someone may wish to post.

The first thing you should do when you use Bullet is get the total number of messages that have been posted. The Index command will give you these figures, like so:

```
*INDEX
2Ø1  SALE messages
124  WANTED messages
183  NOTICE messages
```

Knowing how many messages are posted in each Bullet section will help you to estimate how much time you might spend online reading messages.

There are several ways to read messages that have been posted in Bullet. The first way is to display a one-line summary of each message. This can be done by using the Scan command, like so:

```
*SCAN
   #     From:          Date:          Keyword:
   5     79736,1984     Ø4-Sep-85      FREE!!
  21     72996,535      11-Sep-85      COMAL
  53     7Ø185,976      13-Sep-85      DR WHO
  55     7Ø3Ø5,789      12-Sep-85      MAC
  79     792Ø6,162      15-Sep-85      BIRTHDAY
 1Ø8     78826,2175     14-Sep-85      LOGO
 111     75126,1Ø34     3Ø-Sep-85      V
```

The list that you'll see will be considerably longer than this. Remember, the Index command showed a total of 508 posted messages. That's how many one-line summaries you'll see displayed on your screen. You'll probably want to use Control-S to pause the display and Control-Q to resume it. If you don't, you'll quickly get overwhelmed by the list. By issuing a Control-P, you can interrupt this display to get back to the asterisk prompt. Typing Scan by itself will display message summaries from all three Bullet sections. If you just wanted to look for messages under the Notice section, you'd type **SCAN NOTICE,** like so:

```
*SCAN NOTICE
   #     From:          Date:          Keyword:
   5     79736,1984     Ø4-Sep-85      FREE!!
  21     72996,535      11-Sep-85      COMAL
  53     7Ø185,976      13-Sep-85      DR WHO
 111     75126,1Ø34     3Ø-Sep-85      V
```

Similarly, you could type SCAN WANTED or SCAN SALE. Again, the list that you'll see will be longer than this brief illustration. The Index command previously showed a total of 183 posted messages in the Notice section. The Scan command now shows the essential information you need to read the messages that have been posted. In the column showing User IDs, you can see if someone has made multiple postings. Sometimes a person will repeat his or her message under a different title. It can be irritating to read the same message over and over. By looking at the User ID, you'll be able to skip repetitive messages. Under the Keyword heading you can see the subject of each message. You can see each message's assigned number in the column with the # (number sign) heading.

Going through Bullet with the Scan command means that you'll have to have pen and paper nearby to write down the message numbers that you wish to read. Let's say that you've finished scanning and want to start reading the messages, beginning with message 5. Reading a message is easy. You just type **READ** and the message number, like this:

```
*READ 5
The Computer Phone Book[tm] might
finally publish a newsletter
update of the book. See the notice
at the front of this book!
** 5 [79736,1984] 4-Sep-85 FREE!!
```

This is what a message posted on Bullet looks like. The width of the message will depend on your width setting in Defalt. To read the next message you're interested in, you'll have to type READ and its message number. Unfortunately, Bullet doesn't allow you to pick more than one message at a time to read. In other words, you can't type a command string like READ 5;13;27;34, to read messages 5, 13, 27, and 34 one after the other. Remember, though, that all online systems are constantly undergoing changes. Perhaps a multiple read feature will be available on Bullet by the time this book is published.

The next way of going through the messages posted on Bullet is by using the View command. If you type VIEW by itself, you'll go through all three sections of Bullet. You can narrow View by including one of the section names, for instance, VIEW SALE. Using the View command looks like this:

```
*VIEW
      #     From:          Date:          Keyword:
      5     79736,1984     Ø4-Sep-85      FREE!!
      -- Read (X, Y or RETURN)?
```

The prompt beneath the message summary looks cryptic at first glance, but it's easy to decipher. X stands for Exit. Typing an X will get you back to the asterisk prompt. Y stands for Yes. Typing Y will display the text of the message (which you've already seen in the previous illustration). RETURN stands for pressing your Return key. By pressing Return, you will see the next message summary. Each message summary will have the same prompt. After you've read a particular message, you'll see the next message summary and the same prompt. Using the View command means you won't have to bother writing down message numbers on a piece of paper like you do when using the Scan command. On the other hand, using the View command takes considerably more time than the Scan command, even when you include the amount of time it takes to write down the message numbers on a piece of paper. It's up to you to choose the method you'll use.

The third way of going through the messages posted on Bullet is by using keyword search. Keyword search requires a three-part command. First, either Scan or View; second, the name of one of the Bullet sections—Sale, Wanted or Notice; third, a keyword that you supply. These are all of the keyword search commands that you can use:

- SCAN SALE KEYWORD
- SCAN WANTED KEYWORD
- SCAN NOTICE KEYWORD
- VIEW SALE KEYWORD
- VIEW WANTED KEYWORD
- VIEW NOTICE KEYWORD

KEYWORD is a word that you supply. You've already seen keywords used in Chapter 4, Using BRS After Dark. Keyword searching works much the same way here, although there is a difference. In Bullet, keywords can only be a maximum of 10 letters long. So, for example, if you wanted to look for "Commodore-64," a 12-letter phrase, you'd do better by using just "Commodore," "C64," or "C-64" as your keyword. Keyword searching looks like this:

```
*SCAN NOTICE C64
   #    From:        Date:        Keyword:
   25   79738,19Ø    Ø4-Sep-85    C64 COMAL
   51   72798,639    11-Sep-85    CPM C64
   73   72855,896    13-Sep-85    C64 BBS
   85   74375,789    12-Sep-85    C64 HELP
```

The list that you see would probably be longer than this.

To read any of these, just use the **Read** command, like this:

***READ 25**
If your want to learn more about the best programming language
for your Commodore-64, you should investigate COMAL. It has
the structure and clarity of Pascal, the simplicity of Basic,
turtle graphics like Logo, and the support of a large user
group. We're that group. Write us for more information.
COMAL Users Group, USA, Ltd, 55Ø1 Groveland Terrace, Madison,
WI, 53716.
** 25 [79738,19Ø] 4-Sep-84 C64 COMAL

By using keyword searching, you can see if any Bullet messages contain information about whatever you're interested in or looking for. It's faster than using the Scan or View commands. Keyword searching helps to decrease your connect-time; that means saving money.

Now that you've seen how to summarize, search for, and read the posted messages, it's time to look at how to create a message to place in Bullet. This is done by using the **Compose** command, like so:

***COMPOSE**
[New file Ø24MCN.TMP - ready]

This is the CIS text editor called FILGÉ (FILe Generator and Editor) or EDIT, depending on where you are in CIS. You'll see something very similar to FILGE in Chapter 15, using THE SOURCE. FILGE is also used in the CIS Forums (although you also have the choice of a second text editor) and in the Personal File Area.

FILGE is what is known as a line-oriented editor; that is, it's like using a word processor in some ways. When you use a word processor, you know that you have to place the cursor on the line that you wish to type or edit. In the same way, FILGE gives you an imaginary cursor, called a line pointer. However, instead of using cursor keys to move the line pointer (your imaginary cursor), you tell the system by a direct command where it is to move. This may seem confusing right now, but you'll see an example that will make it clear.

Although FILGE has many commands, the ones you'll use the most are

- /T, which will take you to the Top of a file.
- /P, which will Print the current line or, when combined with a number (for instance, /P10) several lines.
- /C, which will change text in the current line. It's used as /C/old/new.

For instance, to change the word "reel" to "real" in a line, type /C/reel/real.

- /L, which will Locate a word or phrase in a file. For instance, typing /L/reel will locate the word "reel" in a file.
- /N, which will move the line pointer down or up through a file. Typing /N2 will move you down two lines in a file. Typing /N-2 will move you up two lines in a file.
- /EX, which will Exit (close) a file when you're through creating or editing it.

Let's create a sample message to see how these commands work.

```
*COMPOSE
[ New file Ø24MCN.TMP - ready ]
This is a tset of CIS BULLETT.
It use FILGE, which is easy to use.
```

These two lines are enough to show you how to use FILGE. Right now, the line pointer is on the third line of the file, which is a blank line. In order to correct the mistakes on the first line, you have to get the line pointer from the bottom of the file to the top. This is done by using the **/ T** command, like so:

```
*COMPOSE
[ New file Ø24MCN.TMP - ready ]
This is a tset of CIS Bullett.
It use FILGE, which is easy to use.
/T
```

The line pointer is now on the first line. How can you be sure?

Type **/P** to Print the line, like this:

```
*COMPOSE
[ New file Ø24MCN.TMP - ready ]
This is a tset of CIS Bullett.
It use FILGE, which is easy to use.
/T
/P
This is a tset of CIS Bullett.
```

That's one way to move the imaginary cursor. Now, let's correct the mistakes. The first thing to do is change "tset" to "test." This is done by using the /C, for Change, command. Type **/C/tset/test** to make the correction:

```
*COMPOSE
[ New file Ø24MCN.TMP - ready ]
This is a tset of CIS Bullett.
It use FILGE, which is easy to use.
/T
/P
This is a tset of CIS Bullett.
/C/tset/test
```

Now, you have to look at the line again to make sure that the correction was made. This is always a good idea, no matter which text editor you're using on any online system and no matter how familiar you become with a text editor. It's very easy to have new mistakes creep in. To redisplay the line, type **/P** for Print:

```
*COMPOSE
[ New file Ø24MCN.TMP - ready ]
This is a tset of CIS Bullett.
It use FILGE, which is easy to use.
/T
/P
This is a tset of CIS Bullett.
/C/tset/test
/P
This is a test of CIS Bullett.
```

The correction was made. Now, you must change "Bullett" to "Bullet." There are several ways this can be done. The most obvious one is to type /C/Bullett/Bullet. But that's too much typing in my opinion. It's faster and easier just to type **/Ctt/t**:

```
*COMPOSE
[ New file Ø24MCN.TMP - ready ]
This is a tset of CIS Bullett.
It use FILGE, which is easy to use.
/T
/P
This is a tset of CIS Bullett.
/C/tset/test
/P
This is a test of CIS Bullett.
/C/tt/t
/P
This is a test of CIS Bullet.
```

Once you make the change, type **/P** to redisplay the line, as shown.

Now, you must move the line pointer down to the second line. This is done by using the /N command. Since you want to move down one line, type **/N1** and then **/P** to Print the line, like this:

```
*COMPOSE
[ New file Ø24MCN.TMP - ready ]
This is a tset of CIS Bullett.
It use FILGE, which is easy to use.
/T
/P
This is a tset of CIS Bullett.
/C/tset/test
/P
This is a test of CIS Bullett.
/C/tt/t
/P
This is a test of CIS Bullet.
/N1
/P
It use FILGE, which is easy to use.
```

Here, you must change the first "use" to "uses." What would happen if you just typed /C/use/uses? Would it change both instances of "use" into "uses"? The answer is no. FILGE's editor only looks for the *first occurrence* of any letter, word, or phrase in a line and executes the change on that. Before we make any change, though, what if you wanted to change the second "use" into "see"? You could not type /C/use/see because of the explanation just given. But you could type C/use./use. (notice the periods). This would tell FILGE to look for "use."—which is, of course, the second "use" that you want to change. Remember that whenever you need to change a word that has a duplicate in the same line, try to *isolate* the particular word, as just shown. Now, let's make the correction that's needed here:

```
*COMPOSE
[ New file Ø24MCN.TMP - ready ]
This is a tset of CIS Bullett.
It use FILGE, which is easy to use.
/T
/P
This is a tset of CIS Bullett.
/C/tset/test
/P
This is a test of CIS Bullett.
/C/tt/t
```

```
/P
This is a test of CIS Bullet.
/N1
/P
It use FILGE, which is easy to use.
/C/use/uses
/P
It uses FILGE, which is easy to use.
```

The file is done. Type **/EX** to exit it.

```
*COMPOSE
[ New file Ø24MCN.TMP - ready ]
This is a tset of CIS Bullett.
It use FILGE, which is easy to use.
/T
/P
This is a tset of CIS Bullett.
/C/tset/test
/P
This is a test of CIS Bullett.
/C/tt/t
/P
This is a test of CIS Bullet.
/N1
/P
It use FILGE, which is easy to use.
/C/use/uses
/P
It uses FILGE, which is easy to use.
/EX
*
```

After you type /EX, the asterisk (*) prompt will reappear. The message won't be posted until you tell Bullet in which section the message should appear and what keyword it must have. The command string you have to type contains three elements: first, the Post command; second, the name of one of the three Bullet sections—Sale, Wanted, or Notice; third, a keyword of up to 10 letters that you supply.

These are all of the variations of the Post command that you can use:

- POST SALE KEYWORD
- POST WANTED KEYWORD
- POST NOTICE KEYWORD

To place this notice in Bullet under the Wanted section with the keyword "Help" would look like this:

```
*POST WANTED HELP

*
```

Your message is posted once the asterisk (*) prompt reappears.

To confirm that the message is actually posted, type **CHECK**.

```
*CHECK

Your outstanding messages:
1 WANTED messages
```

Bullet tells you how many messages you've posted and in which section(s) they appear. If you've posted several messages in Bullet, you'll need to find out which particular messages are yours. You can do this by using the Check command and one of the three section names, like this:

```
*CHECK WANTED
You have posted the following messages:
 #                    Date:        Keyword:

396                   14-Oct-85    HELP
```

You also have to type both CHECK SALE and CHECK WANTED to list any messages you may have posted in those sections. You can read any of your messages in the same way I've already illustrated: just by typing READ and the individual message numbers.

When you want to delete a message you've posted, the Erase command is used. You type ERASE and the individual message number. If you don't erase a message, don't worry about it cluttering Bullet. A message is automatically erased from Bullet after 14 days. In this case, however, it would be best to erase the test message you've placed in Bullet. It would be inconsiderate to make other subscribers read the message and waste connect-time.

Don't forget that you can abbreviate any command to three letters. CHECK would become CHE, ERASE would become ERA, READ would become REA, and so on.

There's just one more Bullet command you should know about. It's a particularly helpful one. Let's say that you check into Bullet every 5 days. Within that period, there are bound to be some new postings. The trouble is that the new ones are mixed in with the old ones you've already read. There's a way to read just the new ones. You can tell Bullet to show you only the messages that have been posted within a certain number of days.

This is the Age command. For instance, if you wanted to catch up on messages that were posted only in the past 5 days, you type this:

```
*AGE 5

*
```

The Scan, View, and Read commands used after this point would only affect messages that have been on the system 5 days or less. All of the messages that have been in Bullet for 6 days or more aren't shown. If you change your mind and want to look at every message posted in Bullet, just type AGE by itself. This will stop Bullet from screening out the older messages.

To leave Bullet, which is what we'll do now, type **EXIT**.

```
*EXIT
CompuServe            Page PCS-3Ø

COMMUNICATIONS
1 EasyPlex
  (replaces EMail)
2 CB Simulation
3 National Bulletin Board
  (public messages)
4 User Directory
5 Access (public file area).

Last menu page. Key digit
or M for previous menu.
!
```

The next item we'll look at on this menu is 4, User Directory. A user directory is the online equivalent of a telephone directory. If you wanted to communicate with someone by voice phone, you thumb through the White Pages in search of that person's telephone number. A user directory fills a similar purpose, except it lists the User ID of a subscriber so contact through EasyPlex can be made. Like a telephone directory, being listed is up to the individual subscriber. You'll see an example of a (better) user directory in Chapter 15, using THE SOURCE. Like any user directory, you'll have to place yourself in it if you want to be listed. It isn't done for you automatically. I'm not going to show how to use the User Directory because it's very easy and doesn't need an explanation. If you're curious, feel free to venture into it. In fact, I suggest that you list yourself in it. It'll make it easier for your friends to contact you in case they forget or lose your User ID.

The next menu item, Access, is where public domain programs are available for downloading. The programs are for a variety of computers. You'll see Access later in this chapter. For now, let's press **Return** to go back one menu:

```
CompuServe          page PCS-1

PERSONAL COMPUTING SERVICES
1 News
2 Reference
3 Communications
4 Shop at Home
5 Communication Forums
6 Personal File Area

Last menu page. Key digit
or M for previous menu.
!
```

At this menu, type **5** for Communication Forums. You'll see this.

```
CompuServe        Page PCS-5Ø

        Personal Computing SIGS

 1 CP/M SIG               11 PowerSoft's
 2 HUG (Heath)            12 Programmer's
 3 MAUG (Apple)           13 CEM SIG
 4 PDP-11                 14 Writers' SIG
 5 MUSUS p-sys.           15 Commodore
 6 EpsOnLine              16 Atari SIG
 7 TRS80 COCO             17 IBM PC PRO
 8 Panasonic              18 IBM NOVICE
 9 OSI SIG                19 Instructions
10 LSI Users              20 Descriptions
Input a number or key
<ENTER> for more choices
!
```

These are just a few of the Forums available on CIS. Choice 20 will give you a brief description of each Forum. Let's look at the two other menus for the Forums by pressing **Return**.

```
CompuServe          Page PCS-1ØØ

      Personal Computing Sigs

 1 MicroSoft Users Group
```

```
  2 Telecommunications SIG
  3 TRS-80 Model 100 SIG
  4 Computer Art SIG
  5 VAX SIG
  6 OS9 Forum
  7 TRS-80 Professional Forum
  8 Whole Earth Software
  9 Texas Instruments Forum
 10 Kaypro Forum
 11 Digital Research Forum

Input a number or key
<ENTER> for more choices
!

CompuServe          Page PCS-43

  1 RCA Micros
  2 Interex/Hewlett Packard
  3 The World of Lotus
  4 Creative Computing
  5 Family Computing Magazine
  6 ICCA Forum
  7 Orch-90
  8 Computer Language Magazine

Last menu page. Key digit
or M for previous menu.
!
```

What exactly is a Forum (also known as a Special Interest Group or SIG)? A Forum is an area in which subscribers who share a particular interest can meet to exchange messages on a bulletin-board, upload and download public domain software and text files, and engage in online conversations. A CIS Forum is like a miniature version of CIS. CIS has more Forums (also known as Special Interest Groups) than any other online system. (Although you won't see them in this book, because neither system had them ready at press time, both Delphi and THE SOURCE have SIGs, too. See Chapter 8, A Too-Brief Look at Delphi and Chapter 15, Using THE SOURCE.) Don't be surprised if more Forums have been added to the menus than are shown here. CIS is always adding to its Forum roster. As you can see, some Forums are for particular brands of computers, others are for software, and yet others are run by magazines. There's something for almost everyone.

Let's go back to the first Forum menu.

```
CompuServe          Page PCS-5Ø

        Personal computing SIGS

 1 CP/M SIG            11 PowerSoft's
 2 HUG (Heath)         12 Programmer's
 3 MAUG (Apple)        13 CEM SIG
 4 PDP-11              14 Writers' SIG
 5 MUSUS p-sys.        15 Commodore
 6 EpsOnLine           16 Atari SIG
 7 TRS8Ø COCO          17 IBM PC PRO
 8 Panasonic           18 IBM NOVICE
 9 OSI SIG             19 Instructions
1Ø LSI Users           2Ø Descriptions

Input a number or key
<ENTER> for more choices
!
```

Of all of the Forums available on CIS, we'll look at one for Commodore computers. This choice reflects the fact that I use a Commodore-64 and frequently use the Forum I'll be showing you. Also, this Forum is a good microcosm of all CIS Forums. If you aren't a Commodore computer owner or user, don't skip this section. What I'll be illustrating isn't just for Commodore users. All Forums work the same way.

Typing **15** here will display

```
CompuServe          Page PCS-16Ø

    Commodore User Groups

 1 Commodore's Creative Corner
 2 The Commodore 64 Forum
 3 The CBM Programming SIG

Last menu page. Key digit
for M for previous menu.
!
```

Commodore computers are used by many CIS subscribers. The subscriber proportion of Commodore owners is so great that three Forums are needed to handle the demand. In fact, by the time this book is published, there may be more than three Commodore Forums. The only other computer company that has more than one Forum is IBM. (There's a Professional Forum and a Novice Forum. By the time this book is published, there may also be two Apple Forums. One for the Apple II family and one for the Macintosh family.)

Let's type **3** here, to enter the CBM Programming Forum:

```
CompuServe          Page PCS-116

Request Recorded,
One Moment, Please
```

When you choose a Forum to enter, you'll be moved to a particular DISPLA page where you'll be switched to the individual CIS mainframe computer on which the Forum resides. In this case, Page PCS-116 is an entry point for the CBM Programming Forum. You can just type G PCS116 at any "!" prompt to go to this Forum directly. When you choose a Forum to enter, make a note of the particular page number that leads to it. Later, you can just type the page number to get to the Forum faster.

After a few moments, you'll see

```
Thank you for Waiting

Welcome to CBM Programming SIG, V. 3B(25)

New member menu:
1 Purpose
2 Membership Sign Up
3 Instructions
4 Enter CBM Programming SIG
Ø Exit

Enter selection:
```

Let me explain each of these menu choices. The first one, Purpose, will give you an explanation of what the particular Forum is about, what takes place in it, its policies, and who the Forum's sysops (system operators) are. You should always choose this selection first so you can decide if the Forum can be useful. Choice 2, Membership Sign-Up, will be explained in a moment. Choice 3, Instructions, will give you a brief overview of the commands that are used in the Forum. You'll be seeing how a Forum works in the rest of this chapter. Even so, you might want to look at this choice to see if any new commands have been added. Choice 4, Enter CBM Programming SIG, will place you in the Forum. You won't be a Forum member, though, and won't be able to use all of the Forum's commands. Choice 0, Exit, will take you back to the previous menu.

Of all of the choices, you should use number 2, Membership Sign-Up, first. Only a few of the Forums on CIS require you to pay a membership fee, and you'll be told if this is the case before you make any commitment. Remember, if you choose to read the purpose of the Forum first, you'll know if a membership fee is expected. Most of the Forums don't have charges other than connect-time, so feel free to become a member. Members are able to use all of the Forum commands. When you become a Forum member, the only thing that's required is that you conduct yourself in a courteous manner.

Let's join the Forum by typing **2:**

```
Please enter your name:
```

Type your name. Don't use a handle. Most Forums require you to use your real name.

```
Please enter your name: Mike Cane
Mike Cane
Is this correct? (Y/N)
```

The Forum checks to see if you've spelled your name correctly. If you haven't, just type N and start all over.

If your name is correct, type **Y** to see

```
Is this correct? (Y/N) Y

Inserting name and ID...
```

The Forum is placing your name and User ID in the membership roster. In a few moments, you'll be in the Forum and see something like this:

```
Welcome to CBM Programming SIG, V. 3B(4)

Name:        Mike Cane   79736,1984
Last on:     Ø4-Sep-85   Ø1:17:25
High msg#:   Ø

You are user number 8282Ø5
System contains messages
9Ø834 to 91285
```

While you're in a Forum, you might see something like this:

```
Files busy, code Ø-11............
Files busy, code Ø-11............
```

```
Files busy, code Ø-11............
Files busy, code Ø-11............
```

This is CompuServe's cryptic way of informing you that the Forum is currently running at capacity. In other words, the place is so crowded that you'll have to wait your turn for your command to be acted upon. This can happen at any time while you're in the Forum, even when entering. Eventually you'll see

```
Files busy, code Ø-11.............have files (12Ø sec)
```

And then your command will be processed. If you get the "Files busy" message for more than 5 minutes (it's been known to happen), you're justified in hanging up on the system in self- defense. This is a rare instance in which *The Computer Phone Book* sanctions the improper exiting of a system. You should immediately call CIS Customer Support and report the situation. Give them your User ID, describe what happened, and request that the waiting time be deducted from your bill. Once you're back online, also send Feedback to CIS to describe the problem and request a deduction from your bill. (You'll see how to use Feedback later in this chapter.)

After you've entered the Forum, you'll probably see a signon bulletin that will welcome you and let you know what the membership is currently doing. It'll also tell you to type three commands; MI, B and I. When you're in a Forum and type these commands, you'll be able to read text files that will tell you how to use the Forum, tell you about Forum policies, and bring you up to date on Forum activities.

After the bulletin has appeared, you'll get this prompt:

```
Key <ENTER> for menu:
```

This means to hit **Return** so you can see this:

```
CBM Programming SIG

Function Menu
1 (L)     Leave a Message
2 (R)     Read Messages
3 (CO)    Conference Mode
4 (DL)    Data Library (Former XA)
5 (B)     Bulletins
6 (V)     View Member Directory
7 (SS)    Set Sub-topic
8 (OP)    Set User Options
```

```
9 (I)       Instructions
Ø (E)       Exit the CBM Programming SIG
Enter selection or H for Help:
```

When you enter a CIS Forum for the first time, the system will display menus to help you find your way around. Although this can be helpful, it can also be quite a nuisance and run up your connect-time charges considerably. The best way to use a Forum is to be in command mode most of the time. When you're in command mode, you can always display a menu by typing an **H** or a **?** (question mark). I'm going to show you how to use the Forum in command mode; the way to get into command mode is to change your Forum options. This is choice 8 on the above menu. After typing **8,** we'll see:

```
User Options Menu

[ ] represents current setting

1 (MEN)     Use menus [Yes]
2 (BR)      Use brief prompts [No]
3 (ST)      Stop between msgs [Yes]
4 (TWM)     Type waiting msgs [No]
5 (RNS)     Skip msgs you left [No]
6 (T)       Return to Function Menu

Numbers toggle yes/no options.
Commands take yes/no arguments.
Enter selection, or key <ENTER>
for additional options:
```

Your current Forum settings are shown by a [Yes] next to the menu item. To change any of these items from a [No] to a [Yes] (or vice versa), just type the menu number. The entire menu will be redisplayed and you'll see the [Yes] or [No] changed to its opposite meaning.

Let's look at each Forum option. I'll explain which options I use and suggest alternatives that you may wish to explore.

- MEN—*use menus.* This option will give you menus in every part of the Forum. Menus are a time waster and it would be better if you avoided them. It's better to be in command mode at all times. A menu is only a typed **?** or an **H** away in the Forum. Throughout this explanation of the Forum, I'll dispense with the menus except when explaining the commands that are available to you. Feel free to set this option later to see what the menus look like.

- BR—*use brief prompts.* This is an option that we'll set. It'll display shorter prompts, which means you can move through the Forum quicker.
- ST—*stop between msgs.* This option is already set by the Forum. It'll give you a prompt after you read a message. It's best to leave this as it is.
- TWM—*type waiting msgs.* When you enter the Forum, this will display any messages that are waiting for you. If you plan to correspond with other Forum members, you might want to have any messages that are waiting for you typed out automatically when you enter the Forum. Messages addressed to you are called "marked" messages. In other words, the Forum software has been told to let you know of these messages and, if you set this option, automatically display them when you enter the Forum. There is a drawback to using this option, though. Once the Forum starts displaying your waiting messages, you'll have to go through all of them. You won't be able to quit the display without unmarking all of the messages. Imagine having to read over 20 waiting messages when all you want to do is download a short program. It can happen—and often does when you won't want it to. It's best not to select this option. Leaving it as it is will simply display the headers of the messages that are waiting for you, allowing you to read them when you wish to, not when the system forces you to at entry.
- RNS—*skip messages you left.* When you instruct the Forum to display all of the new messages that have been posted, this option will skip messages that you've posted. It'll save you time. I recommend that you set this option.
- T—*return to Function Menu.* This command is used after you've set all of your options. I'll return you to the Forum message area.

Let's press **Return** at this menu to look at the rest of the Forum settings:

```
User Options Menu

1 (LL)    Line length  [4Ø]
2 (CN)    Name [Mike Cane     ]
3 (PC)    Prompt character [ ]
4 (ED)    Editor [Sed]
5 (DS)    Default Sub-topic [0]
6 (B)     Back to prior menu page
7 (T)     Return to Function Menu

Enter selection,
or H for help:
```

- LL—*line length*. The number in parentheses should be the same as the width setting you made earlier in Defalt. You can change it if you wish.
- CN—*name*. If your name has been typed incorrectly or you've decided to add your middle initial, you can use this option to set things right.
- PC—*prompt character*. This doesn't show a prompt character within brackets. If you're using a terminal program that does line-by-line uploading in response to a system prompt, you may need to use this option to tell the Forum the kind of prompt your terminal program requires. It's doubtful that you'll need to set this option since most (good) terminal programs allow you to set a prompt in the software.
- ED—*editor*. The current setting is SED, which is the SIG (Forum) Editor. This is the text editor that the Forum automatically gives you. It's somewhat like the text editor in EasyPlex, and I'll illustrate its use. If you don't care for it, you can always change this setting. The other available text editor is FILGE, which you've just seen at work in Bullet.
- DS—*default sub-topic*. This option will place you in a particular part of the Forum message area. Since you can also accomplish this in the Forum message area with a command, it's not necessary to set this option.
- B—*back to prior menu page*. This is self- explanatory.
- T—*return to Function Menu*. This was explained earlier.

Of all of these options, I suggest that you set yours to look like these two completed menus:

First Menu

User Options Menu

[ ] represents current setting

1	(MEN)	Use menus [**No**]
2	(BR)	Use brief prompts [**Yes**]
3	(ST)	Stop between msgs [**Yes**]
4	(TWM)	Type waiting msgs [**No**]
5	(RNS)	Skip msgs you left [**Yes**]
6	(T)	Return to Function Menu

Second Menu

User Options Menu

```
1 (LL)    Line length [63]
2 (CN)    Name [Your Name ]
3 (PC)    Prompt character [ ]
4 (ED)    Editor [Sed]
5 (DS)    Default Sub-topic [Ø]
6 (B)     Back to prior menu page
7 (T)     Return to Function Menu
```

Once all of the options have been set, type **T** to get this prompt:

```
Are the changes just made
for this session only, or permanent?
Enter S or P, or H for help:
```

Typing **P**, for permanent, will store the settings and return you to the main prompt of the Forum, which is

```
Function:
```

Now that we're topside, let's take a look at the commands that are available. A list of them is only a typed **H** or **?** away. If you forget this simple command, just press **Return** for a reminder:

```
Function: [RETURN]

Use H for list of valid commands.

Function: H

Functions:
B    - bulletins            CO   - conference
D    - delete               DL   - library
E    - exit                 G x  - go to page x
I    - instructions
L    - leave a message
M    - previous menu
MI   - membership information
NEW- new/changes
OFF - log off               OP   - set options
QS   - quick scan           R    - read messages
R x  - run SIG x            RT   -read thread
S    - scan headers
```

```
SD  - scan & display
SEN - send a message
SB  - sub-topic names
SS  - set sub-topic
T   - go DISPLA          U   - user log
UST - current users
V   - interests          X   - database

? x- explanation of function x

Function:
```

These are all of the commands available in the main part of the Forum, called the message area. As the last line of this menu states, you can get an explanation of each command (and how it is used) by typing **?** and the command; for example, **? B** or **? NEW** or **? X**. To save you time (and connect-time charges), I'll explain some of these commands below and illustrate the others as we go along.

- B—*bulletins*. A bulletin is what you'll sometimes see when you enter a Forum. This command can be used to re-read the bulletin if you skipped it with a Control-O or Control-P. If you enter a Forum as a result of buying this book, use this command to read all of the old bulletins that are filed away, as well as new bulletins that contain news about certain portions of the Forum you've entered. This will help you to keep current with Forum happenings. This is also one of the commands you'll be told to use when you enter a Forum for the first time.
- E—*exit*. Takes you out of the Forum.
- G x—*go to page x*. This is a DISPLA command. It will take you to any requested DISPLA page. For example, typing **G** CIS1 will take you to Page CIS-1.
- I—*instructions*. CIS is always improving the Forum software and there will probably be some changes after this book gets to the printer. Use this command to display all of the instructions. This is also one of the commands you'll be told to use when you enter a Forum for the first time.
- M—*previous menu*. This command will take you back to which ever DISPLA menu page you were at before entering the Forum.
- NEW—*new/changes*. This is where you can find out what revised versions of the Forum software can (or can't) do. Along with the "I" command, you'll need to use this command to catch up on new features added to the Forum since this book was published.

- OFF—*log off*. Immediately exits you from not only the Forum but from CIS itself.
- OP—*set options*. You just saw this illustrated.
- R x—*run* SIG x. Although I've been told that this command is being discontinued, it always seems to be available on each new version of the Forum software. Still, adhering to CIS's wishes, I must advise you not to use it.
- T—*go* DISPLA. This will take you to the top page of the DISPLA portion of CompuServe. Unless you set a different page in Default, your top page will be CIS-1.

This brings us to the illustrations of the other commands. The first is the V command. It stands for interests but means view the interests of other users. This is where most users of the Forums place their state, names, and interests. It's a user directory for the Forum members. (You'll also see another example of a user directory in Chapter 15, Using THE SOURCE.) It would be a good idea to list yourself here so that other Forum members will be able to get your User ID so they can leave messages for you.

Let's type **V** to explore this area:

```
Function: V
```

Remember that typing **?** or **H** will display a menu for you.

```
Option: ?
A    - add entry to log
C    - change existing log entry
D    - delete existing log entry
S    - search interest log
T    - return to top command level
Option:
```

Let's type **S** to look at some entries:

```
Option: S
Enter search string
(blank line implies all):
```

Press **Return** here:

```
 75975,428
    NY Andy&Josie, C64 communications with IBM
mainframes
```

```
79385,1595
    CA Kildy Loyers, C64/justice/law/sunshine/plain
english contracts

75995,488
    CT Izzy Simpul, COMAL, EZScript, Master Composer,
Koalapad

79736,1984
    NY Mike Cane, Author of "The Computer Phone
Book[tm]" and die-hard fan of NBC News Overnight (bring
it back!)

79736,1984
    NJ Madeline Simon, TeleComputing, Programming,
Pasc^P

Option:
```

You can interrupt the display at any time by issuing a **Control-P (^P).** Now, type **A** to add yourself:

```
Option A

State:
```

Type the two-letter post office abbreviation of your state. Next, you'll see this.

```
State: NY
Interests:
```

Type your interests. Separate each interest with a comma. You have 142 characters in which to describe your interests. Your name and User ID will be added for you automatically, so don't type them. Entering your interests will look something like this:

```
Interests: telecom, c64,vic2Ø, sid chip[RETURN]
Enter blank line to end
Continue (113 characters remaining)
modems, downloading[RETURN]
Continue <94 characters remaining>
[RETURN]

Option:
```

To see if everything came out correctly, just start the search process again by typing **S:**

```
Option: S

Enter search string
(blank line implies all):
```

This is where your User ID comes in. Type it to have your listing called up immediately, like this:

```
Enter search string
(blank line implies all): 79997,748
79997,748
     PA Your Name telecom, c64, vic2Ø, sid chip,
modems, downloading
```

If your entry isn't the way you want it, you can start all over by typing **C**, like so:

```
Option: C

Current entry reads:
PA Your Name telecom, c64, vic2Ø, sid chip,
modems, downloading
```

And the process will begin again:

```
State:
Interests:
Enter blank line to end
```

After you're through, type **T** to exit:

```
Option: T

Function:
```

The next command we'll look at is SS, set sub-topic. A sub-topic is name for a section of the Forum message area and databases. All CIS Forums are divided into sections, called sub-topics. Each section has a different name to guide the membership in posting certain types of messages. The section names also correspond to databases of files in the DL (formerly called XA) portion of the Forum (to be covered later). Typing **SB** will show the sub-topic section names that are used in this particular Forum:

```
Function: SB

Ø  Welcome to the SIG!
1  B-128, VIC-2Ø & PET
2  High Level Utility
3  Disk Programming
4  Beyond BASIC
5  Technical Tips
6  Club 65XX
7  Terminal Programs
8  The BBS Corner
9  C128 Info Center
1Ø

Function:
```

If you have a general question, you would place it in sub-topic 0, Welcome to the SIG! If you're doing programming with a CBM disk and have some comments or questions, you would put your message in sub-topic 3, Disk Programming. You'll see how to post messages and place them in a particular section soon.

The next Forum command I'll introduce you to is the SS command, for set sub-topic. It'll allow you to access a particular sub-topic of the Forum's message base. In other words, it blocks out all of the other sub-topic sections so you can concentrate on just one. To use it, type **SS** and one of the sub-topic numbers shown above. For instance, to access only sub-topic 4, Beyond BASIC, type **SS4:**

```
Function: SS4

Sub-topic 4 - Beyond BASIC
Function:
```

Once "Sub-topic 4 - Beyond BASIC" is displayed, it means that you'll only see messages in sub-topic 4 of the Forum message base. What good is this? Let's say that you're learning Pascal or COMAL and need help. The best place to look for other programmers would be in sub-topic 4. So, use SS4 to block out the other sections and concentrate your message scanning/reading to that one section. Keep this useful command in mind, later, when I'll illustrate various ways of going through Forum messages.

To go back to assessing all sub-topic sections of the Forum's message base, you have to type **SSALL:**

```
Function: SSALL
```

```
All accessible sub-topics active
for retrieval

Function:
```

Now you're ready to see examples of how to go about retrieving messages posted by other Forum members. First, let's take another look at the Forum menu of commands by typing **H** again:

```
Function: H

Functions:
B     - bulletins              CO  - conference
D     - delete                 DL  - library
E     - exit                   G x - go to page x
I     - instructions
L     - leave a message
M     - previous menu
MI    - membership information
NEW- new/changes
OFF - log off                  OP  - set options
QS  - quick scan               R   - read messages
R x - run SIG x                RT  - read thread
S   - scan headers
SD  - scan & display
SEN - send a message
SB  - sub-topic names
SS  - set sub-topic
T   - go DISPLA                U   - user log
UST - current users
V   - interests                X   - database

? x  - explanation of function x

Function:
```

The first method of looking at the messages posted in the Forum is to just look at the headers. A *header,* as its name implies, is at the top of a message and contains the message number, its author, the author's User ID, the date and time it was posted on the Forum, the message's subject, and whom it is addressed to. (Chapter 12, using MCI Mail, and Chapter 15, Using THE SOURCE, show other formats of message headers.)

To view the headers only, on any Forum, just type **S,** for Scan:

```
Function: S
```

Then you'll see

<F>orward, <R>everse, <A>bort:

This prompt is asking for the direction in which you want to scan the message base. A Forward scan will start with the lowest-numbered message and work its way to the highest number. A Reverse scan will start at the highest-numbered message and go backward to the lowest number.

I'll use a Forward scan as an example:

<F>orward, <R>everse, <A>bort: **F**
System contains messages
158373 to 158852
Starting message number
(N implies since last time on):

Once the direction of the scan has been specified, press **Return** in reply to the final prompt. That'll start the scan at the earliest message. Then you'll see something like this scroll up your screen:

```
#:    158373      Sec. 4 - Beyond BASIC
Sb:   #COMAL Cult!
      Ø3-Sep-85 ØØ:49:Ø4
Fm:   Mike Cane 79736,1984
To:   Madeline Simon 79238,72 (X)

#:    158374      Sec. 3 - Disk Programming
Sb:   1541 DOS
      Ø3-Sep-85 ØØ:49:24
Fm:   Kildy Loyers 79775,1675
To:   Izzy Simpul 79845,1678 (X)

#:    158376      Sec 5 - Technical Tips
Sb:   #Amiga V
      Ø3-Sep-85 ØØ:52:59
Fm:   Diana Visitor 79976,1958
To:   Juliette Parrish 79845,1678 (X)
```

You can continue this scan throughout its several hundred headers or issue a Control-P to get back to the "Function:" prompt. The drawback of doing a scan is that you can't immediately read a message if its header looks interesting.

Before I go any further, it would be best for you to know the parts of a message header. This knowledge will help you to keep track of not only other member's messages to each other but your own messages, too.

Let's take the first header shown above as an example.

```
#:     158373     Sec. 4 - Beyond BASIC
Sb:    #COMAL Cult!
       Ø3-Sep-85 ØØ:49:Ø4
Fm:    Mike Cane 79736,1984
To:    Madeline Simon 79238,72 (X)
```

I'll explain it line by line.

Line 1 is

```
#:     158373     Sec. 4 - Beyond BASIC
```

#: 158373 means this is message number 158373. Sec. 4 - Beyond BASIC means it was posted in sub-topic 4.

Line 2 is

```
Sb: #COMAL Cult!
```

Sb: stands for Subject. "COMAL Cult!" is the subject of the message. But what's the "#" symbol preceding the subject? It's a marker placed by the Forum to indicate that this message has replies to it. Sometimes, you'll also see an actual message number as part of the Subject line, indicating that the exchange of information has gone on for more than two messages. This is an extremely useful piece of information. You'll see how it's used later in this discussion.

Line 3 is

```
Ø3-Sep-85 ØØ:49:Ø4
```

This line is simple enough. The left hand part is the date, the right hand part is the time (in military 24:00 fashion).

Line 4 is

```
Fm: Mike Cane 79736,1984
```

Again, this line is very simple. Fm: stands for From. This is the name and the User ID of the person who authored the message.

Line 5 is

```
To: Madeline Simon 79238,72 (X)
```

This line is virtually self-explanatory. This is, of course, the person to whom the message is addressed. Her name and User ID are shown. But what's the (X) tagging along? This is another Forum marker. This symbol indicates that the person who is supposed to get this message has not only received it but has read it. It's like a little receipt.

In contrast to doing a scan, you can do a Scan and Display. This is SD from the Forum's main menu. It'll let you read any message that you want immediately, like so:

Function: **SD**
System contains messages
158373 to 158852
Starting message number
(N implies since last time on):

Press **Return** to start at the earliest message for a forward scan. Forward scan is the only direction in which Scan and Display works, by the way. You can also specify a particular message number as a starting point.

In this example, I'll use the earliest message:

#:	158373	Sec. 4 - Beyond BASIC
Sb:	#COMAL Cult!	
	Ø3-Sep-85 ØØ:49:Ø4	
Fm:	Mike Cane 79736,1984	
To:	Madeline Simon 79238,72 (X)	

<R>ead <T>op:

The prompt, "<R>ead <T>op," offers three choices: You may read the text of the message by typing **R,** return to the "Function:" (top) prompt by typing **T,** or have the next header appear on your screen by pressing **Return.** At just one press of a key, the SD function will allow you to read a message immediately.

Although this is a better method of accessing messages than just using Scan (S), it's still inefficient. If you'd like to scan all of the messages and read them after the scan, you can. The command is SM (Scan and Mark). Even though it's not listed on the main menu of Forum commands, it still exists. Like Scan (S), Scan and Mark (SM) has the option of going through the message base in forward or reverse order. You can use the command like this:

Function: **SM**
<F>orward, <R>everse, <A>bort:**F**
System contains messages
158373 to 158852
Starting message number
(N implies since last time on):

Press **Return** to start at the earliest message for a forward scan (or the highest message number, if you're going in reverse):

```
#:      158373        Sec. 4 - Beyond BASIC
Sb:     #COMAL Cult!
        03-Sep-85 00:49:04
Fm:     Mike Cane 79736,1984
To:     Madeline Simon 79238,72 (X)
<R>ead <M>ark <T>op:
```

In this instance, the option prompt after the display of a header is similar to that of Scan and Display (SD), except an additional option, <M>ark, is available. Typing **M** in response to this prompt will notify you that the message has been marked for you. You can continue scanning until you get to the last message that's been posted. Then, when you get the "Function:" prompt again, just type **RM.** This stands for "Read Marked [messages]."

Another method of accessing messages isn't much better than Scan except that it comes in very handy if you're in a hurry and just want a general overview of the messages in a Forum. This is the QS command, quick scan. A quick scan will look like this:

```
Function: QS;N
System contains messages
158373 to 158852
158373:   COMAL Cult!           Sec. 4 - Beyond BASIC
         1 reply
158374:   1541 DOS              Sec. 3 - Disk Programming
158376:   Amiga V               Sec. 5 - Hot Topic
         3 replies
```

This will continue to the final message unless you abort it by issuing a Control-P. As you can see, it's not as informative as a Scan or as flexible as a Scan and Display, but it does offer a quick way of getting the gist of what subjects are being bandied about on the Forum.

I hope that you noticed that I skipped a step in issuing the QS command above. I didn't wait for the Forum to ask me if I wanted forward or reverse direction. I just added my choice to the QS command itself, by combining QS with the N (for "new") command by using a semicolon (;). All of the commands available in the message base of the Forum may be truncated by combining the primary command with its secondary options. In other words, you can put the command and its option on the same line in response to one prompt. Just combine them with a semicolon. You've already seen an example of doing this in Chapter 4, Using BRS After Dark. It works the same way here.

In the examples that I've just shown of going through messages, the following commands could have been condensed in this manner:

- Scan Forward as S;F
- Scan Reverse as S;R
- Scan and Mark Forward as SM;F
- Scan and Mark Reverse as SM;R.

Some of these commands may be combined without using semicolons. Just type them as one word, for instance, SMF for Scan and Mark Forward. Combining several commands onto one line will save time (as well as money in connect-time). More examples of combined commands will be shown as we move along.

Finally, we arrive at the heart of retrieving messages, the Retrieve (R) command and its numerous options. Typing **R** will net this response:

```
Function: R

Subcommand:
```

Again, help is only a **?** or an **H** away:

```
Subcommand: ?
<A>bort
<F>orward
<I>ndividual
<M>arked
<N>ew
<R>everse
<S>earch

Subcommand:
```

These are the available options:

- <A>bort, which will take you back to the "Function:" prompt.
- <F>orward and <R>everse, which indicate the direction of the retrieval process.
- <N>ew, which will start at the first (public) message you haven't read yet. (The Forum keeps track of the last message number you've read when you exit.)
- <M>arked and <S>earch will be covered shortly.
- <I>ndividual, which will be illustrated now.

Typing **I** shows this:

```
Subcommand: I
System contains messages
158373 to 15882
Message number (Ø to end):
```

Just type in a message number. You may try any of the ones that fall within the range noted (158373–158852) when on the Forum. For this demonstration, the first message will do. Typing **158373** brings up

```
System contains messages
158373 to 158852
Message number (Ø to end): 8Ø373

#:      158373      Sec. 4 - Beyond BASIC
Sb:     #COMAL Cult!
        Ø3-Sep-85 ØØ:49:Ø4
Fm:     Mike Cane 79736,1984
To:     Madeline Simon 73235,72 (X)
Hey, did you see InfoWorld? Dvorak
called us a cult! Maybe we COMAL
"cultists" should come up with a
password and Secret Handshake?

* Reply:
        158383
(C RE T):
Message number (Ø to end):
```

Notice the "* Reply: 158383" at the bottom of the message. When messages are individually read, you'll be shown if there are any replies to that message and the Forum will also show each reply's message number. At the "Message number (Ø to end):" prompt, you can type in the reply's message number to read it. This is how you go about reading a single message on the Forum. This method, of course, requires that you first know the message number. If you had used the QS (Quick Scan) command initially and made note of interesting messages by their number, you would be able to retrieve the desired messages. Still, this is slow and has a drawback.

Remember that you can string primary commands and their options on the same prompt line. After using QS and noting desired messages, you could retrieve them in the following manner. Let's say you wanted messages 158375, 15839Ø, and 158399. At the prompt, type this:

```
Function: R;I;158375;15839Ø;158399
```

This would automatically retrieve these messages. The drawback, however, is that you cannot reply to one of them without having the Forum "forget" the numbers of the other messages you wanted. So, after reading message 158375 and replying to it (this process will be illustrated shortly), you'd get

```
Message number (Ø to end):
```

The Forum does not remember that you also wanted it to retrieve messages 15839Ø and 158399. These message numbers must be re-entered, like so:

Message number (Ø to end):**15839Ø;158399**

The Forum would then go ahead and fetch them for you. Of course, if you reply to message 15839Ø, it would forget that you wanted it to get message 158399, and that message number must be typed a third time.

What good is the R;I (Retrieve Individual message) command? There may be times when a signon bulletin from the sysops asks the membership to read a certain message. They'll post the number in the bulletin. Using R;I, you can get it quickly and easily.

It's not necessary for me to illustrate either the R;F (Retrieve Forward) or R;R (Retrieve Reverse) features. These work similarly to the Scan (S) command (except that it displays the whole message, not just its header). Also, R;N (Retrieve New) is simply an automatic forward retrieval that starts at the first message you haven't read yet.

The next useful retrieval method is R;S (Retrieve Search). It's a very handy method of retrieving that allows you, in the least amount of time, to get messages of interest. It's used like this:

Function: **R**
Subcommand: **S**

Search field:

Again, type a **?** or **H** for assistance:

Search field:

<F>rom
<S>ubject
<T>o

Search field:

These are the fields on which you can search for a message. In my previous description of a message header, I showed each of these fields. To recap briefly and expand a bit on that explanation, the <F>rom field designates the person who sent the message. This field may be specified by the person's full name, last name, or his or her CompuServe User ID. The <T>o field designates the person to whom the message is sent. It can also be searched the same way as the <F>rom field. The <S>ubject field, of course, designates what the message is about. The difference between this field and the other two is that you don't need to know someone's name or User ID prior to searching; you just need to know the subjects you are interested in.

An example of searching the <S>ubject field for a topic of interest looks like this:

```
Search field: S
Search string:
```

"Search string:" means you should type a keyword for the subject you're interested in. You've already seen keyword searching in Chapter 3, Using BRS After Dark. It almost works the same way here, except a keyword can only be one subject and it must be less than 24 characters long. Multiple keywords require multiple searches on the subject field.

To keep up to date on new BBSs (Bulletin-Board Systems), for instance, type **BBS:**

```
Search string: BBS
System contains messages
158373 to 158852
Starting message number
(N implies since last time on): Ø
```

A zero (Ø) tells the system to start from the first message posted. You could, as mentioned earlier, just press **Return.** The result would be the same. If there are any messages in the Forum for Bulletin-Boards that are specified as the subject keyword "BBS," you'll see something like this:

```
Search string: BBS
System contains messages
158373 to 158852
Starting message number
(N implies since last time on): Ø
```

```
#:    158841        Sec. 8 - The BBS Corner
Sb:   Your 'BBS'?
      Ø4-Sep-85 16:44:11
Fm:   Jim Main 74978,814
To:   Alan Bechtold 79987,1234

Is your BBS still operating?
I can't get it to pick up when I call it.

(C RE T):
```

To see if there are other messages on the same subject, hit Return when presented with the "(C RE T)" prompt. Any subsequent message will follow, and you'll have to press Return again at "(C RE T)." After the final message has been placed on your screen, the "Function:" prompt will reappear. This is an efficient and effective way of getting to messages that discuss topics of interest and may hold answers to questions you may have. If you have a communications program with a buffer, you can use the variations of the R;S command to capture important messages in your buffer one after another. You don't have to bother with quick scanning (QS) or scanning (S). Simply get in, define your subject(s), have the Forum do the search for you, and get out with the least amount of connect-time incurred. Remember, however, to use several variations of a subject to ensure that the Forum does a complete search. For instance, searching for BBSs could be done by defining the subject search string as "BBS," "Bulletin-Board," "Board," or "System." Also, remember that you can string everything together on one line by separating the various elements with semicolons. In the example just shown, you could have typed **R;S;S;BBS** (Retrieve;Search;<S>ubject field;BBS) to get the same result.

Now that you've seen the primary ways of the scanning and retrieval commands, it's time to see how you can join in with your own messages. Leaving a message can be accomplished in two ways: by replying to someone else's message or by composing your own new message. I'll illustrate both ways.

The first method, replying to a message, will be illustrated by using the message that was retrieved using the R;S command, just shown:

```
 #:  158841        Sec. 8 - The BBS Corner
Sb:  Your 'BBS'?
     Ø4-Sep-85 16:44:11
Fm:  Jim Main 74978,814
To:  Alan Bechtold 79987,1234

Is your BBS still operating?
I can't get it to pick up when I call it.
```

```
(C RE T):
```

Once again, to get all of the available options, type a **?** or an **H:**

```
(C RE T): ?
Options:
C - continue              D - delete
M - mark                  NS - No Stop
RE - reply                RP - Read Prev
RR - Read Reply           RT - Read Thread
T - top command level
UA - use address
RETURN or ENTER - continue

? x - explain option x

(C RE T):
```

You can get full explanations of all of these commands while you're online by typing a **?** and the letter of the option (for instance, **? M** for information on "mark"). There are only two options of concern at the moment: T and RE. If you decide not to reply to the message and, in fact, just want to get back to the "Function:" prompt, type **T.** Of course, a **Return** will continue to the next message, if there is one. To reply to the message, however, type **RE**. You'll see this:

```
(C RE T) : RE

1:
```

This is the text entry mode of the Forum message base, using the SIG Editor. Remember, you have your choice of using FILGE (the text editor that's used in Bullet) or the standard SIG (Forum) editor. I'm going to show you how to use the SIG Editor since you've already seen how to use FILGE. Pay attention, because the commands illustrated in this example are precisely the same ones you'll use in creating an original message. Once the REply process has been started, the Forum automatically assigns your message the highest message number available. The Forum also places your name in the "Fm:" ("From:") field described earlier and uses the subject of the message you are replying to in the "Sb:" ("Subject:") field. You don't have to type in anything except your message. The prompt shown above, "1:," designates the first line of the message. Just go ahead and type your message. Make sure that your line isn't longer than 79 characters, though, or you'll get a notice telling you to retype it because it is too long.

It doesn't matter if you type a line that's only 22 columns or as long as 79, the Forum will dynamically reformat the message so it can be easily read on any size screen. You have up to 35 lines for a message. After you've typed a first line and pressed **Return,** you'll see this:

```
1:  Could youlease tell me the number of your BBS?
2:
```

There's a typo. Forget it for the moment. The "2:" shown is a prompt for a second line. Just go ahead and type a second line:

```
1:  Could youlease tell me the number of your BBS?
2:  Thanks very.
3:
```

A prompt is given for the next line. If you're finished typing your message, press **Return** to get the next set of options. Ignore the mistakes you may have made in typing it, as illustrated above.

```
3:  [Return]

Leave option:
```

Again, type a **?** or an **H** for a list:

```
Leave option: ?

A - Abort          C - Continue
D - delete         E - edit
I - insert         L - list
P - preview        R - replace
S# - Store to sub-topic #
SP# - Store Prvt to sub-topic #

Valid sub-topic #s:
Ø        Welcome to the SIG!
1        B-128, VIC-2Ø & PET
2        High Level Utility
3        Disk Programming
4        Beyond BASIC
5        Technical Tips
6        Club 65XX
7        Terminal Programs
8        The BBS Corner
9        C128 Info Center
1Ø
```

? x - explain x

Leave option:

You can get explanations of all of these commands by typing a **?** and the letter of the option (for instance, **? R** for information on "replace"). For now, all you need to know is that if you decide not to send this reply after all, you still have a chance to delete it by typing A, for abort. The system will ask if you're sure that you wish to abort the message; typing a Y in response will break you out of the composing process and return you to your prior command (if you've been scanning or retrieving messages) or the "Function:" prompt.

If you still want to send the message, you'll have to correct the mistakes. This is where the E (edit) command comes in. Type **E** to get this:

Leave option: **E**

Line # to edit:

This is why each line of the message is numbered: to enable you to locate it quickly for editing.

Since line #1 of the message is less than perfect, that is where you should start, by typing **1** in reply:

Line # to edit: **1**
Line 1 reads:
Could youlease tell me the number of your BBS?
String to replace:

You're being asked to type the mistake. A "string" is any collection of letters or number that you've typed. Obviously, "youlease" should be "you please." So, to correct this, type:

String to replace: **youlease**
Replacement string:

"Replacement string:" means to type the correction. So, type

String to replace: youlease
Replacement string: **you please**
Could you please tell me the number of your BBS?
Okay?

The Forum then redisplays the line with the correction in it. If the line still isn't correct, you can type **N** at the "Okay?" prompt to get another chance.

Line #2's "Thanks very." should be "Thanks very much." To correct it, do this:

Leave option: **E**

Line # to edit: **2**
Line 2 reads:
2: Thanks very.
String to replace: **very.**
Replacement string: **very much.**
2: Thanks very much.
Okay? **Y**
Leave option:

Remember the way that commands can be strung together on one line linked by semicolons? The same is true of editing commands. So, we could have done this editing with just two lines, like this:

Leave option: **E1;youlease;you please**

Could you please tell me the number of
your BBS?
Okay? **Y**

Leave option: **E2;very.;very much.**

Thanks very much.
Okay? **Y**

Leave option:

This method is easier for short messages and even for long ones, if you can recall the line numbers that require editing. To make sure that everything is OK, type **L** to list the message, like this:

Leave option: **L**

1: Could you please tell me the number of your BBS?
2: Thanks very much.

Leave option:

If you have a very long message and don't want to wade through all of it just to see if one line was corrected by editing, you can list a single line or a range of lines. The syntax for this command is **L#** (for instance, L1 for "list line 1") or **L#,#** (for instance L4,7 for "list lines 4, 5, 6 and

7"). Another way to look at a message before sending it is to use the P command. P means "Preview," and it'll just show you the message text without the line numbers. The sample message above would look like this:

```
Leave option: P
Could you please tell me the number of your BBS?
Thanks very much.

Leave option:
```

You can't preview a single line or a range of lines. But you can preview the message in a desired screen width. If your Forum screen width is set for 80 columns and you want to see what your message looks like when formatted for a 40-column screen, do this:

```
Leave option: P40
Could you please tell me the number of
your BBS? Thanks very much.

Leave option:
```

Now that the message is done, you must decide how to store it to the Forum. Do you want everyone to read it? If your reply has general interest, you may want others to see it so that they might have the chance to reply to it (someone other than the person the message is intended for may know the answer and post it sooner). If your reply is not of general interest, if, in fact, it is a personal message, by all means store it as a private message. A private message is one that only the recipient may read. Not every Forum allows private messages, so you should test this option before you spend your time typing a message that's meant to be private. Just type a one-line test message to yourself and try to store it privately using the method I'm about to show you.

To store a reply as a public message, type **S:**

```
Leave option: S

Message # 158853 Stored
```

The message is now stored publicly; any Forum member may read it.

To store the message privately so that only the recipient may read it, type **SP:**

```
Leave option: SP

Message # 158853 Stored
```

When the person gets the message, he or she will find the symbol "(P)" next to the message's number. This lets the person know it's a private message. Any message that person makes in a reply will also be private. Once a message is private, all of its replies are private, too. To leave someone a private message, you have to include his or her User ID.

If a Forum doesn't allow private messages, you'll see this:

```
Private messages not allowed!
```

It may sound obvious, but to compose an original message, you need to know who will receive it. If the message is for anyone, address it to "ALL." If the message is for a particular person, you must know that person's name, he or she must be a member of the Forum, and you must know the person's CompuServe User ID. Remember that CompuServe—and any system for that matter—only knows each person by his or her User ID. The system doesn't recognize John Smith, or Jane Doe, or Mike Cane; it only knows them by their individual User ID. If you try to leave a message to someone without the User ID, you're just being sloppy. You can't use any electronic message system without knowing the recipient's ID, and you shouldn't expect to use the Forum's message facility without following the same rule. A few pages ago, you learned about the user directory available in the Forum under the "V" command (View interest log). This is where you can find other Forum members' User IDs, so you don't have an excuse for not knowing a person's User ID. If you aren't listed in the directory, make life easier for your fellow Forum members by placing yourself in it the next time you're online. Then others can find your User ID just by searching for your name.

Let's look at how to leave an original message. We start by typing **L:**

Function: **L**
To:

Type the name and the User ID of the message's intended recipient. This is the correct format:

To: **Mike Cane 79736,1984**

If the message is to be totally public and for everyone, type **ALL:**

To: **ALL**

If you need help from one of the fine Forum sysops, type **SYSOP:**

To: **SYSOP**

This will get your message into the hands of the Forum's sysops. The next thing you'll see is

Subject:

Just type the subject of the message. If it's a public message, try to make it as informative as possible. Subjects such as "Help" and "Assistance needed" are too general to be of use if someone is using the QS (Quick Scanning) command in the message base. It would be better if you were more specific; for instance, "Help with COMAL," or "1541 Save & Replace," or "Review of 1541 Flash". Each of these sample messages contain a narrow, searchable <S>ubject field. No one (except possibly the sysops) would bother searching for the subject "Help." But someone who knows the COMAL programming language would be interested in other messages about COMAL, and "1541" is virtually synonymous with "disk drive" for Commodore owners. Try to keep it simple, make it very descriptive, and most of all, keep it 24 characters or less in length.

After you've filled in the subject, entering and editing a message is the same as replying to a message. You've already seen this, so I won't repeat it. The Forum will automatically insert your name and User ID into the "Fm:" ("From:") field of the message. You don't have to type either of these items in the body of your message. The only new part of this process is when the time comes to store the message.

Aside from specifying whether an original message is to be public or private, you must have to choose which Forum sub-topic section the message is to be placed in. Look at what happens when you just try to store the message without selecting a Forum sub-topic section number:

Leave option: **S**

Enter selection: **3**

Message # 158853 Stored

Function:

The system prompts you for the sub-topic section number and gives the list as a reminder. The purpose of each sub-topic has already been described. To store a private message, type **SP** *plus* the sub-topic section number. For instance, **SP3.** If you leave off the sub-topic number when you type SP, the message won't be stored privately unless you tell the Forum to store it privately a second time when you select a sub-topic. I can't emphasize this enough.

I'll now provide an illustration:

Leave option: **SP**

Sub-topic # required
0 Welcome to the SIG!
1 B-128, VIC-2Ø & PET
2 High Level Utility
3 Disk Programming
4 Beyond BASIC
5 Technical Tips
6 Club 65XX
7 Terminal Programs
8 The BBS Corner
9 C128 Info Center
10

Enter selection: **SP3**

Message # 158853 Stored

Function:

Repeat: Notice that you must type **SP** a second time with the sub-topic number. If the Forum doesn't allow private messages, you'll be told so. Remember to test the private message feature before you try to write a private message.

There are only three other Forum messaging commands to know about. They're used when retrieving messages. They are

- RP, for Read Previous message
- RR, for Read Reply to this message
- RT, for Read Thread of this message

Each of these is used when the "(UA RE T)" prompt appears at the end of any message you've read.

If you're reading a message that has a particular importance, it might be a reply to a prior message. That prior message may also contain information you can use. At the "(UA RE T)" prompt, type **RP** and, if the message is still available, it'll appear on your screen. This is a very useful command to use if you've come in on the middle of an exchange of messages.

Remember that any message that contains the "#" symbol next to the "Sb:" ("Subject:") field indicates that it has at least one reply. The message number of the reply will appear after the message itself. Instead of making a note of the message number and retrieving it individually (R;I), you can read it immediately by typing **RR** at the "(UA RE T)" prompt.

If the message has several replies, you can use **RT** after the "(UA RE T)" prompt. "RT" stands for "Read Thread," and it follows the hierarchy of the initial message and its replies. After you've read the initial message, RT will show you all of the public replies to that message.

A little-known command that can be used at the "(UA RE T)" prompt is **M.** This will mark the message. If you come across an interesting message but don't wish to capture it in your terminal buffer immediately, type **M** and the Forum will hold it until you're ready to get it. When you're ready to read it again, type **RM** (Read Marked messages) at the "Function:" prompt. The "M" command will only hold a message while you're still in the Forum. If you forget to type RM, become accidentally disconnected, or leave the Forum, the marked message will be set free. You'll have to go look for it using any of the techniques I've already described.

I haven't covered every combination of every available Forum message base command in this section. The combinations and variations on a theme are so numerous that trying to describe each and every one of them would only be confusing. What I've given you are the fundamentals. These just may be more commands than you'll ever use, actually. I've presented as many as I thought would enable you to navigate throughout a Forum's message base without running up a large connect-time bill, without having to ask other Forum members how to use the Forum, and without having to feel fear or utter confusion in using a medium that is designed to help you.

Let's look at the other Forum commands, starting with **UST.** This means "User STatus" (also called "USTat"), and it'll display a list of everyone currently using the Forum and what part of it they're in. It's just like the /USERS command you saw earlier, illustrated in the CB Simulator. Using it looks like this:

```
Function: UST

Job   User ID       Node     Prgm.
24    79575,829     T16TAM   SIG
29    79736,1984    TØ4NYC   SIG
32    79745,8Ø8     TØ1PRI   CO
34    75829,963     T41ARL   ACCESS
39    75245,1286    TØ1HOU   CO
45    75879,Ø829    TØ9NYC   CO
48    74885,1959    T27DAL   ACCESS
52    7Ø819,929     TØ2LAN   CO

Function:
```

"Job" is a number assigned to each individual accessing CompuServe. "User ID," of course, is each person's User ID. "Node" refers to the physical telephone connection to the CompuServe computers and has two parts. The first part is a node number and the second part is the city of origin or the packet-switched network being used. The first node, "T16TAM," is node 16 in the city of TAMpa. The column heading "Prgm." is an abbreviation for "program," which tells the part of the Forum each user is in. Generally, one of three programs are listed: "SIG," which stands for the main message base of the Forum; "ACCESS," which refers to the databases of downloadable software; and "CO," which is short for COnference. With the UST command, you can see if any of the people you know on the Forum are presently in it by looking for their User IDs. If you find someone you know, you can send a short message to that person using the **SEN** command. "SEN" is short for "SENd."

It works like this:

Function: **SEN JOB 24 Hello there,**
Madeline! Want to go to CO?

Function:

On Madeline's screen, whatever she is doing on the system will be interrupted by

;; SIG - Job 15: Hello there, Madeline! Want to go to co?

The two semicolons at the start of the message indicate an interruption; "SIG" shows the origin of the message; "Job 15" is the job number of the sender (in this case, yourself), which may be found in USTat. For Madeline to reply, she would have to issue a Control-C or Control-P to terminate her current activity, get a prompt [such as "Function:" or "(UA AR T)"], and then use the same SENd format as you.

It's just as inconvenient as I've described it, more so if you don't wish to be interrupted. Since it's such an inconvenience to terminate your current Forum activity to respond to a SENd, most people use the SENd command sparingly. Try not to use this command on people you don't know; most people won't stop what they're doing to respond to someone they don't know. Wait until you've made some friends in the Forum before attempting an interruption with the SENd command. It's not much fun to have your work interrupted. The only other thing you should know about the SENd command is that you can't use it to send a message to someone in the COnference area or to someone who is busy downloading or uploading a file. If you try to send a message during these situations, the Forum will curtly tell you

```
That Job is busy!
```

The next Forum command is **CO,** which will place you in the conferencing area of the Forum. The conferencing area is similar to the CB Simulator. It uses the same commands and works the same way as CB. You've already read about the CB Simulator, so I won't show the Forum conferencing area. The only thing you need to know about this area is that you shouldn't use a handle in it. As I said earlier, most Forums want you to use your real, full name in any messages you post. The same policy is also in effect when you use the conferencing area.

Back at the "Function:" prompt, there are two other areas of the Forum you should know about. Both are databases and are reached with the D and DL commands that are listed on the main menu. The D databases are text files about the operation of the Forum's various sections. In effect, it's some of what you've been reading about here, in different words. The D databases are labeled to correspond with the various Forum Sections. So, to access a D database that corresponds to Section 1, type **X1** at the "Function:" prompt. I don't have to give an example of using a D database because it's just a text file to be read. If you're curious, try it out once you're in the Forum. You may interrupt the output at any time by issuing a Control-P.

The DL databases are different. Collectively, they are known as the Database Libraries of the Forum. In them, you'll find a variety of public domain programs that may be downloaded into your computer. Each database corresponds to a Forum Section. For instance, in this particular Forum, these are Sections 4 and 7:

```
4 - Beyond BASIC
7 - Terminal Programs
```

In Section 4, you will find programs written in COMAL, PROMAL, Pascal, and other languages available for Commodore computers. In Section 7, you will find various types of terminal programs written and uploaded by the Forum membership. In these sub-topic sections in the message base, you will find messages about these subjects. In the corresponding database sections, you'll find corresponding downloadable programs and text files.

In each Forum you'll find quite a variety of software categories to choose from. The list of text files and programs grows daily as the Forum members contribute their talents and time.

Some people think using the databases is a bit tricky, but I'll give you a solid understanding of their operation so that you'll be able to join the thousands of other CIS subscribers who are busy downloading.

At the "Function:" prompt, type **DL**. You'll see this:

```
Function: DL
Database for which Section:
Ø 1 2 3 4 5 6 7 8 9 1Ø
```

Again, the databases are set up in different sections. Since I didn't specify a particular section, the system is asking for one now. Type the number of the Section you wish to enter. If you know which Section you want to go into at the start, just include that number with the DL command. If you want to enter Section 2, type **DL2** at the "Function:" prompt. The "Database for which Section:" prompt would be skipped and you'll be taken to Section 2 immediately. Since I didn't select a Section, I'll have to supply one now. Section 3, Disk Programming, will do. Typing **3** will get this:

```
Database for which Section:
Ø 1 2 3 4 5 6 7 8 9 1Ø 3
Commodore Programming SIG Database Access
Use ? for help

DL 3:
```

"DL 3:" is the only prompt you'll get. This is due to the OP (set options) command that was used earlier. One of the Forum options that was set was BR, for brief mode. "DL 3:" is the briefest prompt available. Remember, though, that help is always a ? or an H away. Typing **a ?** will give you the full menu of the database commands:

```
DL 3: ?

Valid commands:
PUB  - retrieve from Public ACCESS
NOR  - normal SIG access
DL   - Change to new data library
SB   - Type sub-topic names
S    - Scan
BRO  - browse thru files
R    - read a file
DOW  - download a file
UPL  - upload a file
SUB  - submit a file
KEY  - search keyword list
```

```
ERA  - erase a file
T    - return to function menu
UST  - list users in SIG
SEN  - send message to user
SET  - set menu & brief on/off
DES  - Describe the current data library
OFF  - logs you off

? xxx - explain command xxx

DS 3:
```

I'll explain each of these commands, most of them with examples. When you're online, you can get help with any of these commands just by typing a **?** and the command (for instance, **? NOR** to have the "Normal" command explained).

You don't have to settle for the briefest prompt in the databases. You can temporarily change the options for this portion of the Forum without affecting the way the other parts of the Forum will prompt you. This can be done by using the SET command. The SET command offers the choice of full menus, a short prompt, a brief prompt, and pauses between selections. To find out your current options, just type **SET**:

```
DL 3: SET
Current settings:

     BRIEF
     NO MENU
     NO PAUSE

DL 3:
```

Using these database prompt settings will allow you to get in and out in the least amount of time. But if you plan to use the databases infrequently, you might want to have menus to guide you. In computerese, online options are often set by toggling (using or not using) the word "no" before individual options. This is true in the Forum databases, too. So, to clear the brief mode and get longer prompts, type **SET** and **NO** BRIEF. Similarly, to allow menus, type **SET** and **MENU**. And to throw some pauses into the works, type **SET** and **PAUSE**. You can see the effect of two of these options below.

```
DL 3: SET NO BRIEF

DL 3 - Disk Programming:
```

Immediately, a longer prompt appears. Now you don't have to remember, or look through this book to find out, that DL3 is the Disk Programming database. The system itself will remind you.

The next option will show you this:

```
DL 3 - Disk Programming: SET MENU

1 BRO Browse thru files
2 UPL Upload a new file
3 EXI Exit to CBM Programming SIG
4 HEL Help
5 DL  Change database

Key digit:
```

This is a menu of the five commands you're most likely to use in the Forum databases. If you spend a considerable amount of time in the Forum databases, you'll learn the commands and not require any of the menus.

Let's take a look at what it's like to operate at the menu level. First, type **1** to browse the selections. You'll see something like this:

```
DL 3 - Disk Programming:

1 BRO Browse thru files
2 UPL Upload a new file
3 EXI Exit to CBM Programming SIG
4 HEL Help
5 DL  Change database

Key digit: 1
/AGE:
```

"/AGE:" is a delimiter. It's not important to know what it means just now, only that it'll appear when you use menus. In this example, we'll press **Return** to skip it. Then you'll see this:

```
/KEY:
```

"/KEY:" is a second delimiter. Again, it's not important to know what it means just yet. Another press of the **Return** key, and a selection such as this will appear:

```
[78529,948]
DISKCK.IMG 17-Jun-85 9415(3720) 276

     Keywords: DISK UTILITY GENERAL
```

```
THIS PROGRAM WILL:

    1. GIVE YOU A BAM OF YOUR DISK.
    2. CHECK ALL FILES FOR ERRORS.
    3. CHECK FOR BAD TRACK AND SECTORS.
    4. RECOVER SCRATCHED FILES.
```

```
Disposition:

1 R     Read this file
2 D     Download this file
3 T     Top Access menu

Key digit or ENTER for next:
```

This is an example of what it's like to BROwse through the databases on the menu level. Look at all of the menus. The "Disposition:" menu will appear after every entry. That takes up time. Your best bet is to get rid of all of the menus, relying on this book or the ? and H commands for help. That said, you'll now get a detailed look at how to use the Forum databases. Another look at the main menu of options will help:

```
DL 3: ?

Valid commands:
PUB - retrieve from Public ACCESS
NOR - normal SIG access
DL  - Change to new database
S   - Scan
BRO - browse thru files
R   - read a file
DOW - download a file
UPL - upload a file
SUB - submit a file
KEY - search keyword list
ERA - erase a file
EXI - exit from ACCESS
UST - list users in SIG
SEN - send message to user
SET - set menu & brief on/off
HEL - explains ACCESS
OFF - logs you off

? xxx - explain command xxx

DL 3:
```

Let me explain each of these commands.

- PUB will switch you to a section of CompuServe called "Public ACCESS." It works just like the Forum databases, but it contains programs and files for all types of computers. Once you've mastered the databases, go into Public ACCESS and look around.
- NOR will return you to the Forum databases from Public ACCESS.
- DL was already shown. It was used to get into the Forum databases from the "Function:" prompt. It's also used within the databases themselves to transfer from one database section to another.
- S stands for Scan. When you use this command in the Forum message base, it'll display a very brief description of the messages posted. This command works in a similar way in the databases, as you'll soon see.
- BRO stands for BROwse. You've just seen an example of what it does. It displays complete information programs and text files contained in the databases. You'll see more of this command later.
- R stands for Read, but some of the files in the databases aren't made to be read. You'll see what I mean later.
- DOW stands for DOWnload. This is the command that is generally used to transfer public domain programs and text files to your computer. You'll see how this command works later.
- UPL stands for UPLoad. This is the command that's generally used to transfer your original, public-domain programs and text files into the databases. A short example will appear later.
- SUB means SUBmit. This is another manner of placing programs and text files in the databases.
- KEY stands for KEYword. This is the first of several "switches" (or delimiters) that you may use in the databases. It's very handy to know. It may be used by itself, as KEY, to run through a list of keywords that have been placed in the databases by members who have UPLoaded or SUBmitted files.
- ERA stands for ERAse. This is how to delete any files that you've UPLoaded or SUBmitted to the Forum database.
- EXI stands for EXIt. It'll get you back to the Forum message base.
- UST stands for User STatus. You've already seen how this works in the Forum message base. It works the same way in the Forum databases. It'll display a list of the User IDs currently occupying the Forum and where they are.
- SEN stands for SENd. You've already seen how this works in the Forum message base. It works the same way in the databases.

- SET has just been shown.
- HEL stands for HELp. It'll display explanations of how to use the commands of the database that you're in.
- OFF will disconnect you from CompuServe.
- ? xxx has already been explained.

Now that you've had a crash course in the definitions of the commands, you'll see how they actually work. The first command we'll look at is **BRO**. Typing it at the "DL 3:" prompt will get something like this:

```
DL 3: BRO

[78529,948]
DISKCK.IMG 17-Jun-85 9415(372Ø)      276

     Keywords: DISK UTILITY GENERAL

     THIS PROGRAM WILL:

       1. GIVE YOU A BAM OF YOUR DISK.
       2. CHECK ALL FILES FOR ERRORS.
       3. CHECK FOR BAD TRACK AND SECTORS.
       4. RECOVER SCRATCHED FILES.
```

When the BROwse command is used, the file that was put into the database most recently will appear first. The list will continue in descending order of data. The databases use the LIFO rule: Last In the database is the First one Out. Public ACCESS follows the same rule.

To stop the display of the file descriptions, issue a Control-P. This will take you back to the "DL 3:" prompt. Don't issue a Control-C or you'll wind up back in the Forum message base at the "Function:" prompt.

The above description is a single entry from DL3. It's the actual entry (with the exception of the User ID, which has been disguised at the request of CompuServe). I'll explain this listing item by item, just as I explained a Forum message header earlier.

The fist element, [78529,948] is the PPN of the person who UPLoaded or SUBmitted the file. It's handy to have if you want to leave the person a message on the Forum thanking him or her for the program. Invariably, Forum members usually get complaints from people who wind up with bad DOWnloads of their files. So take some time out to thank these people. After all, they're paying the same amount for their connect-time on CompuServe as you are.

The second element is DISKCK.IMG. This is the *filename*. Filenames are made of two parts: the name itself and an *extension*. Names are limited to six letters. This leads to strange, very unpronounceable, and very hard to remember filenames. Extensions are limited to three letters, and are separated from the filename by a "." (period). Extensions follow a set convention in computing. They are shorthand for the type of information contained in the file. Extensions you'll come across in the databases include the following:

- HLP, which means HeLP, and is a text file that describes how to use a certain part of the Forum
- BAS, which means the file is a BASIC program listing
- SEQ, which means SEQuential file (this is specific to Commodore computers)
- TXT, which means a TeXT file
- DOC, which means DOCumentation and is a text file that gives instructions about using a program file
- BIN, which means BINary and is usually used with CP/M
- HEX, which means HEXidecimal
- SCR, which means SCReen and is primarily used in programming in the FORTH language
- ASM, which means ASseMbler and is usually associated with CP/M
- IMG, which stands for IMaGe and is used by CompuServe for downloading machine-specific program files (more on this later)

17-Jun-85 is the third element. This is the date the file was placed in the database. It may not seem important at the moment, but its purpose will be made clear. Remember, the date on the first entry that comes up on your screen will be that of the latest file that has been entered.

The fourth element is 9415(3720). Like the filename, this is in two parts. It will only be in two parts, though, when the filename has the IMG (IMaGe) extension. This is the size of the file in bytes. In this case, it is a little over 9.4K. The file size is important if you're using a terminal program that has, say, a 26K buffer. If the file you wish to capture is, say, 40K, you might have to do some manual labor in downloading it. IMG files have two file sizes because they have to be converted either during or after downloading. The second figure (in this case 3720) represents the actual number of bytes the program will take up as a runnable program on your disk.

276 is the next element. This is how many Forum members have accessed the file. It's useful if you've placed a file in one of the databases. It's always satisfying to see how many people are enjoying your contribution.

Keywords: DISK UTILITY GENERAL is next. These are the words the Forum member chose to use to describe his or her offering. When UPLoading or SUBmitting a file, you'll be asked to furnish a set of your own keyword descriptions. This Forum member chose only three. In actuality, the following keywords could have been added: 1541 DRIVE C64 64 BAM RECOVER TRACKS SECTORS. The more keywords a file has, the easier it is for everyone to locate it in the database. These keywords also wind up in a sorted keyword directory. You'll see this directory later. Keywords are also used when using the /KEY delimiter in searching the databases. An example of this will also be shown later.

THIS PROGRAM WILL: . . . is the final element of this file. It's the description of the file the Forum member has written to describe his or her file. It is comprehensive yet brief and to the point. Some files note in their description that they were uploaded using CompuServe's Vidtex software, along with the version number.

All of this is what you'll ideally see for each available file when you use the BROwse command to go through a database.

Another way of going through the database is by using the S (Scan) command. It'll display something like this:

```
DL 3: S

[78529,948]
DISKCK.IMG     17-Jun-85 9415(372Ø)            276
LODADR.IMG     17-Jun-85 8Ø5Ø(3168)            175

[739Ø8,9Ø9]
VIDFIL.DOC     1Ø-Jun-85 1Ø75                   93
VIDFIL.IMG     Ø1-Jun-85 12745(5Ø16)            4Ø

[7Ø88Ø,694]
PNTRM1.IMG     25-May-85 9435(372Ø)            166
PNTRM2.IMG     25-May-85 411Ø(1632)            1ØØ
```

To interrupt the output, issue a Control-P to get the "DL 3:" prompt again. You can see that the Scan command gives you a very limited amount of information. The use of this command, by itself, has little practical value. In fact, just using the BROwse command by itself is of little use if you want a particular file that happens to be at the bottom of the list. Both the BROwse and Scan commands are more powerful and useful when they're used with the /KEY: and /AGE: delimiters.

/KEY:, again, stands for KEYword. You may enter the KEY command by itself at the "DL 3:" prompt. You'll get something like this:

```
DL 3: KEY
1541           3
```

64	23
64BASIC	1
ADDRESS	1
AID	4
ALIGNMENT	1
AND	1
ASCII	1

This is just a portion of the actual list of keywords that has been placed in this database by the Forum members. This list, by itself, is of no practical use. The command /KEY: is, however, when used as a delimiter. This is done by combining it with the S (Scan) or BROwse commands, with a slash, and supplying a keyword for a subject you're interested in. For example, if you wanted to get a list of all of the files in this database that are about producing sector errors on a disk for copy protection, you'd use the command in this manner:

DL 3: **S/KEY:ERROR**

or this manner:

DL 3: **BRO/KEY:ERROR**

"Error" is the keyword that has been supplied in this example. By using the /KEY: delimiter, you're telling the database, in the first example: "Give me a Scan of all of the files in this database that contain the keyword 'error' in their description."

In the second example, you are asking the database to let you BROwse the files with the same limitation as the first example. Examples of both Scanned and BROwsed output have already been shown.

The /AGE: delimiter works the same way. This time, instead of furnishing a keyword, you type a number that specifies a certain number of days prior to your current search. For instance, if the last time you were in the databases was 7 days ago, you could tell the system to give you a Scanned or BROwsed list of just the files that have been submitted within the past 7 days. This would help you to keep current with new entries in the least amount of time. Using the /AGE: delimiter in this context would look like this:

DL 3: **S/AGE:7**

or this:

DL 3: **BRO/AGE:7**

Both of these delimiters can be used at once. If you wanted to look for files that contained the keyword "error" in their description but only ones that have been submitted within the past 7 days, you would type one of the following:

DL 3: **S/KEY:ERROR/AGE:7**

or

DL 3: **BRO/KEY:ERROR/AGE:7**

This may look intimidating and complex, but it really isn't. Try these commands when you're online. You'll be surprised at how quickly you become comfortable with them. Don't become discouraged if, after using these, nothing appears on your screen but the DL prompt again. This simply means that the files currently nestled in the system don't meet the requirements you set. It just may be possible that no files about sector errors were placed in the system during your 7-day absence. Try another keyword. Or, better yet, write a program and submit it for others to enjoy.

Before you can place anything into a database, you need to know how to get something out. This brings us to downloading. There are several ways to download from a Forum database. The method that you'll use will depend entirely on your communications software. The commands that may be used are **R** for Read or **DOW** for DOWnload. The first, Read, is sometimes used to examine files before downloading them; to read text files without downloading them; or, alternately, for downloading text files. Both of these commands require a filename and extension to follow them. So, you'd type **R FILENAME.EXTENSION** or **DOW FILENAME.EXTENSION.** "FILENAME. EXTENSION," of course, means the name of the file you wish to download.

Let's look at the description of the first file that was shown with the BROwse command:

```
[78529,948]

DISKCK.IMG     17-Jun-85 9415(372Ø)  276

    Keywords: DISK UTILITY GENERAL

    THIS PROGRAM WILL:

      1. GIVE YOU A BAM OF YOUR DISK.
      2. CHECK ALL FILES FOR ERRORS.
```

3. CHECK FOR BAD TRACK AND SECTORS.
4. RECOVER SCRATCHED FILES.

Notice, again, that the extension on this file is IMG. You'll recall that this means it is an IMaGe file. An IMaGe file is CompuServe's method of storing programs that are machine specific and are, ideally, downloaded to your computer using CompuServe's B-Protocol for error-free transmission. IMaGe files are stored in a hexidecimal format. Using the R (Read) command on such a file will result in the following:

DL 3: **R DISKCK.IMG**

```
: 18ØØØØØØØ4ØØ4343335ØØ1Ø81EØ85AØØ97353332383Ø2C31313A973525
:18ØØ18ØØ333238312C3Ø3A99229993220Ø55Ø864ØØ99221D1D1D1D1261
:18ØØ3ØØØ4449534B2Ø434845434B4552922Ø2Ø2D2Ø4A494D2Ø4255546E
:18ØØ48ØØ5445524649454C4411223A973131373Ø2C3438ØØ9DØ86EØØD9
:18ØØ6ØØØ862Ø41283235352922C43252837372C3238292C4425283129B4
:18ØØ78ØØ2C4E2428323234292C5425283232342C31292C5325283232CE
:18ØØ9ØØØ342C31292C4C2528323234292C5225283737290ØBBØ878ØØ7B
:18ØØA8ØØ4425283Ø29B235383A4425283129B234323A5A24B2C7283Ø71
```

Now you can understand why, in the earlier description of the Read command, I said that some files weren't meant to be read. Also, you should now understand why IMaGe files have two file size listings. The above code, which is in hexidecimal notation, takes up a lot of room! When it's converted into a RUNnable program, it takes up considerably less space on a disk (as reflected by the second, parenthesized, file size listing). Clearly, the Read command is not designed for novices to examine IMaGe files. The Read command is handy when files contain a DOC, TXT, or BAS extension. You'll be able to read the DOCumentation or TeXT file in English or examine a BASIC program listing (10 PRINT"MY PROGRAM", etc.).

The second method of downloading files is with the DOW command. This will download the file to your computer. There are four methods that can be used: Control-R/Control-T buffer control, XMODEM, A-Protocol, and B-Protocol.

- Control-R/Control-T buffer control. This is simply a method of opening and closing the buffer of your terminal program. No error-checking is done, and if you're downloading an IMG file, you'll have to use a separate program to convert the file into its original language (such as BASIC). Not many terminal programs use Control-R/Control-T.

- XMODEM. This is the popular and ubiquitous Christiansen protocol, a mainstay of telecommunications in the CP/M world. CIS recently added this protocol to its system. It allows many more brands of computers to upload and download from CIS. Error- checking is done during the upload and download. There's an XMODEM terminal program for almost every brand of computer. XMODEM terminal programs are available from various sources (including the public domain software libraries of local user groups) for Atari computers, the Apple Macintosh, the Commodore-64, the IBM PC series, the Kaypro series, and the Osborne.
- A-Protocol. This is a protocol devised by CIS. Hardly anyone uses it.
- B-Protocol. This is a proprietary error-checking protocol devised by CIS. It is a standard feature of their Vidtex (sometimes called Executive) terminal programs. It differs from XMODEM in that it will automatically convert an IMG file into its original form (for example, BASIC). XMODEM will not do this and you'll need a separate program to make the translation. At the beginning of this chapter, I showed you where you can order Vidtex on CIS. CIS will license this protocol to terminal program publishers, and at least two terminal programs for the Commodore-64 will be available from a source other than CIS.

The two best methods of downloading from CIS is by using the XMODEM and CompuServe B-Protocols. Each of these methods will ensure that no errors sneak into the transmission from noisy phone lines. Both the XMODEM and B-Protocols use a checksum to make sure that all of the data that are supposed to get to your computer do so without mistakes. Both methods send files to your computer in blocks. Once a block is transmitted, its parts are added to create a numeric sum. This sum is then transmitted back to CompuServe to check against the sum the system possesses. If the two sums match, all is well, and the next block is transmitted. If the two sums do not match, the process starts over, with the erroneous block being erased from your computer and a fresh one sent again by CompuServe. This process will look differently, depending on your communications software. Some versions are presented below.

```
DL 3: DOW DISKCK.IMG

Transfer protocols available,

 1 - XMODEM or MODEM7 protocol
```

```
  2 - CompuServe 'B' protocol
  3 - CompuServe 'A' protocol
  4 - DC2/DC4 capture protocol

  Ø - Abort transfer request

Please make a selection: 4
ICapture Buffer Transfer
No error detection/correction

Opening capture buffer...
: 18ØØØØØØØ4ØØ434333500108 1EØ85AØØ97353332383Ø2451313A973525
```


```
: 18ØØØØØØØ4ØØ43433350Ø1Ø81EØ85AØØ97353332383Ø2451313A973525
:18ØØ18ØØ333238312C3Ø3A99229993220Ø55Ø864ØØ99221D1D1D1D1261
: 18ØØ3ØØØ4449534B2Ø434845434B45529220202D2Ø4A494D2Ø4255546E
:18ØØ48ØØ5445524649454C4411223A97313137302C3438ØØ9DØ86EØØD9
: 18ØØ6ØØØ862Ø41283235352 92C43252837372C3238292C4425283129B4
: 18ØØ78ØØ2C4E2428323234292C5425283232342C31292C5325283232CE
:18ØØ9ØØØ342C31292C4C2528323234292C5225283737290ØBBØ878ØØ7B
:18ØØA8ØØ4425283Ø29B235383A4425283129B234323A5A24B2C7283Ø71
```


```
Capture buffer closed.
DL 3:
```

The second version of DOWnloading a file looks like this:

DL 3: **DOW DISKCK.IMG**

I need a file name for your computer: **DISKCK**

```
3+ + + + + + + + + + + + + + + +Ø:diskck,p,w
4+ + + + + + + + + + + + + + + +5+ + + + + + + + + + + + + + + +6+ + + +
+ + + + + + + + + + + +7+ + + + + + + + + + + + + + + +8+ + + + + + + + +
+ + + + + + + +9+ + + + + + + + + + + + + + + +Ø+ + + + + + + + + + + + +
+ + +1+ + + + + + + + + + + + + + + +2+ + + + + + + + + + + + + + + + +34
```

DL 3:

The third version of DOWnloading a file looks like this:

DL 3: **DOW DISKCK.IMG**

Transfer protocols available,

```
  1 - XMODEM or MODEM7 protocol
  2 - CompuServe 'B' protocol
  3 - CompuServe 'A' protocol
  4 - DC2/DC4 capture protocol

  Ø - Abort transfer request
```

```
Please make a selection: 1
Starting XMODEM transfer

Enter a carriage return when
transfer is complete

DL 3:
```

Quite a difference in appearance, isn't it? What makes this difference? Again, the answer is the terminal program you use to DOWnload files.

The first illustration is of downloading an IMG file; it shows its true form. It is what an IMG file looks like. It is exactly what would be seen on your screen when DOWnloading an IMG file from CIS on most terminal programs. If you're going to download any IMG files from CIS, it is an absolute necessity that your communications software contains a program for converting IMaGe (IMG) files. Also, your software should have a buffer large enough to hold most of the programs available in the databases. If your program has a rather stingy buffer area, you'll have to babysit your computer while it receives files from the databases, then manually close, save the portion of the file to tape or disk, and reopen your buffer in order to download the rest of the file. Once you've downloaded an IMaGe file, you'll have to go offline, load and run the IMG conversion program, convert the file, and then run the program to make sure that no errors entered the program while it was in transit to your machine from CompuServe. This isn't any fun.

The second illustration is what it looks like to DOWnload that very same IMG file using CompuServe's communications software, Vidtex. You don't see the IMG format or any of the file. You don't even have to make a selection from the protocol menu. CIS polls the Vidtex software and automatically selects the appropriate protocol. DOWnloading is accomplished via CompuServe's error-checking B-Protocol. Each plus sign represents a block of data sent to your computer's buffer. Each number represents data being written to your disk during the transfer. As the program is written to disk, it is automatically converted from an IMaGe file to a runnable program. Once the DOW command has been issued, you do not have to watch your computer. When the transfer is complete, you'll have a program on disk that's free from transmission errors and ready to load and run once you're offline.

The third illustration is only partial. It just shows the start and completion of a file download using an XMODEM terminal program. I can't show the whole process because each terminal program is different. Once the process starts, the terminal program displays the process in its own way.

Most XMODEM programs show how many blocks have been received, the status of transmission (Xon/Off), and if any retries are being made.

How does the DOW command work with files that have the TXT, DOC, or HLP extension? Again, it depends on the terminal program being used. Remember, files with the TXT and DOC extensions are simply text files, written in English, that are descriptive in content. They aren't programs. Using the Control-R/Control-T method of downloading would look like this:

```
DL 3:DOW TEST.TXT

Transfer protocols available,

  1 - XMODEM or MODEM7 protocol
  2 - CompuServe 'B' protocol
  3 - CompuServe 'A' protocol
  4 - DC2/DC4 capture protocol

  Ø - Abort transfer request

Please make a selection: 4
ICapture Buffer Transfer

No error detection/correction

Opening capture buffer...
     This is a test of the TeXT file
capability of the databases. You
can store English-language files here.
To let others know what the file
contains, append the TXT extension to
the filename if it is a descriptive text
file or the DOC extension if it is a
file that describes the operation of a
program you have uploaded to the
database.
```

It's that simple. If you're concerned about noisy phone lines sticking errors into the text, just sit at your screen and monitor the transfer. You don't need to know any language other than English to see any erroneous characters in the transfer. How would the transfer look using Vidtex? It would look like this:

```
DL 3:DOW TEST.TXT

I need a file name for your computer: TEST-TEXT
```

```
0:test-text,w
4+++++++++++++++++5++++++++++++++++++6++++
+++++++++++++7+++++++++++++++++8+++++++++
+++++++9+++++++++++++++++++0++++++++++++++
++1+++++++++++++++++2++++++++++++++++34
```

DL 3:

Again, the B-Protocol is used, and the file is automatically saved to your disk during the transfer process.

This is how you DOWnload files from the databases. But how are files put in? There are two methods: the UPLoad command and the SUBmit command. The UPLoad command allows direct transfer of files from your computer to the database. Using CompuServe's Vidtex software, the UPL process will look like this:

DL 3: **UPL NUKE.IMG**

After you type **UPL** and the FILENAME.EXTENSION. Then you will see

Keywords:

Then supply a list of keywords so other SIG members can search for your program using the BRO/KEY: command/delimiter, like so:

Keywords:
64 commodore 64 nuclear nuke graphics
demo color sound power plant

Once finished, hit **Return**, to see

Description (5ØØ chars max, blank line when finished):

This is simple enough. Type a narrative description of the program, up to 500 characters total, such as this:

Description (5ØØ chars max, blank line when finished):

This program is in the public domain
to the best of my knowledge. It is an
interesting demo of the 64's graphics &
color, showing the operation of a
nuclear power plant. It is cute. It is
fun. So what if it is blatant

propaganda? Just duck & cover and enjoy. And have at least 69 blocks free on your disk!!
<hit Return here to make a blank line>

When you're through, the system will repeat what you've typed, like so:

Keywords: C64 COMMODORE 64 NUCLEAR NUKE GRAPHICS DEMO COLOR SOUND POWER PLANT

This program is in the public domain to the best of my knowledge. It is an interesting demo of the 64's graphics & color, showing the operation of a nuclear power plant. It is cute. It is fun. So what if it is blatant propaganda? Just duck & cover and enjoy. And have at least 69 blocks free on your disk!!

Is this okay (Y or N)?

If everything is in order, type **Y** in response. If something is drastically wrong, type **N** and the process will start over. After this step has been completed, the system will prompt you with:

I need a filename for your computer:

The uploading process has not started yet. The file you wish to transfer still resides on your disk, in your drive. You have to tell the database what the name of the file is, such as,

I need a filename for your computer: **NUKE.IMG**

Vidtex will then access your disk drive, the process will begin, and when completed, it will look like this on your screen:

```
Ø:nuke.img
12 + + + + + + + + + 3 + + + + + + + + + 4 + + + + + + + + + 5 + + + + + + + + + 6 +
+ + + + + + + + 7 + + + + + + + + + 8 + + + + + + + + + 9 + + + + + + + + + Ø + + + +
+ + + + 1 + + + + + + + + + 2 + + + + + + + + + 3 + + + + + + + + + 4 + + + + + + +
+ 5 + + + + + + + + + 6 + + + + + + + + + 7+ + + + + + + + + 8 + + + + + + + + + 9 +
+ + + + + + +Ø+ + + + + + + + +1+ + + + + + + + +23
```

```
Copying file to SIG/ACCESS...
Your request will be processed by the
Sysop as soon as possible.

DL 3:
```

Here again, CIS's error-checking B-Protocol is used to ensure that your file reaches the database in its intended form. As this file is received by CIS, it's also translated from its original form into an IMG file because of its IMG extension. If an extension other than IMG had been used, the file would be stored in its original textual format.

The second way of placing a file into the databases is via the SUBmit command. This command is used only after one of two things has been done: either first transferring a file into your personal online disk space on CIS by using the FILTRN facility or by using the UPLoad command to send a file directly into Public/ACCESS.

In this first instance, you must use CompuServe's Vidtex program. Once the file resides in your online disk space, you must enter Public/ACCESS by typing **R ACCESS** at the OK prompt. Then the SUBmit command must be used to transfer the file into the Public/ACCESS database. After 24 hours, once the file has appeared in Public/ACCESS, you must enter the Forum database and use the SUBmit command in the appropriate database section.

This is a good time to leave the Forum and venture back into the rest of CIS so you can see how to access your Personal File Area. Back at the "Function:" prompt, type **G PCS174**. This will let you exit the Forum and take you to your Personal File Area on CIS. When you leave any Forum, you will see an exit notice in this format:

```
Exiting at 21-Sep-85        16:19:52
Last message on system:  158853
High message retrieved:  158123
Thank you for visiting CBM Programming
```

Next you'll see the menu for your Personal File Area. It looks like this:

```
CompuServe            Page CIS-174

       FILE MANAGEMENT

 1 Brief catalog of files
 2 Detailed directory of files
 3 Create & edit files via FILGE
```

4 Type a file's contents
5 Delete a file
6 Rename a file
7 Copy a file
8 Change a file's protection
9 Upload or download a file
10 Print a file ($)
11 Enter command mode

Last Menu page. Key digit
or M for previous menu!

This is the menu for your Personal File Area. Once you've become familiar with using CIS, you can bypass this menu structure and go directly into the personal file area by typing **PRO** at any "!" prompt. Once you've done that, the only prompt that you'll get is

OK

If you get stuck at this prompt, you can type HELP for information. To get back to the menu structure of CIS, you can type EXIT. To go to any menu page, you can type the GO command with a page number. If you want to go to Public/ACCESS, you can type R ACCESS.

The choices on the above menu are virtually self-explanatory, so I'll only show some of them briefly—choices 1 and 2.

Typing **1** will display just the names of the files that are in your CIS personal file area. By this time, you should have this file waiting:

EMAIL.DAT

Key S or <ENTER> to continue!

This is the EasyPlex test message that you sent to yourself earlier. Typing **2** will show you more information about the file:

FILE MANAGEMENT

1 Brief catalog of files
2 Detailed directory of files
3 Create & edit files via FILGE
4 Type a file's contents
5 Delete a file
6 Rename a file
7 Copy a file
8 Change a file's protection

```
 9 Upload or download a file
10 Print a file ($)
11 Enter command mode

Last Menu page. Key digit
or M for previous menu! 2

Name       Blocks     Creation         Access

EMAIL.DAT     2 18:45 08-SEP-85              (4)
TOTAL         2

Key S or <ENTER> to continue!
```

You might think that it would be OK for you to try to read this file by typing 4. You didn't place this file there, however. CIS did. The only way to read it will be through the EasyPlex menu. Whenever you see a file like the above, go to EasyPlex (GO EASY) to read it.

Choice 3, creating and editing a file, will place you in the same text editor that you saw illustrated earlier in using Bullet. I won't repeat that illustration. Refer to the Bullet example. There's only one difference between using the text editor in Bullet and using it here. When you use it in your Personal File Area, you have to give the file a name and an extension, for instance, TEST.DAT or NUKE.IMG. Refer to the extensions that were explained in the Forum database section. Don't use EMAIL.DAT as a filename, though, since CIS uses that when it places an EasyPlex delivery into your message box.

At this point, quickly review the section on EasyPlex. On the main menu for EasyPlex, you'll see a choice for using a file from the PER area. That's what this area of CIS is. You can upload your messages into your personal file space and then send them through EasyPlex. (You can also upload them directly to EasyPlex.) This will help you cut down on connect-time since you won't be typing in your messages while you're online. You can do it while you're offline with a word processor and then upload the completed messages.

Later, when I show you how to read an EasyPlex message, you'll see a menu choice for filing a letter. The filed EasyPlex message will be placed in your personal file area.

Choice 9, upload/download, will give you the same selection of transfer protocols that you just saw in the Forum databases. You can use any of those to transfer a file to or from CIS. If you're using CIS's Vidtex terminal program, you'll automatically get FILTRN, which uses the B-Protocol for error-checking. It'll look like this:

```
CompuServe file transfer program

Select direction -
 1 - Download to your computer
 2 - Upload to CompuServe
 3 - Exit
:
```

Uploading and downloading files will look the same as the illustrations shown in the Forum databases.

Whether you've placed files in your Personal File Area by typing them online or uploading them, you should know that CIS automatically *deletes* files that haven't been accessed in 30 days. So, if you plan on keeping anything important in your Personal File Area, you should read the files at least once a month. It's also a good idea to make sure that you have copies of the files stored on floppy disk, just in case they're deleted from your Personal File Area.

If you've uploaded a file to your Personal File Area that you intend to put into public/ACCESS, you'll have to go to that area and use the SUBmit command. Let's look at Public/ACCESS by typing **G PCS46**:

```
Public File Access System
Use ? for help

Access:

1 BRO Browse thru files
2 UPL Upload a new file
3 EXI Exit from Access
4 HEL Help

Key digit:
```

To get all of the commands, type a **?**:

```
Key digit: ?

Valid commands:
PUR      - purge files
S        - Scan
BRO      - browse thru files
COP      - copy to disk
R        - read a file
DOW      - download a file
UPL      - upload a file
SUB      - submit a file
```

```
KEY     - search keyword list
ERA     - erase a file
EXI     - exit from ACCESS
SET     - set menu & brief on/off
HEL     - explains ACCESS
OFF     - logs you off

? xxx   - explain command xxx

Press ENTER to continue: [RETURN]
Access:

1 BRO   Browse thru files
2 UPL   Upload a new file
3 EXI   Exit from Access
4 HEL   Help

Key digit:
```

Let's say that the file you've placed in your personal file area was NUKE.IMG, from the earlier Forum UPLoad example. To place it in Public/ACCESS, use the SUBmit command, like this:

```
Access: SUB NUKE.IMG
Notice:
    ACCESS is for the distribution
of original software. Submitters
are subject to copyright laws.
    Commercial advertising or
catalogs are not permitted.

Visible (Y or N)?
```

The above warning, issued by CIS, is self-explanatory. The prompt, "Visible (Y or N)?," is asking if you want everyone to see the file and have free access to it. Since your goal is to SUBmit your file to a Forum database, you'd type **Y**. (I will cover invisible files in a moment.) After answering **Y**, you'll be prompted for keywords and a description of your file, just as in the example shown of UPLoading a file directly into the Forum databases. After supplying these, they'll be repeated back for verification or correction, and then you'll see

```
Copying file to ACCESS...
File will be present within 24 hours.
Files are subject to being purged;
see ? PURGE for details.
```

Access:

It'll be at least 24 hours for the file to be placed into Public/ACCESS. This delay is because of the way the file is routed through CIS's computers. After the file has appeared, go back to the appropriate Forum, and in the appropriate database use the SUBmit command as here.

Why would you want to use Public/ACCESS if it takes so long to get your file into a Forum? The advantage is that anyone can get to the file, not just Forum members. Should the Forum the file is in become inaccessible (for instance, while CIS upgrades its software or performs maintenance), the Forum members will still be able to go to Public/ACCESS to get it.

Remember, though, that the SUBmit command doesn't have to be used since the UPLoad command is also available in Public/ACCESS. The SUBmit command is an alternative.

Also remember that neither the FILTRN facility nor CIS's B-Protocol for error-free file transfer can be used if you aren't using Vidtex. In order to UPLoad an IMG file to the Forum databases, a converter program must be used. This program should come with your software to translate files into IMG format. Then, you'll have to load the converted file into your computer's buffer and manually open the buffer to send the file to a Forum database or Public/ACCESS. Instead of seeing plus signs on your screen, the raw hexidecimal code of the IMG file will scroll up your screen.

Before we move on to EasyPlex, I want to mention invisible files in Public/ACCESS. If you don't want your file to be seen by everyone, add **/INV** (slash INV) to the filename; for instance, TEST.DAT/INV or NUKE.IMG/INV. You can leave the keywords and description of the file blank, since no one will be able to read it anyway. In order for other people to be able to download or read your file, you'll have to give them the filename. You can send it via EasyPlex or while in talk mode in CB or the Forum conference area. Invisible files are sometimes used in place of EasyPlex, since EasyPlex can't send long documents or programs. Just put the file up in Public/ACCESS as invisible and distribute the filename to people you want to have access to it.

I'll skip the steps to get to EasyPlex. You should remember that you can get to it from an "!" prompt by typing G EASY.

```
EasyPlex   Main Menu

1 READ, 1 message pending

2 COMPOSE a new message
3 UPLOAD a message
```

4 USE a file from PER area
5 ADDRESS book
Enter your selection number,
or H for more information!

Type **1** to read the message:

EasyPlex

Date: 25-Sep-85 19:Ø3
From: Winston Smith [79736,1984]
Subj: EasyPlex test

This is a test of the EasyPlex system for myself.
It's very easy to use this!

Key S or <ENTER> to continue! **[RETURN]**

EasyPlex Action Menu

** Winston Smith/EasyPlex test

1 DELETE this message
2 FILE it
3 FORWARD
4 REREAD message
5 REPLY

Last menu page. Key digit
or M for previous menu!

All of these choices are almost self-explanatory. When you type 3 to forward the message, you'll be asked to type a user ID. When you reply to the message, it'll automatically be sent to the message's originator. You won't have to type his or her User ID.

Let's type **5** to look at filing a message:

Name of file:

Type a filename and an extension. The extension should be either DAT or TXT to indicate that it is a data or text file, for instance,

Name of file: **TEST.DAT**
Message filed in TEST.DAT

Key S or <ENTER> to continue!

```
EasyPlex   Main Menu

1 READ, Ø messages pending
2 COMPOSE a new message
3 UPLOAD a message
4 USE a file from PER area
5 ADDRESS book
6 SEND last message
7 EDIT last message

Enter your selection number,
or H for more information!
```

The message now resides in your Personal File Area in CIS. If you were to look at a brief catalog, you'd find that EMAIL.DAT was gone and that TEST.DAT is now there. If you wanted to send that file to someone else, you could do so by typing 3 at this menu, for using a file from the PER area. You'd be asked to type the name of the file and then you'd be asked to type the User ID of the recipient and a subject. You shouldn't have any problems using CIS's EasyPlex message system. As you've seen, it's very easy to use yet offers many advanced features.

The next thing I'll show you how to do on CIS is create a customized menu for yourself. This ties in with the discussion and illustration of Defalt at the beginning of this chapter. If you didn't set your logon actions to take you directly to EasyPlex when you had a message waiting, you'll see your personal menu when you enter CIS. The procedure for creating your own first menu starts at Page CIS-9, at Defalt:

```
CompuServe          Page CIS-9

     Welcome to DEFALT

1 Instructions
2 Setting Your Terminal Type
3 Setting Your Logon Actions
4 Setting Delays for Printers
5 View or Change Current
     Terminal Parameters
6 Exit DEFALT
Last Menu Page. Key digit
or M for previous menu.
!
```

Type **3** here to see this:

```
Actions When Logging On:

1  If EasyPlex waiting,              Announce it
2  You now receive                 Short prompts
3  Automatically run                  No program
4  First Service is                     Videotex
5  Create/Edit your Personal                menu

Select item to be changed or
press <ENTER> for no change.
!
```

If item 1 is set for "Go to EasyPlex," you should change it if you want to see your personal menu every time you enter CIS. Change it to "Announce EasyPlex." After that, type **4**:

```
Set first service to:

1 VIDEOTEX
2 Personal file area
3 Personal menu
4 Selected Videotex Top page

Current setting is 1
<ENTER> leaves it unchanged
Key Choice:
```

Type **3** here:

```
Actions When Logging On:

1  If EasyPlex waiting,                 Go to it
2  You now receive                 Short prompts
3  Automatically run                  No program
4  First Service is Personal                menu
5  Create/Edit your Personal                menu

Select item to be changed or
press <ENTER> for no change.
!
```

Type **5** here to start creating your own customized first menu:

```
Your personal menu may contain
up to 1Ø choices. For each
choice, you must enter the page
you wish to access and a menu
```

description. Press <ENTER> at
page number prompt when done.

After this introduction, you'll get this form to fill out:

Menu choice 1
Page number:
Description:

It'll continue (Menu choice 2, Menu choice 3, etc.) until you leave one of the selections blank by pressing Return or until you've filled out all 10 blanks.

To create your personal menu, you should have the names and page numbers of the services that you'd like to be able to access directly when you enter CIS. I'll show you what one of my personal menus is like, and that'll give you some ideas about how you may want to create your own.

Menu choice 1
Page number: **Easy**
Description: **EasyPlex**
Menu choice 2
Page number: **pcs116**
Description: **CBM Programming Forum**
Menu choice 3
Page number: **pcs156**
Description: **C-64 Forum**
Menu choice 4
Page number: **pcs155**
Description: **CBM Creative Corner**
Menu choice 5
Page number: **pcs51**
Description: **MAUG/Apple Forum**
Menu choice 6
Page number: **pcs117**
Description: **WESIG**
Menu choice 7
Page number: **cis9**
Description: **+ + ** DEFALT ** + +**
Menu choice 8
Page number: **cis8**
Description: **--> FEEDBACK! <--**
Menu choice 9
Page number: **bil5**
Description: **$ $ $ $ BILLING! $ $ $ $**
Menu choice 10
Page number: **[RETURN]**

After the process is complete, CIS will repeat your selections so you can check them for accuracy and completeness:

```
CompuServe          Personal Menu

 1 EasyPlex                        EASY-1
 2 CBM Programming Forum           PCS-116
 3 C-64 Forum                      PCS-156
 4 CBM Creative Corner             PCS-155
 5 MAUG/Apple Forum                PCS-51
 6 WESIG                           PCS-117
 7 + + ** DEFALT ** + +            CIS-9
 8 --> FEEDBACK! <--               CIS-8
 9 $ $ $ $ BILLING! $ $ $ $        BIL-5
Change, Insert, Delete or End !
```

If you'd like to change something, it's quite easy. I won't illustrate the process since it's almost identical to changing a line in an EasyPlex or a Forum message.

Once everything is the way you want it to be, type **E** to end the process. CIS will tell you that

```
File MENU.CTL now exists in your
area and contains your Personal
menu.
```

This means that a file named MENU.CTL is in your Personal File Area. If you were to get a brief catalog of your files at PCS-174, you'd see TEST.DAT now joined by MENU.CTL. MENU.CTL has the same limitations as any other file in your personal file area: If it isn't used once a month, it'll be automatically deleted by CIS.

When I sign on to CIS, my personal menu looks like this:

```
CompuServe          Personal Menu

 1 EasyPlex
 2 CBM Programming Forum
 3 C-64 Forum
 4 CBM Creative Corner
 5 MAUG/Apple Forum
 6 WESIG
 7 + + ** DEFALT ** + +
 8 --> FEEDBACK! <--
 9 $ $ $ $ BILLING! $ $ $ $
Key digit or H for help

!
```

At the beginning of this chapter I told you that Page CIS-1 can always be reached by typing T. Creating a personal menu doesn't change that. At the time this book was going to press, CIS hadn't implemented a command to get back to your personal menu once you pass it. The only way possible to get it back is to type PRO and then at the OK prompt to type R MENU.

When you create your personal menu, I suggest that you include Defalt, Feedback, and Billing in it. These are three services that you'll find yourself turning to when you need them—and it's no fun trying to remember their page numbers or going through menus to get to them. By putting them in your personal menu, you can get to them by just selecting them from this menu.

The final item on CIS that I'll show you is Feedback. This is where you lodge your complaints against CIS when you have problems, ask questions when you can't figure out how to do something, or compliment their crack Customer Service Department for their fine work in helping you. Feedback starts at Page CIS-8:

```
CompuServe            Page CIS-8

Request Recorded,
One Moment, Please
Thank you for Waiting

Welcome to FEEDBACK! We
appreciate any comments, ideas,
problems, or suggestions you
send along to us. Your connect
time is credited while you are
in FEEDBACK, although you will
be charged for communication
surcharges. You'll be told upon
exiting FEEDBACK when connect
charges resume.
The Customer Service Represen-
tative will answer via
Electronic Mail as quickly as
possible.

Key S or <ENTER> to continue! [RETURN]
Please enter your name
(Last name, First name)
:
```

You don't have to type your name if you don't want to. It doesn't really matter. CIS's Customer Service Department will look up your name anyway so they know who to address in their EasyPlex reply. After this step, you'll see

```
FEEDBACK Categories
1  Telephone/access problems
2  Billing questions
3  Vidtex software questions
4  User Guides/Products ordered
5  CB Simulator
6  EasyPlex Messages
7  National Bulletin Board
8  Forums (SIGS)
9  Managing/finding files
10  Business & Financial services

Please enter number of item or
press <CR> for more choices ! [RETURN]

FEEDBACK Categories (cont.):

11  Games
12  Home Services
13  Services for Professionals
14  Electronic Mail
15  Change Address/Phone no.
16  General system problems
17  Request additional services
18  Misc. suggestions & comments
19  None of the above
0   Exit FEEDBACK

Please enter number of item or
press M for previous menu !
```

I've displayed all of the Feedback categories here. Placing most of the categories on a menu like this should help you to define the type of problem you're having. If you're not having a problem with one of these services or if you just want to say "thank you," choose 19. Once you've made a selection, you'll be asked to type your message:

```
Please enter your message (press
your carriage return key to end
each line). You may leave up to
43 lines. When done, enter EXIT
at the beginning of a new line.

 1:
```

From this point on, creating and editing a Feedback message is virtually identical to creating and editing an EasyPlex message. I won't repeat an illustration of the process here. The only difference (and it's a puzzling inconsistency at that) is that you type EXIT on a line by itself in a Feedback message, whereas you must type /EXIT (slash EXIT) in EasyPlex. Once you've typed that, you'll see

```
Thank you for your message.

Key S or <ENTER> to continue!
Thank you for using FEEDBACK.
Charges resume on the next page.
```

That's what the CompuServe Information Service is like. Actually, it's only what part of it is like. There's plenty more that I haven't shown you. What you've seen are the most popular parts of a system that is adding more choices for its subscribers every month.

* * *

Additional Information

CONTACT:

CompuServe, Inc., Consumer Information Service, 5000 Arlington Centre Blvd., Columbus, OH, 43220, (614)457-8600, 1-(800)848-8199.

8 A too-brief look at Delphi

Control functions used on this system: Control-C (echoes as Control-Y), system interrupt; Control-H, backspace (nondestructive!); Control Q, resume output (XON); Control-S, pause output (XOFF); Control-Z, end of file/move back to prior prompt.

Delphi (CBP10100), from General Videotex Corporation (GVC), went online in 1982 and was originally known as The Kussmaul Encyclopedia. It was the first publicly available online encyclopedia in the world. The Kussmaul Encyclopedia, which gets its name from Wes Kussmaul (GVC's president), is still a feature of Delphi. Delphi itself has grown from its original single online offering to a full National System offering bulletin-boards, real-time multi-user conferencing, electronic mail, travel and shopping services, and special interest groups.

Delphi is available by direct dial to its Cambridge, Mass., host computer or through the packet-switched networks DataPac, Tymnet, and Uninet. It costs $49.95 for a lifetime subscription to Delphi, which includes an instruction manual. Prime-time hours (called "Office Time" by GVC) are weekdays from 8 AM to 6 PM, local time, at the rate of $16 per hour for 300 or 1200 bps service. Non-prime-time hours are weekdays from 6 PM to 8 AM, local time, at the rate of $6 per hour for 300 or 1200 bps service. Non-prime-time includes all weekend and some holidays. Packet-switched network charges in the continental United States are included in the connect-time charges. Some services and databases cost more than the basic connect-time rates just quoted. The more expensive services will let you know this (but, at the time this book was being written, not before you might accidentally start being charged for them). GVC bills through credit cards and direct billing to individuals. Direct billing has a $3.50 per month additional charge for administrative costs.

Delphi also started offering 2400 bps service in some cities, via Tymnet, and this boosts prime-time rates to $21 an hour and non-prime-time rates to $11 an hour. You should know that Delphi's 2400 bps rate is lower than most systems' 1200 bps rates!

At the time this book was going to press, Delphi started a system-wide overhaul of its software and services. By the time this book gets into your hands, Delphi will look very different than any coverage contained in this book. In other words, Delphi's coverage in this book would be totally outdated. Therefore, Delphi will not, unfortunately, get the amount of coverage that it deserves and that I'd like to give it. Instead, this chapter will focus on showing one of the system's menus and giving a brief overview of the services available at press time. As the title of this chapter states, this will be a too-brief look at Delphi.

When you sign on to Delphi for the first time as a new subscriber you will see something like this:

```
Hello MIKECANE

Welcome to DELPHI
Copyright (c) 1985
General Videotex Corporation

Logon at        : 25-SEP-1985 18:36:19
Last Logon      :
```

In place of "MIKECANE" above, will be your User ID. Delphi, unlike other online systems, allows you to create your own User ID for the system. As you can see, I've chosen my own name as my User ID. It's easier for other people to remember, easier for *me* to remember and type, and says more than a User ID such as 79736,1984 or XYZ984. Most Delphi subscribers use their own names, although some choose to use handles or company names.

The point is, each subscriber is able to have a say in what she or he will be called on Delphi. This is a democratic quality that is not currently found on other systems and is indicative of just how differently Delphi does some things. If you plan to subscribe to Delphi, give some thought to the User ID you would like to use. Once assigned, it is virtually impossible to have it changed according to Delphi Customer Service, so choose wisely.

After this signon notice, as a first-time caller you'll then be taken on a tour of Delphi by the system itself. Delphi will display a tutorial on your screen. As the system explains the Control functions that Delphi uses, you'll be invited to try them out during the tutorial. It's all a part of GVC's way of introducing you to Delphi in the least intimidating way possible. During this guided tour, you'll also be able to make the settings you'll need for your screen display. If you've never done this before, the Delphi tutorial will actually assist you, to make sure you don't set anything you don't want to set. You'll also be given an opportunity to set the length of prompts Delphi will display. As a new subscriber, you should stay with full menus.

After the tutorial and tour is complete, you'll see Delphi's main menu. It'll look something like this:

```
MAIN Menu:

Bulletin Boards         Office Manager
Conference              People on DELPHI
DELPHI Mail             Reviews and Views
Entertainment           Sports
Financial Services      Travel
Groups and Clubs        Using DELPHI
Library                 Workspace
Merchants' Row          HELP
News and Weather        EXIT

MAIN>What do you want to do?
```

When you look at Delphi's main menu, you should be able to see a difference between it and the ones you've seen in Chapters 4–7. Delphi's menu selections are not numbered. To make a selection on the system, you have to type letters. There are obvious limitations to such a design:

- There are only 26 letters in the alphabet.
- No two menu selections can start with the same letter.

The second limitation can be skirted by making subscribers type more than one letter—but that is much more typing than would have to be done if the choices were numbered.

Part of the overhaul being undertaken on Delphi is to make sure that no two selections within the same menu start with the same letter. This can lead to some bizarre names for what would otherwise be plain-English selections on a menu on which the choices were numbered, though, and may create a whole new problem for Delphi's programmers to tackle.

Aside from numberless menu selections, Delphi differs from other

National Systems by allowing you to choose the kind of prompts you'll see. Let's look at the main menu one more time:

MAIN Menu:

Bulletin Boards	Office Manager
Conference	People on DELPHI
DELPHI Mail	Reviews and Views
Entertainment	Sports
Financial Services	Travel
Groups and Clubs	Using DELPHI
Library	Workspace
Merchants' Row	HELP
News and Weather	EXIT

MAIN>What do you want to do?

This is a menu, but it can also be considered a long prompt. There are two other kinds of prompts you can get. The first is a medium prompt. A medium prompt would make the main menu look like this.

MAIN>What do you want to do?

The next level is a short prompt. It would make the main menu look like this:

MAIN>

Once you've mastered Delphi, you can change your menu to a shorter prompt, if you wish. After you've done that, you can still always get a full menu to remind you of your choices just by typing a question mark (?) or by pressing Return.

Let's go through Delphi's main menu choices in alphabetical order:

- *Bulletin Boards*. Delphi's new bulletin-board software will be a hybrid of a traditional bulletin-board (see Chapter 17, Using Bulletin-Board Systems) and a tree-structured conferencing system. This would, in principle at least, make it similar to CIS's Forum message area (see previous chapter).
- *Conference*. This is Delphi's multiuser real-time conferencing facility. It is similar, though far superior, to CIS's CB Simulator. It offers a variety of commands not found on other types of software and also

allows participants temporarily to pop out of a talk to enter the mail system, to read or send mail.

- *DELPHI Mail.* This choice leads to a sub-menu that offers the choice of U.S. Postal Service E-COM, domestic and international Telex, one-way electronic text message sending to CIS and THE SOURCE, and Delphi's own internal main system.
- *Entertainment.* Under this category are collaborative novels written by subscribers, newsletters, the Delphi user directory (which is the best user directory I've ever seen on any online system), the Delphi Oracle (a collection of experts who you can turn to for answers to various questions), online games, and subscriber-generated polls.
- *Financial Services.* An assortment that includes online banking, business news, brokerage and personal financial services from outside firms.
- *Groups and Clubs.* This is Delphi's version of Special Interest Groups. At the time this book went to press, this area was undergoing a total overhaul, with new software being added, some existing SIGs being dropped, and new SIGs being added. It's impossible to give a list of available SIGs, so check with Delphi directly.
- *Library.* This is where you can access Dialog's vast collection of reference databases, access Dialcom's variety of databases, use the Kussmaul Encyclopedia, or use a private firm's research services. (Note that accessing Dialog or Dialcom incurs a charge above Delphi's basic connect-time rates. Also note that Dialog is the full Lockheed-Dialog system, *not* Knowledge Index, which is covered in Chapter 11.)
- *Merchant's Row.* This is where several firms can be found that offer goods for online purchasing. Delphi subscribers can also offer items for sale on a special bulletin-board.
- *News and Weather.* News is via Dialcom; Weather is from Accu-Weather.
- *Office Manager.* This is an online appointment calendar, a business SIG, and an online diary.
- *People on Delphi.* This item had yet to be defined at press time.
- *Reviews and Views.* Advice and reports on sexuality, psychology, autos, wine, health, and movies.
- *Sports.* Sports reports and features.
- *Travel.* Complete travel services from an outside travel agency.
- *Using Delphi.* The irregularly published (online only) Delphi subscriber newsletter; various help files on using Delphi and Dialog; and information about rates and packet-switched networks.

- *Workspace.* This is your private filespace on Delphi and also the area in which all Delphi subscribers may place files for sharing (like CIS's Access; see previous chapter).

That, in a very small nutshell, is Delphi. If any of it sounds interesting to you, give General Videotex a call to inquire about the state of the system and its current services.

* * *

Additional Information

CONTACT

General Videotex Corporation, 3 Blackstone St, Cambridge, MA, 02139, (617)491-3393, 1–(800)544-4005.

9 Using Dow Jones News/Retrieval Service

Control characters used on this system: Control-S (XOFF), pause output; Control-Q (XON), resume output; Control-X, abort current function and return to prompt. Note, this system does not recognize Control-H (destructive backspace) and displays an error message when it is used; Control-X cannot be used in the full-text database (see later in this chapter).

Dow Jones News/Retrieval Service (CPB100125) is the oldest online system discussed in this book. It started operations in 1974 and is designed for business users who are primarily interested in financial information. I'll refer to this system as DJNRS throughout this chapter.

DJNRS has a complicated rate structure that would only confuse you if I tried to describe it in a single paragraph. Instead, I've placed all of this information at the end of the chapter, most of which is in the original form as it appears online on the system itself. Billing is via credit card to individuals and direct billing to businesses.

DJNRS is available via DataPac, Telenet, Tymnet, and Uninet.

The system is both menu and command driven. Command reminders are scattered throughout the system. This is helpful for new subscribers but can sometimes be tiresome for those with experience. The reminders cannot be suppressed and their repetition only causes wasted time. As you already know, online, time is literally money.

Once you have signed onto DJNRS, you'll see this screen:

```
              DOW JONES NEWS/RETRIEVAL
                 COPYRIGHT (C) 1985
              DOW JONES & COMPANY, INC.
                 ALL RIGHTS RESERVED

TYPE //MENU FOR A DATA-BASE LIST.
ENTER QUERY
```

Sometimes a signon notice will accompany this screen, highlighting a new service that has been added or pointing out a late-breaking news story.

As the command reminder in the above screen states, typing //MENU will display a list of choices. Most direct commands on DJNRS are prefixed with two slashes (//). The exception is the full-text databases, which you will see later.

Now, let's type **//MENU:**

//MENU

```
                 Master Menu
              Copyright (C) 1985
           Dow Jones & Company, Inc.

PRESS            FOR
  A          Dow Jones Business And
                 Economic News Services
  B          Dow Jones Quotes
  C          Dow Jones Text-Search
                 Services
  D          Financial And Investment
                 Services
  E          General News And
                 Information Services
  F          Mail Service and
                 Free Customer Newsletter
```

Although this menu's selections are called up by pressing a letter key, the other menus within DJNRS have numbered selections.

Going through the menu structure of DJNRS isn't the most efficient way of accessing the information the system contains. This is especially true because DJNRS's connect-time rates are quite high compared to the other systems described in this book. However, I would like to show you some more menus in this series because they'll illustrate a very nice feature of DJNRS. It's a feature that other page-structured systems should incorporate.

At the above menu, typing **A** will display this:

```
MASTER MENU              PAGE 1 OF 2

           Dow Jones Business
       And Economic News Services
For help, type code and HELP.
    (Example: //DJNEWS HELP)

    TYPE      FOR

//DJNEWS  9Ø-Day News From The
          Broadtape, Selections
          From Barron's And The
          Wall Street Journal
```

[RETURN]

```
MASTER MENU              PAGE 2 OF 2

      TYPE        FOR
//UPDATE     Weekly Economic Up-
             date: A Roundup Of The
             Past Economic Week
//WSJ        Wall Street Journal
             Highlights Online:
             Summaries Of The Past
             Five Editions Of The
             Wall Street Journal
               *   *   *
For an overview, type //DJ HELP
```

At the top of the two new menus, you can see the page number and its relationship to other pages; for instance, "Page 1 of 2." This is a wonderful feature. It lets you know that there's more information beyond the screen you're currently seeing. It also lets you know when you've reached the last page of the series. This format helps you to decide just how far you'd like to read into any single item. You'll see some other examples of this later.

Before going any further, I'd like to list all of the direct commands available on DJNRS and describe the information that each one of them will take you to. I won't be illustrating all of these selections, since some of them are menu-driven and their contents are self-explanatory.

- //DJNEWS This is Dow Jones News. It's a database of news collected from the Dow Jones News Service, the *Wall Street Journal*, and *Barron's*. The news contained in this database is the most recent, with an archive of stories dating back to the past 90 days.

- //WSJ This is The Wall Street Journal Highlights Online. Each morning at 6 A.M., Eastern Time, highlights of the current edition of the *Wall Street Journal* are placed online. Highlights for issues 2 days previous are also available at any given time.
- //UPDATE Weekly Economic Update. This is a summary of important economic statistics that were compiled during the current week. A forecast of economic statistics for the next month is also available.
- //CQ This is Current Quotes. During market hours, there is a minimum 15-minute delay of prices for common and preferred stocks and bonds, mutual funds, and U.S. Treasury issues and options.
- //HQ This is Historical Quotes. Daily volume, price highs, lows, and closes are available, with monthly summaries available back to 1979, and quarterly summaries back to 1978. Specific dates can be used for daily quotes. Composites are available for monthly and quarterly information.
- //DJA This is Historical Dow Jones Averages. Averages for industrials, transportation, utilities, and over 60 stock composites are available for retrieval.
- //TEXT There are two parts to this keyword-search database. The first is the full-text of stories from The Wall Street Journal, from the present day to the previous January of the same year. The second part is Dow Jones News, which contains selected stories, in full-text versions, from the *Wall Street Journal, Barron's*, and Dow Jones News Service. These stories are from the present day and date back to June 1979.
- //EARN This is Corporate Earnings Estimator. It's a database of earnings forecasts for over 3000 of the most-watched companies.
- //DSCLO This is Disclosure II. You'll also find this database on two other systems in this book, CIS and The Source. It contains information on over 9400 public companies, in the form of profiles, 10-K extracts, and SEC filings.
- //MEDGEN This is Media General Financial Services. Financial information for over 4300 companies and 170 industries is available in categories such as revenue, earnings, volume, ratio, price changes, and dividends.
- //MMS This is Economic and Foreign Exchange Survey. Each week U.S. money market and foreign exchange trends are reported in this database.
- //FORBES This is the Forbes directory. This is the Top 500 corporations in the United States.

- //KYODO Japan Economic Daily. Via satellite, this database offers same-day coverage of business, economic, financial, and political news from Japan. Also offered are translated transcriptions of the headlines that appeared in the morning and evening editions of Japan's major newspapers.
- //OAG This is Official Airline Guides. This database is available on other systems described in this book, such as CIS, NewsNet, and The Source. Daily fare information for North American flights is available, as well as schedules for 650 airlines worldwide.
- //MENU This is Master Menu. You've seen this command. It'll always return you to the main menu of DJNRS.
- //ENCYC This is the Academic American Encyclopedia. It's an electronic edition of the print volume, updated twice a year.
- //NEWS This is News/Retrieval World Report. It's domestic and foreign news from the Associated Press, updated at various times each day.
- //SPORTS This is News/Retrieval Sports. Stories and various statistics for major sports, updated every day.
- //WTHR This is News/Retrieval Weather Report. Current and two-day forecasts of weather for major cities, domestic and foreign. It includes temperature highs and lows and weather status. Long-range forecasts are also available.
- //MOVIES This is Cineman Movie Reviews. It has current and recent film reviews, with a database of reviews for films dating back to the 1920s.
- //WSW This is Wall $treet Week Online. It's transcripts of the four most recent editions of the PBS television program.
- //STORE This is Comp-U-Store. This shopping database can also be found on CIS and The Source.
- //SYMBOL This is News/Retrieval Symbols Directory. Over 15,000 symbols are available here for stocks, corporate and foreign bonds, Treasury issues, mutual funds, and options. In addition, codes are available that are used in the Dow Jones News databases and the Media General database.
- //DEFINE This is Words of Wall Street. Over 2000 business and financial terms are defined.
- //INTRO This is Intro. It is a free online newsletter of DJNRS that keeps subscribers up-to-date on system additions, changes, and enhancements.
- //MCI This is MCI Mail. MCI Mail is described in Chapter 12.

- //MEDX This is a database of information about health-related news and prescription drug information.
- //SCHOOL This is *Peterson's Guide to Colleges and Universities*.

Instead of moving through menus, typing any one of these commands will place you within the corresponding database immediately.

The first command I'll illustrate is //INTRO. This is the free newsletter of DJNRS. It features help and information files about system changes. Typing **//INTRO** will display a menu that looks something like the following one. The one you see will be different, of course, because the newsletter is constantly updated.

```
//INTRO

      Welcome to //INTRO, the free
    Newsletter of News/Retrieval.
Press    For
  1  //SCHOOL Introduced On DJN/R
  2  New //MEDX Gets First Update
  3  December Free Time Offers
  4  Investor Profiles In //TRACK
  5  Give a DJN/R Membership Kit
  6  Data Base News For December
  7  Win Prizes Through Uninet
  8  Rate Changes for MCI Mail
  9  HomeBanking, DowPhone Quotes
       & News, DowQuot Available
 1Ø  News/Retrieval Seminars
 11  Customer Information
 12  Dow Jones Software

     MCI Mail Rates to Change
```

Some of these selections may have a sub-menu. Like any menu-structured system, typing the appropriate number key will bring you to your request.

Next, let's look at what I think is the most important feature of DJNRS. It's the symbol directory. I consider it the most important feature because the symbols it contains are used in several of the databases on the system. In effect, it becomes a database that unifies all of the others. By typing **//SYMBOL**, will enter the database:

```
//SYMBOL
                 DIRECTORY OF SYMBOLS
                  COPYRIGHT (C) 1984
               DOW JONES & COMPANY, INC.
```

```
PRESS   FOR
 1      STOCK SYMBOLS
 2      COMPANY NAMES USING STOCK SYMBOLS
 3      STOCK OPTIONS
 4      MUTUAL FUNDS
 5      U.S. CORPORATE BONDS
 6      FOREIGN BONDS
 7      U.S. TREASURY NOTES & BONDS
 8      NEWS/RETRIEVAL CATEGORY CODES
 9      MEDIA GENERAL INDUSTRY GROUP CODES
10      RECENT SYMBOL CHANGES

OR, PRESS RETURN FOR INSTRUCTIONS
```

When you're online, you may want to review the instructions for this database by pressing Return, as the prompt states. This will be necessary if the menu on your screen is drastically different than the one shown here. It would mean that changes have been made to the database, and it would be in your best interest to see just how the changes might affect the way in which you use the database. Of the 10 menu items, I'll illustrate choices 1 and 8.

Typing **1** will display this screen:

```
1

SYMBOL              STOCKS
ENTER QUERY
```

To retrieve a stock symbol, type the name of a company. I'll type **Commodore** in this example:

```
SYMBOL              STOCKS
ENTER QUERY
COMMODORE

SYMBOL              STOCKS      PAGE 1 OF 1

CCT       *COMMODORE CORP. - AM
CBU       *COMMODORE INTERNATIONAL LTD.
             - NY
D.CIU     COMMODORE RESOURCES CORP. - NA
-----------------------------------------------------------
ENTER QUERY
OR PRESS RETURN FOR MAIN MENU
```

Of the above two choices, stock symbol CBU is the one I was looking for. Now, I can use that symbol within DJNRS databases to retrieve stories and financial information about the computer manufacturer, Commodore. If you want to look up another symbol, type another company name.

When you're through retrieving stock symbols, press **Return** to redisplay the main menu of this database:

```
              DIRECTORY OF SYMBOLS
                COPYRIGHT (C) 1984
            DOW JONES & COMPANY, INC.
PRESS       FOR
  1   STOCK SYMBOLS
  2   COMPANY NAMES USING STOCK SYMBOLS
  3   STOCK OPTIONS
  4   MUTUAL FUNDS
  5   U.S. CORPORATE BONDS
  6   FOREIGN BONDS
  7   U.S. TREASURY NOTES & BONDS
  8   NEWS/RETRIEVAL CATEGORY CODES
  9   MEDIA GENERAL INDUSTRY GROUP CODES
 1Ø   RECENT SYMBOL CHANGES

OR, PRESS RETURN FOR INSTRUCTIONS
```

Choice 2 of the above menu will retrieve a company name when you type a stock symbol. I won't illustrate it because the procedure is similar to choice 1, which you've just seen.

Choice 8 is the next important selection. It'll display the category codes that are used in the Dow Jones News (//DJNEWS) database, which you'll see shortly. Typing **8** will display this menu:

```
SYMBOL     NEWS CODE   PAGE 1 OF 1

PRESS      FOR
1          INDUSTRIES
2          STOCK MARKET NEWS
3          ECONOMIC NEWS
4          U.S. GOVERNMENT NEWS
5          FEDERAL REGULATORY AGENCIES
6          GENERAL NEWS
7          FOREIGN NEWS BY AREA
8          ALPHABETICAL DIRECTORY OF NEWS
             CATEGORIES
```

All of the category codes that you can retrieve from the menu choices shown here are available in the DJNRS instruction manual. This database is handy when you don't have the manual with you. It's also helpful to keep track of new codes that have been added. Unfortunately, a menu selection for just new codes wasn't available as this book went to press. The only way to discover new codes would be to keep track of them from DJNRS print publications.

The industry codes are the ones that you'll probably use the most if you're interested in following a certain type of industry, for instance, computers and data processing. From this menu, let's type **1**:

```
SYMBOL     INDUSTRIES   PAGE 1 OF 5

I/FIN      ACCOUNTING
I/TNM      ACQUISITIONS
I/MKT      ADVERTISING
I/ARO      AEROSPACE
I/AIR      AIRLINES
I/TEX      APPAREL
I/ELE      APPLIANCES
I/AUT      AUTOS, AUTO PARTS
I/BCY      BANKRUPTCIES
I/BNK      BANKS
I/TEL      BROADCASTING
I/CNO      CASINOS AND GAMBLING
I/CHM      CHEMICALS
I/EPP      COMPUTERS
```

The list of codes will continue if you press Return. You can also jump ahead to a certain page by typing **P** and the page number. For instance, **P4** will take you immediately to page four. If you want to go back to the main menu of the database from any page of this list, type **T**. T stands for top menu. Unlike the T command you saw in Chapter 7, Using the CompuServe Information Service, the DJNRS T command will take you to a top menu within a database, not to the DJNRS master menu from within a database.

Let's jump now from the symbol directory to Dow Jones News. You can exit almost every DJNRS database (except //TEXT, which you'll see later) just by typing a new database command. Typing **//DJNEWS** will exit the symbol database and go directly to this screen:

```
//DJNEWS

DOW JONES NEWS IS BEING ACCESSED
ENTER QUERY
```

To use Dow Jones News, you'll need to know some of the codes. You can get these from the symbol database, which you've just seen. Some of the most useful codes are the ones listed below. Note that you must type a *period* as each code's first character.

- .A/ This will display all of the news of the current day, starting with the latest and moving back in time.
- .BRRNS This will display shortened versions of feature stories from *Barron's*.
- .I/GEN This will display general news stories; that is, without a business slant.
- ./HOH This will display the headlines of the most important stories that have been added for the current hour.
- .H/ This will display urgent business stories.
- .LABOR This will display labor news.
- .I/ECO This will display news about the U.S. economy.
- .I/EMI This will display statistics of economic indicators.
- .GOVMT This will display general news about the federal government.
- .G/EXE This will display news about the executive branch of government.
- .FORGN This will display general foreign news.

There are quite a few other codes. They cover various aspects of finance, government agencies, and some countries. There are also codes for specific industry categories, such as airlines, banking, computers, electronics, and utilities.

Let's look at how an industry code is used in the Dow Jones News database. The code for the computer industry is **.I/EDP** (again, note that the code starts with a period). Typing this code alone will display the latest news story about the computer industry that's contained in the database. The process will look like this:

```
DOW JONES NEWS IS BEING ACCESSED
ENTER QUERY
.I/EDP

N   I/EDP      Ø1/29 LX   1/1
  /FREST IBM              /EDP  /
     12/24 IBM IS ISSUED LICENSE
  (WJ) FOR A SOUTH KOREA BUSINESS
     NEW YORK — INTERNATIONAL BUSINESS
MACHINES CORP. SAID IT HAS BEEN ISSUED
```

```
A LICENSE BY THE SOUTH KOREAN
GOVERNMENT TO START A BUSINESS IN THAT
COUNTRY.
     AN IBM SPOKESMAN REFUSED, HOWEVER,
TO CONFIRM WIRE SERVICE REPORTS FROM
FINANCE MINISTRY OFFICIALS THAT THE
COMPANY WOULD BUILD A $22 MILLION
COMPUTER MANUFACTURING PLANT IN SOUTH
KOREA.
     ACCORDING TO MINISTRY OFFICIALS,
IBM IS PLANNING A $13 MILLION EQUITY
INVESTMENT FOR THE PROJECT, WHICH WOULD
BE OWNED BY ITS NEW SUBSIDIARY, IBM
KOREA SYSTEMS CORP.
```

This is the end of this particular sample story. Others may not be so brief. You can continue reading any story by pressing Return at the end of each page.

Let me explain the salient points of this screen so you'll be able to get the most out of this database. This is the first line from this screen:

```
N  I/EDP     Ø1/29 LX  1/1
```

The first letter, N, has no significance for you, so it can be ignored. The I/EDP is the code that was typed into the database; in place of I/EDP will be whatever code you've typed. Next, 01/29 means that this story was taken from a list of headlines that is 29 pages long. You'll see a headline list shortly. LX is the code for this individual story; it's an identification code from a list of headlines that you'll see shortly. 1/1 means this story is the first page of a one-page story. In other words, the single screen that you've seen is the entire story.

This is the third line from this screen:

```
/FREST IBM          /EDP  /
```

The first item, /FREST, has no importance to you. Next is IBM; this is the stock symbol of the company mentioned in this story. If a story mentions more than one publicly traded company, the stock symbols of the companies will appear on this line, too. Last, /EDP is the industry code that is represented in the story. A story can have several industry codes listed here, just as it can have several company stock symbols.

The next part of the story we'll examine is the headline:

```
  12/24 IBM IS ISSUED LICENSE
(WJ) FOR A SOUTH KOREA BUSINESS
```

The 12/24 is the date of the story; this is significant if you access the database during the weekend to see if any stories have been added about your category of interest. The story headline itself is next. The (WJ) stands for the *Wall Street Journal*, which is the source for the story. Other source codes include

- BN for *Barron's*
- DJ for Dow Jones News Service
- DW for Dow Jones News Service and the *Wall Street Journal*
- NR for Dow Jones News/Retrieval

Displaying full stories is an inefficient way of searching for information in this database. I've shown how it's done because it comes in handy when you just want to take a look at the latest news story about a given subject. The best way to search this database is to scan the headlines. This is done by typing one of the codes and appending **Ø1** to it. For instance, scanning the headlines for stories about the computer industry would be done by typing **.I/EDP Ø1** (again, note the period), to get a result like this:

```
.I/EDP Ø1

  N  I/EDP
Ø1/29
  LX 12/24 IBM IS ISSUED LICENSE
     (WJ) FOR A SOUTH KOREA BUSINESS
  LW 12/21 COMMODORE INTERNATIONAL SEES
     (DW) LOWER SALES IN 2ND QUARTER
  LV 12/21 DIGITAL EQUIPMENT FILES
     (DW) TRADEMARK SUIT AGAINST C. ITOH
  LU 12/21 WANG LABS SEES 2ND QUARTER
     (DW) RESULTS BELOW ITS GOALS
  LT 12/20 AT&T SIGNS DISTRIBUTION PACTS
     (DJ) WITH 44 RESELLERS
  LS 12/20 AT&T UNVEILS MEMORY CHIP THAT
     (DW) CAN STORE OVER 1 MILLION BITS
  LR 12/19 JUDGE ALLOWS STORAGE TECH
     (DW) TO USE UNIT'S FUNDS
  LQ 12/19 ASHTON-TATE SOFTWARE PACKAGE
     (DJ) ADDS COPY PROTECTION SYSTEM
  LP 12/19 U S WEST UNIT-GENL DATACOMM
     (DJ) IN PACT FOR DATA EQUIPMENT
```

```
LO 12/19 CORPORATE DATA SCIENCES TO
   (DJ) FORM COMPUTER VENTURE IN CHINA
LN 12/19 HITACHI IN ALTERNATIVE SOURCE
   (DJ) PACT WITH MOTOROLA ON COMPUTER
```

To continue to the next screen of headlines, you press Return. Each of these headlines starts with a two-letter code in front of the story's date. In this list, the codes run from LX to LN. The LX-coded headline, at the top, is the one for the sample story on IBM you've just seen. To read the second story, the one about Commodore, for instance, you just type **LW**, like so:

```
LW

  N   I/EDP      01/29 LW   1/5
    /CBU              /EDP   /
      12/21 COMMODORE INTERNATIONAL SEES
    (DW) LOWER SALES IN 2ND QUARTER
    NEW YORK -DJ- COMMODORE
INTERNATIONAL LTD. SAID SALES IN THE
FISCAL SECOND QUARTER ENDING DEC. 31
WILL BE LOWER THAN THE YEAR-EARLIER
QUARTER AND CONFIRMED THAT ITS
HOME-COMPUTER SALES ARE SLOWING.
    THE QUARTERLY SALES DROP MARKS
COMMODORE'S FIRST SUCH DECLINE ON A
YEAR-TO-YEAR BASIS SINCE IT BEGAN
THRIVING IN THE HOME-COMPUTER BUSINESS
MORE THAN TWO YEARS AGO.
    THE COMPANY WOULDN'T ESTIMATE SALES
FOR THE CURRENT QUARTER OTHER THAN TO
SAY THEY WILL BE THE SECOND-HIGHEST IN
ITS HISTORY. THAT WOULD PUT SALES
BETWEEN THE $326.2 MILLION FOR THE
QUARTER ENDED LAST MARCH 30 AND THE
$431.4 MILLION FOR THE QUARTER ENDED
DEC. 31, 1983.
    BUT THE CHRISTMAS SEASON SLOWDOWN
```

To continue to the next screen, you press Return. You can also choose to start reading another story at this point by typing its two-letter code. You can also type another news code, for instance .I/GEN, to read the latest story in that category or do a scan of headlines in another category by typing, for instance, .I/GEN Ø1. You can also jump to a different database, which is what I'll do now, by typing **//WSJ**:

```
//WSJ

        THE WALL STREET JOURNAL
           HIGHLIGHTS ONLINE
          COPYRIGHT (C) 1985
      DOW JONES & COMPANY, INC.

      THIS DATA BASE ENABLES YOU
     TO VIEW ONLINE HEADLINES AND
    SUMMARIES OF MAJOR STORIES IN
     THE WALL STREET JOURNAL. FOR
      DETAILS ON THESE AND OTHER
         STORIES, PLEASE SEE
          TUESDAY'S JOURNAL

PRESS      FOR
  A     TUESDAY'S EDITION
  B     PREVIOUS EDITIONS
```

I won't be showing much of this database because it's very simple to use. I'll just show this menu and the menu for the current edition, which is displayed by typing **A**:

```
WSJ 12/14/85

   THE WALL STREET JOURNAL
   THE EDITION FOR MONDAY,
      DECEMBER 14, 1985

PRESS    FOR

1        FRONT PAGE
2        EDITORIALS
3        FRONT PAGE -- SECTION 2
4        MARKET NEWS
5        BACK PAGE
```

Most of the other databases on DJNRS are menu driven, and I'll skip illustrating them. You've already seen plenty of examples of using menu-driven services in this book. They're so easy to use, you shouldn't have any trouble with them on DJNRS. Within these menu-structured databases, these are the navigational commands:

- T Typing T will take you to the top menu of that particular database.
- Return Pressing Return will move you to the next page.

- M Typing M will take you back to the previous menu, just as it does on CIS.
- R Typing R will move you back a page.
- P Typing P, when combined with a number—for example, P3—will move you ahead the specified number of pages. You can use this command to skip from the first page of a story to the last page, to get a quick overview.

I'd like to illustrate two of the most important features of DJNRS: //TRACK and //TEXT.

//TRACK is a feature of DJNRS that allows you to set up to five lists of up to 25 companies each that will automatically recall stock quotes and news stories on the companies you list. Typing **//TRACK** will start the process, which looks like this:

```
//TRACK

With //TRACK you can create your own
profiles to monitor current quotes and
news on companies of interest.

Each profile can track as many as 25
companies. And you can create up to 5
profiles. //TRACK usage is billed at
the rate you now pay for stock quotes.
A $5 monthly fee for //TRACK will be
waived until February 1, 1985.

To use //TRACK, you'll need to create a
4-digit personal identification number.
Please note your "PIN" for future use.

Now enter any 4 numbers as your PIN.

1234
```

I've used **1234** in this example. I advise you to use a more random set of four numbers.

```
         Dow Jones Tracking Service
              Copyright (C) 1984
         Dow Jones & Company, Inc.

Press   To
  1     Create a Profile
  2     Review or Change the Companies
           In a Profile
```

3 Delete a Profile
4 Execute a Profile Search
5 Learn More About The Dow Jones
 Tracking Service

See //MENU for a description of other
Dow Jones News/Retrieval services

When you're online, you may want to select choice 5 to get an overview of the Tracking Service. In this illustration, I'll show how a Track profile is created by typing **1**:

1

//TRACK provides current stock quotes
and recent business stories. You will
see quotes and then news for each
company in your profile.

Each profile can track as many as 25
companies. Create up to five profiles
so you can track similar companies in
each one.

For the stock symbols you need to
create your profile, see //SYMBOL,
the online directory of symbols.

Press Return to create a profile.

[RETURN]
You must give this profile a unique
name for ease in identifying it later.

You might want to call this profile
BUY if you're tracking companies as
potential investments. If you're
monitoring your company's vendors, you
might want to name your profile:

SUPPLIERS

Enter up to ten letters to name this
profile.

COMP

You can use a full word for a Track profile. I tend to use abbreviations, such as COMP for computers as used here. It's faster to type and I remember them easily.

```
Please enter the stock symbols for the
companies you want to monitor in this
profile. For example, you can:

Enter       DJ  IBM  MGM  RCA  TNDM

To Track    News and quotes for these
            five companies

Enter up to 25 symbols separated by
spaces. When you have finished, press
return.
```

These are the stock symbols I chose:

CBU AAPL RCA IBM TL WCI LOTS

```
YOU CURRENTLY HAVE ROOM FOR 18 COMPANIES
IN YOUR PROFILE. PLEASE ENTER STOCK
SYMBOLS(S) OR ENTER A SINGLE SLASH (/)
```

I don't have any other companies that I'd like to track, so I'll tell DJNRS that I'm finished by typing a slash (/):

/

```
Thanks. Your profile has been created.

For quick access to a specific profile
containing quotes and news stories,
type //TRACK and the profile's name.
          EXAMPLE: //TRACK BUY
To receive headlines rather than full
stories, type //TRACK, the profile name
and "HL" for headlines.
          EXAMPLE: //TRACK BUY HL
To receive only the news added since
you last displayed a profile, type
//TRACK, the profile name and "NO" for
no old news.
          EXAMPLE: //TRACK BUY NO
Press return to continue.
```

[RETURN]

```
PRESS     TO

  1       Create Another Profile
  2       Review Or Change The Companies
            In A Profile
  3       Delete A Profile
  4       Execute A Profile Search
  5       Learn More About The Dow Jones
            Tracking Service

-----------------------------------------------------------------
To search other data bases, type two
slashes followed by the data-base name.
          EXAMPLE: //NEWS
```

This is really a roundabout way of going at this, but I'd like you to see all of the menus in this particular database. Typing **4** will start the Track search:

4

```
     DISPLAYING YOUR PROFILES

  PRESS       TO DISPLAY YOUR

  1    COMPANY PROFILE - COMP

---------------------------------------------------------------------
FOR HEADLINES RATHER THAN FULL STORIES,
TYPE THE PROFILE NUMBER AND HL.
          EXAMPLE:   2 HL   (RETURN)
FOR ONLY THE NEWS ADDED SINCE YOU LAST
USED A PROFILE, TYPE THE NUMBER AND NO.
          EXAMPLE:   2 NO   (RETURN)
```

1

```
DOW JONES STOCK
QUOTE REPORTER SERVICE
STOCK QUOTES DELAYED
OVER 15 MINUTES
*=CLOSE ADJ. FOR EX-DIVIDEND

STOCK                 CBU
BID/CLOSE             18 1/4
ASKED/OPEN            17 3/4
```

```
HIGH                  17 7/8
LOW                   16 3/8
LAST                  16 3/8
VOLUME (1ØØ'S)        4677
```

[RETURN]

```
                      Ø1/Ø2 AS
    N     CBU
1/5
  /CBU              /EDP     /
    12/21 COMMODORE INTERNATIONAL SEES
  (DW) LOWER SALES IN 2ND QUARTER
    NEW YORK -DJ- COMMODORE
INTERNATIONAL LTD. SAID SALES IN THE
FISCAL SECOND QUARTER ENDING DEC. 31
WILL BE LOWER THAN THE YEAR-EARLIER
QUARTER AND CONFIRMED THAT ITS
HOME-COMPUTER SALES ARE SLOWING.
    THE QUARTERLY SALES DROP MARKS
COMMODORE'S FIRST SUCH DECLINE ON A
YEAR-TO-YEAR BASIS SINCE IT BEGAN
THRIVING IN THE HOME-COMPUTER BUSINESS
MORE THAN TWO YEARS AGO.
    THE COMPANY WOULDN'T ESTIMATE SALES
FOR THE CURRENT QUARTER OTHER THAN TO
SAY THEY WILL BE THE SECOND-HIGHEST IN
ITS HISTORY. THAT WOULD PUT SALES
BETWEEN THE $326.2 MILLION FOR THE
QUARTER ENDED LAST MARCH 3Ø AND THE
$431.4 MILLION FOR THE QUARTER ENDED
DEC. 31, 1983.
    BUT THE CHRISTMAS SEASON SLOWDOWN
```

[story continues for several screens and ends . . .]

[RETURN]

END OF NEWS ABOUT CBU

[RETURN]

```
DOW JONES STOCK
QUOTE REPORTER SERVICE
STOCK QUOTES DELAYED
OVER 15 MINUTES
* = CLOSE ADJ. FOR EX-DIVIDEND
```

STOCK	AAPL
BID/CLOSE	27
ASKED/OPEN	27 1/8
HIGH	27 5/8
LOW	27 1/8
LAST	27 1/2
VOLUME (1ØØ'S)	3Ø15

THERE IS NO CURRENT NEWS ABOUT AAPL

[RETURN]

This is what it looks like when DJNRS does a Track search for you. The actual search would go on past this illustration, but this is enough to give you an idea of how it works and what it is like to use.

The quickest way to use //TRACK is to type it as a direct command along with your profile name. For instance, typing **//TRACK COMP** anywhere (except the Free-Text database) within DJNRS would take you directly to the prompt asking you to type in your PIN. Then the Track search would start.

A shorter way of doing a Track search is to request only the headlines of the news stories that have been retrieved. This is accomplished by adding Ø1 to the //TRACK command. For example, //TRACK COMP Ø1. Such a search would look like this:

//TRACK COMP Ø1

DOW JONES STOCK
QUOTE REPORTER SERVICE
STOCK QUOTES DELAYED
OVER 15 MINUTES
*=CLOSE ADJ. FOR EX-DIVIDEND

STOCK	CBU
BID/CLOSE	18 1/4
ASKED/OPEN	17 3/4
HIGH	17 7/8
LOW	16 3/8
LAST	16 3/8
VOLUME (1ØØ'S)	4677

[RETURN]

N CBU
Ø1/Ø2
AS 12/21 COMMODORE INTERNATIONAL SEES
(DW) LOWER SALES IN 2ND QUARTER

[RETURN]

END OF NEWS ABOUT CBU

[RETURN]

DOW JONES STOCK
QUOTE REPORTER SERVICE
STOCK QUOTES DELAYED
OVER 15 MINUTES
*=CLOSE ADJ. FOR EX-DIVIDEND

STOCK	AAPL
BID/CLOSE	27
ASKED/OPEN	27 1/8
HIGH	27 5/8
LOW	27 1/8
LAST	27 1/2
VOLUME (1ØØ'S)	3Ø15

[RETURN]

THERE IS NO CURRENT NEWS ABOUT AAPL

[RETURN]

DOW JONES STOCK
QUOTE REPORTER SERVICE
STOCK QUOTES DELAYED
OVER 15 MINUTES
*=CLOSE ADJ. FOR EX-DIVIDEND

STOCK	RCA
BID/CLOSE	35 5/8
ASKED/OPEN	35 3/8
HIGH	35 3/4
LOW	35 3/8
LAST	35 3/4
VOLUME (1ØØ'S)	1145

It would, of course, continue. Once a Track search has been completed, DJNRS will tell you that you've reached the

```
                END OF PROFILE COMP

PRESS RETURN FOR THE //TRACK MENU OR
TYPE //TRACK AND ANOTHER PROFILE NAME.
        EXAMPLE: //TRACK BUY

TO REACH A DATA BASE, TYPE TWO SLASHES
AND THE DATABASE NAME.
        EXAMPLE: //NEWS
```

There are two other things you should know about //TRACK. If you check into it several times a day, you might want to add NO to the //TRACK command, for example, //TRACK COMP NO. This will only show you the stories that've been added since the last time you performed a search. Second, I hope you noticed how many times the Return key had to be pressed in the illustrations. This can be awfully time consuming. At the time this book was written, DJNRS did not have a command to let you tell it to display the Track search continuously. To get around this design shortsightedness, you can press Return more than once when it's first required. The extra Returns will be obeyed by the system when it needs them. This will help you to get through a Track search faster. Be careful about how many you put in at one time, though, or you might overshoot the end of the profile and get command reminders from DJNRS which will eat up the time you were trying to save. I suggest pressing Return no more than four times at any one point. If you experiment, you'll be able to find the best way for your own profiles.

The final DJNRS database we'll look at is also the most powerful one. It's the Free-Text database, //TEXT. It's similar in some respects to BRS After Dark (see Chapter 4, Using BRS After Dark) and Knowledge Index (see Chapter 11, Using Knowledge Index). Accessing it is as easy as typing **//TEXT**:

```
//TEXT
     DOW JONES TEXT-SEARCH SERVICES
            COPYRIGHT (C) 1984
        DOW JONES & COMPANY, INC.

PRESS    FOR

  1      THE WALL STREET JOURNAL:

    FULL-TEXT VERSION
    FROM JANUARY 1984
```

```
         * * A NEW SERVICE * *
  2         DOW JONES NEWS:
    BROADTAPE, AND SELECTED
    STORIES FROM BARRON'S AND
    THE WALL STREET JOURNAL
    FROM JUNE 1979

  1

DJ/NRS - SEARCH MODE - ENTER QUERY
1_:
```

This is the only prompt in this database. It's the signal to start your search by typing a search statement. You've already seen how a search service works in Chapter 4 (Using BRS After Dark; you may want to refer back to that chapter to refresh your memory before continuing here). Let me run through a search in this illustration. I'll be looking for documents that mention the IBM PC, the telecommunications company Rolm, and Japan. First, though, I'll start by typing **..SET DETAIL=ON**. This command will display how many times a search word appears in the database. It can be useful for focusing on a search. It won't be too useful in this particular illustration, but you may find the command to be useful and showing how it works here will help you to become familiar with it.

```
    1_:  ..SET DETAIL=ON

R4001 * SET-COMMAND HAS BEEN EXECUTED; PRESS ENTER KEY TO CONTINUE.
[RETURN]
```

This example will be longer than any actual search should be in order to show you the framework that supports a search. The first step is to type **IBM**:

```
1_:    IBM

DJ/NRS     - SEARCH MODE
00001  IBM
IBM                                        718 DOCUMENTS
RESULT          718 DOCUMENTS
```

Next, I'll look to see if IBM's full corporate name has more mentions than its abbreviation:

```
2__:     INTERNATIONAL ADJ BUSINESS ADJ MACHINES

DJ/NRS      - SEARCH MODE
ØØØØ2 INTERNATIONAL ADJ BUSI
INTERNATIONAL                                    7325 DOCUMENTS
BUSINESS                                         9141 DOCUMENTS
MACHINES                                         138Ø DOCUMENTS
RESULT         8Ø5 DOCUMENTS
```

I'll set these results aside for the moment and move onto looking for mentions of personal computers or, as IBM's is called, the letters PC. I'll tell the system to look for the words "personal" and "computer" only when they are next to one another. This is done by using the search command, ADJ, which you've seen in the illustrations of using BRS After Dark's search service.

```
3__:     PERSONAL ADJ COMPUTER OR PC

DJ/NRS      - SEARCH MODE
ØØØØ3 PERSONAL ADJ COMPUTER
PERSONAL                                         2185 DOCUMENTS
COMPUTER                                         289Ø DOCUMENTS
PC                                                161 DOCUMENTS
RESULT         42Ø DOCUMENTS
```

There are now 420 documents that have either the phrase "personal computer" or "PC" in them. I'll combine this search statement with my first one that just looked for mentions of "IBM." This can be typed as a whole search statement, but it's really unnecessary. The database remembers whatever it's been asked, so I don't have to type the word search statement out. I just have to tell it which search statement numbers to refer to and how I want these statements to be used. To use the first and third search statements, I just have to refer to the numbers 1 and 3. Since I'm looking for documents that contain the phrases from both statements, I'll use the connector "AND." This is boolean logic, which you've seen in Chapter 4.

```
4__:     1 AND 3

DJ/NRS         - SEARCH MODE
ØØØØ4 1 AND 3
1          IBM                                    718 DOCUMENTS
3          PERSONAL ADJ COMPUTER                  42Ø DOCUMENTS
RESULT         225 DOCUMENTS
```

Out of the combined 1138 documents, 225 contain the phrases I'm looking for. Now I want to see how many of the documents from my second search statement would also qualify. Again, I can do this just by telling the database to refer to numbers 2 and 3. Again, I'll use "AND" as the connector:

```
5_:     2 AND 3

DJ/NRS     - SEARCH MODE
00005 2 AND 3
2          INTERNATIONAL ADJ BUSI                805 DOCUMENTS
3          PERSONAL ADJ COMPUTER                 420DOCUMENTS
RESULT             222 DOCUMENTS
```

Of the combined 1225 documents, 222 qualify for my search so far. Now let's weed through the total of 447 documents and see how many of these still qualify. This will also dispose of any duplicate documents. I'll have the system compare the two and tell me how many are unique.

```
6_:     4 AND 5

DJ/NRS     - SEARCH MODE
00006 4 AND 5
4          1 AND 3                               225 DOCUMENTS
5          2 AND 3                               222 DOCUMENTS
RESULT             174 DOCUMENTS
```

Of the 447 documents, only 174 are unique. Now let's narrow the search further by seeing how many of these contain a mention of the company, Rolm:

```
7_:     6 AND ROLM

DJ/NRS     - SEARCH MODE
00007 6 AND ROLM
6          4 AND 5                               174 DOCUMENTS
ROLM                                              57 DOCUMENTS
RESULT             8 DOCUMENTS
```

Only 8 documents qualify so far. Now, for the final step—weeding out the ones that don't have a mention of Japan in them. At this point, I'll use the word "Japan" as a stem followed by a wild card. In this database, the wild card is a dollar sign ($). This will allow documents that contain "Japan" and "Japanese" to qualify:

```
8_:     7 AND JAPAN$

7       6 AND ROLM
R1      JAPAN$                       2286 DOCUMENTS
R3      JAPAN***                        1 DOCUMENT
R4      JAPAN-AMERICAN                  1 DOCUMENT
R5      JAPAN-BASED                     8 DOCUMENTS
R6      JAPAN-BASHING                   1 DOCUMENT
R7      JAPAN-BOUND                     1 DOCUMENT
R8      JAPAN-CHINA                     1 DOCUMENT
R9      JAPAN-RELATED                   1 DOCUMENT
R10     JAPAN-SOVIET                    1 DOCUMENT
R11     JAPANESE                     1757 DOCUMENTS
R12     JAPANESE-AMERICAN               3 DOCUMENTS
R13     JAPANESE-AMERICANS              5 DOCUMENTS
R14     JAPANESE-BUILT                  2 DOCUMENTS
R15     JAPANESE-CANADIANS              1 DOCUMENT
R16     JAPANESE-CAR                    1 DOCUMENT
R17     JAPANESE-CURRENCY               1 DOCUMENT
R18     JAPANESE-DESIGNED               3 DOCUMENTS
R19     JAPANESE-ENGLISH                1 DOCUMENT
R20     JAPANESE-HANDLED                1 DOCUMENT
R21     JAPANESE-INSPIRED               1 DOCUMENT
R22     JAPANESE-LANGUAGE               3 DOCUMENTS
R23     JAPANESE-LED                    1 DOCUMENT
R24     JAPANESE-MADE                  15 DOCUMENTS
R25     JAPANESE-MARKET                 1 DOCUMENT
R26     JAPANESE-OPERATED               1 DOCUMENT
R27     JAPANESE-OWNED                  2 DOCUMENTS
R28     JAPANESE-STYLE                  4 DOCUMENTS
R29     JAPANESE-YEN                    1 DOCUMENT
R30     JAPANESES                       1 DOCUMENT
R31     JAPANESQUE                      1 DOCUMENT
R32     JAPANS                          2 DOCUMENTS
R33     JAPANSPEAK                      1 DOCUMENT
R34     JAPANTOWN                       1 DOCUMENT
DJ/NRS  -SEARCH MODE
00008 7 AND JAPAN$
RESULT      2 DOCUMENTS
```

As you can see, more than just the word "Japanese" starts with "Japan"! The database has displayed every word or phrase that starts with the stem "Japan." I've done this to bring home a very important point: *never* use the ..SET DETAIL=ON option with wild cards. It'll only make your search take longer than it should, and the list of words the database displays could go on for quite some time. For instance, the list would be very, very long if the stem "compute" had been used with a wild card. If you happen to use a stem only three or four letters long, you'll probably watch a list displayed for several hours.

As for the search, it's been narrowed down to just two documents. To display a document, type **..P** (period period P), like so:

```
9_:  ..P
          DOCUMENT=        1 OF       2       PAGE =       1 OF      15
AN     841204-0110.
HL         Companies Unveil Computer-Telephones
         But Potential Customers Seem Lukewarm
         ---
         By John Marcom Jr.
         Staff Reporter of The Wall Street Journal
DD     12/04/84
SO     WALL STREET JOURNAL (J)
IN     COMPUTERS (EDP)
       TELECOMMUNICATIONS, BROADCASTING, TELEPHONE, TELEGRAPH (TEL)
                                  - MORE -
```

At the - MORE - prompt, you must press Return to continue reading the document. If you want to print the whole document nonstop, type **..CP**. *Warning:* Once you type ..CP, you cannot abort the display. Even if you disconnect from DJNRS by hanging up the phone, the display will continue being sent by the system, and this could result in a crash of the system. Use ..CP very, very carefully. This is a very bad database design and Dow Jones should have their programmers correct this. You shouldn't have to worry about clogging or crashing a system, especially at the connect-time rates that DJNRS charges.

If you want to skip this document at any point (again, except when ..CP has been typed), you can type **..P/DOC= 2** to skip to the first page of the second document. This command is an obtuse way of telling the system to start printing the second document, like so:

```
..P/DOC=2
          DOCUMENT=      2 OF     2     PAGE =      1 OF     20
AN     840313-0035
HL         IBM Beefs Up European Operations
         ---
         By Beth Karlin
         Staff Reporter of The Wall Street Journal
DD     03/13/84
SO     WALL STREET JOURNAL (J)
CO         IBM EUROP RM AMH BGH
IN     COMPUTERS (EDP)
       MONETARY NEWS, FOREIGN EXCHANGE TRADE (MON)
                                  - MORE -
```

Once you've completed a search, you might want to review the steps you took in order to see if there were possibilities that you didn't take advantage of. Typing **..DISPLAY ALL** will display a list of your search statements and the number of occurrences and documents that the database found:

```
..DISPLAY ALL
SEARCH - QUERY
ØØØØ1 IBM
    NUMBER OF OCCURRENCES = ØØØ3558    NUMBER OF DOCUMENTS = ØØØØ718
SEARCH - QUERY
ØØØØ2 INTERNATIONAL ADJ BUSINESS ADJ MACHINES
    NUMBER OF OCCURRENCES = ØØØØ828    NUMBER OF DOCUMENTS = ØØØØ8Ø5
SEARCH - QUERY
ØØØØ3 PERSONAL ADJ COMPUTER OR PC
    NUMBER OF OCCURRENCES = ØØØ1145    NUMBER OF DOCUMENTS = ØØØØ42Ø
SEARCH - QUERY
ØØØØ4 1 AND 3
    NUMBER OF OCCURRENCES = ØØØØ225    NUMBER OF DOCUMENTS = ØØØØ225
SEARCH - QUERY
ØØØØ5 2 AND 3
    NUMBER OF OCCURRENCES = ØØØØ222    NUMBER OF DOCUMENTS = ØØØØ222
SEARCH - QUERY
ØØØØ6 4 AND 5
    NUMBER OF OCCURRENCES = ØØØØ174    NUMBER OF DOCUMENTS = ØØØØ174
SEARCH - QUERY
ØØØØ7 6 AND ROLM
    NUMBER OF OCCURRENCES = ØØØØØØ8    NUMBER OF DOCUMENTS = ØØØØØØ8
SEARCH - QUERY
ØØØØ8 7 AND JAPAN$
    NUMBER OF OCCURRENCES = ØØØØØØ2    NUMBER OF DOCUMENTS = ØØØØØØ2
                    ****   END OF DISPLAY, RETURN TO CONTINUE   ****
```

There are other avenues that could've been taken in this search, but this illustration (combined with the ones in Chapter 4, Using BRS After Dark, and Chapter 11, Using Knowledge Index) should be enough to get you started on your own.

In displaying a list of your search statements and their results, you can also limit the display to just a few of the statements, as the following two illustrations show:

```
    13_:   ..DISPLAY 1,3
SEARCH - QUERY
ØØØØ1 IBM
    NUMBER OF OCCURRENCES = ØØØ3558    NUMBER OF DOCUMENTS = ØØØØ718
```

```
SEARCH - QUERY
00002 INTERNATIONAL ADJ BUSINESS ADJ MACHINES
    NUMBER OF OCCURRENCES = 0000828      NUMBER OF DOCUMENTS = 0000805
SEARCH - QUERY
00003 PERSONAL ADJ COMPUTER OR PC
    NUMBER OF OCCURRENCES = 0001145      NUMBER OF DOCUMENTS = 0000420
                        ****   END OF DISPLAY, RETURN TO CONTINUE   ****

[RETURN]
    10_:    ..DISPLAY 1-3
SEARCH - QUERY
00001 IBM
    NUMBER OF OCCURRENCES = 0003558      NUMBER OF DOCUMENTS = 0000718
                        ****   END OF DISPLAY, RETURN TO CONTINUE   ****
[RETURN]
SEARCH - QUERY
00002 INTERNATIONAL ADJ BUSINESS ADJ MACHINES
    NUMBER OF OCCURRENCES = 0000828      NUMBER OF DOCUMENTS = 0000805
                        ****   END OF DISPLAY, RETURN TO CONTINUE   ****
[RETURN]
SEARCH - QUERY
00003 PERSONAL ADJ COMPUTER OR PC
    NUMBER OF OCCURRENCES = 0001145      NUMBER OF DOCUMENTS = 0000420
                        ****   END OF DISPLAY, RETURN TO CONTINUE   ****
[RETURN]
SEARCH - QUERY
00004 1 AND 3
    NUMBER OF OCCURRENCES = 0000225      NUMBER OF DOCUMENTS = 0000225
                        ****   END OF DISPLAY, RETURN TO CONTINUE   ****
[RETURN]
```

By typing **..DISPLAY 1,3** in this first illustration, the database displayed the results of the first three search statements, without pausing between each one. In the second illustration, typing **..DISPLAY 1-3** displayed the results of the first three search statements, with a pause between each one.

If these commands seem odd to you, it's because they are. Traditionally, a command such as ..DISPLAY 1,3 should only display the results to search statements 1 and 3. Typing ..DISPLAY 1-3 should display the results of search statements 1, 2, and 3. The syntax is convoluted and is another flaw in the design of DJNRS. Businessmen may be used to dealing with bureaucracy in their jobs and so may tolerate the convolution in DJNRS's command structure. However, there is no reason for such inconsistency, especially when dealing with computers that can be set right just by changing their software instructions. It's clearly poor design. DJNRS is running on IBM mainframe computers, which may account for some of these problems. Still, they are inexcusable and should have been attended to a while ago.

Finally, let's look at how the illustrated search could've been carried out in just one statement:

```
1_:      IBM AND (PERSONAL ADJ COMPUTER OR PC) AND ROLM AND JAPAN$/..P HL,DD,CO

RESULT                2 DOCUMENTS
                    DOCUMENT=       1 OF       2   PAGE =        1 OF       1
HL                  Companies Unveil Computer-Telephones
                  But Potential Customers Seem Lukewarm
                    ---
                  Staff Reporter of The Wall Street Journal
DD                12/Ø4/84
                      END OF DOCUMENT

[RETURN]

                    DOCUMENT=       2 OF       2   PAGE =        1 OF       1
HL                  IBM Beefs Up European Operations
                  ---
                  By Beth Karlin
                  Staff Reporter of The Wall Street Journal
DD                Ø3/13/84
CO                  IBM EUROP RM AMH BGH
RØ6Ø1 * END OF DOCUMENTS IN LIST - ENTER RETURN OR ANOTHER COMMAND.
```

At the end of the search statement is a print command that's been delimited. The database was told to display the first two documents of any match. The display was limited to only the following items: headline (HL), date (DD), and company codes (CO) (if any). These delimiters can be used at any time when displaying documents that have been retrieved. So, when you want to print a retrieved document, you can add any of these delimiters to the print command (**..P**):

- AN, which is the ascension number of the story (a unique index code the database uses to arrange the stored documents).
- HL, which is the headline of the document (this will include bylines if the document is from the *Wall Street Journal*).
- DD, which stands for date of the document.
- SO, which is the source of the document. Source codes are:
  - B for *Barron's*
  - J for the *Wall Street Journal*
  - N for News/Retrieval Service
  - T for Dow Jones News Service
  - W for the *Wall Street Journal* and Dow Jones News Service
- CO, which is the Dow Jones company code.

- IN, which is the Dow Jones industry code and description.
- GV, which is the Dow Jones government code and description.
- TX, which is the text of the document.

Examples of using these combinations are as follows:

- ..P HL,DD, which will print the document headline (HL) and date (DD).
- ..P HL,CO,TX, which will print the document headline (HL), company code (CO), and text (TX).
- ..P DD,SO,CO,GV, which will print the document date (DD), source (SO), company code (CO), and government code and description (GV).

When you're through using the Free-Text database, type **..OFF** (period period OFF) or **&OFF** (and-sign OFF) to return to the rest of DJNRS. These commands will not disconnect you from the system. They'll just allow you to exit from the Free-Text database, like so:

```
..OFF

TEXT-SEARCH SERVICES SIGNOFF COMPLETE

TO REACH ANOTHER DATA BASE, TYPE TWO
SLASHES (//) AND THE DATA-BASE CODE.

        EXAMPLE: //NEWS (RETURN)

OR, TYPE //MENU FOR A DATA-BASE LIST.
```

From this point, you can jump to any other DJNRS database you wish. When you are finished using DJNRS, you must type **DISC** to log off. Neither OFF nor BYE will disconnect you. Only DISC will.

Dow Jones News/Retrieval Service provides excellent financial information and news databases for business people. However, its inconsistent command structure and repetitive display of help prompts detract from the service. The inability of the system to recognize a Control-H as a correction is a glaring example of poor database design and software engineering. If you can put up with these shortcomings, you'll find DJNRS to be worth the investment. Even if you can't put up with them, DJNRS can't be beat by any other system in this book for the scope of financial information and news services it offers.

* * *

Additional Information

CONTACT:

Dow Jones & Company, Inc., P.O. Box 300, Princeton, NJ, 08540, (609)452-1511, 1–(800)257-5114.

NEWS/RETRIEVAL PRIME AND NON-PRIME TIME

Usage rates for customers accessing News/Retrieval directly are divided into prime-time and non-prime-time hours as follows:

Time Zone	*Prime*	*Non-Prime*
Eastern	6 AM–6 PM	6:01 PM–4 AM
Central	5 AM–6 PM	6:01 PM–3 AM
Mountain	4 AM–6 PM	6:01 PM–2 AM
Pacific	3 AM–6 PM	6:01 PM–1 AM

Note. If you log on before 6:01 PM local time, the entire session will be billed as prime time.

Usage rates for those who access News/Retrieval through the MCI gateway are divided into prime and non-prime hours as follows:

Time Zone	*Prime*	*Non-Prime*
Eastern	6 AM–9 PM	9:01 PM–4 AM
Central	5 AM–8 PM	8:01 PM–3 AM
Mountain	4 AM–7 PM	7:01 PM–2 AM
Pacific	3 AM–6 PM	6:01 PM–1 AM

Note: If you log on before non-prime time begins in your time zone, the entire session will be billed as prime time.

Weekends, New Year's Day, Washington's Birthday, Memorial Day, Independence Day, Labor Day, Thanksgiving and Christmas Day are billed at non-prime rates. News/Retrieval is available 22 hours per day, 7 days a week, from 6 AM to 4 PM Eastern Time.

The below prices apply only in the 48 contiguous states and at a transmission speed of 300 bps. A transmission speed of 1200 bps provides data up to four times faster, at a price two times higher than 300 bps rates.

Connect times are rounded to the nearest minute.

Usage in Alaska and Hawaii is billed at $1 per minute. The $1 price holds regardless of data base or time.

NEWS/RETRIEVAL SUBSCRIPTION PRICES

Standard Membership

- $75 one-time start-up fee per location
- $12 annual or $3 monthly service fee per account

Blue Chip Membership

- $75 one-time start-up fee per location
- $95 annual subscription fee
- 33 1/3% discount on non-prime usage
- No service fee

Executive Membership

- $50 monthly subscription fee per location
- 33 1/3% discount on prime and non-prime usage
- No service fee

Blue Chip and Executive memberships guarantee 6 hours of free usage each year (1/2 hour each month) to be used in selected databases. See //INTRO, our free online newsletter, at the beginning of each month for free time offer.

NEWS/RETRIEVAL CONNECT-TIME CHARGES

Prime-Time	Non-Prime Time
90¢/minute	20¢/minute
($54/hour)	($12/hour)

NEWS/RETRIEVAL CONNECT-TIME SURCHARGES

The following databases carry a 30¢/minute ($18/hour) surcharge during prime time and a 60¢/minute ($36/hour) surcharge during non-prime time:

- Official Airlines Guide
- Standard & Poor's Online
- Media General
- Dow Jones News*
- Merrill Lynch
- Disclosure II
- Corporate Earnings Estimator
- Economic and Foreign Exchange Survey

*There is no surcharge for Dow Jones News in non-prime time.

Real-Time Quotes (//RTQ) offers quotes, with no delay, from the New York, American, Midwest and Pacific stock exchanges and composite quotes.

//RTQ also features a News Alert that refers investors to current-day market news from the Dow Jones News Service.

To receive Real-Time Quotes, you must sign a separate contract and pay a special monthly exchange fee of $18.50.

The Dow Jones Tracking Service, //TRACK, gives you the ability to easily monitor news and quotes for up to 125 companies through the creation of online profiles. There is a $5 monthly storage fee per password for //TRACK.

//TEXT offers both the full text of The Wall Street Journal since January 1984 and an archive of the Dow Jones 90-day news data base since June 1979. //TEXT is available 7 days a week from 6 AM to 4AM Eastern time, with the full text of the *Wall Street Journal* updated each business day at 6 AM Eastern Time.

//DSCLO carries an access fee of $5 for each company search in prime time or $2 in non-prime tme. It is not voided by free time offers and also must be paid by those who receive free time with the purchase of software packages published or authorized by Dow Jones.

Program and usage costs may be tax-deductible. Consult your tax adviser.

//INTRO is the free customer newsletter of News/Retrieval and provides free online information on News/Retrieval data bases, software developments and enhancements, special application suggestions, and customer service information.

For //MCI rates, see Chapter 12, "Using MCI Mail."

10 Using EasyLink

> Control characters used on this system: Control-H, backspace; Control-Q (XON), resume output; Control-S (XOFF), pause output; Control-X, erase typed line; Break, system interrupt.

EasyLink (CPB100150), which started operations in 1982, is Western Union's foray into microcomputer communications. Western Union is the leader in U.S. Telex communications, a primitive yet widely used means of communicating between, mostly, teletype machines. EasyLink can be viewed more as an upgrade and enhancement to the existing Telex network rather than as a service solely for microcomputer users. In 1984, Western Union spent well over $100 million to improve and promote the service. In short, Western Union is counting on EasyLink succeeding.

I first saw EasyLink a little over a year after its introduction. Its thin instruction manual was worse than some amateur publications I've seen. The system itself consisted on a single, baffling prompt: PTS. "PTS" means "Proceed To Select." How obvious. EasyLink's design could only be considered to be an embarrassment.

Two years later Western Union announced it had discovered menus and would shortly incorporate them into EasyLink. This would make EasyLink, well, easier. Apparently, however, someone in the Western Union marketing department unfortunately thought that the word "menu" wasn't good enough for Western Union. Thus, "menu" became two words: session control.

Luckily, this same pattern of thought did not spread to the new EasyLink manual. Western Union contracted the firm of Baker & Sakowski to write it. They produced a manual that stands as a model for all online system manuals. It's clear, complete, easy to grasp, and startlingly logical in its arrangement. It makes EasyLink look better than it is.

Another plus on Western Union's side is a a terminal program from Kensington Microware, called The EasyLink Instant Mail Manager. Although it can be used with any online system, it is specially crafted to act as a front end—as sort of interpreter—to EasyLink. Using it means you won't have to remember the plethora of special commands, formats, and limits of each type of EasyLink message format. Instead, the software handles all of that. The program isn't perfect, but it, too, makes EasyLink look better than it actually is.

Let me make it clear here: There is nothing functionally wrong with EasyLink. It simply has a sloppy, patchwork design that does not live up to the image of Western Union. The menus and help files were placed on the system last, as if they were a brief afterthought—and it shows.

EasyLink is available through direct-dial local numbers in 16 cities, Tymnet, and a Western Union 800 number. There is an additional charge for using the 800 number.

EasyLink's pricing structure is complex and depends on the way in which you're connected to the system, the speed of transmission, and the type of message being sent. For instance, calling EasyLink via a Western Union or local access number at 300 bps will cost $18 per hour in connect-time, plus additional charges depending on the type of message being sent. Using the FYI information service databases, which are part of EasyLink, costs $49 per hour in connect-time, plus a 15¢ charge for each transaction. Rates for messaging services only are reduced by 40 percent between the hours of midnight and 7 AM Eastern Time on weekdays, all day Saturday and Sunday, and certain holidays. (Again, like all prices for all systems covered in this book, check with the individual system for their current rates.)

When you subscribe to EasyLink, you'll be issued an EasyLink ID, password, a mailbox address, and a Telex number and Answerback code. You'll get a User Name, which you may choose for yourself. Also, you'll be issued a terminal type code. This code will tell EasyLink how it should react to your particular terminal; for instance, whether or not it should send a linefeed with a carriage return at the end of a line. EasyLink doesn't allow you to change this once you're online, and this is another serious flaw in the system's design. Trying to communicate with EasyLink in a manner other than that specified by the terminal type code has unpredictable results.

EasyLink allows for a variety of messages to be sent and information to be retrieved. Messages can be sent to EasyLink electronic mailboxes or to any terminal in the world that's connected to the Telex network. You can also send Mailgrams, telegrams, cablegrams, InfoCom (private Telex network) messages, Computer Letters, E-Com (United States Postal Service's Electronic-Computer Originated Mail), and Overseas Priority Letters. Information that can be retrieved through the FYI collection of databases includes the UPI news wire, financial information, and a variety of general interest files (such as best-seller lists).

EasyLink also offers an online directory of both Telex and EasyLink mailbox addresses. (Note that these are domestic addresses only. For foreign mailbox and Telex addresses, you must call Western Union's 800 number for operator assistance.) Also available is the ability for two terminals of any type (for instance, a teletype and a microcomputer) to converse in real-time. You've seen an example of this type of online communicating in Chapter 7 (Using the CompuServe Information Service) in the illustrations of CB and talk. EasyLink's real-time communication is somewhat like CIS's CB Talk mode.

When you've connected with EasyLink, you may see a brief signon notice announcing a new service or feature. Western Union will be improving EasyLink, so some of what I'll be illustrating here may change. After the signon notice, you'll see something like this:

```
9299899A 2ØNOV85 12:33 EST
PTS
```

This is the infamous PTS prompt. If you'd like to get a rundown of all of the commands that are available on the system, type **/HELP** (slash **/HELP**):

```
9292862A 2ØNØV85 12:35 EST
PTS /HELP
THE FOLLOWING INSTRUCTIONS ARE AVAILABLE TO HELP YOU USE EASYLINK.

TO DISPLAY ANY OF THESE INSTRUCTIONS ENTER THE COMMAND FOR THE
DESIRED INSTRUCTION FOLLOWED BY A CARRIAGE RETURN OR A CARRIAGE
RETURN AND A LINE FEED.

     HELP INSTRUCTIONS                              COMMAND

INTRODUCTION TO EASYLINK                            /HELP INTRO

ADDRESS TYPES
  HOW TO SEND TO A TELEX I, TELEX II
    (TWX) OR EASYLINK NUMBER                        /HELP ADDRESS
```

```
HOW TO SEND A WORLDWIDE
  TELEX NUMBER                                    /HELP WUW

HOW TO SEND A MAILGRAM                            /HELP ZIP
```

This list will continue for quite a long time, since there are many help files that can assist you in using the system and its various features. At the end of the list, you'll see

```
REQUEST TERMINATED
EASYLINK
9292862A 2ØNOV85 12:38 EST
PTS
```

To get to the session control feature—which is usually known as a menu—you have to type **/EXIT** (slash EXIT). (Although common sense dictates that a command called /EXIT would sign you off of a system, common sense isn't always used in designing online systems—or most anything that has to do with operating a computer.)

```
EASYLINK
9292862A 2ØNOV85 12:38 EST
PTS

/EXIT

        EASYLINK SERVICE

1       EASYLINK INSTANT MAIL SERVICE (IMS)
2       FYI REPORTS (FYI)
3       DIRECTORY INFORMATION SERVICE (DIS)
4       ON-LINE CONVERSATION TO TELEX
7Ø      HELP FOR EASYLINK SERVICE MENU
75      HELP FOR ON-ONE CONVERSATION TO TELEX
8Ø      NEWS ABOUT EASYLINK
9Ø      SIGN-OFF FROM EASYLINK

ENTER NUMBER OF SELECTION DESIRED   (RETURN)
```

- Choice 1, EasyLink Instant Mail Service (IMS), is the messaging system.
- Choice 2, FYI Reports (FYI), is the collection of EasyLink databases and text files.
- Choice 3, Directory Information Service (DIS), is the online Telex/EasyLink address directory.

- Choice 4, On-Line Conversation to Telex, is for real-time terminal-to-terminal communications between compatible terminals.
- Choice 70, Help for EasyLink Service Menu, is a brief explanation of the menu selections. Instead of this, type /HELP (slash HELP) at any prompt to get the longer help message that lists all of the help files.
- Choice 80, News About EasyLink, is an explanation of new features and services that've been added to the system.
- Choice 90 is self-explanatory. Typing /QUIT (slash QUIT) will also disconnect you. Remember, /EXIT will display the menu; it will not disconnect you from the system.

Let's look at how to send an EasyLink message. Some EasyLink messages start with just an address, whereas others start with a command. There are also different address formats for each message as well as limitations in the length of messages and the number of characters per line. The EasyLink manual is scrupulously complete in its explanation of how to compose each type of message.

It's doubtful that you'll need to know how to send more than two or three types of messages, so I'll just illustrate the ones I think are the most popular. They are

- Sending a message to another EasyLink mailbox
- Sending a domestic Telex
- Sending a WorldWide (foreign) Telex

To start a message to another EasyLink mailbox, you must know the mailbox address. If you don't have the address handy, you can look it up in the online directory by typing 3 at the menu:

```
        EASYLINK SERVICE

1       EASYLINK INSTANT MAIL SERVICE (IMS)
2       FYI REPORTS (FYI)
3       DIRECTORY INFORMATION SERVICE (DIS)
4       ON-LINE CONVERSATION TO TELEX
7Ø      HELP FOR EASYLINK SERVICE MENU
75      HELP FOR ON-LINE CONVERSATION TO TELEX
8Ø      NEWS ABOUT EASYLINK
9Ø      SIGN-OFF FROM EASYLINK

ENTER NUMBER OF SELECTION DESIRED  (RETURN)
3
```

```
ØØØ1417325 124Ø ET

ENTER: NAM, NBR, ANS, HELP OR QUIT.
```

The NAM command will find a mailbox or Telex number and Answerback code when you only know the subscriber's name and state, for instance, NAM NJ WESTERN UNION. The NBR command will find the subscriber name and Answerback code when you only know the EasyLink or Telex number, for instance, NBR 7314185. The ANS command will find the subscriber name and EasyLink or Telex number when you only know the Answerback code, for instance, ANS USCOMP.

Let's take a look at finding a mailbox number when the subscriber doesn't have one. This will give you an idea of how the directory operates:

```
ENTER: NAM, NBR, ANS, HELP OR QUIT

NAM NY CANE

NAM NY CANE
DIRECTORY INFORMATION AS FOLLOWS

INQUIRED NAME NOT FOUND
THESE NEAR MATCHES FOUND IN DATABASE

CANAAN LABS

CANADA BELT CO

CANADA BELT CO

CANADA CONSULATE GENERAL

CANADA DRY BOTTLING CO

MORE?
N

ENTER NEXT REQUEST OR TYPE NONE
```

You can see that the director displays entries that may be close to the one you've typed.

Let's look at a successful search now:

```
ENTER NEXT REQUEST OR TYPE NONE
NAM NY MIKE CANE
```

```
NAM NY MIKE CANE
DIRECTORY INFORMATION AS FOLLOWS

MIKE CANE
NEW YORK NY (MCANE1) TLXI 592735
ESL 62999999

ENTER NEXT REQUEST OR TYPE NONE
```

This is an imaginary listing, since I don't subscribe to EasyLink. You can see two (imaginary) addresses. The first is a Telex I number. That number is 592735 and its Answerback code, which is found in parentheses, is MCANE1.

Using these imaginary addresses, I can now show you how to send two types of EasyLink messages. Let's exit the Directory Information Service and at the same time introduce you to a new command. Remember that some of the main menu selections had three-letter codes in parentheses? When you type one of these codes with /EXIT, you'll be taken directly to that service. These are EasyLink's versions of direct commands. The direct commands that may be used to move from one part of the system to another are

- /EXIT IMS, which will bring you to the message system
- /EXIT DIS, which will take you to the Telex directory
- /EXIT FYI, which will take you to the FYI databases

Note that you cannot use these commands to move from real-time online conversational mode between terminals, though.

To go from the Directory Information Service (DIS) to the EasyLink Instant Mail Service (IMS), type **/EXIT IMS**, like this:

```
ENTER: NAM, NBR, ANS, HELP OR QUIT

/EXIT IMS

93Ø6355A 2ØNOV85 12:45 EST
PTS
```

This is the PTS prompt again. You would think that since you typed /EXIT, you'd get a menu again. This is not so. In IMS, you have to type a new command to a menu. That command is /PROMPT.

As the PTS prompt shows, EasyLink is ready for you to start your message. Let's start by sending a message to the EasyLink electronic mailbox. There are two ways this can be done:

- In menu mode
- In command mode, with just the PTS prompt

Let's see how sending a message looks with a full menu. Type **/PROMPT** for the IMS menu:

```
9306355A 20NOV85 12:45 EST
PTS
/PROMPT

*** SELECT FUNCTION ***

 1 - - Send message
 2 - - Forward (resend) message
 3 - - Get mail
 4 - - Disconnect or exit to other services
 5 - - Guidelines for using EasyLink without prompts
 6 - - Help
 7 - - Leave Prompt and go to Command mode

Enter a number 1 - 7   <RETURN>
```

Choice 1, Send message, is what we want:

```
Enter a number 1 - 7   <RETURN>
1

*** SELECT ADDRESS TYPE ***

  1 - - EasyLink Mailbox
  2 - - Telex I or II
  3 - - Worldwide Telex
  4 - - Mailgram
  5 - - Telegram (Public Message Service)
  6 - - International Cablegram
  7 - - Express Document - 2 Hour
  8 - - Express Document - Overnight
  9 - - Return to *** SELECT FUNCTION ***
 10 - - Help

Enter a number 1 - 10   <RETURN>
```

Let's look at how to send a message to another EasyLink mailbox by type **1:**

```
Enter a number 1 - 10   <RETURN>
1
*** ENTER EASYLINK MAILBOX ADDRESS ***
```

EXAMPLES:

62999999+ If last address, end with plus (+)
62999999, If another follows, end with comma (,)

Enter 8-digit number beginning with 62 or /HELP <RETURN>

As you can see from this address prompt, this type of message begins by typing the EasyLink mailbox address of the recipient followed by a plus sign (+). The plus sign tells the system that you are finished entering destination addresses. In these illustrations, I'll be using imaginary addresses. You should use your own EasyLink address to send a message to yourself. As for Telex numbers, you might consider sending a test message to your company's Telex machine.

If you need more help than the above prompt gives, press Return and then type /HELP. I'll dispense with that and enter the imaginary EasyLink mailbox address:

62999999+

GA

ADDRESS ENTERED

*** ENTER TEXT ***

Enter text of message below.
When finished, press <RETURN> then enter one of these commands:

LLLL <RETURN> To send message and stay connected, or
MMMM <RETURN> To send message and disconnect

To get help, press <RETURN> then enter /HELP <RETURN>

This is where you might need additional help, so I'll show you the help menu and one of its text files. I'll start by pressing **Return** and typing **/HELP.**

[RETURN]
/HELP

< < < SELECT HELP > > >

1 - - How to finish text and send a message
2 - - How to correct a typographical error

3 - - How to cancel a message
4 - - Return to *** ENTER TEXT ***

Enter a number 1 - 4 <RETURN>

Let's take a look at the first help file. It'll give you some idea of EasyLink's help facility. Type **1:**

Enter a number 1 - 4 <RETURN>
1

< < < HOW TO FINISH TEXT AND SEND A MESSAGE > > >

To send a message:
Press <RETURN> then enter

LLLL <RETURN> to send message and stay connected or
MMMM <RETURN> to send message and disconnect

EXAMPLE: This is the body of the message. <RETURN>
This is the last line of the message text. <RETURN>
LLLL <RETURN>

END of HELP - Press <RETURN>
[RETURN]
< < < SELECT HELP > > >

1 - - How to finish text and send a message
2 - - How to correct a typographical error
3 - - How to cancel a message
4 - - Return to *** ENTER TEXT ***

Enter a number 1 - 4 <RETURN>

No other help file is needed for this illustration, so I'll type **4** to get back to composing the message:

4

Begin entering your text:

Terrahawks.
Stay on this message.
This is an emergency!

Once the message is finished, you have to let EasyLink know that it should speed it to its destination. This is done by typing four L's, which can be in lowercase or uppercase (llll or LLLL). You can also type four M's (mmmm or MMMM). The difference between these two commands is that the four L's will send your message, bring you back to the menu, and keep you online. The four M's will send your message and then immediately disconnect you from the system. Until you're sure of how to use EasyLink, you should use four L's, like so:

```
LLLL

ACCEPTED 93Ø6355
EASYLINK
93Ø7345A 2ØNOV85 12:49 EST
PTS

Press <RETURN> to continue
```

Pressing Return here will take you back to the IMS menu. I'll skip that, and the remaining illustrations of using EasyLink will be in command mode.

If, after a PTS prompt, you decide that you'd rather cancel the message process, press your Break key. If you don't have a Break key on your terminal, you can type, on a line by itself, a plus sign followed by four E's (+eeee or +EEEE). To cancel the process after a GA prompt, that is, once you have started typing your message, press your Break key. If you don't have a Break key, type four E's (eeee or EEEE) on a line by itself to cancel the message.

In the previous illustration, remember that an *imaginary* EasyLink mailbox address was used. You should restrict your message sending to real mailboxes. If you happen to send a message to a mailbox or other address that doesn't exist, EasyLink will intercept the message and send a notice to your mailbox letting you know of the undelivered message. You'll see an example of such a notice later in the chapter.

Right now, let's look at how to send a domestic Telex:

```
93Ø7345A 2ØNOV85 12:51 EST
PTS
```

At the PTS prompt, type the Telex number. This can be either a Telex I or Telex II (TWX) number. If you want verification of the message delivery, include the Answerback code in parentheses following the Telex number. Don't put any spaces between the Telex number and the Answerback code. Again, after you've finished entering the address, conclude with a plus sign (+) to let the system know that you're through.

If you're sending a Telex to Mexico, you have to prefix the Telex number with a zero (Ø). If you're going to send a Telex to a terminal other than Telex I or Telex II (for instance, ITT, RCA, or Graphnet), you have to prefix the number with a 71.

Using the imaginary Telex number 592735 and the imaginary Answerback code MCANE1, sending a domestic Telex looks like this:

```
93Ø7345A 2ØNOV85 12:52 EST
PTS

592735(MCANE1)+
GA
```

The GA from EasyLink means "Go Ahead." Why the system doesn't just print "GO AHEAD," in full, is another example of poor design. There is an insignificant amount of additional work that would have to be done for the system—for *any* system—to give you full English prompts.

After the GA prompt, type your message. A message can be up to 200,000 characters long. Each line, though, can only be up to 68 characters wide; for instance,

```
Terrahawks.
Stay on this Telex.
This is an emergency!
LLLL
```

Typing four L's (llll or LLLL) on a line by itself at the end of the message signals the system to dispatch the message. Remember that you can also type four M's (mmmm or MMMM) to disconnect from the system immediately after your message is sent.

A Telex can take up to 2 hours to deliver. It may take longer if the recipient terminal is otherwise engaged. Note that the above process is what an EasyLink subscriber would also go through to send a Telex to an MCI Mail subscriber (see Chapter 12, Using MCI Mail).

Sending a WorldWide Telex, which is to a country outside of North America, is simple. First, you must type **/WUW** and a space. This lets the system know that this message is to be a WorldWide Telex. Following that is a three-digit Country Code. After that, the procedure is the same as for a domestic Telex; that is, a Telex number and directly following without a space the Answerback code in parentheses. Conclude with a plus sign (+), as usual. Such an address would look like this:

9307345A 20NOV85 12:55 EST
PTS

/WUW 123592735(MCANE1)+
GA

Type your message. It can be up to 200,000 characters long. Each line can be up to 68 characters wide. When it's finished, type **LLLL** to tell the system to send the message or **MMMM** to be disconnected from the system once the message has been sent.

So far what you've seen are illustrations of composing messages while directly online to EasyLink. You can also prepare messages offline and upload them into the system. The command to let EasyLink know you are uploading is **/BATCH,** which follows any PTS prompt. After you've typed /BATCH, immediately start the uploading process. EasyLink will not give you a GA prompt. You may include the LLLL command at the end of a message. When the /BATCH upload is complete, you must conclude with MMMM. Although these four M's will usually disconnect you from EasyLink, in the case of using the /BATCH command, you'll get a new PTS prompt. This is a jarring inconsistency.

These three types of messages should enable you to get a good deal of use out of the EasyLink system. If you're a subscriber to the Business Computer Network (BCN, see Chapter 5, A Brief Look at the Business Computer Network), you should now be able to use EasyLink without having to arrange for the separate purchase of an EasyLink manual.

There are two additional commands you may wish to use in certain situations. These commands will work only with the three types of messages I've just outlined. The first command is /NTF. This will place a notice in your EasyLink mailbox to verify that your message was delivered. The second command is /PRI. This will arrange priority delivery of a message. These commands can be used with the three types of messages you've just seen illustrated: EasyLink mail, Telex, and WorldWide Telex. Each command is typed on a line by itself prior to entering an EasyLink mailbox address or Telex number; for instance, like this:

9306355A 20NOV85 12:59 EST
PTS

/NTF
62999999+

GA

Or, with the second command, like this:

```
93Ø6355a 2ØNOV85 12:59 EST
PTS

/PRI
62999999+

GA
```

You may also combine these commands to arrange for both a delivery receipt and priority delivery. The combination would look like this:

```
93Ø6355A 2ØNOV85 12:59 EST
PTS

/NTF PRI
62999999+

GA
```

There are other types of EasyLink messages that may be sent and other message-handling features that may be used. However, if you don't send many Telexes or if your EasyLink mailbox correspondence is infrequent, the examples I've shown will be enough to enable you to send messages without worry.

The other side of using EasyLink is handling the messages that you've received. You can receive messages from other EasyLink subscribers and other Telex users. This would include subscribers of Delphi (see Chapter 8, A Too-Brief Look at Delphi) and The Source (see Chapter 15, Using THE SOURCE) when the subscribers use the available Telex resources of each system. Both of these systems offer Telex services, and Telex messages can be sent to your EasyLink Telex number and appear in your EasyLink mailbox. You cannot, however, send a reply back to Delphi or The Source. It's a one-way street—one that's unlikely to change any time soon.

When you have messages in your EasyLink mailbox, they'll remain there for 10 days, waiting to be read. After that time period, Western Union will automatically send them to you as Mailgrams, via the U.S. Postal Service, and charge you for this forwarding. It can be argued that this is tantamount to interference with your communications, but the other side of the argument is that you may be missing some important messages by not checking your mailbox regularly. A 10-day grace period is quite sufficient in my opinion.

There are several ways of accessing your EasyLink mailbox. To find out if you have any messages waiting, type **/SCAN** at the PTS prompt, like this:

```
EASYLINK
9369106A 20NOV85 13:19 EST
PTS
/SCAN

NO. LINES ACCEPTED ON ORIGINATOR                    (REFERENCE)

P  1    5 20NOV 13:02 WESTERN UNION EASYLINK         (This is a test)
   2   16 20NOV 12:58 WESTERN UNION TELEGRAPH CO     (TO: MIKE CANE)
   3    8 20NOV 13:02 EASYLINK NOTIFICATION          (DELIVERY)
THERE IS ONE PRIORITY MESSAGE AND 2 NORMAL MESSAGES

MAILBOX SCAN COMPLETED
EASYLINK
9369106A 20NOV85 13:20 EST
PTS
```

This is self-explanatory for the most part. The only item that may be unclear is the text within parentheses. This is usually the first line of the message.

You can read your messages in several ways:

- Individually by typing /READ and a message number or numbers
- All at once by typing /READ ALL
- All at once by typing /MBX

Reading only the first message would look like this:

```
EASYLINK

9369405A 20NOV85 13:24 EST
PTS

/READ

EASYLINK MBX 9306355A001 20NOV85 13:19/13:26 EST
PRIORITY MESSAGE
FROM:    62819794
         WESTERN UNION EASYLINK
TO:      62999999

Terrahawks.
Stay on this message.
This is an emergency!
MMMM
READ REQUEST COMPLETED
```

Although this message was not sent with the priority command used in its previous illustration, I did send it that way originally in order to illustrate what a priority message looks like when received. At the end of a message, EasyLink displays four M's (MMMM). This signifies the end of the message. It would be better if EasyLink just displayed END OF MESSAGE. Once you've read a message, EasyLink takes it out of your mailbox and places it in your "hold" box. It'll remain there up to 3 days. After that, it'll be automatically deleted. Have a floppy disk handy to capture and save EasyLink messages if you think you'll need a copy of them for reference.

You can see the change in your mailbox after reading one message by typing **/SCAN** again:

```
EASYLINK

9369405A 20NOV85 13:26 EST
PTS

/SCAN

NO. LINES ACCEPTED ON ORIGINATOR                      (REFERENCE)
  1   16 20NOV 12:58 WESTERN UNION TELEGRAPH CO       (TO: MIKE CANE)
  2    8 20NOV 13:49 EASYLINK NOTIFICATION            (DELIVERY)

MAILBOX SCAN COMPLETED
```

The message that was read is no longer in your mailbox. To read every message at once, use the **/MBX** command:

```
EASYLINK

9369405A 20NOV85 13:29 EST
PTS

/MBX

EASYLINK MBX 9297473A001 20NOV85 12:58/13:31 EST
FROM:     62900100
          WESTERN UNION TELEGRAPH CO
TO:       62999999
TO:       MIKE CANE

WE CANCEL THE FOLLOWING MESSAGE:

MESSAGE:  9292862A001
TIME  IN:  20NOV85 12:52
ADDRESSED TO:  L2819794
```

REASON: INVALID DESTINATION NUMBER

REPEAT: WE CANCEL

INTERCEPT DEPT EASYLINK
BRIDGETON MO

MMMM

EASYLINK MBX 9307346A001 20NOV85 13:49/13:32 EST
FROM: EASYLINK

TO: 62999999

DELIVERY NOTIFICATION:

RE MESSAGE NUMBER: 9306355A001
INPUT ADDRESS: 62999999
DELIVERED TO: 62999999
DELIVERED AT: 20NOV85 13:49 EST

MMMM

YOUR MAILBOX IS NOW EMPTY

Here you can see two other types of messages. The first is an intercept notification, telling of the cancellation of a message because it was sent to an address that doesn't exist. This is the kind of notice you'll get if you try to use any of the imaginary addresses in these illustrations. The second type of message is a delivery receipt. This is what you'll receive if you use the /NTF command when you send a message.

Now that all of the messages have been read and your EasyLink mailbox is empty, we can look at the last two commands you can use in your mailbox. These are

- /SCAN HOLD, which will scan the contents of your mailbox hold file
- /MBX HOLD, which will read all of the contents of your mailbox hold file

You can combine both of these commands with a display command in order to view a specific number of lines before EasyLink prompts you to press Return to continue the display. Adding CRT to either of these commands will display 24 lines at a time. Instead of CRT, you can add any number from 10 to 99 to tell EasyLink how many lines it should display before pausing the display with a prompt. The variations of these commands look like this:

- /SCAN HOLD CRT
- /SCAN HOLD 20
- /MBX HOLD CRT
- /MBX HOLD 55

Using the /SCAN HOLD Command looks like this:

```
EASYLINK

9369405A 20NOV85 13:52 EST
PTS

/SCAN HOLD

NO. LINES ACCEPTED ON ORIGINATOR                    (REFERENCE)

  1    8 20NOV 13:49 EASYLINK NOTIFICATION          (DELIVERY)
  2    5 20NOV 13:49 WESTERN UNION EASYLINK         (This is a test)
  3   16 20NOV 12:58 WESTERN UNION TELEGRAPH CO     (TO: MIKE CANE)

HOLD FILE SCAN COMPLETED
EASYLINK

9369405A 20NOV85 13:54 EST
PTS
```

Your hold file contains every message that you've read in your mailbox. Remember, though, that EasyLink will only hold the messages you have read for 3 days. Store them on disk when you read them initially so you can be sure you have a copy.

Finally, let's go to the FYI Reports databases by typing **/EXIT FYI** at the PTS prompt:

```
EASYLINK

9369405A 20NOV85 13:54 EST
PTS

/EXIT FYI

WU FYI BGTN

ENTER CATEGORY NAME
```

If you type **HELP** at this prompt, you'll be told to

```
PLEASE ENTER EITHER NEWS SPORTS MARKET STOCKS OR CATALOG
```

Typing CATALOG will display all of the keywords that may be used in FYI. This list is reproduced at the end of this chapter. FYI is the easiest part of EasyLink to use. You choose from the list of keywords and type the keyword for the information you want to retrieve. This is similar to using StarText, which you'll see later in Chapter 18, Using Local Systems.

These are some FYI keywords:

- UPIINDEX is an index to sections of the United Press International news wire.
- HOLIDAYS is a list of holidays within a month for countries around the world.
- CONSUMER is a table of contents for articles from *Consumer Reports* magazine.

Let's look at each of them briefly:

```
ENTER CATEGORY NAME
UPIINDEX

UPIINDEX

**   ELECTRONIC NEWSPAPER INDEX   **

TYPE  FOR     SECTION

U001          GENERAL NEWS
U002          SPORTS
U003          FINANCE
U004          EUROPE NEWS
U005          LATIN AMERICA NEWS
U006          MIDEAST/AFRICA NEWS
U007          ASIA/FAR EAST/PACIFIC NEWS
U008          DOMESTIC/INTERNATIONAL WEATHER

TO SCAN TODAY'S HEADLINES IN ANY OF THE SECTIONS ABOVE, TYPE U001,
U002 ETC. WHEN SYSTEM ASKS FOR YOUR CATEGORY.

ENTER CATEGORY NAME
```

Seeing the news category headlines is accomplished just by typing one of the codes listed above, such as **UØØ3** for financial news:

```
ENTER CATEGORY NAME
UØØ3
UØØ3---Financial News (all update times EST)

  name
  U33Ø   Esso and Shell abandon 3rd well in S China Sea, 2:30 pm
  U329   Blue named Frontier Horizon Airlines presidnet, 2:30 pm
  U328   Accord may be near in General Dynamics strike, 2:15 pm
```

To read an individual story, just type one of its codes.

Let's move on to the **HOLIDAYS** keyword:

```
ENTER CATEGORY NAME
HOLIDAYS

HOLIDAYS

MANY DIFFERENT HOLIDAYS ARE CELEBRATED ALL OVER THE WORLD
DURING THE YEAR. WESTERN UNION HAS CREATED A LIST OF WORLD
HOLIDAYS TO HELP YOU CONDUCT YOUR INTERNATIONAL BUSINESS MORE
EFFECTIVELY. TO FIND OUT THE HOLIDAYS DURING A GIVEN MONTH IN
1984 PLEASE TYPE THE APPROPRIATE CATEGORY NAME.

HAPRIL          HJULY           HOCTOBER
HMAY            HAUGUST         HNOVEMBER
HJUNE           HSEPTEMBER      HDECEMBER
```

Let's look at one of these months, **HNOVEMBER:**

```
ENTER CATEGORY NAME
HNOVEMBER

NOVEMBER

1.   ALL SAINTS DAY -
          ANGOLA, AUSTRIA, BELGIUM, BURUNDI, CENTRAL AFRICAN
          REPUBLIC, CHAD, CHILE, COLOMBIA, CONGO, EQUATORIAL
          GUINEA, FRANCE, GABON, FEDERAL REPUBLIC OF GERMANY,
          GUATEMALA, HOLY SEE, ITALY, IVORY COAST,
          LIECHTENSTEIN, MADAGASCAR, MONACO, MAURITIUS,
          PARAGUAY, PERU, PHILIPPINES, POLAND, RWANDA,
          SAN MARINO, SENEGAL, SEYCHELLES, SPAIN, SWEDEN,
          TAHITI, TOGO, UPPER VOLTA, VENEZUELA
     FEAST OF ALL SAINTS - PORTUGAL
     NATIONAL DAY - ALGERIA
```

The list, of course, continues.

Finally, let's look at the **CONSUMER** keyword:

```
ENTER CATEGORY NAME
CONSUMER
```

CONSUMER REPORTS	CATEGORY NAME
4 WHEEL DRIVE VEHICLES - PART I AND PART II	(AUTO)
WHAT TO DO IF A TOY IS 'SOLD OUT'	(GENERAL)
HOME SECURITY: DOOR LOCKS - BRAND NAME RATINGS AND HOW TO MAKE A DOOR MORE KICKPROOF	(PRODUCT)
PROBLEM: CLEANING PATIO BLOCKS WITHOUT DAMAGING SURROUNDING PLANTS: REMOVING CARPETING; CLEANING GROUT FROM TILES; REMOVING SCOTCH TAPE FROM WALLS	(QUESTION)

TO SELECT A REPORT, TYPE IN THE CATEGORY NAME(S) DISPLAYED IN PARENTHESIS.

Reading an article by *Consumer Reports* is the same as reading a UPI story. Type the code, and the story will be displayed on your screen.

To return to the menu, type /EXIT at any prompt within FYI. Or, if you prefer to sign off, type /QUIT.

In addition to the services you've seen briefly illustrated here, EasyLink also offers overnight and 2-hour hardcopy delivery of documents that have been typed online or uploaded into the system. Check with Western Union for the latest rates for these services.

Western Union is marketing EasyLink primarily to businesses. It's probably not a service you'll want to subscribe to for yourself, as an individual. It is, though, a service you should be familiar with. If you're a subscriber to the Business Computer Network (BCN) (see Chapter 5, A Brief Look at the Business Computer Network), you'll have access to your own individual EasyLink mailbox.

Western Union still has quite a way to go before the system can live up to the Western Union reputation. It would seem that Western Union introduced EasyLink before it was fully developed in order to preempt its competition, which helps neither Western Union nor its potential customers.

* * *

Additional Information

CONTACT:

The Western Union Telegraph Company, One Lake Street, Upper Saddle River, NJ, 07458, (201)825-5000.

FYI DATABASE KEYWORDS

CATALOG

All reports are updated Monday to Friday unless otherwise noted. All times are eastern time.

NEWSLINE

UPIINDEX	Access complete reports behind the day's top news, sports, and financial stories by typing UPIINDEX. Updated 8AM–midnight, 7 days a week.
NEWS	UPI news bulletins updated hourly on the half hour, Monday–Saturday, 7:30 AM to 8:30 PM.
SPECIAL	In-depth report on topics making news. Updated 8 AM, 1:30 PM, 4:30 PM.
FINANCE	Business-related bulletins from 9 AM to 7 PM. Updated hourly on the hour.
CONGRESS	Reports on legislation affecting business from U.S. Chamber of Commerce. Updated 10:30 AM.
SPORTS	Latest scores, stories, bulletins. Updated hourly on the hour, Monday–Saturday, 8 AM to midnight.
EMBARGO	Weather-related and regular railroad embargoes, car disability, track conditions. Updated 3 PM.

MONEY

STOCK	Prices on NYSE, ASE, and NASDAQ stocks/stock options. Updated continuously during trading days.

OPTIONS	Instructions to access a stock option through FYI; a reference to be kept for future use.
COMMENTARY	In-depth survey of foreign exchange market sentiment and development. Updated 11:00 AM, 3:30 PM.
CURRENCY	Domestic money rates at 9 AM, 5 PM. Foreign exchange rates, spot gold prices updated at 9, 11 AM, 1, 3, 5 PM.
MARKET	Stock market commentary 9:00 AM to 10:59 AM. Latest market averages from 11 AM to 5 PM. Updated on the hour.
LATIN	Latin American currency rates. Updated 11 AM.
COMMODITIES	
TRADE	International business clearinghouse linking you to a worldwide network of businesses wishing to buy, sell, or exchange goods and services. Updated continuously.
FUEL	The day's gasoline, propane, and oil prices plus analysis of the overall fuel market. Updated 10:30 AM, 3:30 PM.
BONDS	Treasury bonds futures. Updated 10 AM, 1:30 PM, 3:30 PM.
GNMA	Government national mortgage association futures (GNMAS). Updated 10 AM, 1:30 PM, 3:30 PM.
NOTES	Treasury notes futures. Updated 10 AM, 1:30 PM, 3:30 PM.
CASH	Spot prices of 22 agricultural products. Updated 5 PM.
GOLD	Futures prices updated 10:30 AM, 1:30 PM, 4 PM.
METALS	First-session London metal market 8:30 AM. Opening comex on gold, silver, copper 10:30 AM. Second session 1:00 PM. Closing COMEX on gold, silver, copper 4:00 PM.

FISH	Seafood and exvessel prices and tonnage from Boston and New Bedford auctions. Updated 12:30 PM.
SUGAR	Sugar, coffee, cocoa futures prices. Updated 11 AM, 1:30 PM, 4:00 PM.
COTTON	Futures prices updated 11:30 AM, 1:30 PM, 4:00 PM.
GRAIN	Commentary from 4:15 PM to 10:59 AM. Wheat, corn, oats, soybeans futures prices updated 11:30 AM, 2 PM, 4 PM.
LIVESTOCK	Cattle, hogs, and pork bellies prices and volumes. Updated 10:55 AM, 12:45 PM, 2:45 PM.
LUMBER	Plywood futures updated 12 noon, 2 PM, 4 PM.
FORECAST	
CITIES	Two-day condensed forecast for 25 major U.S. cities. Updated Monday–Saturday, 8 AM, 8 PM.
HURRICANE	Tropical weather outlook for the Atlantic, Gulf of Mexico, and the Carribean Sea, in season June 1 through November 30. Updated daily at 5:30 AM, 11:30 AM, 5:30 PM.
WEATHER	Detailed 2-day forecasts for numerous U.S. cities. All reports updated throughout the day, 7 days a week.
HUMAN INTEREST	
BIBLE	Passages from King James version. Updated 5 AM.
BOOKS	Best-seller list, hardcover (top 20), paperback (top 10). Updated 9:00 AM Wednesday.
CONSUMER	Analyses of variety of products and services from publishers of *Consumer Reports* magazine. Updated Monday 7 AM.
DIAL 100	DIAL 100 bulletin board. Info on DIAL 100 events from discounts to tips to gifts. Updated Monday.

ENTERTAINMENT	Nine reports covering Hollywood—its business, music, cinema, TV, celebrities. Updated 3 PM.
GAMES	A quiz a day to test your mental mettle. Updated 8 AM.
GREETINGS	List and description of greetings, including availability dates and explanation of how to resend as Mailgrams.
HOROSCOPE	Horoscope with all 12 Zodiac signs. Updated 7:30 AM.
MOVIES	Minireviews of latest releases, current films, coming attractions. Updated Monday 12 noon.
REVIEWS	In-depth reviews of new releases in movies category. Updated Monday 12 noon.
RECORDS	Best-selling singles. Updated Monday 7:30 AM.
SKIING	Explanation of how to access any of 25 ski reports by state.
BABY	To greet new arrival.
BIRTHDAY	Birthday greeting.
CGNS	Congratulatory greeting for many occasions.
GETWELL	Messenger with flowers wishing a speedy recovery.

You can arrange to have the FYI report(s) of your choice delivered automatically to your terminal or mailbox. Type SUBSCRIPTION for explanation of how to subscribe.

11 Using Knowledge Index

Control characters used on this system are Control-H, backspace; Control-Q (XON), resume display; Control-S (XOFF), pause display; Break, system interrupt.

Knowledge Index (CPB100350) is from Lockheed-Dialog Information Services, which is one of the leading business-oriented online database companies. Knowledge Index, which started operations in 1982, offers subsets of several of the databases that are available on the larger Dialog Information Retrieval Service system.

Knowledge Index is comprised of 15 different sections, each with one or more databases. It is available through Telenet, Tymnet, Uninet, and Dialnet at a flat $24 an hour, at either 300 or 1200 bps, and regardless of the individual database you may access. There are no monthly minimum charges. Registration is $35, and connect-time is billed to your credit card.

You can order copies of articles that are referred to in the system's databases. Copies of articles are $6.25 in North America and $8.25 outside of North America. There is also a 20¢ per page charge for photocopies. Copies of documents (which may be seminar papers, symposium briefings, and the like) are $6.25 in North America and $8.25 outside of North America plus the actual cost of the document. Rush orders for copies of either articles or documents cost an additional $6. You may place your order online, as you'll see later in this chapter.

Knowledge Index is available Monday through Thursday from 6 PM to

5 AM; Friday from 6 PM to midnight; Saturday from 8 PM to midnight; and Sunday from 3 PM to 5 AM. All times are your local time.

When you subscribe to Knowledge Index (referred to as KI in the remainder of this chapter), you'll receive a large looseleaf-bound manual that's filled with examples of how to use the system. Although the manual seems intimidating at first, it is clearly written, logically arranged, and very easy to read and understand. The manual is obviously written to help subscribers get the most out of the system in the least amount of connect-time charges. When you get the manual, read it through completely before you go online. As you read the manual, write down, on a sheet of paper, the commands you think you'll be using when you go online. This method will enable you to refer to your own notes on a single sheet of paper, rather than thumbing through the manual.

Like BRS After Dark, KI uses boolean logic. This means you can use words such as "AND," "OR," and "NOT" in your search statements (see Chapter 4, Using BRS After Dark, and Chapter 9, Using Dow Jones News/Retrieval Service, for more information).

When you connect to KI, you'll be greeted with

```
WELCOME TO KNOWLEDGE INDEX
```

Following this may be some brief signon notices, letting you know if any databases have been added or if any databases are temporarily unavailable due to updating. After this, you'll see the KI prompt, which is a question mark:

```
?
```

This is the KI system, before you've entered any of the various databases. Typing **HELP** here will bring this response:

```
?
HELP

HELP HELP
     Knowledge Index has an online HELP
feature designed to provide a brief
explanation of the many options on the
Knowledge Index System. Simply enter
the word HELP followed by the term for
which you are seeking an explanation.
     The online HELP feature of Knowledge
```

```
Index contains the following options:
General
     HELP KI            HELP COMMANDS
     HELP HELP          HELP SECTIONS
Commands
     HELP BEGIN         HELP PAGE
     HELP FIND          HELP ORDER
     HELP COST          HELP KEEP
     HELP DISPLAY       HELP AU=
     HELP RECAP         HELP JN=
     HELP EXPAND        HELP PY=
     HELP LOGOFF        HELP UD=
Sections
     HELP AGRI          HELP GOVE
     HELP BOOK          HELP LEGA
     HELP BUSI          HELP MAGA
     HELP COMP          HELP MATH
     HELP CORP          HELP MEDI
     HELP EDUC          HELP NEWS
     HELP ENGI          HELP PSYC
                        HELP REFR
System Information
     HELP HOURS
     HELP RATES
     HELP BILLING
     HELP TELECOM
     HELP TERMINAL
     HELP SERVICE
     HELP ERICCOD
     HELP NTISCOD

?
```

These are the help files that are available on the system. All of them are clearly written and concise and can help you use the service if you happen to be accessing the system when your manual (or your copy of this book) isn't at your side.

KI is the third example of a search service in this book and works in a similar—though not identical—fashion to BRS After Dark and the Free-Text Search database of Dow Jones News/Retrieval Service. Since Chapters 4 and 9 have already detailed the ins and outs of online searching, this chapter will be brief and focus on other aspects of online searching.

To enter any of the databases on the system (which are listed at the end of this chapter), you must type **BEGIN** (or just **B**) and a database name at any ? (question mark) prompt, like so:

```
?
BEGIN COMP2

10/20/85  18:40:09 EST
Now in COMPUTERS & ELECTRONICS (COMP)
                Section
    Intl. Software (COMP2) Database
    (Copyright 1985 Imprint Software Ltd.)

?
```

This particular database in an online directory of software for microcomputers of all types and brands. Unlike both BRS After Dark and the Free-Text Search database of DJNRS, once you're in this database you can't just type a search statement. This is because in KI you can use the HELP command in any of the databases at any ? (question mark) prompt, whereas if you were to type HELP while in a database in BRS After Dark or the Free-Text Search database of DJNRS, the system would think you wanted to find all of the occurrences of the word "help." In a KI database, you must use a distinct command. This command is **FIND.**

Let's look at a sample search in which all appearances of the terms "Commodore" and "64" are requested:

```
?
FIND COMMODORE AND 64

                1971 COMMODORE
                1358 64
    S1    1296    COMMODORE AND 64

?
```

This search statement could have been typed as "FIND COMMODORE 64," leaving out the "AND" connector. I put the connector in to get a tally of the occurrences of each word. This is sometimes very useful in trying to narrow or expand a search. When you've thought through your search beforehand offline and you're in a hurry to keep down your connect-time costs, leave out the "AND" connector when you're searching for two or more words that are usually found together, for instance, Commodore 64, Apple Macintosh, United States, Great Britain, and word processing.

Out of over 2300 occurrences of the words "Commodore" and "64," only 1296 of these occurrences have the two words appearing together. Before going on, let's examine what this means. First, there are 1971 occurrences of "Commodore." This is over 600 more than qualify for the search statement. Obviously, there may be some software titles that have the word "Commodore" in them. Also, many of those occurrences are for "Commodore PET" or "Commodore VIC-20." Out of 1358 occurrences of "64," a little under 100 of them don't qualify. Again, some software titles may contain "64," and "64" may appear as a RAM requirement for some of the programs (as in "64K required").

Of the 1296 occurrences of "Commodore" and "64," it's very unlikely that you'll want to display all of the software titles retrieved. It'd be cheaper to buy several Commodore 64 software directories. Plus, the titles that have been retrieved are not in any particular order. Let's display the first seven of them to see the order they're in.

Displaying retrieved documents on KI is very similar to the way it's done on BRS After Dark (see Chapter 4). To display a retrieved document, type

- **DISPLAY** (or just **D**)
- The search number (also called a "Set" number)
- The format length you want,
- The document numbers

These elements look like this:

- DISPLAY (or D)
- S and the appropriate number, such as S1, S2, S3
- S for short format, M for medium, and L for long
- The appropriate numbers, such as 1 or 1-7 or 1,2,3,4,5,6,7

These variations would look like these sample commands:

- DISPLAY S1/S/1—To display the result of the first search statement (S1), in short form (S), with only the first document being shown (1)
- D S5/M/1-4—To display the result of the fifth search statement (S5), in medium form (M), with only the first four documents being shown (1-4) with a pause between each document
- D S1Ø/L/1,2,3—To display the result of the tenth search statement (S1Ø), in long form (L), with only the first three documents being shown (1,2,3) without a pause between each one

Don't worry if this seems a bit confusing. You'll see some illustrations as we go along. These commands are very similar to the ones used in BRS After Dark and are just as easy to use.

Let's display (D) from the first search statement (S1), in short form

(S), the first seven (1,2,3,4,5,6,7) results without a pause between each. The command and its result look like this:

D S1/S/1,2,3,4,5,6,7

```
                    Display 1/S/1
Ø19445     957Ø91ØØ
     YOUR PERSONAL NET WORTH
                    Display 1/S/2
Ø19444     957Ø9Ø8Ø
     SONGWRITER
                    Display 1/S/3
Ø19443     957Ø9Ø7Ø
     RUN FOR THE MONEY
                    Display 1/S/4
Ø19441     957ØØ5Ø
     PHI BETA FILER
                    Display 1/S/5
Ø1944Ø     957Ø9Ø4Ø
     PATTERNMAKER
                    Display 1/S/6
Ø19439     957Ø9Ø3Ø
     MASTERTYPE
                    Display 1/S/7
Ø19266     8665Ø2ØØ
     KMMM PASCAL VERSION III.9

?
```

The titles aren't grouped by program function. This list is composed of programs for personal finance, music, game playing, filing, education, typing, and programming. Let's narrow it down by looking for programs for communications, otherwise known as terminal programs. You don't have to retype "Commodore and 64." KI, like BRS After Dark, remembers your previous request. You refer to it just by its search number, S1. So, the second search statement would look like this:

F S1 AND TERMINAL

```
                    1296   S1
                     566 TERMINAL
          S2           4   S1 AND TERMINAL

?
```

Let's take a look at these:

```
?
D S2/S/1-4

                Display 2/S/1
Ø17Ø35     739252ØØ
    OMNICOMM
?
```

Although I told the system to display all four, it paused after the first one. This is a flaw in KI's design.

Although common sense dictates that the command 1-4 should display items 1 through 4 without a pause, KI has it backward. That method of requesting documents places a pause between each document. Conversely, on KI typing 1,2,3,4 would not place a pause between each document, as illustrated in the previous request. Most systems use the hyphen format (i.e., 1-4) to indicate no pause between each item and use the comma format (i.e., 1,2,3,4) to indicate a pause between each item. When you take this to its logical conclusion, if you wish to display more than 10 documents without a pause, you have to type *each* document number *and* a comma. It is not fun nor sensible to have to type a command such as

D S1/S/1,2,3,4,5,6,7,8,9,10,11,12,13,14,15. . .etc.

It'd be better and more logical to be able to type D S1/S/1-25 to get all 25 documents to display one after the other without a pause. This glaring design flaw, though, is the *only* one on KI, which only makes it all the more baffling.

In our illustration, you must type **D** at the subsequent ? (question mark) prompt in order to display the next document in sequence. The whole series looks like this:

```
?
D S2/S/1-4

                Display 2/S/1
Ø17Ø35     739252ØØ
    OMNICOMM
?D
                Display 2/S/2
Ø15693     663871ØØ
    C64-LINK
?D
```

```
                    Display 2/S/3
Ø13244     53625100
    SMART 64 TERMINAL + 3 (THE)
?D
                    Display 2/S/4
ØØ5797     21400250
    TERMINAL ZONE
?
```

The result of this search brings up another important point: Always use more than one term, if possible, to identify what you're looking for. Of the four titles listed above, only the first and third are terminal programs. The second, C64-LINK, is not a terminal program but an IEEE interface. What about number four? Let's display it in full:

D S2/L/4

```
                    Display 2/L/4
ØØ5797     214ØØ25Ø
    TERMINAL ZONE
    CYBERIA INC
    233Ø LINCOLN WAY
    AMES, IA 5ØØ1Ø
    (515)292-7634
    COMMODORE 64/5-1/4-inch disk/14.95$
    Country of Currency: USA
    Source Code Available: NO
    Integrated Packaging: NO
    Updates: YES
    Class of Computer: MICRO
    Date of Release: 83Ø2ØØ   Warranty: LIMITED
    This is a game of skill and precision. You are the commander
of a high performance bomber on a dangerous mission to the
Terminal Zone, the site of the greatest concentration of
nuclear warheads on Earth. In this game of skill and precision,
you must destroy all the warheads and avoid the deadly fire of
anti-aircraft missile launchers.
    530 GAMES/ARCADE

?
```

It's a game, not a terminal program. But it still fits my search criteria, which was to retrieve anything that had "Commodore and 64 and terminal" together somewhere within a document. There are actually more than two communications programs for the C64, and they'd probably be discovered by using "communications" or "online" or "modem" in subsequent search statements.

Let's switch databases now and look at another telltale search:

```
?
BEGIN COMP3

1Ø/2Ø/84   18:48:26 EST
Now in COMPUTERS & ELECTRONICS (COMP)
                  Section
     Microcomputer Index (COMP3) Database
      (Copyright 1984 Micro Info. Serv. Inc.)

?
```

In this database, I intend to see if the previous edition of this book is listed at all. Knowing that if my book is mentioned, I should be too, I'll start out by searching for my own name and see what the results are:

```
?
FIND MIKE AND CANE

                    16 MIKE
                     1 CANE
      S1         Ø   MIKE AND CANE

?
```

My name is not listed, although there is one "Cane" present. That, however, could also be "cane," as in the walking aid (actually, that's what it turned out to be!). Undaunted, I decide to see if the book itself is mentioned:

```
?
FIND COMPUTER AND PHONE AND BOOK

                  9412 COMPUTER
                   113 PHONE
                  1695 BOOK
      S2             2   COMPUTER AND PHONE AND BOOK

?
```

Although the chances are slim, I decide to call up the documents:

```
?
D S2/S/1,2

                  Display 2/S/1
Ø2638      81Ø6Ø49
     PAN: one activity of the PCNET project
```

```
                Display 2/S/2
20181     8102097
     Electric phone book

?
```

I'm familiar with PAN (Performing Artists Network) and PCNET (which Steve Levy details in his excellent book, *Hackers*), so I know that it's doubtful that the first document will contain a mention of this book. Still, I choose to display it:

```
?
D S2/L/1

                Display 2/L/1
020638     8106049
     PAN: one activity of the PCNET project
     Caulkins, Dave; Harris, David
     Dr. Dobb's Journal , Feb 1981 , v6 n2 p17+ , 2 pages
     Languages: English
     Document Type: Article
     Geographic Location: United States
     Reports on the activities of PCNET which
include:    1)
development of a protocol for any personal
computer to
communicate with different computer; 2)
publishing of the
"Electric Phone Book"; 3) PAN electronic mail system.
     Descriptors:     *Telecommunications;     *Online
Systems;
*Electronic Mail
     Identifiers: PCNET Project

?
```

I've boldfaced the terms that fit my search criteria. From reading this first document, I can see that the second document will cover more of the same because of its "Electric Phone Book" title.

I showed you this search to illustrate this point again: Don't use the "AND" connector if the terms are usually found together. If I'd typed "F COMPUTER PHONE BOOK," I would've been given a zero number of retrieved documents from the start and saved time. My first search statement (FIND MIKE AND CANE), however, was designed to save time; this was done by searching for the same item but by a different set of terms. Remember and put into practice these two important points and you'll be able to cut down on the amount of time and money you spend in online searches.

Let's look at another aspect of online searching—looking for people:

```
?
B MAGA1

10/20/84 18:56:51 EST
Now in MAGAZINES (MAGA) Section
     Magazine Index (MAGA1) Database
(Copyright 1984 Information Access Corp)

?
F LINDA AND ELLERBEE

               1542 LINDA
                  8 ELLERBEE
     S1           8   LINDA AND ELLERBEE

?
```

When you use an online system to do research about a particular person, it's always best to use the "AND" connector. Although this particular illustration doesn't show it, there will be times when you'll come across more instances of the person's last name than the number of documents retrieved. This is because writers tend to mention a person by his or her full name at the beginning of an article and then by the last name afterward. If you ever use a full-text database (which contains "electronic reprints" of actual articles, as opposed to bibliographic databases, which only contain summaries of articles and documents), you'll be more effective in your searches by separating the given name and surname of individuals with the "AND" connector.

Sometimes you'll come across the problem of people with unusual names. Say, for instance, that you were researching the singer, Sting. Adding the name of his group, The Police (without the "The"), would help narrow the search:

```
?
F STING AND POLICE

                246 STING
               2798 POLICE
     S2          27   STING AND POLICE

?
```

Displaying the first three results will bring this surprising result:

```
?
D S2/S/1,2,3
```

```
                Display 2/S/1
1714984
     Alone at the top: the Police took a solitary road to success in 1983.
                Display 2/S/2
1712360
     Sting: rock 'n' roll intellectual.
                Display 2/S/3
1662824
     Stung. (Florida police chief caught by sting operation)
(illustration)
?
```

The third document is not about Sting of The Police but about an officer caught in a sting operation! To get around a problem like this, additional phrases such as "rock" and "music" should be added to the search statement. For anyone who is looking up police involved in sting operations, adding phrases such as "law," "arrest," and "indictment" would help to avoid documents about New Wave music groups.

You can also search for people as authors. For instance, if you were in the Books in Print database and wanted to get a list of all books authored by Ayn Rand, the search statement would look like this:

```
?
F AU=RAND, AYN
```

The delimiter, AU=, tells the system to find anything that has "Ayn Rand" in the author field of the document. This command can be used in any database. The key to its use are these limitations:

- Don't put a space between AU= and the name
- Type the name as surname comma space first name (i.e., Rand, Ayn) or surname comma space first initial or partial first name with wildcard (i.e., Rand, A? or Rand, Ay?).

If you'd first like to see if the person's name is listed in the database, use the EXPAND command, like this:

```
?
EXPAND AU=RAND, AYN
```

The system will then display a list of names surrounding the name. The name that you've typed will be highlighted with an asterisk next to it. The EXPAND command is very handy if you forget the first name of an author or have two authors confused. For instance typing **EXPAND AU=ELLISON,**

? will display both ELLISON, HARLAN and ELLISON, RALPH (among others).

Another useful command is JN=. This stands for journal and will display a list of journal titles (magazines, newspapers, and so on). Its use has the same limitations as the AU= command. It would come in handy, for instance, if you knew of two magazines with similar titles or if you weren't sure how a particular journal was being cited in a particular database. It's unlikely that you'll use it, but it's helpful if you need it.

When you've found a list of documents in a search, you can order a photocopy of any of the documents. The copy will be sent to your billing address and charged to your credit card. To see how this works, let's take a list of documents retrieved in the previous example, STING AND POLICE:

```
D S2/S/1,2,3

                    Display 2/S/1
1714984
    Alone at the top: the Police took a solitary road to success in 1983.
                    Display 2/S/2
1712360
    Sting: rock 'n' roll intellectual.
                    Display 2/S/3
1662824
    Stung. (Florida police chief caught by sting operation)
(illustration)
?
```

The first step in the ordering process is to get KI to remember the items you want. Let's say you wanted to get a copy of the first article. It's from the second search statement (S2) you used in the database. You'd have to instruct KI to **KEEP** that particular item, like so:

```
?
KEEP S2/1
          KEEP S2/1

?
```

Your command is confirmed by KI repeating it. To order this document, type **ORDER KI,** like so:

```
?
ORDER KI
1 Item Ordered
Order #359783
```

Item 1
1714984
Alone at the top: the Police took a solitary road to success in 1983.

After this, you can type **ORDER LIST** to see the status of the order.

If you change your mind, you can cancel the order by typing **ORDER CANCEL** and the **ORDER NUMBER**. For the order just placed, the cancellation would look like this:

?
ORDER CANCEL 359783
Order cancelled

Warning. The ORDER and CANCEL commands can only be used under the following circumstances.

ORDER

- You must place an order before you use the BEGIN (or B) command to enter a new database. Once you've entered a new database, everything that you've placed in the KI memory area with the KEEP command will be erased.
- Make sure that you *write down* the Order Number when you've placed an order. If you don't have the Order Number, you won't be able to use the ORDER CANCEL command.
- Remember that copies of articles are $6.25 in North America and $8.25 outside of North America. There's also a charge of 20¢ per page for photocopies. Copies of documents (which may be seminar papers, symposium briefings, and the like) are $6.25 in North America and $8.25 outside of North America *plus* the actual cost of the document. Rush orders for copies of either articles or documents are an additional $6.

CANCEL

- You should type **ORDER LIST** to see the status of your order. If the order has *already been transmitted*, you *cannot* cancel the order.

Make sure that you are *sure* that you want to order something—and that you've used the ORDER command before you've switched to a new database.

After you've been doing a series of searches in a database, you may lose track of the phrases you've used. This is where the RECAP command comes in. Typing **RECAP** will bring up your "searching scorecard":

```
?
RECAP

In MAGA1 database:
     S1       8  LINDA AND ELLERBEE
     S2      27  STING AND POLICE
     S3       Ø  GERRY AND ANDERSON
     S4     368 TERRAHAWKS
     S5      18 PUPPET?
     S6      18 MARIONET?

?
```

You're told the database you're currently in, the search numbers, the number of results each statement generated, and the terms you've used.

Although I haven't illustrated it, the wildcard that's used on KI is a ? (question mark). You can see it used in the RECAP list above in the last two search statements used. I've already covered wildcards in Chapters 4 and 9, so I won't repeat that coverage here.

Another very handy command that's available on KI is COST. Typing **COST** will display how much money you've spent online so far.

Lastly, KI allows you to use the same type of complex search statements that were illustrated at the conclusion of Chapters 4 (using BRS After Dark) and 9 (Using Dow Jones News/Retrieval Service). Statements such as

F VIDEO AND (CASSETTE? OR TAP?) AND (RENTAL? OR LEAS?)

are allowed. In fact, if you use more statements like that, you'll cut down on your connect-time, increase your chances of finding what you want, and get the most out of systems such as Knowledge Index.

Once you're through with KI, type **LOGOFF**, and you'll be able to see what your total bill for the session comes to:

```
?
LOGOFF

1Ø/2Ø/85 19:Ø2:52 EST
Session total: Ø.637 Hours $   15.29   User U43122
```

Knowledge Index, as you've seen, can be a powerful tool for getting to information that you need in a hurry, provided that you take the time to plan your search strategies before you go online. Choosing between it and BRS After Dark (or even Dow Jones News/Retrieval's, Free-Text databases) is more a matter of your own needs and budget than of comparing the two systems head-to-head.

* * *

Additional Information

CONTACT:

Knowledge Index, Dialog Information Services, Inc., Marketing Dept., 3460 Hillview Ave, Palo Alto, CA, 94304, 1-(800)528-6050 ext. 415, 1-(800)352-0458 ext. 415 (in Arizona), 1-(800)528-0470 ext. 415 (in Alaska and Hawaii).

SECTIONS

There are 14 different sections available in KNOWLEDGE INDEX. Each section contains one or more databases. For an explanation of the database(s) in each section, enter HELP followed by the first four letters of the section name. The database name is the same as the section name, except that it's followed by a number.

SECTION NAME	DATABASE NAME
AGRI–AGRIculture	
Database: AGRICOLA	AGRI1
BOOK–BOOKs	
Database: BOOKS IN PRINT	BOOK1
BUSI–BUSIness Information	
Database: ABI/INFORM	BUSI1
Database: TRADE AND INDUSTRY INDEX	BUSI2
COMP–COMPuters and Electronics	
Database: INSPEC	COMP1
Database: INTERNATIONAL SOFTWARE DATABASE	COMP2
Database: MICROCOMPUTER INDEX	COMP3
Database: THE COMPUTER DATABASE	COMP4

SECTION NAME	DATABASE NAME
CORP–CORPorate News	
Database: STANDARD & POOR'S NEWS	CORP1
Database: ICC BRITISH COMPANY DIRECTORY	CORP2
EDUC–EDUCation	
Database: ERIC	EDUC1
ENGI–ENGIneering	
Database: ENGINEERING LITERATURE INDEX	ENGI1
GOVE–GOVErnment Publications	
Database: GPO PUBLICATIONS REFERENCE FILE	GOVE1
Database: NTIS	GOVE2
LEGA–LEGA1 Information	
Database: LEGAL RESOURCE INDEX	LEGA1
MAGA–MAGAzines	
Database: MAGAZINE INDEX	MAGA1
MATH–MATHematics	
Database: MATHFILE	MATH1
MEDI–MEDIcine	
Database: MEDLINE 1980+	MEDI1
Database: MEDLINE 1973-79	MEDI2
Database: MEDLINE 1966-72	MEDI3
Database: INTERNATIONAL PHARMACEUTICAL ABSTRACTS	MEDI4
Database: BIOSIS PREVIEWS 1981+	MEDI5
Database: BIOSIS PREVIEWS 1977-1980	MEDI6
Database: BIOSIS PREVIEWS 1969-1976	MEDI7
Database: DRUG INFORMATION FULLTEXT	MEDI8
NEWS–Newspapers	
Database: NEWSREACH	NEWS1
Database: NATIONAL NEWSPAPER INDEX	NEWS2
PSYC–PSYChology	
Database: PSYCINFO	PSYC1
Database: MENTAL HEALTH ABSTRACTS	PSYC2

12 Using MCI Mail

Control characters used on this system are Control-H: backspace; Control-L: begin a new page; Control-Q (XON): resume display; Control-R: redisplay typed line; Control-S (OFF): pause display; Control-W: erase single typed word; Control-X: erase current typed.

MCI Mail (CPB100400) is from MCI Communications Corp., which is known as one of the leaders in discount long-distance voice telephone service. In 1983, MCI introduced MCI Mail, an electronic mail service aimed squarely at microcomputer owners and users. Using a blitz advertising campaign on television and in print, the concept of electronic mail was introduced to the public in a way never before attempted.

At press time, MCI Mail had local telephone access numbers in 60 cities, a number that has probably increased at the time you're reading this. These local access numbers are MCI's own packet-switched telephone network and don't have a connect-time charge. Outside of the 60 cities, access to the system is via an 800 number, which has a connect-time charge of 15¢ a minute or via Tymnet in over 500 cities at a charge of 5¢ per minute ($3 an hour).

MCI Mail is available in two forms at different subscription rates. There is the Basic Service and the Advanced Service. A subscription to the Basic Service is $18 a year for one mailbox. A subscription to the Advanced Service is $18 a year for one mailbox plus $10 each month. You can use the service at 300, 1200, and 2400 bps without additional charge.

The cost of sending an electronic letter—called MCI Mail Instant Letters—is 45¢ for up to 500 characters. That's a little over 12 lines of 40 characters each or a little under 7 lines of 80 characters each. Instant Letters between 501 to 7500 characters are $1 each.

MCI Mail also offers a domestic and foreign courier service, a domestic and European overnight letter service, and a domestic and foreign letter service, in which printouts of MCI Mail letters are sent through the local postal system (this is similar, in principle, to the Mailgram service).

Also available is domestic Telex at only 25¢ a minute. Foreign Telex rates vary according to the destination country and message length.

In this chapter, I'll show you examples of the Basic Service, since this is what most people subscribe to at first.

Once you've signed onto MCI Mail, you'll be greeted with

```
Welcome to MCI Mail!
MCI Mail Version 2.3
    There are no messages waiting in your INBOX.

Press <RETURN> to continue
```

Following this will be some signon messages informing you of new services and changes and additions to the system. Once you've sent some letters, you'll also see a message letting you know of any waiting mail. Such a message may look like this:

```
  Your INBOX has 3 messages ( 1 PRIORITY ).

Press <RETURN> to continue
```

Once inside the system, you'll see the main menu, which looked like this at press time:

```
You may enter:

SCAN            for a summary of your mail
READ            to READ messages or LISTS
PRINT           to display messages nonstop
CREATE          to write an MCI Letter
CREATE LIST     to make a distribution list
DOWJONES        to Dow Jones News/Retrieval
ACCOUNT         to adjust terminal display
HELP            for assistance

Command (or MENU or EXIT):
```

You can return to this menu at any time, from any prompt, just by typing **MENU**. All of MCI Mail's menus are numberless, requiring you to type from two letters to almost two words, depending on the individual menu. Although MCI Mail is very easy to use, it'd be even easier if its menu selections were numbered. It'd save typing time. Numberless menus aren't practical unless you can just type *one* letter to make a selection. (See Chapter 8, A Too-Brief Look at Delphi.)

As with most online systems, you should first investigate if there's a way of customizing the system for your computer. MCI Mail's command for this is ACCOUNT, which, once typed, displays this:

```
ACCOUNT
Do you wish to see your current ACCOUNT settings?
YES or NO:
```

Typing **Y** will display this:

```
TERMinal type:    VIDEO
LINE length:      8Ø
PAGE depth:       24
TIME zone:        EST
CR padding:       Ø
LF padding:       Ø

ACCOUNT setting you wish to change:
```

These are the settings that all MCI subscribers are first given. Any of them may be changed by typing at least the first two letters of any setting; for instance, TE for TERMinal and LI for LINE length. Making a change will look like this:

```
TERMinal type:    VIDEO
LINE length:      8Ø
PAGE depth:       24
TIME zone:        EST
CR padding:       Ø
LF padding:       Ø

ACCOUNT setting you wish to change: LI
Please enter the line length: 4Ø

LINE length: 4Ø
ACCOUNT setting you wish to change: [RETURN]
```

Are settings PERManent or TEMPorary: **P**
New ACCOUNT settings are now in effect.

Press <RETURN> to continue

You may change any setting at any time. Selecting "Permanent" simply means that the system will remember the new setting when you sign off and will automatically give you that setting the next time you log on. Selecting "Temporary" means that the system will forget the setting once you sign off.

Here is a description of each setting:

- TERMinal may be either Video or Paper. Typing Video will pause the display after a screen has been filled, requiring you to press Return to continue the display. Typing Paper will give you a nonstop display (which may be paused manually with Control-S and resumed with Control-Q).
- LINE length means the number of characters in a single line. You can type a number between 39 and 132.
- PAGE depth means the number of lines that can fit on your screen. you can type a number between 16 and 100.
- TIME zone will place the local time of messages you send and receive. All messages that you send and receive will be stamped with the time according to the U.S. eastern time zone. If you'd rather have your local time, you may change this setting. Many different local time zone settings are available, reflecting both MCI Mail's international access and standard and daylight savings times. You may type any of these three-letter time zone codes: AST, AHS, AHD, BST, CDT, CST, EST, EDT, GMT, MST, MDT, PST, PDT, YST, and YDT.
- CR padding is usually called "nulls," which are blank characters that are sent after a Carriage Return signal is sent. It's doubtful that you'll need to change this setting. If you ever need to, you can type a number between 1 and 7.
- LF padding is another way of receiving nulls, except they'll be sent after a Line Feed signal is transmitted. MCI Mail offers two ways of getting nulls in order to accommodate a variety of terminals. Again, it's doubtful that you'll ever need to change this setting. Still, in case you ever need to, you may type a number between 1 and 7.

Once your terminal settings have been completed, you'll return to the main menu, as shown here:

```
You may enter:

SCAN            for a summary of your mail
READ            to READ messages or LISTS
PRINT           to display messages nonstop
CREATE          to write an MCI Letter
CREATE LIST     to make a distribution list
DOWJONES        to Dow Jones News/Retrieval
ACCOUNT         to adjust terminal display
HELP            for assistance

Command (or MENU or EXIT):
```

MCI Mail is filled with online help files that can help you use even the most arcane aspects of the system. Since MCI Mail doesn't have a per-minute connect-time charge (except for WATS line access), you should take the time to read these files and print out the ones you think you'll need. This is particularly important if you get a subscription to the Advanced Service, since more options are available and direct commands—not menus —are used. For your convenience, the index of MCI Mail help files are reprinted at the end of this chapter.

Of the items on the main menu, I won't be showing you the DOWJONES command. This is a gateway to the Dow Jones News/Retrieval Service, which has already been illustrated in Chapter 9 (Using Dow Jones News/Retrieval Service).

Let's start using MCI Mail by creating a message. Type **CR** at the main menu to get this prompt:

```
Command (or MENU or EXIT):  CR
TO:
```

At the TO: prompt, you may enter an MCI Mail electronic address for Instant Mail or the name of an individual or company. Typing an MCI Mail electronic address is the fastest way to address an Instant Mail letter. If you don't have the recipient's MCI Mail electronic address at hand, you can type the recipient's name or company name and search through the online directory. Let's look at all of these methods.

First, we'll look at typing an MCI Mail electronic address. The address in this illustration is fictitious, so don't use it:

```
TO:       713-3408
      713-3408     Mike Mercury     MCIC     Supercar Lab     Black Rock NV
TO:
```

Once you've typed an MCI Mail electronic address, the system will display the address and the recipient's name and location. This allows you to confirm that you've typed the address correctly. After that, the TO: prompt will appear again to allow you to type another address. This is useful if you want to send the same message to more than one person.

If you only want to sent an Instant Letter to the first person, press **Return** to get the next prompt:

```
TO:     [RETURN]
CC:
```

The CC: prompt means Carbon Copy. You can send a copy of the letter as a "carbon," instead of as an original. A carbon copy will let the copy's recipient know who else received the Instant Mail letter. If you don't want to use this feature, press **Return** to type the letter's subject, which we'll do in a moment.

Now, let's look at the alternate way of addressing MCI Mail, still using Mike Mercury as the recipient. This is done by typing any one of the following items; a corresponding example for each is shown in parentheses:

- The person's last name (MERCURY)
- The person's first initial and last name (M MERCURY)
- The person's name and company (MERCURY/ORG: SUPERCAR)
- The person's name and location (MERCURY/BLACK ROCK)
- The person's MCI Mail user name (MMERCURY)

In our example, I'll use last name only:

```
TO:    MERCURY

There is more than one:

No. MCI ID            Name                        Organization Location
   Ø NOT LISTED BELOW. DELETE.
   1 NOT LISTED BELOW. ENTER AN ADDRESS.
   2 397-8156       Carl Mercury                          Salinas, CA
   3 635-182Ø       Dale B. Mercury                      Bellevue, WA
   4 378-5356       Deb Mercury                            Fresno, CA
   5 793-1828       Frank R. Mercury                        Aurora, IL
   6 936-6349       H M Mercury            Midland Trust Memphis, TN
   7 713-34Ø8       Mike Mercury         Supercar Lab  Black Rock, NV

Please enter the number:
```

To select the correct Mercury, type the number to the left of it. If the name you're looking for isn't on the list, try another spelling by typing **0**. Number 7 is the one we're looking for. Once **7** has been typed, the TO: prompt will reappear for another addressee. When that's skipped by pressing **Return**, the CC: prompt will appear. After that's been skipped by pressing **Return**, we'll be able to type the message's subject, like this:

CC: **[RETURN]**

Subject: **Vacation**
Text: (Enter text or transmit file. Type / on a line by itself to end.)

As the prompt explains, you can now start uploading a message into the system or start typing while online. At the end of the message, type a /(slash) on a line by itself. The whole process will look like this:

Mike:

We're looking forward to you, Dr. Beeker, Prof. Popkiss, Jimmy, and Mitch arriving tomorrow.

Steve and Venus, Troy and Marina, and Scarlet and Destny have just arrived. The Tracy's will be in day after tomorrow. Tiger, Mary, Kate and Hawkeye will be coming, too. Kate has also promised to sing.

John Tracy and Hiro won't be coming, though. John's stuck in TB5 on duty and Hiro is on call in Spacehawk.

Straker won't be coming, either. Something about a SID malfunction. Alas.

Otherwise, All Systems Are Go!

FAB and Ten-Ten,

Mike Cane

After your message is complete, this menu will appear:

```
You may enter:

READ          to review your letter
READ PAPER    to review your letter for paper
EDIT          to correct your letter
SEND          Postal delivery for paper; instant electronic delivery
SEND ONITE    OVERNIGHT courier for paper; PRIORITY electronic delivery
SEND 4HOUR    FOUR-HOUR courier for paper; PRIORITY electronic delivery
HELP          for assistance

Command (or MENU or EXIT):
```

If your letter has some typos you'd like to correct or if you'd like to add some text, type **ED**, for EDIT. Let's look at how editing works:

```
Command (or MENU or EXIT): ED

You may enter:

ENVELOPE    to EDIT TO, CC, or SUBJECT
TEXT        to EDIT the TEXT
PAPER       to prepare paper mail
LEAVE       when you've finished editing
HELP        for assistance

Command (or MENU or EXIT):
```

These selections are self-explanatory. The editing process is very similar, though not identical, to the one used in CIS's EasyPlex message system (see Chapter 7, Using the CompuServe Information Service). You shouldn't have any problems editing a letter, so my illustration will be brief. Let's type **TE** to edit the letter's text:

```
Command (or MENU or EXIT): TE

You may enter:
    READ, ADD, DELETE, CHANGE,
    FORMAT, CANCEL, or STOP

Your Edit command:
```

These choices are self-explanatory. Let's type **RE** to READ the letter, so the system will provide line numbers:

Your Edit command: **RE**

1 Mike:
2
3 We're looking forward to you, Dr.
4 Beeker, Prof. Popkiss, Jimmy, and
5 Mitch arriving tomorrow.
6
7 Steve and Venus, Troy and Marina, and
8 Scarlet and Destny have just arrived.
9 The Tracy's will be in day after
1Ø tomorrow. Tiger, Mary, Kate and
11 Hawkeye will be coming, too. Kate has
12 also promised to sing.
13
14 John Tracy and Hiro won't be coming,
15 though. John's stuck in TB5 on duty
16 and Hiro is on call in Spacehawk.
17
18 Straker won't be coming, either.
19 Something about a SID malfunction.
2Ø Alas.
21
22 Otherwise, All Systems Are Go!
23
24 FAB and Ten-Ten,
25
26 Mike Cane

Press <RETURN> to continue

Your Edit command: **[RETURN]**

You may enter:
READ, ADD, DELETE, CHANGE,
FORMAT, CANCEL or STOP

Your Edit command:

Let's correct line 8, on which "Destny" should be "Destiny." To make a correction, type **CH**, for CHANGE, and the line number, like this:

Your Edit command: **CH 8**

Old text: **Destny**
New text: **Destiny**

```
     8       Scarlet and Destiny have just arrived.
1 change
Your Edit command:
```

Once you've finished, type **ST**, for STOP:

```
Your Edit command: ST
You may enter:

ENVELOPE     to EDIT TO, CC, or SUBJECT
TEXT         to EDIT the TEXT
PAPER        to prepare paper mail
LEAVE        when you've finished editing
HELP         for assistance

Command (or MENU or EXIT):
```

Notice that there isn't a command you can use to send the edited, finished, message immediately. You have to go back another menu for that. Is this bad software design? No, it's very shrewd software design; you'll learn why at the end of this chapter.

At this menu, type **LE**, for LEAVE, to get to the message sending menu:

```
Command (or MENU or EXIT): LE

You may enter:

READ           to review your letter
READ PAPER     to review your letter for paper
EDIT           to correct your letter
SEND           Postal delivery for paper; instant electronic delivery
SEND ONITE     OVERNIGHT courier for paper; PRIORITY electronic delivery
SEND 4HOUR     FOUR-HOUR courier for paper; PRIORITY electronic delivery
HELP           for assistance

Command (or MENU or EXIT):
```

These selections are self-explanatory. Let's type **SE**, for SEND:

```
Command (or MENU or EXIT): SE

One moment please; your message is being posted.

Your message was posted: Fri Dec 7, 1985 12:54 pm EST.
There is a copy in your OUTBOX.

Press <RETURN> to continue
```

That's how an MCI Mail Instant Letter is created and sent to any other MCI Mail subscriber.

One thing that I advise you *always* to do when you're sending an MCI Mail Instant Letter is to use the option for getting a receipt. This will let you know when (and especially if) the message has been read. To get a receipt, type **(RECEIPT)** after the recipient's name, as these examples illustrate.

- 713-3408 (RECEIPT)
- MIKE MERCURY (RECEIPT)
- MMERCURY (RECEIPT)
- MERCURY/ORG: SUPERCAR (RECEIPT)
- MERCURY/BLACK ROCK (RECEIPT)
- M MERCURY (RECEIPT)

The importance of this option should not be overlooked. It tells you

- That your mail is not being lost (it can happen on any online system, and usually does)
- That your letter, although not answered, *was* at least read
- How diligent or negligent the recipient is in checking his or her mailbox

If I had to sum up one rule for using MCI Mail (and, indeed, *any* electronic mail service), it would be this: *always use the receipt option.*

Sending printed mail or a Telex to someone who isn't an MCI Mail subscriber is equally easy. Each message is typed (or uploaded), edited, and sent in the same manner as the illustration just shown. Each type of message is different in the way it's addressed. Let's look at each of these processes briefly.

Once you've started the CREATE process and get the TO: prompt, you can address a message that'll be printed on paper and sent via the U.S. Postal Service in these ways:

- By typing (PAPER) after the recipient's name, if the recipient is not an MCI Mail subscriber
- By typing (ADDRESS) after the recipient's name, if the recipient is an MCI Mail subscriber
- By waiting for MCI Mail to prompt you for an address, when the recipient is not in the MCI Mail online directory (in other words, when the recipient is not an MCI Mail subscriber)
- By typing (PRINT) after the recipient's name, if the recipient is an

MCI Mail subscriber (the printed letter will be sent to the subscriber's address that MCI Mail has on file)

In each of these methods, the address cannot be longer than 44 characters per line.

Let's look at the first method:

```
TO:               MIKE CANE (PAPER)
Enter country of recipient. Press RETURN if USA.

Country:          [RETURN]
Destination is USA.


Title/Company:    THE COMPUTER PHONE BOOK
Address Line 1:   175 FIFTH AVE
Address Line 2:   STE 3371
City:             NY
State:            NY
Zip Code:         10010

TO:               MIKE CANE (PAPER)
                  THE COMPUTER PHONE BOOK
                  175 FIFTH AVE
                  STE 3371
                  NY
                  NY
                  10010

Is this address correct (Yes or No)? Y
```

In the above illustration, you can skip an Address Line if you don't need it by pressing Return. Once you're through with the address, the message writing, editing, and sending process is the same as the previous illustration.

The second method looks like this:

```
TO:              MIKE CANE (ADDRESS)
                 (Please enter address)
                 THE COMPUTER PHONE BOOK
                 175 FIFTH AVE STE 3371
                 NY NY 10010
                 [RETURN]
TO:
```

You have five lines for an address, any of which can be passed by pressing Return. The rest of the process is identical to the original illustration.

The last process looks like this.

```
TO:        TIGER NINESTEIN
           (TIGER NINESTEIN not found. Enter a postal address or TLX: (telex
           address) type HELP, or press RETURN to delete.)
           HAWKNEST
           175 FIFTH AVE, STE 3371
           NY NY 10010
           [RETURN]
TO:
```

Here, too, you have up to five lines for an address, and any line may be skipped by pressing Return.

There are two ways to send a Telex via MCI Mail. They are

- By typing (TELEX) after the recipient's name
- By typing TLX: and the Telex number, when being prompted for it

Let's look at each of these.

```
TO:          MIKE CANE (TELEX)
Enter country name or country code of recipient. Press RETURN if continental
United States.

Country: [RETURN]

Please select appropriate destination:

No. CODE        COUNTRY NAME
  0             NOT LISTED BELOW. DELETE.
  1 -           MCI/WUI (OR OTHER IRC TELEX NETWORK)
  2 0           WESTERN UNION TELEX I NETWORK
  3 5           WESTERN UNION TELEX II (TWX) NETWORK

Please enter the number:
```

At this point, you'll need to know which carrier your Telex recipient is on and type the appropriate menu number, like so:

```
Please enter the number: 1
Destination is MCI/WUI (OR OTHER IRC TELEX NETWORK).
```

```
Telex No:      8000000
Answerback:    90000 CPBBOOK

TO:         MIKE CANE (TELEX)
            TLX: 8000000 90000 CPBBOOK

Is this address correct (Yes or No)?
```

You're prompted for the Telex number and the Answerback code separately, so you shouldn't type them on the same line. The system will then redisplay the address for you to confirm it. The remainder of this process is like sending MCI Mail. *Note*: Telex messages can only be 68 characters wide, so keep that in mind when you prepare your message.

The alternate way of sending a domestic Telex via MCI Mail looks like this:

```
TO:         GERRY ANDERSON
            (GERRY ANDERSON not found. Enter a postal address or TLX: (telex
            address), type HELP, or press RETURN to delete.)
            TLX:80000000 ANDERBURR
```

Once you've been prompted to enter a Telex number, type **TLX**: and the number without leaving a space between TLX: and the Telex number. You may also include the Answerback code, leaving a space between the code and the Telex number. With this method, if you're sending a Telex to a Telex-I terminal, you must prefix the Telex number with a 0 (zero). If you're sending it to a Telex-II (TWX) terminal, you must prefix the Telex number with a 5. Thus, the Telex number in the above illustration would look like this:

- To a Telex-I terminal
  TLX:080000000 ANDERBURR
- To a Telex-II (TWX) terminal
  TLX:580000000 ANDERBURR

Sending an international Telex is similar to both of these methods, only one of which I'll illustrate here.

```
TO:         ED STRAKER (TELEX)
Enter the country name or country code of recipient. Press RETURN if
continental
United States.


Country:    ENGLAND
Destination is GREAT BRITAIN AND NORTHERN IRELAND (UK) (851).
```

Telex No: 851-

The system automatically types the proper country destination code. All that you have to do is to type the Telex number, without leaving a space between the hyphen and the number, like this:

```
Telex No:      851-80000
Answerback:    HSTUDIOS
```

```
TO:     ED STRAKER (TELEX)
TLX:    85180000 HSTUDIOS
```

Is this address correct (Yes or No)?

When you send a Telex—domestic or international—your own Answerback Code is automatically printed on the Telex by MCI Mail so there's no need for you to include it yourself. You'll also receive a receipt in your MCI Mailbox when the Telex has arrived at the recipient's terminal. Whenever possible, though, try to use the recipient's Telex Answerback code. The receipt will let you know that your Telex was delivered to *a* terminal, but the Answerback ensures you that your Telex was delivered to the *correct* terminal.

Now let's look at how to handle mail that you've received. Whether a message is an MCI Mail Instant Letter or a Telex it is handled the same way. When you've been notified at signon of waiting mail, you might want to scan the messages first, like this:

```
You may enter:

SCAN           for a summary of your mail
READ           to READ messages or LISTS
PRINT          to display messages nonstop
CREATE         to write an MCI Letter
CREATE LIST    to make a distribution list
DOWJONES       to Dow Jones News/Retrieval
ACCOUNT        to adjust terminal display
HELP           for assistance

Command (or MENU or EXIT): SC

You may enter:
INBOX      to SCAN your unread messages
OUTBOX     to SCAN messages you sent
DESK       to SCAN messages read before
```

DRAFT	to SCAN your DRAFT message
ALL	to SCAN ALL your messages
LIST	to SCAN your LISTs
HELP	for assistance

Command (or MENU or EXIT):

Let me briefly explain these menu selections:

- INBOX: This is your mailbox. It's where all Instant Letters and Telexes arrive for storage until you sign on to read them.
- OUTBOX: This is a temporary holding area for copies of all mail (electronic print, and Telex) that you send. A copy of a message will be held here for 24 hours and then automatically deleted.
- DESK: This is a temporary holding area for messages that you've already read. In other words, when you read a waiting message in your INBOX, it's then taken out of the INBOX and placed on your DESK. After 24 hours, the DESK copy is automatically deleted.
- DRAFT: This is a message that hasn't been sent out yet. It'll stay on the system for 24 hours and then will be automatically deleted.

Let's look at scanning a message in the INBOX:

Command (or MENU or EXIT): **IN**

1 message in INBOX

No. Posted	From	Subject	Size
1 Dec 7 14:51	Mike Mercury	On Our Way	277

Press <RETURN> to continue **[RETURN]**

You may enter:

READ	to READ the scanned messages
PRINT	to display messages nonstop
SCAN	to SCAN for other messages
HELP	for assistance

Command (or MENU or EXIT):

I won't illustrate the READ process, since it's not a difficult function. Once you've read a message, you'll be presented with this menu, which is also quite elementary:

```
You may enter:

READ          to READ this message again
ANS           to ANSWER the message sender
ANS EACH      to ANSWER the message sender and each recipient
NEXT          to go on to the NEXT message
HELP          for assistance

Command (or MENU or EXIT):
```

There are other aspects of MCI Mail that I won't illustrate here, such as the online advertisements, how to create a mailing list, and toll-free boxes. As you've seen in this chapter, MCI Mail is simple to use. If you think you'll still need help with some aspects of the system, read one of the numerous help files that are in the index at the end of this chapter.

Now that you've seen how MCI Mail's Basic Service operates and how many menus you'll have to go through, you might want to opt for the Advanced service. Remember, though, that costs $18 per mailbox plus $10 a month. That would be a total of $138 a year. I've heard some people complain about this fact, and I can't let it go by any longer without a comment.

For one, MCI Mail is the *only* nationwide electronic mail service that does *not* charge for reading mail. Can you imagine how far the postal system would've gotten if you had to pay to send a letter and your friend had to pay to read it when he or she got it? Can you imagine how long you'd keep your telephone service if you had to pay when someone called you? You already know the answers to these questions, but I doubt you've ever heard the questions themselves. It has always been—and always will be—a sore point with me that the message/mail services on other online systems (some of which are in this book) require both the sender and receiver to pay when a message is transmitted.

Second, MCI Mail isn't forcing anyone to pay for Advanced service. Nothing is *that* important that you can't afford to spend 2–3 minutes (if even that!) going through menus—especially when you're not being charged for having to do it. If something *is* that important, I can only say there's something that's faster—and will always be faster—than MCI Mail (and any electronic mail system). It's called the telephone. No menus there.

If anything, MCI Mail should be appreciated for keeping intact its Basic service, for not charging you to read mail, for not charging you just for the ability to see if you have mail, and for providing on one system—at a relatively low cost—more than just a terminal-to-terminal message system.

Now here comes the kicker. Remember that earlier in this chapter I pointed out the menu that you see when you're through editing a letter? Remember that I pointed out that it'd be nice if it had a send command on it so you could immediately send the edited letter? Well, it could very well be that it's omitted on purpose. Having to go through two menus before you can send your edited letter is such an irritating thing, that I can't shake this idea that it was designed that way—as a way of making you want to get the Advanced service. Very shrewd.

You've now seen two systems that are solely dedicated to electronic mail and Telexes: EasyLink and MCI Mail. Both have the vast Telex network that's already in place, allowing messages to be passed between EasyLink and MCI Mail subscribers through that common network. With EasyLink going after the business market and MCI Mail seeming content to pursue the mass market, the U.S. electronic mail market seems to have all the players that it needs right now.

* * *

Additional Information

CONTACT:

MCI Communications Corp, 1133 19th St NW, Washington, DC, 20036; 1-(800)624-6245

HELP FILES

On-line assistance is available at almost any point by typing HELP. In addition, the following information is available at Main Menu level.

HELP ACCOUNT	Set your MCI Mailbox to fit your terminal
HELP ADDRESS	Envelope-address options
HELP ADS	Shop the online ADS
HELP ADS INDEX	See a list of advertisers
HELP ADVANCED	Benefits of Advanced Service
HELP ANSWER	Reply to a message
HELP CHARGE	Use billing codes for your messages

HELP CONTROL	Lists control keys and their functions
HELP CREATE	Originate a message
HELP DOWJONES	How to use this information supplier
HELP EDIT	Editing options
HELP EXIT	Leave MCI Mail
HELP FORMAT	Adjust lines of text when editing
HELP 4HOUR	Details of 4-hour courier posting
HELP GIFTS	Count points toward valuable gifts
HELP GRAPHICS	Use of letterhead and signature
HELP HANDLING	Special handling options
HELP HOLIDAY	Free graphic for Advanced Service users
HELP INDEX	List of MCI Mail HELPs
HELP MCI LETTER	For discount pricing schedule
HELP NEWS	MCI Mail's weekly online newsletter
HELP NEXT	Using the NEXT command
HELP OLD NEWS	Last two issues of online newsletter
HELP ONITE	Details of overnight courier posting
HELP PAPER	Details on posting laser-printed mail
HELP PARAMETER	Settings for your device
HELP PC	Use your personal computer with MCI Mail
HELP PHONES	List of local access phone numbers
HELP POST	If your message can not be posted
HELP PRINT	Explains how to use the PRINT command
HELP READ	Explains the READ command
HELP READ PAPER	See how your letter will look when laser printed
HELP RECEIPT	How to receive notification of delivery
HELP REFERRAL	To enroll your business associates on MCI Mail
HELP REQUEST	Receive additional MCI Mail information
HELP SALES	Phones and addresses of MCI Mail sales offices
HELP SCAN	Get a summary of your mail

HELP SEND	Tells how to SEND a message
HELP TELEX	Tells how to use Telex Dispatch
HELP TEXT	Explains how to write text
HELP TOLLFREEBOX	To set up a toll-free (recipient pays) in box
HELP [STATE]	Type HELP and state name for deliverable zip codes; *Note*: NEWYORK, NEWMEXICO, NEWJERSEY are one word; other unique spellings are: NCAROLINA, NDAKOTA, SCAROLINA, SDAKOTA, WVIRGINIA
HELP VOLUME	Information about high-volume mailings

13 Using NewsNet

Control characters used on this system: Control-H, backspace; Control-P, system interrupt; Control-Q (XON), resume display; Control-S (XOFF), pause display; Break, system interrupt.

NewsNet (CPB100500) started operations in 1982, offering electronic editions of printed business newsletters. It currently has over 200 newsletters online, some of which are only available in electronic form via NewsNet.

NewsNet is available through Telenet, Tymnet, Uninet, and direct dial. A subscription costs $24, which may be deducted from the first month's bill. Billing is by invoice to company and individual accounts. There is a $15 a month additional subscription charge, regardless of whether or not the system has been accessed during the month.

NewsNet prime-time hours are from 8 AM to 8 PM, Monday to Friday and non-prime-time hours are from 8 PM to 8 AM, Monday to Friday and all weekend. All times are eastern. Prime-time connect charges are $24 an hour for 300-bps service, $48 an hour for 1200-bps service, $72 an hour for 2400-bps service, and $96 for 4800-bps service. Non-prime time rates are $18 an hour at 300 bps, $36 an hour at 1200 bps, $54 an hour at 2400 bps, and $72 an hour at 4800 bps. These connect-time rates do *not* include the price of reading any portion of the contents of any online newsletter, since each publisher sets its own connect-time rate. Publisher rates are set to two scales: nonsubscriber and subscriber. Subscribers to the print edition of a newsletter that's being read online are charged a lower connect-time rate than nonsubscribers who read the same newsletter online. For example, a subscriber may be charged $24 an hour, whereas a nonsubscriber may be charged $48 an hour.

NewsNet also has additional charges for special services such as the Official Airline Guides Electronic Edition (a database of airline flights and rates) and B.R.A.I.N. (a research organization).

Signing onto NewsNet looks like this:

```
NET9Ø8Ø (user 37) logged in Saturday, Ø6 Oct 85 ØØ:1Ø:28.
Last login Tuesday, 25 Sep 85 17:35:56.

***************
* NEWSNET * for the Business Information Edge
***************


Copyright NewsNet 1985. Copying prohibited without prior
written permission. For details, refer to 'Terms and
Conditions of NewsNet Use' and the NewsNet Pocket Guide.

At any time, touch <RETURN> for assistance,
or type HELP for detailed instructions.

Enter command or <RETURN>
—>
```

There may also be a bulletin about new services and newsletters that've been added to the system. Plus, if you've used the electronic mail feature to contact NewsNet or a publisher (this capability is covered later in this chapter), you'll be told if a reply is waiting for you.

Pressing **RETURN** at the above prompt will bring up the NewsNet main menu, which looks like this:

```
Enter command or <RETURN>
—> [RETURN]

*** COMMAND MENU ***

READ.....Read full text               FLASH...Update NewsFlash profile
SCAN.....Scan headlines               OAG......Official Airline Guides
SEARCH..Search for keywords           MAIL.....To publishers or NewsNet
HELP.....Detailed instruction         ORDER....Print subscriptions
PAGING..Display one page at a time

LIBRARY..Low-cost browsing            PASSWORD.Change your password
BACK.....Return to previous prompt    PRICES..Complete price list
QUIT.....Return to main prompt        INFO.....Information on services
OFF......Sign off                     LIST.....Services by subject category

Enter command or <RETURN>
—>
```

Most of these selections are self-explanatory; they will be illustrated in the course of this chapter.

What you will do on NewsNet when you sign on for the first time will depend on your individual needs. You might want to jump right in and start reading the full text of newsletters or just scan their headlines. The best way to make use of NewsNet, though, is by using its keyword search capabilities.

NewsNet's keyword search is similar to the keyword searching you've seen illustrated in the chapters about search services (Chapter 4, Using BRS After Dark; Chapter 9, Using Dow Jones News/Retrieval Service; and Chapter 11, Using Knowledge Index). Although it's similar, it's *not* identical. NewsNet is *not* a search service, despite what anyone may tell you. First, you cannot refer back to a prior search statement during a search. This is a feature search services have. (See Chapter 4, "Using BRS After Dark" and Chapter 11, "Using Knowledge Index.") NewsNet does not have this capability. Second, there are only two search terms that may be used on NewsNet: AND and OR. NOT isn't available. Also not available is the ability to construct complex search statements, such as

(MICRO OR PERSONAL) AND COMPUTER AND (HARD OR FLOPPY) DISK

NewsNet's keyword search capability is just a bit more advanced than the Search feature that's available on word processors (or word processing software). Let's go through an actual search that was conducted on NewsNet to see how this is so.

First, you must know something about how the NewsNet system is designed. Newsletters are categorized by the industries they cover. First each industry is given a two-letter code. Each newsletter within that industry has the two-letter industry code plus a two-number code. The complete list of NewsNet industry codes is given at the end of this chapter. For the purpose of the illustrations you'll be seeing, you need to know these industry codes:

- EC—Electronics and Computers
- EL—Entertainment and Leisure
- PB—Publishing and Broadcasting
- TE—Telecommunications

Following these industry codes, a newsletter in the EC category would be coded as for instance EC01. A newsletter in the EL category would be EL01, and so on.

When you conduct a search on NewsNet, you start by typing **SEARCH** and one of three things:

- ALL, to search all of the newsletters on the system
- Up to three industry codes
- Up to three newsletter codes

The command variations would look like this:

- SEARCH ALL
- SEARCH EC PB TE
- SEARCH EC27 PB21 E31

In this search, I used three industry codes:

```
At any time, touch <RETURN> for assistance,
or type HELP for detailed instructions.

Enter command or <RETURN>
—> SEARCH EL TE EC
Enter LATEST for the latest issue, or other date options
```

This last line is the next prompt in the Search process. Note that this comes after you've specified the portion of the system you're conducting the search in. Here, you may enter a date in any of the following ways:

- 1/1/86, for just the issue or issues dated January 1, 1986 (or any other month, day, year)
- 1/1/86-3/15/86, for just the issues published between January 1, 1986, and March 15, 1986 (or any other month, day, year)
- 1/1/86-, for just the issues published after January 1, 1986 (or any other month, day, year)
- -1/1/86, for just the issues published before January 1, 1986 (or any other month, day, year)
- LATEST, for the latest issue(s)
- EARLIEST, for the earliest (oldest) issue(s)
- ALL, for all of the issues.

In this illustration, I'll be searching for instances of "Computer Phone Book," to see if the previous edition of this book was mentioned in any of the newsletters in the system. When you know what you're looking for, you can disqualify a great deal of the newsletters on the basis of time. For instance, the previous edition of this book did not exist before September 1983, so any newsletter published before then would not have written about it. Only newsletters published after that date qualify for searching. By narrowing the criteria in this manner, you'll be able to reduce your connect-time and perform more efficient searches.

```
Enter LATEST for the latest issue, or other date options
—>9/1/83-

Enter Keyword(s)
```

This is the final prompt, at which point you type your keywords. You can use * (an asterisk) as a wildcard in a keyword. (You've already seen wildcards illustrated in Chapters 4, 9, and 11.) When you type more than one keyword, NewsNet suggests that the most general term should be first in the list. This belies another flaw in the system, one that is very serious: It doesn't matter what order your search terms are in, because the system searches for the *occurrences of the individual words not for the words as a phrase*. I'll expand on this point later, after the results of this search.

When you type your keywords, you can use AND or OR as search qualifiers. If you type more than two keywords without AND connecting them, NewsNet assumes that AND is present. The ramifications of this design will become evident as we progress.

```
Enter Keyword(s)
—>COMPUTER AND PHONE AND BOOK
!...!.!..!..........!..........!.!..!.......!!!.!!
...!!!.!....!!.!!...!!..........

 43 Occurrences

Enter HEAD for headlines, TEXT for full text, ANALYZE for occurrences in each
service, BACK for new keyword(s)
—>
```

After the keywords have been entered, NewsNet searches through the qualifying newsletters. Each ! (exclamation point) represents one or more occurrences of the keywords within a particular newsletter title. Each . (period) represents a particular newsletter title that has been searched. This "visual feedback" is a very nice feature and lets you know that the system is acting upon your request. After the search has been completed, you're told how many occurrences of your keywords have been found. Then you're given a prompt that tells you the various ways in which you can access the retrieved information. At this point, you may be tempted either to read the retrieved headlines or jump right in and read the full text of the articles. Both of these options are costly. Although reading headlines does not incur any charge past NewsNet's basic connect-time rates ($24 and $18 an hour), the display of the headlines takes time, especially when there are more than 10. If you jump right into reading the full text of the retrieved articles, you start incurring the additional connect-time charges for each newsletter, which varies from newsletter to newsletter. This rate can be anywhere from $24 to $120 an hour.

Your best bet with *any* NewsNet search is first to take the time to analyze the results by using the ANALYZE command. It looks like this, which is the actual result that was obtained from the search in our illustration:

```
—> ANALYZE
    *** NEWSNET SEARCH ANALYSIS SAT, Ø6 OCT 1985 ØØ:18:1Ø ***
    ==================================

    KEYWORDS              CATEGORIES           DATE RANGE
    *****************     *****************    ******************
    COMPUTER              EL TE EC             9/1/83-
    PHONE
    BOOK

CODE                 NEWSLETTER NAME              OCCURRENCES
===                  ===========                  =========

    ELØ1   VIDEO WEEK                                       2

    LØ9    HOLLYWOOD HOTLINE                                3

    PB11   TRAVELWRITER MARKETLETTER                        3

    TEØ1   COMMUNICATIONS DAILY                             2

    TE2Ø   ON-LINE COMPUTER TELEPHONE DIRECTORY             1

    TE42   TELEPHONE ANGLES                                 2

    ECØ3   PERSONAL COMPUTERS TODAY                         1

    PBØ7   ONLINE DATABASE REPORT                           1

    SSØ4   RFC NEWS SERVICE                                 1

    PB99   NEWSNET ACTION LETTER                            5
```

EC1ØE	THE COMPUTER COOKBOOK	1
EC28	JAPAN HIGH TECH REVIEW	1
EC32	DATA BASE INFORMER	2
PBØ1	TELEVISION DIGEST	1
PBØ5	THE SEYBOLD REPORT ON PUBLISHING SYSTEMS	2
PB15	IIA FRIDAY MEMO	1
EC27	COMPUTER BOOK REVIEW	2
ECØ9	MINI/MICRO BULLETIN	1
EC11	MICRO MOONLIGHTER	4
EC2Ø	SEYBOLD REPORT ON PROFESSIONAL COMPUTING	1
EC22	THE BUSINESS COMPUTER	4
MTØ3	OFFICE AUTOMATION UPDATE	1
OFØ3	THE SEYBOLD REPORT ON OFFICE SYSTEMS	1
TOTAL	OCCURRENCES	43

Enter HEAD for headlines, TEXT for full text, ANALYZE for
occurrences in each
service, BACK for new keyword(s)
—>

That's quite an impressive lineup of publications that mentioned my book, I thought.

Let's go further into this search by looking at the headlines of these retrieved articles:

Enter HEAD for headlines, TEXT for full text, ANALYZE for
occurrences in each
service, BACK for new keyword(s)
—> **HEAD**

1) 9/12/83 ELØ1 VIDEO WEEK
COLECO PLANS COMPUTER VIDEO, AT&T SOFTWARE

2) 11/21/83 ELØ1 VIDEO WEEK
Computer software market turmoil isn't stopping companie

3) 3/ 5/84 ELØ9 HOLLYWOOD HOTLINE
Soap Opera Summaries-Ø3/Ø2/84

4) 3/16/84 ELØ9 HOLLYWOOD HOTLINE
Soap Opera Summaries-Ø3/15/84

5) 8/31/84 ELØ9 HOLLYWOOD HOTLINE
Entertainment News-Ø8/31/84

6) 4/ 1/84 PB11 TRAVELWRITER MARKETLETTER
MARKETWATCH -- A-E

7) 5/ 1/84 PB11 TRAVELWRITER MARKETLETTER
MARKETWATCH -- A-F

8) 9/ 1/84 PB11 TRAVELWRITER MARKETLETTER
MARKETWATCH -- N-S

9) 11/25/83 TEØ1 COMMUNICATIONS DAILY
FCC APPROVES DETARIFFING AND TRANSFER OF IN-PLACE EQUIPMENT TO AT&T-IS; REQUIRES SEPARATE BOC SUBSIDIARY FOR COMPETITIVE EQUIPMENT OR SERVICES

10) 12/14/83 TEØ1 COMMUNICATIONS DAILY
OAK & TIMES FIBER IN ADDRESSABILITY JOINT VENTURE

By this point, you may be wondering what a mention of *The Computer Phone Book* would be doing in a summary of soap operas. No doubt you're imagining something along the lines of this:

"General Hospital" (Thursday): Laura leaves Luke for a hacker she found on a BBS from a listing in *The Computer Phone Book*. Luke fashions a letter bomb to send to the author. . . .

Of the 43 occurrences cited by NewsNet, only *2* were about *The Computer Phone Book*. They were headlines number 21 and 31 . . . in a list of 43. What did NewsNet retrieve? Something along the lines of this:

"General Hospital" (Thursday): Laura buys a new **computer** for Luke but couldn't get him the **book** he wanted. The **phone** rang while she was wrapping his present, and a voice from her past revealed itself. . . .

I've highlighted the words NewsNet found. NewsNet did *not* look for the phrase "Computer Phone Book." It looked for the words "computer," "phone," and "book," *regardless of their order or proximity to each other.*

The point is, NewsNet cannot look for *phrases*. It can only look for words. Even when the AND connector is left out, NewsNet operates on the premise that AND is present. In other words, it breaks the phrase into its component parts and searches for occurrences of each component within the text, regardless of the order of the components, their proximity, or the actual context. Plain and simple, as you've just seen illustrated, you run the grave and very real risk of *not* finding what you want—while still incurring connect-time in the process of discovering that what you wanted doesn't exist in the system.

Does this make NewsNet useless? Not entirely. However, it does make NewsNet a very risky proposition for keyword searching. It means that you'll have to think out your search strategy in more ways and with more precision as well as more flexibility. Although that may sound contradictory, it isn't. For instance, while our search for "Computer Phone Book" was, by any sane standards, a miserable failure, using the keywords "Mike Cane" was a great success, only retrieving the pertinent items in the system.

This tremendous flaw in NewsNet could be corrected with the addition of one simple search command: ADJ. ADJ, as you saw in Chapter 9 (Using Dow Jones News/Retrieval Service), means "ADJacent," and instructs the system that the keywords being requested must be next to one another in the precise order in which they were typed.

Although NewsNet would be drastically improved by the addition of this one simple command, putting it into the system is easier said than done. NewsNet is using mainframes that aren't best suited for the type of application NewsNet is offering. (THE SOURCE uses the same brand of mainframes; see Chapter 15, Using THE SOURCE.)

Another flaw of NewsNet you should be aware of is the list of words that cannot be searched. All search services have such a list, and the list varies from system to system. On NewsNet, one of the words on the unsearchable list is "at." This is entirely understandable, and NewsNet is not the only system with this restriction. You may think this is a minor point, but let me add just two letters and capitalize all of them: PC AT. Since "at" cannot be searched for, capital AT is also unsearchable. (NewsNet, like some other search services, does not distinguish between uppercase and lowercase in keywords. This has been common practice for some time in the industry, and NewsNet should not be singled out for the practice.)

This means that you cannot search for occurrences of the IBM PC AT computer unless you do so in a roundabout way. One such way would be to limit your search to issues of newsletters that were published after the introduction of the AT. Another way would be to search for occurrences of PC combined with a word or words that describe a PC AT attribute or exclusive feature or an AT-specific software package. As I mentioned earlier, keyword searching on NewsNet can be very challenging. The more you consider your search terms when you're offline, the better your chances will be in finding the information you need.

Aside from keyword searching, you can choose to scan the headlines of newsletters or to read their full text. Using the SCAN command is similar to using the SEARCH command. You must specify an individual newsletter by its two-letter industry code and specific two-number ID code. Scanning looks like this:

```
Enter command or <RETURN>
—>SCAN TE99
Enter LATEST for the latest issue, or other date options
—>LATEST

Copyright
NATIONAL PHREAKBUSTERS NEWS
            October 1985

+ + + + + +
+  Jailings  +
+ + + + + +
  1) CALIFORNIA BELL TAPPER SENTENCED TO TEN YEARS

  2) NY COURT FINDS GANG OF HACKERS GUILTY UNDER CONSPIRACY LAWS

+ + + + +
+  Busts  +
+ + + + +

  3) "THE LONG CRACKER" SHARES A CELL WITH HIS 'TONTO'

  4) AT&T SECURITY NABS TWO RIFLING TRASH BINS; ESS PLANS FOUND

+ + + + + +
+  Cracks  +
+ + + + + +

  5) UNITEL SWITCHES TO CALL-BACK MODEMS AFTER 'LOCKPICKINGS'

+ + + + + + + +
+  Legislation  +
+ + + + + + + +

  6) CALENDAR OF PENDING DATA CRIME BILLS NATIONWIDE

Enter Item numbers to read, AGAIN, MORE for more issues, BACK,
STOP or HELP
—>
```

At this prompt, you can read any of the corresponding articles by typing the appropriate number. Although there may be a need for a newsletter like the one shown above, you won't find it on NewsNet—at least not as shown here, since this example was created for this illustration.

Using the READ command is easy and I will not illustrate it here.

The last part of NewsNet that you'll see is the NewsFlash service, which automatically retrieves the headlines of new articles according to a set of keywords that you specify. Once you type **FLASH**, setting up a NewsFlash file looks like this:

```
Enter command or <RETURN>
—>FLASH
Enter ADD, ALTER, INQUIRY, NOTICES, QUIT, or <RETURN>
—>
```

To place keywords into the NewsFlash file, type **ADD**:

```
Enter ADD, ALTER, INQUIRY, NOTICES, QUIT, or <RETURN>
—>ADD

Enter service code, ALL, STOP or HELP
—>
```

You can type a business category code or a newsletter code here. It's best to type **ALL** to select all of the newsletters, unless your field of interest is very narrow:

```
Enter service code, ALL, STOP or HELP
—>ALL
Enter exception to service code, DONE or HELP
—>
```

This is the start of the delimiting process. You can either type four business category codes or four newsletter codes for NewsFlash to skip when it searches for your keywords. The process looks like this:

```
Enter exception to service code, DONE or HELP
—>SSØ1
```

The process is terminated like this, when you've finished entering one code at a time:

```
Enter exception to service code, DONE or HELP
—>DONE
Enter keyword(s), keyword phrase(s), or <RETURN> for help
—>
```

The NewsFlash search method is different than the one the SEARCH command uses. In NewsFlash, the search is accomplished literally; that is, as if there were an ADJ (ADJacent) command available. The keywords that you type will be looked for in the exact order in which they are typed. The sole exceptions are uppercase and lowercase (which is not distinguished) and the list of unsearchable words (i.e., PC AT).

Keyword phrases used in NewsFlash must follow these rules:

- Words that are found together must be separated by a space with a + (plus sign) between them.
- The * (asterisk) wildcard may be used but only at the end of a phrase.
- A keyword phrase may be up to 50 characters long, but the entire line may not exceed 70 characters and may not contain more than 7 keywords.
- Only 10 keyword phrases may be contained in a NewsFlash file at any one time.

Let's look at what a keyword phrase is and how it's built. The first one I'll illustrate is simple—a name:

```
Enter keyword(s), keyword phrase(s), or <RETURN> for help
—>MIKE + CANE

Enter CONTINUE to continue, STOP, or HELP
—>CONTINUE
Enter service code, ALL, STOP or HELP
—>ALL
```

The process of elimination starts all over again when a new keyword phrase is entered. Having to repeat this process can be annoying, although it allows you the flexibility of changing your mind with each new phrase.

Once you've done that, you'll get this prompt again:

```
Enter keyword(s), keyword phrase(s), or <RETURN> for help
—>COMPUTER + SOFTWARE + DOWNLOAD*
```

This is an example of the proper use of the * (asterisk) wildcard. If you had typed COMPUTER + SOFT* + DOWNLOAD*, the system would have only looked for articles that had the words "computer soft . . ." and continued until the word "download . . ." was discovered. For instance, the system may have found the sentence "*Computer software* is getting more expensive while more people choose to *download* public domain software." The correct phrase would find a sentence such as "Several firms are offering methods for *computer software downloading* to retailers."

Once you've added the phrases that you need, type **STOP** to go on to the next step in the process.

```
Enter CONTINUE to continue, STOP, or HELP
—>STOP

Enter ADD, ALTER, INQUIRY, NOTICES, QUIT, or <RETURN>
—>
```

To look at the keywords and category/newsletter exclusions you've placed in your file, type **INQUIRY** and you'll see your list:

```
Enter ADD, ALTER, INQUIRY, NOTICES, QUIT, or <RETURN>
—>INQUIRY

YOUR NEWS FLASH KEYWORDS/KEYWORD PHRASES

 # CODE      KEYWORD PHRASE
=====        ===========

 The following keyword sets will become effective at midnight

 1  ALL      MIKE + CANE
   -SSØ1
   -SSØ5
   -SSØ2
   -SSØ3
 2  ALL      COMPUTER + SOFTWARE + DOWNLOAD*
   -SSØ1
   -SSØ2
   -SSØ3
   -SSØ5
 3  ALL      VIDEOCASSETTE + RENT*
   -SSØ1
   -SSØ2
   -SSØ3
   -SSØ5
 4  ALL      APPLE + MAC*
   -SSØ1
   -SSØ2
   -SSØ3
   -SSØ5

Enter ADD, ALTER, INQUIRY, NOTICES, QUIT, or <RETURN>
—>
```

If you've typed less than 10 phrases, you can add others by typing **ADD**. If you change your mind at any point, you can type **ALTER** to change a phrase. When you're through building your NewsFlash file, type **QUIT**.

Now, when you sign onto NewsNet and NewsFlash has retrieved an article for you, you'll see this bulletin:

```
                         NEWSFLASH NOTIFICATION
************************************************************************************
   1 Total Newsflash hits. Use STOP to stop and delete all.
  New Hits = 1        Saved Items =       Ø

TE99     1Ø/1/84     = = COMPUTER + SOFTWARE + DOWNLOAD* = = Headline #1
  HACKERS DISTRIBUTE 'MAD DIALER' VIA DOWNLOADING

Enter Headline numbers or ALL to read, MORE, AGAIN, SAVE, STOP, or HELP
—>
```

When you have more than one headline, each one will have a number. To read the article for a corresponding headline, type the individual number, like so:

```
Enter Headline numbers or ALL to read, MORE, AGAIN, SAVE, STOP, or HELP
—>1

Headline #1

Copyright
NATIONAL PHREAKBUSTERS NEWS
          November 1985

HACKERS DISTRIBUTE 'MAD DIALER' VIA DOWNLOADING

      Across the US, a new flurry of activity has been uncovered in the
covert distribution of various terminal programs that will allow a
microcomputer to randomly dial telephone numbers in search of a modem
carrier signal.
      Distribution is being accomplished via computer software
downloading on hundreds of Bulletin-Board Systems (BBSs) in major
cities and small towns.
```

Once the article is through, you'll get this prompt:

```
Enter Headline numbers or ALL to read, MORE, AGAIN, SAVE, STOP, or HELP
—>
```

Typing **HELP** at this point will give you the full list of options that you may use:

```
Enter Headline numbers or ALL to read, MORE, AGAIN, SAVE, STOP, or HELP
—>HELP

ALL---------Read ALL of the above stories
ALL* -------Read ALL of the above stories plus any/all others,
            deleting each story as it is read
1 3-5-------Read stories #1, and stories #3, #4, and #5
2 1 3-------Read stories #2, #1, and #3, in that order
SAVE------SAVE some or all of the current stories, then
            display more headlines (if any)
HEAD* -----Display all HEADlines, save stories without reading
MORE------Delete current stories, review MORE headlines
STOP-------Delete ALL NewsFlash stories (you should then type
            ALTER to review and revise your current phrases)
AGAIN-----Display the current headlines AGAIN
HELP-------Display this message

Enter Headline numbers or ALL to read, MORE, AGAIN, SAVE, STOP, or HELP
—>
```

Choose whichever option you desire.

Another feature of NewsNet is the ability to contact both NewsNet system staff and newsletter publishers by electronic mail on the system. I won't illustrate the process here, since NewsNet's electronic mail system is very similar to THE SOURCE (see Chapter 15, Using THE SOURCE).

Typing **MAIL NEWSNET** or **MAIL PUBLISHER** will start the process. To send electronic mail to a newsletter publisher, you must have the newsletter's ID code on hand to act as the address when you're prompted for it. Once you're in the enter text mode, typing **.HELP** (period HELP) will list your options. You can abort by typing **.QUIT** (period QUIT) or send it by typing **.SEND** (period SEND).

Another NewsNet feature is the ability to place an order with a newsletter publisher by typing **ORDER** and following the specific prompts from that point. The ORDER process is similar to the electronic mail feature.

NewsNet can be a good addition to any researcher's online toolkit, if used carefully and wisely. Although it doesn't offer the power nor the flexibility of a true search service, it offers something no other online system does—a wealth of industry-specific publications filled with time-sensitive, market-specific information. Too often, online systems are used to dig up facts about the past. NewsNet allows you to keep track of the present and project into the future.

* * *

Additional Information

CONTACT

NewsNet, Inc., Customer Service, 945 Haverford Rd., Bryn Mawr, PA, 19010, 1–(800)345-1301; (215)527-8030 in Pennsylvania.

Industry Categories/Codes and Newsletter Titles/Codes

Advertising and Marketing (AD)

AD01–Media Science Reports

AD02–Source

Aerospace (AE)

AE01–Satellite Week

AE02–Defense Industry Report

AE03–Defense R&D Update

AE04–Space Calendar

AE05–Space Commerce Bulletin

AE06–Japanese Aviation News: Wing

Automotive (AU)

AU01–Electric Vehicle Progress

AU02–Runzheimer on Automotive Alternatives

Building and Construction (BC)

BC06–Surplus Alert

BC07–Engelsman's Construction Cost Indexes

Corporate Communications (CC)

CC01–The Corporate Shareholder

CC02–Sid Cato's Newsletter on Annual Reports

Chemical (CH)

CH1Ø–Hazardous Waste News

CH12–Toxic Materials News

CH13–Sludge Newsletter

Electronics and Computers (EC)

ECØ2–S. Klein NL on Computer Graphics

ECØ3–Personal Computers Today

ECØ6–Communications & Distributed Resources

ECØ8–Computer Market Observer

ECØ9–Mini/Micro Bulletin

EC1Øe–The Computer Cookbook

EC11–Micro Moonlighter

EC13–Unique: Your Independent UNIX/C Advisor

EC14–Interactive Video Technology

EC16–Robotronics Age Newsletter

EC2Ø–Seybold Report on Professional Computing

EC22–The Business Computer

EC24–Electronic Mail News

EC27–Computer Book Review

EC28–Japan High Tech Review

EC31–McGraw-Hill New Business Books/Software

EC32–Data Base Informer

EC35–Semiconductor Industry & Business survey

EC37–Software Review

EC41–Artifical Intelligence Report

EC43–Japan Semiconductor Quarterly

Education (ED)

EDØ1–College Press Service

Entertainment and Leisure (EL)

ELØ1–Video Week
ELØ2–The Gold Sheet
ELØ5–The Fearless Taster
ELØ6–Ken Winslow's Videoplay Report
ELØ9–Hollywood Hotline

Environment (EV)

EVØ1–World Environment Report
EVØ2–Land Use Planning Report
EVØ3–Nuclear Waste News
EV1Ø–Air/Water Pollution Report

Energy (EY)

EYØ1–Daily Petro Futures
EYØ2–Petroleum Information International
EYØ7–Energy Management Online Network
EY1Ø–Energy & Minerals Resources
EY11–Solar Energy Intelligence Report

Farming and Food (FF)

FFØ1T–Agri-markets Data Service
FFØ6–Washington Beverage Insight

Finance and Accounting (FI)

FIØ1–Federal Reserve Week
FIØ2–Washington Credit Letter
FIØ3–Financial Management Advisor
FIØ6–Credit Union Regulator
FIØ7–Banking Regulator
FIØ9T–Fintex All-Day Foreign Exchange Monitor
FI1Ø–American Banker
FI11–EFT Report

FI12–Corporate EFT Report

FI16–Japan's Monthly Finance Review

General Business

GBØ2–International Intertrade Index

GBØ3–Update/The American States

GBØ6–Midwest Technology

Government and Regulatory (GT)

GTØ3–Grants & Contracts Weekly

GTØ3#–Grants & Contracts Alert

GTØ6–PACs & Lobbies

GT1Ø–Access Reports/Freedom of Information

GT12–U.S. Census Report

GT14–Compliance Management Report

GT15–Compliance Alert: Federal Register Digest

GT2Ø–Congressional Activities

Health and Hospitals (HH)

HHØ1–Health Benefit Cost Containment

HHØ2–Diack Newsletter

HHØ5–Prescription Drug Update

Insurance (IN)

INØ2–IMS Weekly Marketeer

International (IT)

ITØ4–The Exporter

ITØ5–Tax Notes International

IT13T–Fintex International Economic Summaries

IT15–Africa News

IT17–United Nations Report

IT18–APS Diplomat

IT21–High Tech

IT22–Japanese Trade & Industry Briefs

IT23–Mid-East Business Digest

IT24–Japan Weekly Monitor

Investment (IV)

IVØ1–Ford Investment Review

IVØ3–Tax Shelter Insider

IVØ5–Daily Industrial Index Analyzer

IVØ6–Biotechnology Investment Opportunities

IVØ7–The Stanger Report

IVØ8–Wall St. Monitor: Weekly Market Digest

IV13–Penny Stock Preview

IV14–Low-Priced Stock Digest

IV17–Insight: Monthly Economic Report

IV18–Fedwatch

IV2Ø–Howard Ruff's Financial Success Report

IV21–Gary North's Remnant Review

IV22–The Wellington Letter Alert

IV22#–The Wellington Alert Bulletin Service

IV23–The Wellington Letter

IV24–Stock Search

IV25–B&S Investment Focus: Applied Technology

IV26–Futures Focus

IV27–APS Review

IV28–Wall Street S.O.S.

IV33–The Wellington Commodity Technician

IV34–Trendvest Ratings

Law (LA)

LAØ4–Industrial Health & Hazards Update

LAØ6–Reports of Interest to Lawyers

Medicine (ME)

MEØ1–Medical Abstracts Newsletter

ME04–Micro MD Newsletter

Metals and Mining (MM)

MM01–Daily Metals Report

Management (MT)

MT01–Entrepreneurial Manager's Newsletter
MT02–Executive Productivity
MT03–Office Automation Update
MT04–Altman & Weil Report to Legal Management
MT10–Healthcare Action Report
MT11–Executive Action Report
MT12–Government Action Report

Office (OF)

OF03–The Seybold Report on Office Systems
OF04–Automated Office Systems

Publishing and Broadcasting (PB)

PB01–Television Digest
PB03–NA Hotline
PB04–Public Broadcasting Report
PB05–The Seybold Report on Publishing Systems
PB07–Online Database Report
PB08–Worldwide Videotex Update
PB09–Viewdata/Videotex Report
PB11–Travelwriter Marketletter
PB12–The Photoletter
PB13–Editors Only
PB15–IIA Friday Memo
PB16–Wiley Book News
PB18–Copyright Management
PB99–NewsNet Action Letter
PB99#–NewsNet's Online Bulletin

Power Generation (PG)

PGØ1–Utility Reporter

Politics (PO)

POØ2–Legislative Intelligence Week

POØ4–Frost & Sullivan's Political Risk Letter

Public Relations (PR)

PRØ1t–PR Newswire

PRØ6–PR Hi-Tech Alert/Video Monitor

Research and Development (RD)

RDØ2–Research Monitor News

RDØ4–Hi Tech patents: Laser Technology

RDØ5–Hi Tech Patents: Fiber Optics Technology

RDØ6–Hi Tech Patents: Data Communications

RDØ7–Hi Tech Patents: Telephony

RDØ8–Techline

RDØ9–Innovator's Digest

RD1Ø–Federal Research Report

RD12–Invention Management

Real Estate (RE)

REØ3–Real Estate Investing Letter

Social Sciences (SS)

SSØ1–Behavior Today

SSØ2–Marriage and Divorce Today

SSØ3–Sexuality Today

SSØ4–RFC News Service

SSØ5–Churchnews International

SSØ6–United Methodist Information

SSØ7–RNS Daily News Reports

Tobacco (TB)

TBØ1–TMA National Bulletin

TBØ3–TMA Executive Summary

TBØ4–TMA State Bulletin

TBØ5–TMA Leaf Bulletin

TBØ6–TMA Issues Monitor

TBØ8–TMA International Tobacco Report

TBØ9–TMA Smoking; Chewing and Snuff

TB1Ø–TMA Cigarettes and Cigars

Telecommunications (TE)

TEØ1–Communications Daily

TEØ2–Cablenews

TEØ3–Satellite News

TEØ4–Telephone News

TEØ7–ISIS New Electronic Media Newswire

TEØ8–Fiber Optics & Communications

TEØ9–Fiber Optics & Communications Weekly News

TE1Ø–LAN

TE12–VideoNews

TE15–DBS News

TE16–Telecommunications Counselor

TE18–Viewtext

TE19–SMR News

TE2Ø–On-Line Computer Telephone Directory

TE21–Cellular Radio News

TE22–Data Channels

TE24–Interconnection

TE25–Mobile Phone News

TE26–Common Carrier Week

TE27–Videotex Products

TE28–Satellite Television Newsletter

TE29–Fiber/Laser News

TE31–NTT Topics

TE41–International Videotex Teletext News

TE42–Telephone Angles

Taxation (TX)

TXØ1–IRS Practice & Procedures

TXØ2–Corporate Acquisitions & Dispositions

TXØ3–Employee Retirement Plans

TX1Ø–CCH Tax Day–A Digest of Federal Taxes

TX12–Tax Notes Today

TX13–CCH State Tax Week (State Tax Review)

TX14–Charitable Giving Techniques

TX15–The Small Business Tax Review

United Press International (UP)

UPØ1–United Press International

UPØ2–United Press International

UPØ3–United Press International

UPØ4–United Press International

UPØ5–United Press International

14 A brief look at PlayNet

PlayNet (CPB100700) started operating in late 1984, providing two-player online color graphic games, several bulletin-boards, real-time online conferencing, electronic mail, and software uploading and downloading. PlayNet is the first of two systems covered in this book that primarily offers games. (See Chapter 16, Using Local Systems, for information on GameMaster.)

PlayNet is unlike most systems in this book in that it requires a special terminal program and a set of floppy disks with special programs on them. All of this is furnished by PlayNet and, at the time this book went to press, was only available for the Commodore-64 computer (although it will probably also run on the new C64-compatible Commodore-128 computer).

PlayNet plans to convert their software to operate on the Apple //e and //c computers. A version for the Commodore Amiga and the Apple Macintosh might also be available sometime late in 1985 or early 1986.

Joining PlayNet costs $49.95, which covers the price of its instruction manual, three floppy disks for the Commodore-64, and 90 minutes of connect-time. PlayNet's manual is easy to understand and is filled with photographs of displays from the system. PlayNet is available via Telenet or direct-dial from 6 PM to 7 AM, on weekdays and 24 hours on weekends and holidays. There is a $8 a month subscription charge. This is offset, though, by the fact that the connect-time charge is an incredibly low $2.75 an hour.

The version of PlayNet discussed in this chapter is for the Commodore-64, although PlayNet will work identically on any computer for which there is PlayNet software. The keys on each computer that are set aside for PlayNet commands will be different.

Briefly, the Commodore-64 (C64) has eight keys on the right side of its keyboard, labeled F1 through F8. Four of these keys are set aside for the execution of PlayNet commands. An overlay is provided by PlayNet to show subscribers which of the keys are used for system functions. On the C64, the function keys perform these tasks:

- F1–Select, which tells PlayNet to carry out the selection you made from a menu window
- F3–Talk/Move, which tells PlayNet that the game move you just selected should be executed and also switches between making a game move and being able to "talk" (by typing) to your opponent
- F4–Cancel, which removes a menu window display
- F5–Menu/Help, which opens a menu window and also opens an individual help window for any command

Another key on the C64 that's significant is the up/down-arrow cursor key, which highlights an individual menu item and performs vertical scrolling in electronic mail, bulletin-boards, and a few other displays.

For game playing, the keys surrounding the "S" key are used, as shown here:

Q W E
A S D
Z X C

Pressing the Q key, for example, will move a game piece diagonally toward the upper left. Pressing the X key, for example, will move a game piece straight down.

The three disks that are provided with the PlayNet manual are one System disk and two Game disks. The System disk is placed in the drive and loaded by typing **LOAD"PLAYNET",8,1** on a C64. After about 10–15 seconds, a Copyright screen is displayed, which states that any key may be pressed to continue. After a key is pressed, a graphic screen of a TV set is displayed with a countdown timer that starts at 1:29. (This loading time will probably be shorter on your own disks, since PlayNet was tightening the program code on their disks for faster loading.)

The next display asks if you wish to connect to the system via Telenet or direct-dial. Once that choice is made and the complete signon procedure is finished, a new graphic screen is displayed, showing a game board with the system selections:

- Electronic File Transfer
- People, Games & More

- PlayNet Shopping Center
- Update PlayNet Disks
- Bulletin-Boards
- PlayNet System Information
- Sign Off PlayNet
- Account Information and Billing

You can see this screen, displayed in Figure 1.

Any one of the selections can be chosen by pressing one of the keys surrounding the "S" key; this will move a game piece over the selection. F1 (Select) is then pressed, and that instructs the system to call up that item. When an item is called up, the disk drive is polled for the current disk in residence, and then the appropriate disk file is loaded into the C64. This will display a new graphic screen with a countdown timer as the program loads.

The color graphic loading screens are some of the best I've seen on a C64 and serve their purpose well—to distract the subscriber while the slow 1541 drive transfers the program into the C64's RAM.

Usually, subscribers start by selecting People, Games & More. This part of the system is where games are played, electronic mail is received

Figure 1. PlayNet's main screen.

and sent, and online conferencing takes place. The graphic loading screen for this part of the system is a door with a mat that says "Welcome."

Once inside People, Games & More, the screen is divided into three parts:

- The first part is a status bar at the top, which shows the name of the "room" you're in. Reception is the room you'll probably wind up in first. Also displayed in the status bar are the names of the other subscribers currently in the room.
- The second part is a conferencing display, which shows the dialog going on between subscribers who are chatting online. When you play a game, this portion of the screen will display the game board.
- The third part is a buffer strip, which shows what you're typing in for conferencing. After you press Return, what you've typed will appear in the conferencing display. This way, what you type is not interrupted. Also in this area is a small box that will have the word "MAIL" in it if you have any.

By pressing F7 (Menu/Help), a menu window opens up below the status bar at the top of the screen, showing some of the commands that you may choose. The menu is only partially displayed and has to be scrolled vertically by using the up/down-arrow cursor key. As a selection passes through the center of the window, it's highlighted. When a selection is highlighted, pressing F1 (Select) will tell the system to execute that choice.

Figure 2 is a photo showing the Reception room with the menu window opened and one of the selections (Games Menu) highlighted.

The complete list of selections on this menu window are as follows:

- *Identify someone*. This will let you type in the name of another PlayNet subscriber and get the city and state the person lives in.
- *List all people in current room*. This will display a complete list of everyone in the room (the status bar at the top cannot fit every name).
- *Locate someone*. If the subscriber you're looking for is currently on the system, this selection will tell you where he or she is.
- *Games menu*. This opens up to a second window of games-oriented selections.
- *Go to a public room*. This allows you to create a new room by typing any name you wish, up to 20 characters. Any other subscriber may join you in the room by freely moving to it.
- *Go to a private room*. This allows you to create a new room by typing any name you wish, up to 20 characters. A private room will not let any other subscriber enter unless invited by you. Moving to a private

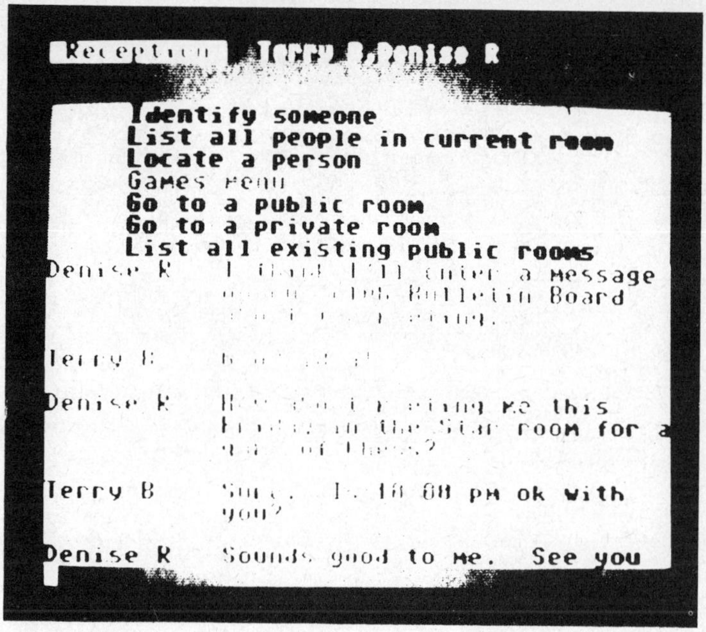

Figure 2. PlayNet's Reception room with menu window.

room is useful if you want to read or send electronic mail without being disturbed.

- *List all existing public rooms*. This will show a list of the names of the public rooms and how many people are in them.
- *On-line messages and electronic mail*. This opens to a new menu window, which allows you to send private live messages or electronic mail.
- *PlayNet announcements*. This is news about upcoming events or system changes.
- *Highlight someone's messages*. This will prominently display an individual subscriber's conference dialog.
- *Remove highlighting*. This turns the previous command off.
- *Ignore someone*. This is like the /SQUelch command in CIS CB (see Chapter 7, Using the CompuServe Consumer Information Service).
- *List people being ignored*. This will show you a list of the subscribers who are being squelched by you.
- *Stop ignoring someone*. This will reverse the Ignore command.
- *Change to a new account*. This is a feature in which parents may set up several separate accounts for their children and move from their account to their child's account without signing off the system.

- *Return to main menu selections*. This will display a menu window of the PlayNet entry selections (Electronic File Transfer, and so on).

Another example of how PlayNet's program does windowing on the C64 (and will do so similarly on Apples), is Figure 3, which is a photo of the Reception room, showing an electronic text message being written in a window placed over the main conferencing window.

The games that are available on PlayNet include these:

- Backgammon
- Boxes
- Capture the Flag
- Checkers
- Chess
- Chinese Checkers
- Contract Bridge
- Four-in-a-Row
- Go
- Hangman
- Quad 64
- Reversi
- Sea Strike

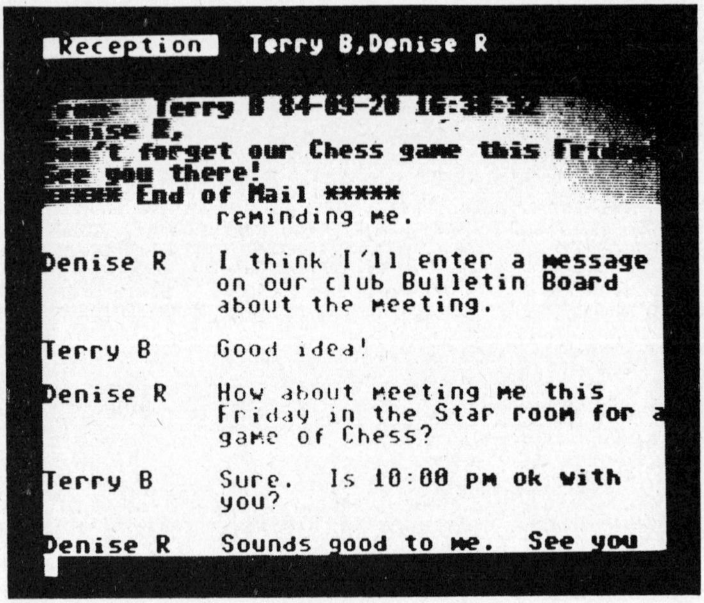

Figure 3. PlayNet Reception room with mail window.

Most of these games are probably familiar to you. Quad-64 is a game in which there are 4 boards of 16 squares each. A player has to be the first to fill in 4 squares with one color in order to win. Sea Strike is like the board game Battleship.

All of the games feature striking color graphics in high resolution with some sound.

While you play a game, you can "talk" (by typing) to your opponent online. Other subscribers can also enter the room (if the room is public) and join in the chatting. In the near future, PlayNet plans to offer a feature by which others can watch two subscribers playing a game.

Also coming up in PlayNet's future is the ability to buy software and other items from your computer. Of course, more games are being planned, too.

One of PlayNet's nongame features is a sort of online social calendar: Certain nights of the week are set aside for certain things. For instance, one night may be Bridge Night and another a COMAL night. On these nights, subscribers can get together to play in tournaments or listen to a guest speaker in one of the conferencing rooms. In the PlayNet newsletter sent to subscribers each month, a full calendar of planned events is printed, showing all of the special event nights. It's quite amazing that such a new system could have so much activity on it.

Trying to describe PlayNet in print, with few actual screen displays, is a frustrating task. The system's color displays are vibrant, and the games are fun to play. Watching a Commodore-64 do window displays is amazing in and of itself. The best thing about PlayNet, though, is its simplicity. The only time you have to type is when you're communicating a private message, electronic mail, or real-time conference. Most of the time, all you have to do is scroll through a menu and press one key to make PlayNet execute any command. This method of doing things makes command typos a thing of the past, doesn't require you to remember a long list of arcane and confusing commands, and puts PlayNet solidly ahead of the other systems in this book for ease of use and innovative design. If there was an award for online system design, PlayNet would win it.

Even though I've never been a fan of computer games—or using computers to play games—PlayNet is still more than worth the price of admission. It's easy, inexpensive, and plenty of fun.

* * *

Additional Information

CONTACT:

PlayNet, Inc., POB 596, Wynantskill, NY, 12198-0607; 1-(800)PLAYNET.

15 Using THE SOURCE

Control characters used on this system: Control-H, backspace; Control-P, system interrupt; Control-Q (XON), resume display; Control-S (OFF), pause display; Break, system interrupt; ESCape, system interrupt.

THE SOURCE (CPB100800) was the first National System designed for and made available to the general public that used microcomputers at home or at work. It was created by William von Meister and his company, Telecomputing Corporation of America in 1979. In 1980, The Source was purchased by Reader's Digest Association, which then sold a share of it to Control Data Corporation in 1983.

The Source started out as a system that used nothing but direct commands. With the Reader's Digest purchase, menus were overlayed onto the existing system, new bulletin-board software was written, and a whole new operating system was created. This entailed a rewrite of most of the system's software. Although many changes have taken place over the course of the years on The Source, each step was a very slow and very long process.

In late 1983, the latest management team that was brought in to run The Source decided to change the system's image and positioning in the market. This led to the design and use of a new logo and a new subtitle for the system. Advertisements no longer proclaimed the virtues of THE SOURCE, America's Information Utility. The ads now aggressively proclaimed the merits of The Source Information Network.

Aside from these cosmetic marketing changes, The Source has been in the forefront of adding news and business services to its system. It now offers several keyword-searchable news wire services, real-time stock quotes, a portfolio management system, and the ability to purchase stocks online virtually instantly.

For microcomputer users, The Source is planning to add what it calls "PC Information Exchanges." These will most likely be Special Interest Groups, which will cover specific brands of microcomputers and feature special member-only bulletin-boards and other services. As this book went to press, The Source could not yet comment on the shape the PC Information Exchanges would take. The planning had not yet been completed. (For other online Special Interest Groups, see Chapter 7, Using the CompuServe Information Service, and Chapter 8, Using Delphi.)

A change that came to The Source in March 1984 was a new set of menus. The 3-year-old ones were dropped in favor of new ones. You'll see several examples of these new menus later in this chapter.

The Source costs $49.95 for a subscription, which includes 1 hour of connect-time and an instruction manual. The Source is available through DataPac, SOURCENet, Telenet, and Uninet. Prime-time hours are from 7 AM to 6 PM weekdays. Non-prime-time hours are from 6 PM to 4 AM weekdays and from 6 AM to 4 AM weekends and holidays. Prime-time connect-time charges start at $21.80 an hour at 300 bps and $25.80 an hour at 1200 bps, with additional charges for certain premium services. Non-prime-time connect-time charges start at $8.40 an hour at 300 bps and $10.80 an hour at 1200 bps, with additional charges for premium services. Billing for individuals is to a credit card and for businesses is by an invoice. There was still a $10 a month minimum charge at the time this book went to press.

Since the management of The Source doesn't like its trademark to be used in the possessive (i.e., "The Source's"), I'll use "STC" interchangeably with "The Source" in this chapter.

Signing onto The Source will display this:

```
DEF999 (user 26) logged in Wednesday, 30 Oct 85 06:15:56.
Welcome, you are connected to THE SOURCE.

Last login Sunday, 20 Oct 85 23:54:36.

(C) COPYRIGHT SOURCE TELECOMPUTING CORPORATION 1985.

—>

WELCOME TO THE SOURCE

1 Using The Source <INTRO> ** FREE **
```

2 Menu of Services <MENU>
3 Member Information <INFO> ** FREE **
4 Today from The Source <TODAY>

(Q or QUIT will take you to Command Level.)

Enter item number, (H)ELP or (Q)uit

This is the first menu of The Source. It's not, however, the main menu and shouldn't be confused with it. This menu is only shown at signon and cannot be returned to once you're in the system.

Like other menus you've seen in this book, this one has its choices numbered. Unlike other menus, following the selection in angle brackets is the direct command that corresponds to the menu choice. This is STC's way of weaning its subscribers from using the menu structure. After seeing the direct command X number or times, it'll probably sink in and the subscribers will use the direct command instead of the menu for faster access.

Another unique part of The Source itself is the free services that are offered to all subscribers. Choices 1 and 3 have ** FREE ** next to them, indicating there are absolutely no connect-time charges associated with these selections. The selections are tutorials on using various parts of The Source. This is something I've been hoping online systems would do for years now. Frankly, I'm surprised to see The Source taking the initiative in this area, but I'm very pleased to see that at least *one* online system has seen the wisdom in offering such a service.

This menu may look slightly different by the time this book is published. STC has removed the menu choice that would remove the menu structure and place subscribers at command level. Instead, (Q)UIT is the sole hint that such a choice exists. This is confusing, though, because new users may think that typing Q will sign them off the system. STC may yet reinstate that menu selection, with QUIT, in parentheses, as the direct command next to the selection. Just remember that typing Q will place you at command level (shown shortly) and not sign you off the system.

Typing **2** will call up the main menu of The Source, which looks like this:

MENU OF SERVICES <MENU>

1 Today from The Source <TODAY>
2 News, Weather, and Sports <NEWS>
3 Business and Investing <BUSINESS>
4 Communications Services <COMM>

5 Personal Computing <PC>
6 Travel Services <TRAVEL>
7 Shopping, Games, and Leisure <HOME>
8 Member Information <INFO> ** FREE **

Enter item number, (H)ELP or (Q)uit

Again, the choices are numbered, and each choice has its corresponding direct command in parentheses. The title of the menu also has a direct command: MENU. Typing **MENU** at any prompt, whether in the menu structure or at command level, will display this main menu again.

The first thing you should do is drop into command level briefly to execute an important command. Type **Q** to get the command level prompt, like this:

Enter item number, (H)ELP or (Q)uit **Q**
—>

The arrow is the command level prompt. At this arrow you can enter any of the direct commands shown in the menus to get to a part of the system faster. The first direct command you should type is **CHAT -OFF**. Make sure there is a space between "CHAT" and "-OFF" or the system won't understand the command:

—> **CHAT -OFF**
—>

I'll tell you what this command means later in this chapter. For now, you only have to understand that it's important for you to insert this command when you sign onto The Source for the first time as a new user.

Let's go back to the main menu now by typing **MENU**:

—> **MENU**

MENU OF SERVICES <MENU>

1 Today from The Source <TODAY>
2 News, Weather, and Sports <NEWS>
3 Business and Investing <BUSINESS>
4 Communications Services <COMM>
5 Personal Computing <PC>
6 Travel Services <TRAVEL>
7 Shopping, Games, and Leisure <HOME>
8 Member Information <INFO> ** FREE **

Enter item number, (H)ELP or (Q)uit

I won't be showing you every part of The Source, just the parts that are tricky to use or particularly interesting. Let's briefly look at choice 1 from this menu, Today from The Source:

TODAY FROM THE SOURCE <TODAY>

1 Hour's Top News <BULLETIN>
2 Business Update <BIZDATE>
3 Sports, News, and Scores <SPORTS>
4 Today's Features <FOCUS>
5 What's New on The Source <NEW>

Enter item number, (H)ELP or (Q)UIT

This is one of the best-kept secrets on The Source. Each day, STC's editors pore through the various news and wire services available on the system and pick out the most important stories in the categories shown above. Instead of subscribers having to go to various parts of the system to catch up on daily events, they can access TODAY and find everything they need in one place. It's almost like having a daily electronic newspaper. It's more timely than any printed newspaper can be, though, because it's updated regularly throughout the day. Plus, choice 1, <BULLETIN>, follows important stories as they come across the many wire services carried by STC.

Let's look at a menu structure command now. Let's go back to the main menu to make another selection. Instead of typing MENU, just type **P**. This stands for "Previous," and will call up the prior menu:

Enter item number, (H)ELP or (Q)UIT **P**

MENU OF SERVICES <MENU>

1 Today from The Source <TODAY>
2 News, Weather, and Sports <NEWS>
3 Business and Investing <BUSINESS>
4 Communications Services <COMM>
5 Personal Computing <PC>
6 Travel Services <TRAVEL>
7 Shopping, Games, and Leisure <HOME>
8 Member Information <INFO> ** FREE **

Enter item number, (H)ELP or (Q)uit

Like the tour of CIS (in Chapter 7), the first thing you'll be shown how to use is electronic mail. STC has the best electronic mail system of any National System listed in *The Computer Phone Book.* That includes both EasyLink and MCI Mail. Type **4** to display the communications menu (COMM):

COMMUNICATIONS SERVICES <COMM>

1 SourceMail
2 Bulletin Boards
3 Chatting Online
4 Computer Conferencing <PARTI>
5 Member Directory <MEMBERS>
6 Members Currently Online <ONLINE>
7 ECOM and Mailgram Messages
8 Member Publishing <PUBLIC>
9 How to Prepare Text to Send
Enter item number, (H)ELP or (Q)UIT

Since communications is the most exciting aspect of using online systems, you'll be seeing several of the selections featured on this menu. The first one is SourceMail, which is commonly called SMail by subscribers. Typing **1** will display its menu:

SOURCEMAIL (MAIL)

1 Overview
2 Instructions
3 Mail Check <MAILCK>
4 Begin Mail
Enter item number, (H)ELP or (Q)UIT

These selections are self-explanatory. If you're signing on for the first time, you won't need to check for mail because you won't have any waiting.

You should become familiar with the mail system by sending a letter to yourself. Type **4** to start the process:

Enter item number, (H)ELP or (Q)UIT **4**

<S>end,<R>ead,<SC>an,<D>isplay, or <Q>uit?

These are the SourceMail options.

Let's type **S** for <S>end. That'll give you this prompt:

To:

Type your own User ID, like so:

To:**DEF999**
Subject:

Type a subject, like so:

Subject: **TEST**

Enter text:

Type some text for your letter, like so:

Enter text:
This is a tsetof the mail system for myselff.
It will show me how esay it is to use SMail.

Some of the same typos that you made back in Chapter 7 on CIS are here again. You'll have to edit the letter. In doing so, you'll see the differences and similarities of the text editor you used in editing text on CIS (FILGE) and the text editor that's present on The Source. To go into edit mode in SMail, type **.ED** (period ED) on a line by itself:

Enter text:
This is a tsetof the mail system for myselff.
It will show me how esay it is to use SMail.
.ED
EDIT

You're now in the STC text editor. The STC text editor uses some of the same commands used by CIS's FILGE text editor, except the commands are not preceded by a slash (/) in the STC editor. The similar commands are these:

- T, which will place you at the top of the file.
- N, which will move you down or up a specified number of lines of the file. For example, typing N5 will move the line pointer *down* five lines in the file. Typing N-5 will move the line pointer *up* five lines in the file.
- P, which will display the current line.
- B, which will place you at the bottom of the file.
- C, which is used to change characters and words.

Let's look at some of these commands in use, starting with **T.** Remember, STC text editor commands don't begin with a slash.

```
Enter text:
This is a tsetof the mail system for myselff.
It will show me how esay it is to use SMail.
.ED
EDIT
T
.NULL.
```

Unlike CIS's FILGE text editor, typing **T** in the STC text editor does not place you at the first line of text in a file. Instead, it places you one line *above* it. This is so if you wish, you can place additional text before your first line. .NULL. means you are currently looking at a blank line in the file. To get to the first line of text in order to edit it, you have to instruct the text editor's line pointer to move down one line in the file. This is done by using **N** command and the number 1, like so:

```
Enter text:
This is a tsetof the mail system for myselff.
It will show me how esay it is to use SMail.
.ED
EDIT
T
.NULL.
N1
This is a tsetof the mail system for myselff.
```

You can see a difference between CIS's FILGE and this text editor right here. In CIS's FILGE, you have to type /P to display the new line. In the STC text editor, when you move to a new line, it's automatically displayed for you. You don't have to type a second command.

Changing text with the STC text editor is similar to changing text with CIS's FILGE text editor. At this point, you shouldn't need a full description of changing text, so I'll just provide an illustration. You can always refer to the coverage of FILGE for a full explanation (see Chapter 7, Using the CompuServe Consumer Information Service).

```
This is a tsetof the mail system for myselff.
C/se/es
This is a testof the mail system for myselff.
/C/to/t o
This is a test of the mail system for myselff.
C/f./.
This is a test of the mail system for myself.
```

To edit the second line, move the line pointer down one line by typing

N1 again:

```
C/f./.
This is a test of the mail system for myself.
N1
It will show me how esay it is to use SMail.
/C/sa/as
It will show me how easy it is to use SMail.
```

To redisplay the entire file, type **T** to go to the top, and then instruct the text editor to display more lines than the file has, using the **P** command, like this:

```
/C/sa/as
It will show me how easy it is to use SMail.
T
.NULL.
P100
.NULL.
This is a test of the mail system for myself.
It will show me how easy it is to use SMail.
BOTTOM
```

"BOTTOM," like FILGE's "%FLGEOF—End of File" notice, indicates that you're at the last line of text in the file. Your first SMail letter is complete.

To get back into the SMail text entry mode, press **Return** *twice*:

```
.NULL.
This is a test of the mail system for myself.
It will show me how easy it is to use SMail.
BOTTOM
[RETURN]
[RETURN]
Enter text:
```

Although I haven't shown blank lines in this example of text editing, I'll explain how to insert them when you're in the STC text editor. You've seen how the Return key switched you from the text editor into text entry. If you're in the text editor and want to start a new paragraph of text by putting in a blank line, press your space bar once to insert a blank space; then press your Return key to start the first line of text. After you've edited a letter and you're back in text entry, use this method, too, or you'll wind up back in the text editor.

When you're finished creating your letter, use the commands shown below to perform various functions. Don't forget that each must be typed on a line by itself and must start with a period (.).

- .S to send the letter; this is the last command you should use.
- .H to get help. You can type this when you're entering text or when you're in the text editor.
- .DI to display the text of the letter.
- .DI TO to display the TO: field, in other words, the User ID the letter is being sent to.
- .DI SU to display the SUBJECT: field, in other words, the subject of the letter that you typed earlier.
- .SU to change the SUBJECT: field, in other words, to replace your old subject with a different one.
- .Q to abort the whole SMail process and not send the letter.
- .SA [FILENAME] to save the letter in a file with a name you give it. For instance, typing .SA TEST will store the letter online in a file called TEST.
- .LOAD [FILENAME] to load a file into SMail. If you decide that you want to send the letter to another person after you've used the .SA command to store it as a file named TEST, you can load it back into SMail by typing .LOAD TEST.
- .FILE [FILENAME] to store the letter in a file in the SMail system.
- .AR to get a receipt in your SMail box when the recipient has read the letter. AR means "acknowledgment requested."
- .EX to send the letter EXpress. This will place the letter first in the recipient's SMailbox.
- .CC [USER ID] to send a "carbon copy" of the letter to another User ID. Typing .CC DEF234, for instance, will send a "carbon copy" to DEF234.
- .BC [USER ID] to send a "blind copy" to another User ID. The recipient won't know that another User ID has also gotten a copy of the letter. Typing .BC DEF234, for example, will send a "blind copy" to DEF234.

Now that you've seen the list of commands you can use, let's look at sending this letter to yourself with a "carbon copy," a "blind copy," an acknowledgment, and express delivery:

```
Continue:
.EX
Continue:
.AR
```

```
Continue:
.BC DEF999
Continue:
.CC DEF999
Continue:
.S
Wait. . .

Sent to - DEF999        --EXPRESS--
Sent to - DEF999
Sent to - DEF999

<S>end,<R>ead,<SC>an,<D>isplay, or <Q>uit?
```

Of course, make sure that you type *your* User ID, not the fictional User ID DEF999 shown in this illustration. After the letter is sped on its way, you'll get the SMail prompt again:

```
<S>end,<R>ead,<SC>an,<D>isplay, or <Q>uit?
```

Don't read your letter yet. It takes a few minutes to get delivered.

Let's look at another way of contacting other subscribers of The Source. It's called Chat. It's similar to CIS's /Talk command in CB; that is, only two people at a time can chat together. The Source has yet to implement a multiuser conferencing system like CIS's CB or Delphi's Conference system.

To locate someone to Chat with, you first have to see a list of who's currently on the system. Let's leave SMail and get back to command level. Type **Q** to get the command level prompt:

```
<S>end,<R>ead,<SC>an,<D>isplay, or <Q>uit? Q
—>
```

Now type **ONLINE**. This will give you a list of the subscribers currently online. The list will look like this:

```
—> ONLINE
DEF123 DEF234 DEF456 DEF789 DEF999 GHI231
GHI543 GHI777 GHI99Ø  PQR111 PQR357 PQR359
PQR567 PQR613 PQR65Ø PQR888 PQR979 PQR989
—>
```

The actual list may be much longer, depending on the hour and day you're on the system. it's not unusual to see a list with over 100 User IDs.

To Chat, you'll first have to type **CHAT -ON** at command level. At the start of this chapter, I told you to type CHAT -OFF. This prevented other subscribers from interrupting you with Chat requests while you were exploring the system and writing a SMail letter. Now that you're ready to Chat, you have to turn that function back on, like so:

```
—> CHAT -ON
—>
```

Remember to leave a space between "CHAT" and "-ON" so the system will understand the command.

Now pick one of the User IDs you saw in the Online list and type it preceded by CHAT, like this:

```
—> CHAT DEF123
```

If DEF123 has issued the CHAT -OFF command on his or her end, you'll see this:

```
—> CHAT DEF123
NOT AVAILABLE FOR CHAT
```

If DEF123 has CHAT -ON, you'll see this:

```
—> CHAT DEF123
Please remember that entering your
password is required only at signon,
and never in CHAT.

Enter:
```

Take that warning to heart: *Never* give anyone your password on any system. Some of the scams that are used on online systems to gain passwords illegally include these:

- Impersonating a system employee in online conversations and asking for your password so a "check" can be run on your account
- Gaining your phone number through online conversations (or directory assistance!) and calling you by voice phone, impersonating a customer service rep
- Sending phony system error messages and signon notices while in online conversations in an attempt to make you think you have to sign on so you'll type your password.

You can be held liable for the connect-time charges someone runs up while using your account illegally, so guard your password.

To get back to chatting, once you see the "Enter:" prompt, it means you can start typing a message to the other person. It means that you're in contact with that subscriber, but the other subscriber still hasn't entered CHAT on the other end.

—> CHAT DEF123
Please remember that entering your
password is required only at signon,
and never in CHAT.

Enter:
Hello there! Care to Chat?

Don't follow up with a second line immediately. The other person may be busy doing something more important online and may not wish to chat. Even if the other person does wish to chat, it may take a few minutes to complete the task you've interrupted and enter Chat mode. Chat protocol requires that you wait between 3 and 5 minutes after asking for a chat. If you don't get any response after that time, abort the chat process by issuing a Control-P or pressing your ESCape or Break key. Don't harass someone if you don't get a response.

If the other person does wish to chat, you'll see this on your screen:

** CHAT FROM DEF123 **
Hi, Mike!!! Was in the middle of a letter!

Like /Talk mode on CIS, if you type while the other person is sending something, your typing will be interrupted. Wait for the other person to finish before you start to type. Chat protocol requires that you signal when you're through typing by pressing **Return** twice. A Chat exchange will look like this on your screen:

Sorry!
[RETURN]
[RETURN]
No problem. I have to re-enter it anyway.
[RETURN]
[RETURN]
Long time no chat. What's new?
[RETURN]
[RETURN]
Nothing much. And u?
[RETURN]
[RETURN]

Of course, you won't see the Returns on your screen, just the blank lines they produce. When both of you are through with the chat, one of you will terminate the Chat command by issuing a Control-P or pressing the ESCape or Break key. You'll see this on your screen when the other person presses ESCape:

```
BYE BYE...FROM DEF123
```

Pressing Break or issuing a Control-P will just return you to the command level prompt and won't bring that "bye bye" message.

Another way to contact subscribers of The Source is to look up over 10,000 subscribers in The Source Member Directory and then contact any of them via SMail. The Source Member Directory is similar to Delphi's PeopleNet directory (see Chapter 8, Using Delphi). (If Delphi had not been under renovation at press time, you would have seen its PeopleNet user directory for yourself. Unfortunately, you'll have to take my word for it. Delphi, by the way, designed PeopleNet long before STC revised its Member Directory.) Like any other user directory, being listed in it is entirely voluntary.

The directory is reached by typing **MEMBERS** at command level:

```
—> MEMBERS
THE SOURCE Member Directory.

1    Search the Directory
2    Add Your Entry
3    Modify Your Entry
4    Replace your Entry
5    Delete Your Entry

<I>nstructions

Enter Item Number or <H>elp:
```

To find out about other subscribers, type **1** for Search the Directory:

```
Enter Item Number or <H>elp:1

Search by:
<ME>mber ID <NA>me <CI>ty <ST>ate <CO>untry
<O>ccupation <MI>cro <IN>terest or <ALL>:
```

You can search for other subscribers using the list of entries shown in this prompt. Let's look at how it works by searching for subscribers who own or use the Apple Macintosh computer. Type **MI** for <MI>cro:

Search by:
<ME>mber ID <NA>me <CI>ty <ST>ate <CO>untry
<O>ccupation <MI>cro <IN>terest or <ALL>:**MI**

Enter Micro:**MAC**
Searching...
199 items found.

<N>arrow <E>xpand <SC>an <ME>nu <C>ancel:

There are two ways of looking at subscriber information: by typing **SC** for <SC>an and getting a complete listing about a subscriber or by typing **ME** for <ME>nu and getting a list of subscribers from which you can choose to read individual listings. Let's type **ME**:

<N>arrow <E>xpand <SC>an <ME>nu <C>ancel:**ME**

1 TIGER NINESTEIN (PQRØ67) HAWKNEST SOUTH AMERICA
2 JOHN TRACY (DEF623) TRACY ISLAND SP UNITED STATES
3 STEVE ZODIAC (GHI174) SPACE CITY AZ UNITED STATES
4 MIKE MERCURY (PQR467) BLACK ROCK AZ UNITED STATES
5 TROY TEMPEST (DEFØ45) MARINEVILLE CA UNITED STATES

This list will continue until about 21 choices are displayed and the following prompt appears:

Enter Item(s) or Return for more:

At this point, you can type one number or several (with each number separated by a space) or just press Return to continue the list. If you choose to press Return and continue getting a menu of choices, the numbers will continue in sequence until you hit the last one, number 199, and the prompt you just saw. As the menu of choices is being displayed, you can write down the numbers for which you'd like to see the full listings. Once you reach number 199 and the prompt, you can start to type the numbers of the listings you'd like to see. Even if you only want to see listing 1, you can type it at that prompt after choice 199. The point is, you're not forced to choose only the ones that are currently displayed on your screen.

Let's go back to the previous prompt by typing **P**:

Enter Item(s) or Return for more:**P**
199 items valid (MAC)

<N>arrow <E>xpand <SC>an <ME>nu <C>ancel:

Let's type **C** here to <C>ancel the search and go back to the top menu of the directory:

```
<N>arrow <E>xpand <SC>an <ME>nu <C>ancel:C

THE SOURCE Member Directory.

1    Search the Directory
2    Add Your Entry
3    Modify Your Entry
4    Replace Your Entry
5    Delete Your Entry

<I>nstructions

Enter Item Number or <H>elp:
```

Now, let's look at how you can place yourself in the member directory so other subscribers can contact you. The process starts by typing **2**.

```
Enter Item Number or <H>elp:2
STC reserves the right to remove MEMBERS
entries which are abusive, unlawful or
otherwise objectionable.

To protect the privacy of your account,
avoid entering ANY information which may
provide "clues" to your password. CHANGE
YOUR PASSWORD REGULARLY.

Enter your name:
```

Each prompt is self-explanatory. You just type the information that's called for. I'll fill out the form without any further explanation:

```
Enter your name:SGT MJR ZERO

Do you live in the US?Y

What City?NEW YORK

Enter State, 2 letter code, or <L>ist:NY

Occupation:ZEROID

Enter micro:ZEROID
Enter up to 7 interests, with each on a
```

```
separate line. Press return when done.
: MARY FALCONER
: VIDEO GAMES
: KATE KESTREL'S MUSIC
: FIGHTING ZELDA
: MAINTAINING HAWKNEST
: FLYING BATTLEHAWK
Enter one more interest, or press
Return to send your entry.
: FOLLOWING HE WHO MUST BE OBEYED
```

After the form is completed, it'll be displayed in its entirety for your approval:

```
User id:DEF999 Name:SGT MJR ZERO From:NEW YORK NY UNITED STATES
Occupation:ZEROID Micro:ZEROID Interests: MARY FALCONER, VIDEO
GAMES, KATE KESTREL'S MUSIC, FIGHTING ZELDA, MAINTAINING HAWKNEST,
FLYING BATTLEHAWK, FOLLOWING HE WHO MUST BE OBEYED

Is this the way you'd like it?
```

This is the kind of listing you'll see for a subscriber when you use the <SC>an command in searching the directory.

If you don't approve of the way your listing looks or if a mistake is present, you can start over again by typing **N** in response to this prompt. Typing **Y** will bring this response:

```
Is this the way you'd like it?Y

Your listing will be added to
the directory shortly.

1     Search the Directory
2     Add Your Entry
3     Modify Your Entry
4     Replace Your Entry
5     Delete Your Entry

<I>nstructions

Enter Item Number or <H>elp:
```

As you can see from this menu, you can go back any time to change or erase your listing. It's not permanent.

Let's go back to command level and look at another way of communicating between subscribers. It's the bulletin-board system of The Source and it's called POST:

```
Enter Item Number or <H>elp:Q
Quitting..
—>
```

At the command level prompt, type **POST** to enter the bulletin-board system:

```
—> POST

Do you want instructions ?
```

Let's skip this by typing **N**:

```
Do you want instructions ?N

<R>ead,<PO>st,<PU>rge,<S>can, or <H>elp:
```

The best way to go through the bulletin-board system is first to <S>can the listings. Notice that Scan has only its "S" highlighted (<S>can) rather than the "SC" (<SC>an) as in SMail and the member directory.

Type **S** to start the process:

```
<R>ead,<PO>st,<PU>rge,<S>can, or <H>elp:S

<C>ategory,<U>ser ID,<D>ate,<K>eyword
```

These are the elements by which you can search the bulletin-boards. You can search by a specific category (which means a specific bulletin-board; the full list of categories are at the end of this chapter), a specific User ID, a date, or a subject keyword.

Let's look at a specific bulletin-board, by typing **C** to narrow the search further:

```
<C>ategory,<U>ser ID,<D>ate,<K>eyword:C
Categories, or <H>elp:
```

This is the prompt at which you type the specific name of the category you wish to scan. You can type more than one category name, as long as the list doesn't go over 80 characters in length. You can also type H at this prompt to get a full, updated list of bulletin-board categories.

At this prompt, type **BULLETIN-BOARD** to scan that individual category:

```
Categories, or <H>elp:BULLETIN-BOARD
Searching. . .
37 notices valid.
<N>arrow, <E>xpand or Return for all :
```

It's not unusual to find over 100 notices on some STC bulletin-boards (the Apple board is a good example). Once you know how many notices are in the individual category, you can decide whether you want to narrow the search any further. If you choose to narrow the search, you'll get the previous prompt asking for a category, User ID, date, or keyword. This same prompt will also appear if you choose to expand your search.

Press **RETURN** to start scanning the notices:

```
<N>arrow, <E>xpand or Return for all :[RETURN]
Wait. .
1    29 OCT DEF123  TERRAHAWKS!(BULLETIN-BOARD)
2    29 OCT PQR536  —> SPACE:1999 <—(BULLETIN-BOARD)
3    29 OCT GHI698  ***UFO***(BULLETIN-BOARD)
4    28 OCT DEF15Ø  -CAPTAIN SCARLET-(BULLETIN-BOARD)
5    28 OCT PQRØ54  THUNDERBIRDS ARE GO!(BULLETIN-BOARD)
6    28 OCT GHIØØ1  INTERNATIONAL RESCUE(BULLETIN-BOARD)
7    28 OCT DEFØ92  STINGRAY!(BULLETIN-BOARD)
8    28 OCT GHIØ9Ø  FIREBALL XL5(BULLETIN-BOARD)
9    27 OCT PQRØ92  SUPERCAR(BULLETIN-BOARD)
```

This list will continue until 21 choices have been displayed; then this prompt will appear:

```
Enter item(s),<H>elp,or Return for more :
```

Notice that although this is the same kind of list you saw when you used the <ME>nu command in the directory, here it is displayed when you use the <S>can command. The POST software was the first new software written especially for The Source. Why their programmers chose to ignore its structure and turn <S>can into <ME>nu is a mystery. A scan command on a system should be the same throughout the system. Consistency is the highest virtue that should be sought in designing an online system. Once internal consistency is in place, using the system is that much easier.

Once again, let's look at the prompt that was just displayed:

```
Enter item(s),<H>elp,or Return for more :
```

At this point you can type one number or several (with each number separated by a space) or just press Return to continue the list. If you choose to press Return and continue getting a menu of choices, the numbers will continue in sequence until you hit the last one, number 37, and this prompt again. As the menu of choices is displayed, you can write down the numbers for which you'd like to see the full listings. Once you reach number 37 and the prompt, you can start to type the number of the listings you'd like to see. Even if you only want to see listing 1, you can type it at that prompt after choice 37. Like using the member directory, you're not forced to choose only the ones that are currently displayed on your screen.

Let's type **1** to look at the first notice:

Enter item(s),<H>elp,or Return for more :**1**
Category:BULLETIN-BOARD
Subject:TERRAHAWKS!
From:DEF123
Posted:28 OCT 12:13 am

<N>ext,<PO>st, or Return for text-

Even though you've told the system that you want to read this notice, you're forced to tell it that again, by pressing Return. This, too, is poor system design. Once the system is instructed to display notices, it should only interrupt with a prompt *after* a notice has been displayed in its entirety. Curiously enough, The Source does it backward. It pauses *before* a notice has been displayed. After a notice has been displayed in its entirety, it'll merrily continue on to the header of the next notice. Again, this is poor system design. While the system works just fine, the design doesn't take into account logic or the way in which people use the system.

Pressing **Return** will display the notice's text, like so:

<N>ext,<PO>st, or Return for text-**[RETURN]**
Terrahawks!

Read this notice!

This is an emergency!

At Command Level Type: PUBFILE DEF123

For Information about Gerry Anderson's new Supermacromation TV
series!

This is a 1Ø-9Ø!!

Ten-Ten

-End-

Since only one notice was selected for display, POST prints the "-END-" notice to let you know you've completed your task.

Press **RETURN** at this point to return to the previous prompt:

-End-**[RETURN]**
37 notices valid.

<N>arrow, <E>xpand or Return for all :

Then type **P** to move back to the prompt before this one:

<N>arrow, <E>xpand or Return for all :**P**

<C>ategory,<U>ser ID,<D>ate,<K>eyword:

Type **P** again to move back to the top prompt:

<C>ategory,<U>ser ID,<D>ate,<K>eyword:**P**

<R>ead,<PO>st,<PU>rge,<S>can, or <H>elp:

Let's look at how to place a message on a bulletin-board, by typing **PO** for <PO>st:

<R>ead,<PO>st,<PU>rge,<S>can, or <H>elp:**PO**

Enter category or <H>elp:

Let's add the notice called Bulletin-Board to the bulletin-board we just scanned:

Enter category or <H>elp:**BULLETIN-BOARD**
Searching. . .

STC reserves the right to remove POSTed material
which is irrelevant to a category, abusive, un-
lawful, or otherwise objectionable. All notices
are purged automatically by STC after 7 days.
Duplicate notices/advertisements may be removed
at STC's discretion.

Enter a brief subject line
Please do not exceed 32 characters

Type the message's subject, like so:

Enter a brief subject line
Please do not exceed 32 characters
ZEROIDS!
Please enter the text of your notice
No more than 23 lines please!
Type ".S" to post your notice, or ".H" for help
Enter text:

Follow these instructions by typing your notice. STC's bulletin-board software will not reformat your message the way CIS's Forum message area and Bullet bulletin-board do. So, when this prompt states you should enter no more than 23 lines, it means it. It doesn't matter whether the lines are 22 characters wide or 80 characters wide; it only counts the number of lines, and 23 is the limit.

Please enter the text of your notice
No more than 23 lines please!
Type ".S" to post your notice, or ".H" for help
Enter text:
I WANT TO GET SMAIL FROM ANYONE WHO HAS BUILT THEIR OWN TERRAHAWKS ZEROID!

ARE THERE MANY ROBOTICS PEOPLE ON STC?

PLEASE SMAIL DEF999

TEN-TEN!

.S
Wait. .
Notice received.
It will be posted shortly.

<R>ead,<PO>st,<PU>rge,<S>can, or <H>elp:

Immediately, you can go back and read the notice by typing **R**:

<R>ead,<PO>st,<PU>rge,<S>can, or <H>elp:**R**

<C>ategory,<U>ser ID,<D>ate,<K>eyword:

At this prompt you could type U, and then at the next prompt you could type your own User ID. That'd be a faster way of seeing your posted notice. But if you've made several posts over a period of a few days, all of them will be called up. It's therefore better to search by the individual bulletin-board category, which is what I'll do here by typing **C:**

<C>ategory,<U>ser ID,<D>ate,<K>eyword:**C**

Categories, or <H>elp:**BULLETIN-BOARD**
Searching. . .
38 notices valid.

<N>arrow, <E>xpand or Return for all :**[RETURN]**
Wait. .
Category:BULLETIN-BOARD
Subject:ZEROIDS!
From:DEF999
Posted:3Ø OCT 6:48 am

<N>ext,<PO>st, or Return for text-**[RETURN]**
I WANT TO GET SMAIL FROM ANYONE WHO HAS BUILT THEIR OWN TERRAHAWKS ZEROID!

ARE THERE MANY ROBOTICS PEOPLE ON STC?

PLEASE SMAIL DEF999

TEN-TEN!

Category:BULLETIN-BOARD
Subject:TERRAHAWKS!
From:DEF123
Posted:29 OCT 5:14 am

<N>ext,<PO>st, or Return for text-

Here you can again see the folly of STC's bulletin-board software design. Not only must you press Return once to instruct the system to let you read your own notice after already asking for it, but you have to suffer through the header for the message that follows. Let's erase this message now.

First type **P** for the previous prompt:

<N>ext,<PO>st, or Return for text-**P**
38 notices valid.

<N>arrow, <E>xpand or Return for all :

Now type **P** again:

<N>arrow, <E>xpand or Return for all :**P**

<C>ategory,<U>ser ID,<D>ate,<K>eyword:

Type **P** just one more time:

<C>ategory,<U>ser ID,<D>ate,<K>eyword:**P**

<R>ead,<PO>st,<PU>rge,<S>can, or <H>elp:

The command to erase a notice you've posted is PU for <PU>rge. Type **PU**:

<R>ead,<PO>st,<PU>rge,<S>can, or <H>elp:**PU**
Searching . . .
1 entry valid.
Wait..
1 30 OCT DEF999 ZEROIDS! (BULLETIN-BOARD)

<D>elete item(s),<H>elp,or Return for all : **[RETURN]**
Category:BULLETIN-BOARD
Subject:ZEROIDS!
From:DEF999
Posted:30 OCT 6:48 am

<D>elete or Return for more-**D**
Purge notice received.
It will be purged shortly.

-End-

The notice is then erased.

If the illustrations of POST looked like it took more effort than it was worth to go through the messages, you're right. Throughout, I used the prompt mode of POST. From command level, you can type command strings to bypass the prompts. Let's look at the various command formats:

- POST S [CATEGORY] will automatically scan the bulletin-board you name. For example, POST S APPLE will scan the Apple bulletin-board.
- POST R [CATEGORY] will automatically read the notices in the bulletin-board you name. For example, POST R COMMODORE will read the Commodore bulletin-board.

- POST S K [KEYWORD] will search all of the bulletin-boards for the keyword you type and display a list of qualifying messages. For example, POST S K BBS will search all of the bulletin-boards looking for the keyword "BBS" in the "subject" field and then display the list of any messages that do.
- POST R K [KEYWORD] will search all of the bulletin-boards for the keyword you type and display the messages that qualify. For example, POST R K COMAL will search all of the bulletin-boards looking for the keyword "COMAL" in the "subject" field and then display any messages that do.
- POST S U [USER ID], will search all of the bulletin-boards for the User ID you type and display a list of messages that qualify. For example, POST S U DEF123 will search all of the bulletin-boards looking for DEF123 in the "from" field and then display any messages that do. Likewise, POST R U [USER ID] will do the same except it will display the message text.
- POST PO [CATEGORY], will start the process to post a message in the bulletin-board you name. For example, POST PO VIDEO will start the process for posting a notice in the VIDEO bulletin-board.
- POST PU [YOUR USER ID], will start the process to erase the notices you've posted on the various bulletin-boards. For example, POST PU DEF999 will erase your notices if your User ID is DEF999. (You cannot erase other subscribers' notices, so don't try typing someone else's User ID.)

STC's bulletin-boards are where most of the action is on the system. They always make for interesting reading and are sometimes filled with news that you can't find anywhere else or won't hear of anywhere else for a few months. The list of bulletin-board categories at the end of this chapter testifies that many interests are served by this medium. Don't hesitate to read the notices and don't be shy about posting your own. You'll meet more people and get more SMail in your box than you thought possible.

Type **Q** now to get back to the command level prompt.

```
-End- Q
—>
```

The last service we'll look at on The Source is a marvelous research aid called Microsearch. It's a database of article and review abstracts from many different computer publications and magazines. If you don't want to subscribe to BRS After Dark or Knowledge Index just to have access to a few computer-oriented databases, Microsearch may be just what you want, and it alone could justify a subscription to The Source.

Type **MICROSEARCH** at the prompt:

—> **MICROSEARCH**

MICROSEARCH (tm)
Copr. 1984 Information, Inc., Wash. D.C. All rights reserved.

1 About MICROSEARCH (tm)
2 Abstracts
3 Product Literature
4 Manufacturers Directory

<I>nstructions
Enter Item Number or <H>elp:

Microsearch has abstracts of articles from over 90 publications. (The complete publication index is printed at the end of this chapter.) This is not to say it's all encompassing. It has gaps in it, but its contents far outweigh the gaps. Abstracts remain online for a year from the time they are added. Abstracts are added on a weekly basis.

Type **2** to start searching the abstracts:

Enter Item Number or <H>elp: **2**

MICROSEARCH (tm)
Abstracts

1 Articles
2 Instructional Articles
3 Book Reviews and Columns
4 Hardware Reviews
5 Software Reviews
6 Firmware Reviews
7 User Reviews and Interviews
8 Search all abstracts

Enter Item Number or <H>elp:

In this example, I'll search all of the abstracts by typing **8**:

Enter Item Number or <H>elp:**8**
<K>eyword,<PU>blication,<TI>tle,<AU>thor,
<D>ate,<MI>cro,<O>perating System,
<MA>nufacturer, or <H>elp:

These are the various ways in which you can search the abstracts. I'll use a keyword in this example:

```
<K>eyword,<PU>blication,<TI>tle,<AU>thor,
<D>ate,<MI>cro,<O>perating System,
<MA>nufacturer, or <H>elp:K

Keyword(s) or <H>elp:ROBOT
Searching . . .
40 items found.

<N>arrow, <E>xpand or RETURN for all :[RETURN]

<R>ead,<SC>an,<ME>nu,<PR>int,<C>ancel:
```

At this prompt, this is what each command will do:

- <R>ead will display each abstract and pause after each one.
- <SC>can will display the headers of each abstract.
- <ME>nu will give you a numbered list of choices, as you saw in the earlier illustration of The Source Member Directory.
- <PR>int will display all of the abstracts one after the other without a pause until the final one has been displayed.
- <C>ancel will stop the search and return you to the previous menu.

Let's type **ME**, for <ME>nu, to display a list of article headlines:

```
<R>ead,<SC>an,<ME>nu,<PR>int,<C>ancel:ME
Wait..
1       KAREL THE ROBOT
2       RobotWar-Review and Challenge
3       Mr. Robot and His Robot Factory
4       AMCALL: A Multipurpose Communication Program
5       Hardware Reviews: U.S. Robotics Password Modem
6       The Game Reserve
7       Top of the Line Standalone Modems
8       Infectious Fun and Rebellious Robots: Robotron: 2084
9       212 S Modems: A Comparison
10      Robotron:2084
11      Thirteen Great New Games: Robotron: 2084
12      Robotron: 2084
13      Pac-Man, Donkey Kong, Centipede, and Robotron: 2084
14      Occam's Edge
15      Robot Runner for the TI
16      The Robots are Coming! Tasman Turtle
17      The Robots are Coming! Topo II
18      Build Your Own Gladiator
```

```
19      MODEM MARKET, THE
20      TRANSPORTER, FILE-TRANSFER PROGRAM FOR THE IBM PC
21      ROBOT BATTLE
22      ROBOTTACK

Enter Item(s) or RETURN for all:
```

I'll display the first abstract by typing **1**:

```
Enter Item(s) or RETURN for all:1

1          Title:  KAREL THE ROBOT
          Source:  MICROCOMPUTING  (Vol. 7, No. 5, P. 143/2),May 1983

Enter Item(s) or RETURN for more:1
                 Title:  KAREL THE ROBOT
                Source:  MICROCOMPUTING ( 1 MAY 1983 )
               Vol-Pag:  VOL. 7, NO. 5, P. 143/2
                Author:  DERRY, JIM

KAREL THE ROBOT IS A SIMPLE APPLE II GAME CAPABLE OF STARTING NEOPHYTES ON
THE ROAD TO PROGRAMMING COMPETENCY, EVEN WITHOUT THEIR KNOWING IT.
DISPLAYED ON YOUR CRT, KAREL HAS NORTH-SOUTH AVENUES AND EAST-WEST STREETS
ON WHICH TO TRAVEL. . . .
```

The abstract continues, but this should be enough to give you an idea of what a Microsearch abstract is like. When abstracts are retrieved, the latest one is the first and the others are listed in descending order of date.

Let's look at another search of the abstracts, this time by looking for material about a certain microcomputer:

```
MICROSEARCH (tm)
Abstracts
1     Articles
2     Instructional Articles
3     Book Reviews and Columns
4     Hardware Reviews
5     Software Reviews
6     Firmware Reviews
7     User Reviews and Interviews
8     Search all abstracts

Enter Item Number or <H>elp:8
```

<K>eyword,<PU>blication,<TI>tle,<AU>thor,
<D>ate,<MI>cro,<O>perating System,
<MA>nufacturer, or <H>elp:

Here, type **MI** for <MI>cro:

<K>eyword,<PU>lication,<TI>tle,<AU>thor,
<D>ate,<MI>cro,<O>perating System,
<MA>nufacturer, or <H>elp:**MI**

Enter Micro, Micro Manufacturer,
Operating System or <L>ist:

Whatever you do, *don't* type L for a list at this prompt! The list is made up of all three items—microcomputers, manufacturers, and operating systems—and is very long. There are over 70 items to go through before Apple is displayed, and that's just part of the A's!

I'll type **TIMEX 1000:**

Enter Micro, Micro Manufacturer,
Operating System or <L>ist:**TIMEX 1ØØØ**
Entry does not match - try again

Enter Micro, Micro Manufacturer,
Operating System or <L>ist:

Apparently, my way of typing the name of the computer is not in the Microsearch index, so I'll type the name of the manufacturer, **TIMEX:**

Enter Micro, Micro Manufacturer,
Operating System or <L>ist:**TIMEX**
1 TIMEX TS1ØØØ
2 TIMEX/SINCLAIR
3 TIMEX/SINCLAIR 1ØØØ
4 TIMEX/SINCLAIR 15ØØ
5 TIMEX/SINCLAIR 2ØØØ
6 TIMEX/SINCLAIR 2Ø48
7 TIMEX/SINCLAIR 2Ø68
8 TIMEX/SINCLAIR ZX8Ø
9 TIMEX/SINCLAIR ZX81

Enter item number or <H>elp:

Instead of having to wade through the seemingly endless list of micros, manufacturers, and operating systems that Microsearch has online, it has given me a list of choices. Every Timex computer name is displayed, along with the variations of the way the TS1000 is listed in the Microsearch index. All that I have to do is choose one by typing its number. I'll choose and type **3:**

```
Enter item number or <H>elp:3
Searching. . .
93 items found.

<N>arrow, <E>xpand or RETURN for all :
```

Going through 93 items, even as a menu, is not something I'd like to do, so I'll narrow my search by typing **N:**

```
<N>arrow, <E>xpand or RETURN for all :N

<K>eyword,<PU>lication,<TI>tle,<AU>thor,
<D>ate,<MI>cro,<O>perating System,
<MA>nufacturer, or <H>elp
```

Here I'll type **K** for <K>eyword:

```
<K>eyword,<PU>lication,<TI>tle,<AU>thor,
<D>ate,<MI>cro,<O>perating System,
<MA>nufacturer, or <H>elp:K

Keyword(s) or <H>elp:
```

Now I'll use a word that describes an application the machine can do. I'll type **FILE.** Actually, I could also type database, filing, catalog, and other similar terms. Each result would be different, though. File will suffice.

```
Keyword(s) or <H>elp:FILE
Searching. . .
6 items found.

<N>arrow, <E>xpand or RETURN for all :[RETURN]

<R>ead,<SC>an,<ME>nu,<PR>int,<C>ancel:ME
Wait. . .
1    THE ORGANIZER
2    INVENTORIES
3    PROGRAM COLLECTIONS
4    ADDRESS AND PHONE LISTS
```

5 A Small Wonder
6 PERSONAL DATA BANK

Enter Item(s) or RETURN for all:

I won't illustrate reading an abstract again.

There's one big limitation to Microsearch: It acts like NewsNet when you do a keyword search. (See Chapter 13, Using NewsNet.) In other words, if you type more than one keyword as a phrase, Microsearch will retrieve any entry with that phrase as well as any entry that has each word in it. For example if "Computer Phone Book" is the keyword phrase, it will retrieve any abstracts that have the book title "Computer Phone Book" in them, as well as any abstract that has the words "computer," "phone," and "book" in them—regardless of their order or proximity to one another.

Like NewsNet, Microsearch shouldn't be thought of as a search service. For most applications, though, Microsearch will suffice for general information about any subject. It's very useful and is the lowest-priced database of its kind in the online industry. It's a bargain that can't be beat and, as I said, may be reason enough to subscribe to The Source.

The last part of The Source we'll see is the mail system, where you will learn how to read and dispose of letters you receive. At command level, type **MAILCK.** This stands for "Mail Check" and will tell you if you have any mail waiting for you. It may take a few moments, so be patient.

—>**MAILCK**
1 Unread Express, 2 Unread, 3 TOTAL
—>

The three letters are actually the letter you sent to yourself at the outset of this chapter, a "carbon copy," and a "blind copy." Now type **MAIL SC.** This stands for "Mail Scan" and will display the headers ("envelopes") of the letters:

—>**MAIL SC**

```
  1) From: DEF999      2-Lines --EXPRESS--
On:Ø5 OCT 1985 At: ØØ:35
To: DEF999
Subject: TEST

  2) From: DEF999      2-Lines
On:Ø5 OCT 1985 At: ØØ:35 Copy: BC
To: DEF999      Cc: DEF999
Subject: TEST
```

```
  3) From: DEF999      2-Lines
On:Ø5 OCT 1985 At: ØØ:35 Copy: CC
To: DEF999      Cc: DEF999
Subject: TEST

<R>ead or <D>elete by number:
```

Only the first letter is significant, so you can go ahead and type 2 and 3 (**2 3**) to delete the copies. After that, type **R** to read the remaining letter. It'll look like this:

```
From: DEF999      2-Lines --EXPRESS--
On:Ø5 OCT 1985 At: ØØ:35
To: DEF999
Subject: TEST

-More-[RETURN]
Wait. . .

Sent to -- DEF999 --
Acknowledged

This is a test of the mail system for myself.
It will show me how easy it is to use SMail.

Disposition:
```

The next time you look in your SMailbox, you'll have a receipt for this letter, showing that it was delivered and read. That's how the .AR (period AR; Acknowledgment Requested) command works.

Now that you're through reading the letter, you have to decide how to dispose of it. These are your options at a Disposition prompt:

- D to delete the letter.
- Q to return to the main prompt in SourceMail.
- N to go on to the next letter (if there is one).
- RE to reply to the letter. (The To and Subject fields will be filled out with the recipient and same subject.)
- FO to forward the letter to another person. You'll be able to add text at the beginning of the letter. For example, typing FO DEP123 will forward a copy to the User ID DEF123.
- A to display the letter again.
- FILE to file it in a general SMail area file.

- FILE [NAME] to store it in a SMail area file with a name you give it (up to 20 characters long); for example, FILE LETTER1.
- SAVE [FILENAME] to store the letter in your general online file area under a name that you give it. This will save the whole letter; for example, SAVE LETTER2.
- SAVE TEST [FILENAME] to store the letter's text only in your general online file area under a name that you give it. This will save just the text of the letter, not the header; for example, SAVE TEXT LETTER3.
- SAVE IN [FILENAME] to store the letter in a file that already exists and has other contents in it. This is like placing a letter into a folder of letters; for example, SAVE IN LETTER4. The file called LETTER4 was created previously and already contains other SMail in it.
- SAVE TEXT IN [FILENAME] to store just the text of the letter in a file that already exists and has other contents in it. It's like the above command.
- UN to "un-read" the letter. This means it'll remain in your SMailbox and will appear as a new letter when you do a MAILCK.
- Press RETURN to leave the letter in your SMailbox and go on to the next letter (if there is one).

Let's look at how the FILE command works. You can just type **F** to use it:

Disposition:**F**
You do not have a filing cabinet!
Would you like one created? **Y**
A minimum of 16 storage blocks will be
created. Shall I continue? **Y**
Creating Your Filing Cabinet
Filed

Disposition:

The letter is now filed away. Actually, it isn't. A *copy* of it is. The "original" is still in your SMailbox. That's why the Disposition prompt reappeared. Let's place it in your general file area, too, with the SAVE command:

Disposition:**SAVE LETTER1**

Disposition:

And now let's delete it, by typing **D:**

Disposition:**D**
No More Mail

<S>end,<R>ead,<SC>an,<D>isplay, or <Q>uit?

To look at the letter that was saved in your SMail file cabinet, type **D** for Display at this prompt:

<S>end,<R>ead,<SC>an,<D>isplay, or <Q>uit?**D**

<F>iles or <D>istribution lists?

Now type **F** for <F>iles:

<F>iles or <D>istribution lists?**F**

You have 1 one letter in your filing cabinet and 1
filing category.
Categories are:
MAIL.UFD
<S>end,<R>ead,<SC>an,<D>isplay, or <Q>uit?

To read or scan the letter, type **R MAIL.UFD** or **SC MAIL.UFD**. You'll be given the chance to delete the letter if you wish.

From command level, you can get to this SMailbox file with these commands:

- MAIL R F MAIL.UFD to read the contents of the file
- MAIL SC F MAIL.UFD to scan the contents of the file

You can also create other SMailbox files with different names. When you do that, the command strings would be as follows:

- MAIL R F [FILENAME] to read the contents of the file; for example, MAIL R F LETTER9
- MAIL SC F [FILENAME] to scan the contents of the file; for example, MAIL SC F LETTER1Ø

Let's go back to command level and look at how to display the letter you placed in your general file area:

<S>end,<R>ead,<SC>an,<D>isplay, or <Q>uit?**Q**
—>

At command level, type **FILES** to see a directory of all of your online files. This will include both your general files and your SMailbox files, as this list shows:

```
—> FILES
<USR14B>DEF>DEF999 (ALL), Records= 2, Quota= 22 / 1000
Files= 1.
ALL          1 sam          30 Oct 85 00:44:40    LETTER1
Directories= 1.
ALL          20 dir      0  30 Oct 85 00:44:20    MAIL.UFD
—>
```

You can see the names of the files—LETTER1 and MAIL.UFD, the creation date and time, and the number of storage blocks each file has used. To read any file that's in your general file area, type **TY [FILENAME]**. In this case it'd be **TY LETTER1**:

```
—>TY LETTER1
From: DEF999     2-Lines --EXPRESS--
On:05 OCT 1985 At: 00:35
To: DEF999
Subject: TEST

This is a test of the mail system for myself.
It will show me how easy it is to use SMail.
—>
```

If you ever want to edit this file, type **ED [FILENAME]**. In this case it'd be **ED LETTER1**. This would put you in the STC text editor, which you saw at work earlier in this chapter.

If you want to delete the file, type **DEL [FILENAME]**. In this case it'd be **DEL LETTER1**, like so:

```
—>DEL LETTER1
LETTER1 Deleted.
—>
```

The final feature of The Source I'll illustrate is a bit advanced. Don't try it until you're familiar with The Source manual. I'm illustrating it to give you an idea of just how the system can be customized for your own purposes. As you become conversant with the system, you can build upon the ideas about to be shown.

I'm not very fond of the command level prompt of The Source. The —> (arrow) symbol is just too impersonal for me. Since I use command level most of the time, I have to see that arrow a lot within one session. At least I did until I changed it. In a fit of humanizing the inhuman, this

—>

became this

Hi, Dear:

I'm now assured that I can get a least one kind word a day just by signing onto The Source and watching it purr, "Hi, Dear:" to me as a prompt.

Also, whenever you make a mistake in typing a command at command level, the "—>" prompt becomes "?>". Who needs that? Now, when I mistype something at my lovely "Hi, Dear:" prompt, The Source gently corrects me with "Oopsie, Dear!:".

To change the prompt, be it to something more aesthetic, more compatible with your terminal software, or more compatible with your personality, type **RDY -RB NEWPROMPT**. NEWPROMPT can be an asterisk, a semicolon, a hyphen, an exclamation point, or one word. If you want to change "—>" to "Yeah?," for instance, type

—>**RDY -RB Yeah?**

Don't forget to place a space between **RDY** and **-RB** and **NEWPROMPT**.

If you want the new prompt to be *two* words (as mine is), you must surround the new prompt with single quotes, like so:

—>**RDY -RB 'Hi,Dear:'**

To change the command level error prompt of "?>" to something else, type

—>**RDY -EB NEWPROMPT**

The same format rules apply in changing the regular command level prompt.

This is a nice feature but you would have to *retype* RDY -RB NEWPROMPT and RDY -EB NEWPROMPT every time you signed onto The Source. The system doesn't remember these commands after you have logged off. To change the prompt permanently by making The Source remember these commands, a SID file must be created. A SID file is activated whenever you sign onto The Source. Aside from automatically activating a command (such as changing the command level prompt) or several commands (such as changing both prompts), it'll also place you directly at command level unless you tell it not to. Setting up a SID file is a bit tricky. Consult The Source manual for full details. I'll give you a brief outline and let your imagination (and determination in learning the instructions in the manual) do the rest.

At command level, type **ENTER SID**, followed by the two commands to change your prompt. You can also add commands to scan the bulletin-boards, if you wish. A command such as **POST SCAN MACINTOSH** will perform a scan of the Macintosh bulletin-board and leave you at the POST program. If you don't want that, you can type **MENU** into the SID file in order to have the system activate the menu structure once the prompt has been changed. When you're through, press **Return** to complete the SID file. Both of these options look like this as a complete SID file:

```
—>ENTER SID

Enter Text

RDY -RB NEWPROMPT
RDY -EB NEWPROMPT
POST SCAN MACINTOSH
[RETURN]
—>
```

or

```
—>ENTER SID

Enter Text

RDY -RB NEWPROMPT
RDY -EB NEWPROMPT
MENU
[RETURN]
—>
```

Don't forget that NEWPROMPT stands for whatever the new prompt is to be. To see the SID file work, log off The Source and sign back on. If there's a mistake in the file or something goes awry, start from scratch by typing **CLOSE SID** at command level and then **DEL SID** when the command level prompt appears a second time. Then create a new SID file.

This is just part of what a SID file can do. The Source manual you'll receive as a subscriber will help you get the most out of the SID options. The manual is full of examples of how to use SID files.

The Source offers many more services and features than I've illustrated here. Type PUBLIC at command level to see the many electronic magazines and newsletters that are written and published by other subscribers. The best two are Newsbytes and SourceTrek. (*Note:* At press time, Newsbytes is no longer a User Publication but an actual service. By the time this book is published, you'll be able to access it just by typing **NEWSBYTES** at command level; —>.) A complete list of publications by subscribers, along with the commands to access them from command level, can be found at the end of this chapter.

Although The Source still has some rough edges, it's clear that work is being done in a genuine effort to smooth things out. The many services and features that've been added in just the past year shows that The Source has yet to concede to any of its competitors. If what you've seen in this chapter looks good to you, don't hesitate to subscribe. The Source is a world of its own.

* * *

Additional Information

CONTACT

Source Telecomputing Corporation, 1616 Anderson Rd., McLean, VA, 22102. 1-(800)336-3366; 1-(800)572-2070 (in Virginia); 1-(703)734-7500 (outside the continental United States.).

POST Bulletin-Boards

These are the POST bulletin-boards (categories). For an updated list, type **POST R HELP** at command level.

Antiques, Apartments, Apple, Atari, Automobiles, Aviation, Books/Publications, Bulletin-board, Businesses, CADO, Chatter, Clubs, Collectables, Commodore, CP/M, CPA, CTSlate, DEC, Documentation, Education, Epson, Games, Gripes, Ham-radio, Hardware, Hayes, Heath, Help-wanted, Hewlett-Packard, Hobbies-and-crafts, IBM, Investments, Kaypro, Macintosh, Merchandise, Music, NEC, Novation, Office-equipment, Osborne, PARTI, Personal, Photography, Plato, Politics, Programming, Public, Public-files, Real-estate, Services, Soap-operas, Software, Source, Sports,

Tandy, Taxes, Teens, TI, Transend, Travel, Victor, Video, Visicalc, Xerox, Zenith.

Microsearch Magazine Index

These are the magazines that are abstracted by Microsearch. This is the Microsearch magazine index, with the spellings (or misspellings) transcribed intact.

68' Micro Journal; 80 Micro; 80 U.S.; 99'er Home Computer; A +; A.N.A.L.O.G. Computing; AAMI Journal; Access; Ahoy!; Alternate Source, The; Antic; Apple; Apple Magazine; Apple Orchard; Apple's Apprentice; Atari Connection; Basic Computing; Broderbund Software; Inc.; Business Computer Systems; Business Computing; Business Software; Businessweek; Byte; Call – A.P.P.L.E; Call-A.P.P.L.E.; CAP; CAP Magazine; Classroom Computer Learning; Classroom Computer News; Color Computer; Color Computer Magazine; Color Computer News; Commander; Commodore; Commodore Microcomputers; Compute!; Compute!'s Gazette; Compute!'s PC+PCjr; Compute!'s PC+PCjr Magazine; Computer + Software News; Computer Accessories and Peripherals; Computer Business News; Computer Buyer's Guide; Computer Buyer's Guide and Handbook; Computer Decisions; Computer Digest; Computer Games; Computer Gaming World; Computer Graphics News; Computer Graphics World; Computer Language; Computer Merchandising; Computer Shopper; Computer Trader Magazine; Computer Update; Computer User; Computer!'s Gazette; Computers + Electronics; Computers + Programs; Computers; Computers 84; Computers and Electronics; Computers in Accounting; Computerworld; Computronics; Consumer Reports; Consumer Reports Computers at Home; Core; CP/M Review; Creative Computing; Creative Computing Buyer's Guide 1983; Creative Computing Software Buyer's Guide; Creative Software; Databased Advisor; Data Communications; Datamation; Desktop Computer; Desktop Computing; Digital Review; Dr. Dobb's Journal; Dun's Business Month; Eastern Review; Easy Home Computer; Economist, The; Educational Computer; Educational Computer Magazine; Educational Computing; Educational Learning; Educational Technology; Electronic Fun; Electronic Games; Electronic Learning; Family Computing; Fareastern Economic Review; Financial + Investment Software Review; Forbes; Forth Dimensions; Fortune; Futurist, The; Government Computer News; Hampton's Buyer's Guide to Small Computers; Hardcore Computist; Hi-Res; Hi-Res Magazine; High Technology; Home and Educational Computing!; Home Computer Magazine; Home Magazine; Hot

Coco; IBM PC Update; IEEE Micro; Inc.; Incider; Industry Week; Info-64; Info - 64; Information + Records Management; Infoworld; Inside Washington Apple PI; Interface Age; ISO World; Journal of Financial Software; Journal of Pascal; ADA + Modula-2; Journal of PASCAL;ADA;+Modula-2; Journal of Pascal; ADA; and MODULA-2; Jr; K-Power; Lifelines; Linkup; Link-Up; LinkUp; List; M.D. Computing; MACWorld; Media + Methods; Media and Methods; Media Methods; Micro; Micro Communications; Micro Computing; Micro Computer Printout; Microcomputing; Microkids; Microsystems; Midnite Software Gazette; Mini-Micro Systems; Money; MUG Quarterly; New in Computing Magazine + Buyer's Guide; New in Computing Magazine and Buyer's Guide; New York Times; Newsweek. Nibble; Nibble Express; OC; Office Administration and Automation; Office, The; Online Today; Passages; PC; PC Magazine; PC Products; PC Report; PC Retailing; PC Software; PC Tech Journal; PC Tech Review; PC Week; PC World; PCjr; PCjr Magazine; Peanut; Peelings II; Personal and Business Computer Handbook; Personal and Professional; Personal Computer Age; Personal Computer Handbook; Personal Computing; Personal Software; Popular Computing; Popular Science; Popular Software; Portable 100; Portable Computer; Power of: ES, The; Power/Play; Power/Play Computing; Power/Play Magazine; Pro/files; Professional Computing; ProFiles; Programmer's Journal; Publishers Weekly; Radio-Electronics; Rainbow; Rainbow, The; Reference; Run; Run Magazine; Sextant; Small Business Computers; Small Systems World; Soft Sector; Softalk; Softline; Softside; Software; Software Buyer's Guide; Software Magazine; Software Merchandising; Software Retailing; Software Supermarket; SourceWorld; ST.Game; ST.Mac; Sync; Syntax Quarterly; Systems + Software; Systems and Software; Technology Illustrated; TI Professional Computing; Time; TLC; Today; TPUG Magazine; TRS-80 Micro Computer News; U.S. 80; U.S.News + World Report; Unix/World; User's Guide; User's Guide to CP/M Systems + Software; User's Guide to Systems + Software; Venture; Veterinary Computing; Wall Street Computer Review; Wall Street Journal; Washington Apple PI; Washington Post; Washington Post, The; Washington Times; Whole Earth Software Review.

USER PUBLICATIONS

These are the electronic publications that are produced by subscribers of The Source. To get an updated list, type **PUBLIC 7** at command level. From Command Level, type **PUBLIC** followed by a space and the location number.

TITLE	LOCATION NUMBER
AINetwork	119
Anne's Annals	159
Apple City	113
Christology Course	124
Dial-a-Date	122
Digital Decisions	118
Eater's Digest	156
Elephant Walk Computers	172
First Byte Software	117
Gourmet Diner's Club	127
Image Micro Catalog	171
Independent Record Releases	175
Jobhunter's Handbook	126
Kaypro-Knews	182
The Muses	151, 114
Mylar's Warp	161
New Tech Times	125
Online Educator	157
Oxbridge Legal Forms	123
Product Reviews	116
Public Access Systems	112
Real Times Magazine	111
Religion Online	128
S.A.U.G. Magazine	115, 133
S.A.U.G. Libraries	22
S.I.G.O.P. Library	21
SourceTrek	152
Subfile99	181
Teleresource	174
Vault of Ages	141
W-i-n-k Magazine	154, 131

16 Using local systems

Local Systems are classified as such by *The Computer Phone Book* according to these criteria:

- The system must be running on a supermicro or larger computer.
- The system must have multiple phone lines for access.
- The system must not be available through a nationwide packet-switched telephone network, such as Tymnet or Telenet.

Aside from these three points, it doesn't matter if the system is free or has a per-hour, monthly, or other fee for access. The system can be a "glorified BBS." As long as it meets the criteria, it's classified as a Local System.

In this chapter, we'll look at three Local Systems that are unique and are worth exploring:

- GameMaster
- MicroShare
- StarText

GameMaster

This system, based in Chicago, Illinois, started operations on the very same day that The Source did. That and the fact it's an online system are about all it has in common with The Source, though.

GameMaster offers lots of games. It has small games to pass the time and large games that span galaxies and require teams of people to play.

A subscription to GameMaster is available in two forms:

- $20, which includes 4 hours of connect-time and 8 pages of instructions
- $50, which includes 10 hours of connect-time and a large instruction manual that covers the rules for the whole system and every game on it

There's a $3 per month minimum and $3.60 an hour connect-time charge. Some special, large multiplayer games also have a one-time fee to set up an account. (Again, as with all systems covered in this book, check with the individual companies for their latest rates.) Billing is to credit cards, or prepayment can be arranged. Since GameMaster is not connected to a packet-switched network, you have to call the system long distance and pay for the call yourself. This is standard for all Local Systems.

GameMaster is designed as a large mansion, and moving through it is like playing one huge adventure game. The following are the floors and the rooms in the GameMaster mansion. At one time or another a room will be "closed for renovation," meaning a new game is being written to be placed in that room.

LOWER LEVEL

Mind Room, Locker Room, Time Room, War Room, Club Room, State Room, Engine Room, Board Room, Game Room, Chamber

FIRST FLOOR

Foyer, Kitchen, Parlor, Banquet Room, Mailroom, Door (Front), Greenhouse, Pantry

SECOND FLOOR

Bedroom, Conservatory, Library, Store Room

THIRD FLOOR

Newsroom, Guest Room, Balcony, Dark Room, Three Conference Room(s)

FOURTH FLOOR

Gallery, Archive (Library), Junk Room, Bulletin Board, Classroom, Magic Blackboard

TOP FLOOR

Observatory, Divination Room

Found in these rooms are the following games:

- Airflight Simulator (1 player)
- All/None (1 or 2 players)
- Backgammon (2 players)
- Caverns (1 player multilevel)
- 18-Wheeler (1–6 players)
- GM Air Freight (1–6 players)
- GameMaster Baseball (1 or 2 players)
- GameMaster's Den [Dungeon Game] (multiplayer)
- GameMaster Football (1 or 2 players)
- Makin' Tracks (1–6 players)
- Mini-Dungeon (1 player)
- Nuke Strike!! (2 players)
- Oil Baron (2–4 players)
- Powerplay (1 or 2 players)
- Rack Up (1 or 2 players)
- Eamon (1 player)
- Scavenger Dungeon (1 player, competitive)
- Cosmic Cartels (multiplayer, competitive)

Signing onto the GameMaster system is an adventure in itself. I won't narrate each step here, since most of it is self-explanatory.

```
[GM Doorkeeper]
COM ON IN AND HAVE SOME FUN.

ARE YOU A REGISTERED MEMBER OF THE
GAMEMASTER SYSTEM ?Y

THE MANSION AWAITS. . .
['PLEASE IDENTIFY YOURSELF']

ACCOUNT NUMBER ?
PASSWORD ?
WEDNESDAY, OCTOBER 26, 1984 10:06:44 PM
CURRENT CREDIT BALANCE = 5,000
```

3 MEMBERS CURRENTLY VISITING. . .

WELCOME MIKE

P.A.---------------------------------------
'MEMBER ENTERING MANSION'
----

1. COSMIC CARTELS IS UNDERWAY.
TURNS ARE NOW BEING PROCESSED DAILY.
GET YOUR ORDERS IN A.S.A.P. IF YOU HAVE
NOT ALREADY DONE SO. GOOD LUCK!!

2. SCAVENGER DUNGEON IS STILL BURIED
UNDER A TON OF RUBBLE. WORKING ON IT!

3. THE MAIL ROOM IS NOW OPEN, CASHIER IS
OPEN. LOOK 'UP' IN MAILROOM TO GET INFO
ON MAILBOXES AND CREDITS.

4. FIVE CARD DRAW AND 5 CARD STUD CONTESTS
WILL BE ENDING AT MIDNIGHT DEC. 31ST.

5. EAMON CONTEST POSTPONED INDEFINITELY.

DO YOU WANT TO SEE WHO IS
IN THE HOUSE RIGHT NOW ?**Y**

* G a m e M a s t e r GUEST BOOK *

>> S. CLAUS
>> HARLOW D. STEVENS JR.

= =

DO YOU WANT TO SEND A MESSAGE ON THE
P.A. SYSTEM TO ALL THOSE IN THE HOUSE ?**Y**

OK, YOU WILL NOW BE ALLOWED TO SEND ONE
MESSAGE OF UP TO 70 CHARACTERS TO ALL IN THE MANSION.

INPUT YOUR MESSAGE NOW. .>
Hello from "The Computer Phone Book"[tm]!

THIS THE WAY YOU WANT IT ? —>
Hello from "The Computer Phone Book"[tm]!

Y

```
-------[FOYER ENTRY P.A. SYSTEM]------
Hello from "The Computer Phone Book"[tm]!
======================
```

This message is broadcast throughout the mansion for everyone to "hear." Other subscribers make P.A. announcements as well, giving the mansion setting some life. Then the entryway of the mansion is described:

```
YOU ENTER UPON A GRAND FOYER. THERE ARE
DOORS ON EITHER SIDE OF YOU AND A HALL
IN FRONT OF YOU. THE STAIRWAY TO THE
SECOND FLOOR IS UP FROM HERE.

IF YOU'RE NOT SURE HOW TO USE THE SYSTEM
YET OR IF YOU NEED ASSISTANCE, TYPE HELP
WHEN ASKED FOR CHOICE IN THE FOYER.

What would you like to do
in the FOYER ?
```

You can type **H** at mansion prompts for help:

```
What would you like to do
in the FOYER ? H

IF THIS IS YOUR FIRST VISIT TO THE
GAMEMASTER'S MANSION HERE ARE A FEW
HELPFUL HINTS.

1) YOU CAN MOVE AROUND THE HOUSE EITHER
BY WALKING OR ACTIVATING THE PORTAL
DEVICE WHICH WILL "TRANSPORT" YOU FROM
ANY "ROOM" TO ANOTHER "ROOM". THE WALK
COMMANDS ARE FORWARD, BACK, LEFT, RIGHT,
UP, AND DOWN. THIS IS INPUT WHEN ASKED
FOR "WHICH DIRECTION WOULD YOU LIKE TO
MOVE?". TO USE THE PORTAL, TYPE PORTAL
FOR A DIRECTION WHILE IN A ROOM. THE
FOYER IS CONSIDERED A ROOM FOR USING THE
PORTAL DEVICE. IT IS ALSO RECOMMENDED
THAT YOU HAVE A MAP OF THE HOUSE WHICH
WILL GREATLY HELP IN LOCATING INDIVIDUAL
ROOMS.

2) A LIST OF ALL THE ROOMS AND THEIR
STATUS CAN BE FOUND BY MOVING DOWN ONCE
YOU'RE IN THE MAILROOM. THE MAILROOM
```

CAN BE ACCESSED BY MOVING "RIGHT" FROM HERE.

3) A DETAILED LISTING OF THE EACH ROOM IS LOCATED IN THE LIBRARY WHICH IS ON THE SECOND FLOOR. YOU CAN REACH THE LIBRARY BY MOVING UP, THEN LEFT WHEN YOU REACH THE TOP OF THE STAIRS AND THEN TURN RIGHT WHEN YOU REACH THE END OF THE HALL, OR YOU CAN PORTAL DIRECTLY TO THE LIBRARY. THE LIST IS TO THE LEFT. MOVING TO THE RIGHT, THERE ARE "BOOKS" WHICH CONTAIN INFORMATION ON USING THE FUNCTIONS OF THE HOUSE AND IN PLAYING THE GAMES.

4) IF YOU ARE STILL HAVING TROUBLE, CALL THE HOTLINE (328-9ØØ9) OR LEAVE A NOTE IN THE GAMEMASTER'S MAILBOX OFF THE LEFT IN THE MAILROOM.

5) THERE IS ALSO A LIST OF SPECIAL FOYER FEATURES THAT ARE SEEN BY LOOKING "DOWN."

What would you like to do
in the FOYER ?

Taking a cue from that last hint, let's "look down" by typing **D:**

What would you like to do
in the FOYER ? **D**

```
...............................................................
********  F O Y E R   M E N U  ********
^^^^^^^^^^^^^^^^^^^^^^^^^^^^^^^^^^^^^^^^^^^^^^^^^^^^^^^^^^^^^^^

(F)ORWARD    [==]  MOVES DOWN THE HALL.

(B)ACK       [==]  LEAVE THE HOUSE.

(L)EFT       [==]  ENTER PARLOR.

(R)IGHT      [==]  ENTER MAILROOM.

(U)P         [==]  MOVE UPSTAIRS.

(D)OWN       [==]  GET FOYER MENU.

(P)ORTAL     [==]  ACTIVATE THE PORTAL.
```

```
(PA)P.A.        [==]  TURN YOUR P.A. ON/OFF.

(G)UEST         [==]  CHECK ON OTHER GUESTS.

(H)ELP          [==]  GET HELP INFORMATION.

(CALL)          [==]  REQUEST FOR HELP SENT
                      TO GM STAFF MONITOR.

(S)EE           [==]  GET FOYER DESCRIPTION.

(T)IME          [==]  TIME SPENT IN HOUSE.

(X)PERT         [==]  TOGGLE EXPERT/NOVICE
                      USER MODE.

(HAN)DLE        [==]  CHANGES YOUR P.A. NAME.

(CH)AT          [==]  MOVE INTO PARLOR TALKER.

(M)AIL          [==]  FOR OPENING YOUR MAILBOX.

(DIP)LO         [==]  FOR DIPLOMACY PLAYERS.

What would you like to do
in the FOYER ?
```

If you ever get tired of "walking" through the mansion or get lost, you can use a command to transport yourself from one room to another instantly. The command is **PORTAL,** and this is how it works:

What would you like to do
in the FOYER ? **PORTAL**

E N E R G I Z E ! !
[PORTAL ACTIVATED]
WHAT ROOM ARE YOU THINKING OF ?**PARLOR**

You are now in the Parlor. . .

What would you like to do ?**H**

You are currently in the PARLOR.

Options are --

(B)ACKWARD   TO FOYER
(D)OWN   EMPTY

```
(E)XIT          LEAVE THE HOUSE
(F)ORWARD       SIT & TALK
(L)EFT          SIT & TALK
(H)ELP          THIS MENU
(P)ORTAL        ACTIVATE PORTAL
(Q)UICK         ROOM NAME & TITLE
(R)IGHT         SIT & TALK
(S)HOW          ROOM DESCRIPTION
(T)ALK          VISIT WITH OTHERS
(U)P            EMPTY
```

What would you like to do ?**T**

GRAB A SEAT MIKE .

PARLOR P.A.-------------
'Mike Cane WALKING INTO PARLOR'

Need info ? (Y/N)

The Parlor is a room in which other subscribers can "sit" and talk to one another. It's like CIS's CB and Delphi's Conference system, but it doesn't have any of the extra commands those systems have. (See Chapter 7, Using the CompuServe Consumer Information Service and Chapter 8, Using Delphi.)

When you're on the system, you can ask for additional information at this point. I'll pass it by in this example:

Need info ? (Y/N) **N**
What name do you wish to use ?**MIKE CANE**
Confirm ? —> [Mike Cane] (Y/N)**Y**

** HARLOW **
HI MIKE
HI HARLOW!

That's a brief snippet of what it's like to talk in the Parlor.

As brief as this glimpse of GameMaster is, you should be able to see just how different this system is from the others that are discussed in this book.

If you can't get enough of computer games, pack your bags and spend a few nights in the GameMaster mansion. It'll be the best electronic trip you've ever made.

MicroShare

The second Local System we'll look at also specializes in providing a single service—a large library of CP/M programs that are available for downloading to your CP/M or CP/M-compatible computer.

MicroShare has a $10.00 registration fee and charges $2.25 per hour. The system is available for 300 or 1200 bps, with no additional charge for 1200-bps service. Payment is by credit card or prepayment. For any month in which MicroShare is used, there is a $3 minimum charge.

Located in Milwaukee, Wisconsin, MicroShare has been operating for 3 years and offers, on a rotating basis, the complete public domain software libraries of the following:

- CACHE, The Chicago Area Computer Hobbyist Exchange
- CP/MUG, The CP/M Users' Group
- SIGM, The Special Interest Group/Microcomputers of the Amateur Computer Group of New Jersey

These three libraries are placed on the system one at a time for a full week. The rotation is in the order they're listed above. The placement is made during the MicroShare system maintenance hours, which is between noon and 2 PM Milwaukee local time. MicroShare has a storage capacity of 30 megabytes of disk space.

In addition to these rotating libraries, MicroShare maintains a System Library of programs that are always requested, such as various versions of the MODEM (XMODEM, MODEM7, etc.) terminal program.

Like most online systems, MicroShare allows you to customize the system to work well with whatever machine you're using. These are the commands that may be used:

- 40COL for 40-character lines
- 64COL for 64-character lines
- 80COL for 80-character lines
- BACKSPAC to display a prompt for selecting Video, Printer, or Normal (CP/M) backspace mode
- CASE for UPPER CASE ONLY or UPPER/lower
- DUPLEX for Full or Half Duplex
- NULLS to provide 0 to 9 nulls after a carriage return.

These are some of the commands that can be used on the system:

- ED for the CP/M Text Editor
- LIB to display the Library files (those currently online)

- MLIB to display all Library files (including those currently offline)
- NEWS to display system news
- STATS to display your system use statistics
- TIME to display time of day and date
- TYPESQ to type a squeezed file
- XMODEM to transfer files (up/downloading)

To use any of these commands, just type them at the system prompt.

Signing onto MicroShare looks like this:

```
PORT   1   1Ø/1Ø/85   1Ø:2Ø
WELCOME TO MICROSHARE!
PLEASE ENTER YOUR NAME OR "INFO" FOR
INFORMATION ABOUT THIS SYSTEM.
NAME: MIKE CANE
ACCOUNT CODE:

Hello, Mike.
You are logged on at 1Ø:2Ø.

A>
```

The "A>" (capital A and greater-than sign) is the MicroShare system prompt. This is the standard prompt that is used by the CP/M operating system. It indicates that the "A" disk drive is currently available to the caller. To switch to another drive, type the drive's letter and a colon, like this:

```
A>B:
B>
```

You're now in the B drive. This is a standard CP/M command.

CP/M is an operating system for microcomputers. When it's offered online through a system such as MicroShare or an RCP/M (which means Remote CP/M; as in "remote control"), it's still an operating system. Many, if not all, of the commands that you can use on your CP/M computer are also available to be used online on an RCP/M through your computer. Many of these functions aren't needed and aren't used. What's mainly used is the ability of CP/M to wade through large directories of disk files to locate requested programs.

CP/M online is used to transfer files (downloading and uploading; see Chapter 2, Beginners Start Here). These files can be text (instructions, articles, and so on) or programs (in BASIC, assembler, machine language, Pascal, and so on). Transferring the files requires the use of a special terminal program that does error checking. This enables the files to be transferred in their original form, without any errors in them. The program that's used for transferring is called MODEM, which has many names, such as AMODEM, JMODEM, and MODEM7. Each version is a bit different from the others, and some versions will only work on specific computers.

There's much more to CP/M than I've touched on here. There are whole books that explain how it works, and I suggest that you purchase one of them if you want more details.

MicroShare has an extensive help facility for users who are unfamiliar with CP/M and RCP/M operation. Typing **HELP** brings up the first file:

```
A>HELP

HELP.Ø

This is the HELP function of MICROSHARE. It offers information
and instructions for the use of the major functions of the
MICROSHARE system. Please select one of the following topics
for additional information:

    1) Orientation for first time users.
    2) Hours of operation.
    3) Major MICROSHARE system functions.
    4) MICROSHARE system utilities.
    5) How to use the HELP function.

Type 1-5 for more help, or Ø to quit:
```

Let's type **1** here so you can see just how extensive this help facility is:

```
Type 1-5 for more help, or Ø to quit: 1
FIRST.Ø

Welcome to MICROSHARE!

This system is designed to help the personal computer user get
the most out of his or her system. MICROSHARE offers you
access to a large library of public domain software--programs
which you can transfer to your own computer to run or adapt to
your own requirements. We are also in the process of building
a library of games which you can run on this system. Scheduled
for the future are an electronic mail/bulletin board system and
personal programming in several languages including BASIC,
FORTRAN, PASCAL, and COBOL.
```

```
Select one of the following for more information:

    1) More information for the first time user.
    2) How to configure this system to match your terminal.
    3) Restart the "HELP" system.

Type 1-3 for more help, or Ø to quit:
```

As you can see, there are many ways in which you can approach the help facility and move within it. It'd be worth your time to read the help files if you're hesitant about using the system.

On most RCP/Ms, there are just a handful of commands that will keep you out of trouble if you've never used CP/M at all before. They are the following:

- DIR, which will call up a directory of files on the current disk.
- LIB, which, on MicroShare, will display a directory of the current disk that only has the files currently available online for downloading.
- TYPE [FILENAME.EXT], which will display (TYPE) a file that has the extension .TXT or .DOC.
- XMODEM, which starts the Xmodem protocol downloading process. You shouldn't use this command unless you have the right terminal program.
- BYE or OFF, which will log you off the system if you become lost or frustrated.

Since you really have to use CP/M—or at least read a good book—in order to know about it, I'd rather not go into any further detail about how MicroShare or other RCP/Ms operate. These systems are for people who know how to use that particular operating system. As a non-CP/M user, you'd only become frustrated, confused, or intimidated if you tried to use an RCP/M or MicroShare based on this brief overview. So, my advice is don't try.

When you're ready to use RCP/Ms, consider a subscription to MicroShare. Its connect-time rates are low and it offers thousands of programs. Although these programs are available via RCP/Ms that don't charge for connect-time, MicroShare can guarantee one thing an RCP/M can't—no busy signal.

Startext

Startext has been operating since 1982 and has gone through two generations of hosts and three generations of software.

Serving the Ft. Worth-Dallas MetroPlex, Startext has a flat monthly fee of $9.95. Subscriptions for 3-, 6-, and 12-month periods are available. Startext also publishes a tabloid newsprint "newsletter" titled Startext INK. It's the best publication I've seen an online system produce and contains the flavor that makes Startext a success as an online system.

Startext doesn't use menus. It's a totally keyword-driven system. Type the keyword for the information you want and it'll appear. Startext is always adding new keywords and features. A complete list of Startext keywords can be found at the end of this chapter. Startext also has an electronic mail system, but that won't be illustrated in this chapter. After seeing all of the other electronic mail services in this book, you should have no problem using the one that's available on Startext.

Startext is the largest Local System in the United States. It's also the biggest bargain that can be found in any online system that has a fee.

Signing onto Startext for the first time looks something like this:

```
Time:   8:42 AM
(ØØ4)
Good Morning.
Welcome to
S.T.A.R.T.E.X.T.

You have       Ø new
mail messages. ( Ø)

-----------------
(1Ø/1Ø-Ø8:39)
= = = = = =
SYSTEM HIGHLIGHTS:
   * U.S. suffers
record trade
deficit: (BIZ9)
   * OPEC agrees to
cut oil prices,
Saudi oil minister
says: (OIL)
= = = = = =
   FORECAST: Turning
windy, colder
today. Freezing
rain tonight with
mercury dipping
into the low 5Øs.
See (WEATHER) for
details.
= = = = = =
```

```
   PREVIOUS
STARVOTE: "Do you
think of STARTEXT
as part of the news
media?" 589 YES, 96
NO.
   STARVOTE: "Do you
currently have a
membership to an
athletic facility?"
Vote YES or NO at
any request line.
   ======
   * Copyright 1985,
Fort Worth
Star-Telegram
   * STARTEXT is a
registered trademark

REQUEST:
```

This is the system prompt. It's at this point that you type a keyword to retrieve information. You make a request of the system.

As a first-time caller, you should take the opportunity to vote in the Starvote question just polled. You can do this by typing YES or NO at the first REQUEST prompt, like so:

```
REQUEST:NO
Thank you. Your
STARPOLL response
has been recorded.
REQUEST:
```

Next, you should look at the way the system is set up to work with your computer or terminal. This is done by typing **SHOW.ALL.** This will display all of the system's current settings:

```
REQUEST:SHOW.ALL

User operating mode
is: STANDARD
Your screen is set
to: 24 lines by  20
columns.
Pause after each
frame is:  5
seconds.
```

```
You have no Home
Cursor sequence set
up.
You have no Clear
Screen sequence set
up.
Your display mode
is: Ø (Scroll from
bottom).
You will NOT
disconnect after a
Profile.
Display   Ø NULL
characters at the
end of each line.
Your Nickname is:

Your Delete key is
ASCII decimal code:
   8.
Your Suspend key is
ASCII decimal code:
   19.
Your Resume key is
ASCII decimal code:
   17.
Your Backspace is
ASCII decimal code:
   8.
Your Terminator
sequence is:   13,
1Ø
Your Escape key is
ASCII decimal code:
   27.
Your profile A is:
A1  :
A2  :
A3  :
A4  :
A5  :
A6  :
A7  :
A8  :
A9  :
A1Ø:
A11:
A12:
```

```
A13:
A14:
A15:
A16:
Your profile B is:
B1 :
B2 :
B3 :
B4 :
B5 :
B6 :
B7 :
B8 :
B9 :
B10:
B11:
B12:
B13:
B14:
B15:
B16:

REQUEST:
```

That's quite a lot of information to deal with in your first call. Don't be intimidated by it, though. You can probably ignore most of the technical material. Plus, there are plenty of help files on Startext to aid you in setting up the system to work with your equipment. Since Startext doesn't charge you for the time that you're connected, take your time reading all of the help files so you can become more comfortable with the way the system operates.

The first thing you should do is customize the display to suit your screen. As you've seen from SHOW.ALL, the system is currently set to display 24 lines that are 20 characters wide. Type **SET.SCREEN** to change this. You'll be prompted to type new screen dimensions. I've already filled out the form, which doesn't need any further explanation:

REQUEST:**SET.SCREEN**

Your screen is set
to: 24 lines by 20
columns.
Lines> **24**
Columns> **62**
Your screen has been reset to: 24 lines by 62 columns.

REQUEST:

You can see the change immediately. The next item you'll probably want to fix is the pause between screens. You can't see it on paper, but after 24 lines have been displayed, Startext pauses for 5 seconds. If you'd like to keep this pause, then ignore what I'm about to show you. If you'd like to decrease the amount of pause time or get rid of the pause altogether, here's how to do it. Type **SET.PAUSE** and you'll be prompted to fill in the new setting. Again, I've already filled it out in the illustration:

```
REQUEST:SET.PAUSE

Pause after each frame is:  5 seconds.
Pause> Ø
Pause after each frame is:  Ø seconds.

REQUEST:
```

This will get rid of the pause until you want to change it by typing SET.PAUSE again.

If your computer keyboard doesn't have an ESCape key, you'll have to let Startext assign one of your other keys for that purpose. The ESCape key is what Startext uses as a system interrupt and to send electronic mail. Without it, you'll have to look at material you'd otherwise be able to skip, and you won't be able to send any mail. Type **SET.ESCAPE** to reassign one of your keys:

```
REQUEST:SET.ESCAPE

Your Escape key is ASCII decimal code:  27.
Press the key you wish to become your escape key.
<@
As a result of your desired settings, your account has been
forced into EMULATION mode.
Your Escape key is ASCII decimal code:  64.

REQUEST:
```

In this example, I've assigned the @-sign (at-sign) key as my ESCape key. It's best to assign the ESCape function to a key that you hardly ever use, preferably a nonalphanumeric (A–Z, 0–9) key at that.

Briefly, I'll show you what it's like to retrieve information on Startext using keywords. I'll use the keyword **MAC** to show you what kind of information is available for users of the Apple Macintosh computer:

```
REQUEST: MAC

------------------
(10/10-10:08)

                    MacRumors

                    Paul Dobbs
                    MC 25369
                    ***

This week, I have a short review of a game that I liked, a
few words about what Apple announced this week, and then the
full text of Apple's press releases about the new Mac stuff.

REQUEST:
```

Of course, it continues from this point. But it'd be pointless to display any more because the material would be too dated by the time you read it. You should get the idea, though. Type a keyword and the information is displayed.

Here's another example, using the keyword **TIMEX**:

```
REQUEST:TIMEX

------------------
(10/10-09:20)

                    TIMEX NEWS
                  By Julie Barrett
                     MC 51572
             COPYRIGHT 1985, STARTEXT

Speech Synthesis (at last); List of Companies Supporting
Timex Available

     Okay, I admit it, I love gadgets that talk. Our car
talks, one of our clocks talks, and now, my computer talks.
A few weeks back I wrote about my talking 2068, and I had
several requests for details on getting the 1000 to speak. I
found just the book for you.

REQUEST:
```

Again you can see how easy it is to use Startext.

Don't get the idea, though, from these two brief examples that Startext only has information about computers. That's just a small part of Startext. The system features airline flight information; weather; and business, local, national, and foreign news. There's information about the stock market and commodities and several leisure columns. Go through the Startext index at the end of this chapter and you'll get a better idea of what Startext has to offer.

Startext also offers something that no other online system has. Startext can be customized to help lower your phone costs when you call long distance. Startext can be set to call up certain files automatically and then disconnect you. This is accomplished by setting the PROFILE feature. Profile allows you to select up to 32 keywords in two files (A and B) that the system will retrieve once you're online and type the Profile command (PROFILEA or PROFILEB). You don't have to search through Startext's keyword list or your memory to find keywords for files that you usually access. Just place these keywords into Profile once and let the system do the remembering, and work, for you. For example, this is what part of an A file might look like:

```
A1 = COMEXCH

A2 = COMQUIZ

A3 = STARTEXT
```

When you log on to Startext, typing **PROFILEA** will activate the A file. The system will then retrieve the three files shown in this example A file. To get full information about setting up your A and B files, type **HELP.PROFILE** when you're online.

Startext's low price, ease of use, flexibility, and ever-growing list of contents makes it the ideal choice for a first online system subscription.

* * *

Additional Information

CONTACT:

GameMaster, P.O. Box 6056, Chicago, IL, 60204. (312)884-6630.

CONTACT:

Microshare, P.O. Drawer 11N, Milwaukee, WI, 53201, (414)241-4321.

CONTACT:

Startext, P.O. Box 1870, Ft. Worth, TX, 76101, (817)390-7832.

* * *

Startext Keyword Index

Keywords carry these notations: an update code, specifying how often that keyword is updated; the keyword itself, when it's available, a synonym that keyword can also be accessed with, and a brief description of the file.

UPDATE CODE GUIDE

(D) Updated daily

(W) Updated weekly

(S) Updated seasonally

(A) Updated as needed

(MC) Mail code where questions can be addressed to

Words in parentheses are keyword synonyms.

SPECIAL SERVICES

EXCHANGE (MC 1027)–The Computer Exchange. Buy, sell or trade computer ads.

INFO–The Information Exchange, lists of subscribers by computer type.

HOMEWORK–Bulletin board to offer or receive homework help.

MAIL–Electronic mail. For details, request (HELP.MAIL).

MAILPALS (MC 1027)–A list of readers wanting Starmail penpals.

POSTIT (MESSAGES) (MC 1027)–Bulletin board area for noncommercial messages.

STARVOTE–Details on how to vote on special poll questions.

STATS–Your personal usage statistics on Startext

TALKBACK (MC 1027)–The Communication Exchange. Subscribers interested in computer-to-computer communication.

TIME–Request this to get current time plus the line channel you are phoning on. Include channel numbers when reporting line problems.

VOTETOTALS–Totals of previous STARVOTEs.

SPECIAL INDEX FILES

CCINDEX–Classified keywords.

DALINDEX–Dallas listings.

HELP.COMPUTERS–Index to online computer help files.

SUMS–Guide to main summaries by topic.

WRITERS–Complete list of subscriber-written columns.

SPECIAL STARTEXT FILES

(D) COMMENTS (COM)–Message replies. For previous comments, request OLDCOMMENTS or OLDCOM.

(A) FORUMSURVEY–Results of periodic Subscriber Forum questions.

(A) HELP–Using Startext.

(A) INDEX–Current keyword list.

(A) MANAGER–Manager's newsletter.

(A) NEWKEYWORDS (NEWKEYS)–Keyword additions.

(A) RENEW–Facts about renewing your subscription.

(W) STARTEXT (STAR)–Startext Newsletter (updated weekly).

(A) SUBSCRIBE–Online application form.

(A) TOPKEYS–Top five requested keywords every month.

(A) UPLOAD–How to upload files to Startext.

(A) USERGUIDE–Startext online User Guide.

SPECIAL COMPUTER COLUMNS

HOMECOMP–New each Monday.

COMPTALK–New each Tuesday.

HITECH–New each Wednesday.

HOMECOMP–New each Monday.

ONLINE–New each Wednesday.

USER GROUP NEWSLETTERS AND FILES

ATARI–NTACT news.

DALACE–Dallas Atari User Group Newsletter.

DALUG–Dallas User Group Directory.

FWKUG–Fort Worth Kaypro User Group Newletter.

FWUG–Fort Worth User Group Directory.

MCCC–Mid-Cities Commodore Club Newsletter.

TIMEX–Timex Newsletter.

TRSUSER–Mid-Cities TRS-80 Users Group Newsletter.

SPECIAL COMPUTER FILES

WEEKDAY COMPUTER FORUMS–A special file featuring discussion of various computer topics. Request: MFORUM, TFORUM, WFORUM, THFORUM, and FFORUM.

HELP.COMPUTERS–Index to online computer help files.

APPLECHAT (MC 15718)–Apple tips.

APPLESET–Apple settings for Startext.

ATARICHAT (MC 57834)–Atari news.

BBS (MC 52473)–Reviews of local Bulletin Board Systems.

BOARDS–Metroplex Computer Bulletin Boards.

COCOCHAT (MC 65Ø58)–Color computer news.

COMBIZ–Commodore business program reviews.

COMBOOKS–Books about Commodore.

COMCHAT (MC 26Ø91)–Commodore news and ideas exchange.

COMEXCH (MC 3669)–Commodore Exchange, news and reviews.

COMGAMES–Commodore game reviews.

COMHARDWARE–Commodore hardware reviews.

COMPUTERS (COMP)–Summary of computer news on Startext.

COMPWORDS–Special Computer Dictionary.

COMQUIZ (MC 3669)–Commodore questions and answers.

COMSET–Startext commodore settings.

COMTERM–Commodore terminal software reviews.

COMUTIL–Commodore utility programs.

EPSON (MC 73898)–Epson news.

FOR80 (MC 3114)–News and views for TRS 80 owners.

KAYPRO (MC 61758)–Kaypro news.

MAC (MC 25369)–Macintosh rumors and news.

MICROSCOPE (MC 26Ø19; 45678)–Generic computer column.

PASCAL (MC 1Ø311)–Tips on using Pascal.

PCBOOK (MC 23Ø2)–IBM book reviews.

PCCHAT (MC 34779)–IBM PC reviews.

PCTALK (MC 23Ø2)–IBM Newsletter.

SOFTWARE–Weekly software review.

STARUSER–Profiles of individual Startext subscribers.

TI (MC 8762)–TI Newsletter.

TICHAT (MC 511Ø7)–TI news and ideas.

TI2 (MC 62364)–Second TI newsletter.

TIPRO (MC 2473)–TI Professional column.

STARTEXT HELP FILES

HELP.BACK–Setting your backspace.

HELP.CLASS–How to use classified.

HELP.CLEAR–Defining clear screen operation.

HELP.CODE–Displaying decimal code.

HELP.COMMAND–Using the system commands.

HELP.DELETE–Setting your delete key.

HELP.DELTA–How to use Delta schedules.

HELP.EMULATE–How emulation mode works.

HELP.ESCAPE–Setting your ESCape key.

HELP.HOME–Defining home operation.

HELP.KEYS–How the keywords work.

HELP.MESSAGE–How to send a message.

HELP.MAIL–How to use electronic mail.

HELP.MODE–Defining your mode.

HELP.NICKNAME–How to define a nickname.

HELP.NULL–Setting your printer null codes.

HELP.PAUSE–Setting your pause.

HELP.PROFILE–Setting your Profiles.

HELP.RESUME–Setting your resume key.

HELP.RETURN–Setting your Return key.

HELP.SCREEN–Setting your screen size.

HELP.STANDARD–How Standard Operating Mode works.

HELP.STOCKS–How to get stocks.

HELP.SUSPEND–Setting your suspend key.

HELP.TERM–Setting your termination code.

HELP.UPLOAD–How to upload columns to Startext.

DELTA AIR LINES SCHEDULES

HELP.DELTA–How to use Delta schedules.

DELTACITIES–Alphabetical list of cities Delta serves.

DELTAINDEX–Alphabetical list of airport codes for cities Delta serves.

GENERAL NEWS

(D) Request day of month (1) , (2) , etc., for Today in History file or (TODAY) for current file.

(D) Request (NEWS) plus day of month (NEWS1), (NEWS2), etc., for historical news reports.

(D) AMUSEMENTS (AMUSE)–Amusements news summary.

(D) BRITES–News on the light side.

(D) BUSINESS (BIZ)–Business news summary.

(D) DEATHS–National obituaries of note.

(D) EVENING–Wrapup of the afternoon news.

(D) FORBRIEFS–Foreign news briefs.

(D) LIFESTYLE (LIFE)–Lifestyle summary.

(D) MED–Health and medical news.

(D) METRO–Metro news summary.

(D) MORNING–Stories to start your day.

(D) NATION–National news summary.

(D) NEWS–Day's top stories.

(D) NEWSTIP–Editor's choice.

(S) POLITICS–Political news.

(W) RELIGION–Religion in the news.

(D) SCIENCE (SCI)–Science news.

(D) SCORES–Latest scores.

(D) SPECIAL–Special news summary.

(D) SPORTS–Sports news summary.

(D) STATE–Texas news summary.

(W) SUNDAY–Sunday edition summary.

(D) SURPRISE–Guess what?

(D) TODAY–Current Today in History file.

(D) WORLD–World news stories.

(D) USBRIEFS–National news briefs.

(D) VOICES–Letters to the editor/editorial comment.

WEATHER FILES

(D) FORECASTS–Texas forecasts.

(D) GLOBE–Worldwide weather.

(A) PHONECASTS–Phone forecasts for various U.S. cities.

(D) POLLEN–Pollen count totals, available weekdays.

(D) TEXTEMPS–Texas temperatures.

(D) USTEMPS–U.S. temperatures.

(D) USWEATHER (USWEA)–U.S. weather roundup.

(D) WEATHER (WEA)–Weather news summary.

TELEVISION KEYWORDS

Startext features complete 24 hour TV listings for regular TV and cable programs. Each day's listings are divided into 6-hour listings: 6 AM to noon, noon to 6 PM, 6 PM to midnight, and midnight to 6 AM. Schedules are normally carried 1 week in advance.

Here are the special keywords for TV listings:

Monday: M6A, M12P, M6P, M12A

Tuesday: T6A, T12P, T6P, T12A

Wednesday: W6A, W12P, W6P, W12A

Thursday: TH6A, TH12P, TH6P, TH12A

Friday: F6A, F12P, F6P, F12A

Saturday: SA6A, SA12P, SA6P, SA12A

Sunday: SU6A, SU12P, SU6P, SU12A.

(W) NIELSENS (NIEL)–Nielsen ratings

(W) TVQUIZ–TV questions and answers

STOCK DATA BASES

Request these keywords to use the stock data bases. You can match them by symbol for closing prices. Request (HELP.STOCKS) for more information.

AMX–American Stock Exchange.

NY–New York Stock Exchange.

OTC–NASDAQ Over the Counter stocks.

MUTUAL FUNDS: Request MFA through MFZ for the alphabetical listing of the Mutual Funds of your choice.

BUSINESS KEYWORDS

(D) BONDS–Closing bonds report.

(D) DOLLAR–Dollar trading.

(D) DOW–Markets summary.

(D) FOREXCH–Foreign Exchange rates.

(D) FUTTRADE–Closing commodity tables.

(D) FUTURES (FUT)–Commodity report.

(D) GOLD–Gold prices.

(D) GOLDSIL–Gold and silver futures.

(D) MONEYRATES (MON)–Money rates.

(W) M1–Money supply report.

(W) OIL–Oil industry news.

(W) REALESTATE–Real estate news.

(D) SILVER–Silver prices.

(D) STOCKS–Latest Wall Street report. Updated four times daily Monday to Friday.

SPORTS KEYWORDS (Available seasonally)

BASKETBALL KEYWORDS

(S) BBTOP20–College basketball top 20.

(S) MAVERICKS (MAVS)–Mavericks story.

(S) MAVGAMES–Dallas Mavericks schedule.

(S) NBASTANDINGS (NBA)–NBA standings.

OTHER SPORTS KEYWORDS

(W) FISHING–Texas fishing report.

(S) HOCKEY–Hockey roundup story.

(W) LOCAL FISH–Local fishing report.

(W) SALTFISH–Texas saltwater fishing report.

(S) COLOSKI–Colorado ski report.

(S) NMEXSKI–New Mexico ski report.

SPECIAL SPORTS REPORTS

OLYHIS–Special report on history of the Olympics.

SUPERBOWL–Facts, figures, and records.

COURT REPORTS

(S) CRIMCOURT–Texas Court of Criminal Appeals rulings.

(S) HIGHCOURT–Texas Supreme Court rulings.

(S) SCOTUS–Supreme Court Roundup (when in session).

SCIENCE REPORTS

LUCY1–Special Report on Evolution.

TWISTINDEX–Special Report on Tornadoes.

FEATURE KEYWORDS

(W) BILLBOARD (BILL)–Billboard top 10s.

(W) BOOKS–Book review index plus list of top 10 books.

(A) BOOKREVIEWS (BOOKREW)–10 current book reviews.

(A) COOK–Index to Electronic Cookbook.

(W) DINING–Dining review.

(W) HOTWAX–Record reviews.

(A) NAMES–Names in the news.

(A) PEOPLE–People in the news.

(A) SKYWATCH–Astronomy calendar.

(W) SUNVID–Sunday video game column.

(W) VIDEOPLAY (VP)–Lou Hudson's video game column.

(W) VIDEOGAMES (VIDGAMES)–Billboard's top video games.

(W) VIDEO–Billboard's top selling and renting video.

(W) WHATEVER–Whatever happened to. . .

(A) WHO–Abbott's and Costello's "Who's on First" routine.

FEATURE COLUMNS

(W) ANTIQUES–Questions about antiques.

(W) CHILD–Feature article about children's activities.

(W) COINS–Coin collecting.

(W) DOGS–Pet column.

(W) PARENTS–Advice about kids.

(W) PLANTPRO (PRO) (MC 1643)–Garden advice from Dr. Ricks Pluenneke.

(W) PHOTO–Photography column.

(W) SPERRY–Neil Sperry gardening column.

(W) STAMPS–Stamp collecting.

(W) TEXKIN (MC 33878)–Texas ancestors.

(W) WINE–Wine questions and answers.

MOVIE KEYWORDS

(W) DALMOV–Dallas movies by theater.

(W) FWMOV–Fort Worth movies by theater.

(W) MOVIEGUIDE (MGUIDE)–Gene Siskel's capsule guide to first run films.

(A) MOVIEINDEX–Guide to movie reviews.

(W) MOVIES–Fort Worth movie listings.

(A) MOVIE1-MOVIE2Ø–Movie reviews.

ENTERTAINMENT COLUMNS

(W) ALBUMS–Record reviews.

(W) BMOVIES–"B" movie column.

(W) HOMEVID–Metroplex home video column.

(W) OLDIES–Nostalgia column.

(W) RECORDS–Classical record reviews.

(W) SUDS–Soap opera personalities.

(W) VCR–Tips on using a videocassette recorder.

(W) VIDCLIPS–News and charts for top music videos.

ENTERTAINMENT LISTS

(W) CALENDAR–Metroplex calendar of events.

(W) CONCERTS–Metroplex concert calendar.

(W) FINEARTS (FINE)–Metroplex classical music listings.

(W) MUSVID–Music video schedule.

(A) POINTS–Points of interest.

(W) ROCKMUSIC (ROCK)–Live music performances.

DALLAS AREA LISTINGS

(W) DALCLUBS–Dallas night clubs.

(A) DALGAL–Dallas art galleries.

(W) DALMOV–Dallas movie listings.

(A) DALMUSEUMS (DALMU)–Dallas area museum listings.

(W) DALTHEATERS (DALDRAMA)–Dallas theaters.

FORT WORTH AREA LISTINGS

(W) FWCLUBS–Fort Worth nightlife.

(A) FWGAL–Fort Worth art galleries.

(W) FWMOV–Fort Worth movie listings.

(A) MUSEUMS–Fort Worth museum listings.

(W) THEATERS–Fort Worth theater listings.

SPECIAL COLUMNS

(D) EDBRICE (ED)–Ed Brice's column.

(W) CASEY (MC 1Ø81)–Casey's Place.

(W) DAVE–Humor by Davc Barry.

(W) DEARSONYA–Advice on human relationships.

(D) DOLAN–George Dolan's column.

(A) HAMRADIO (MC 46962)–List of ham radio users on Startext.

(W) JACKSON (EJ) (MC 1125)–Ed Jackson's editorial forum for subscribers.

(A) PSYCOL (MC 35152)–Psychology column. Input invited.

(W) SEX–Sex advice.

(A) SHERROD–Katie Sherrod's commentary from the Star-Telegram.

(W) SUMMERS–Roger Summers' editorial column.

(W) TEENTALK (MC 24468) and (MC 40584)–Teen interest column.

(W) TEENVIEWS (MC 62364)–Views of teens.

(W) YOUNGBLOOD–Bill Youngblood's editorial column.

17 Using bulletin-board systems

It seems that everyone is getting into the act as far as BBSs are concerned. A flood of new BBS software has been hitting the market recently, with each author claiming his or her incarnation is tantamount to manna from heaven. When all the hype has cleared away, only one thing is still evident: The systems that are illustrated in this chapter are still the best-designed systems around. Most recent BBS software caters to sysops at the expense of the caller. The sysops get to see easy, understandable prompts on their side of the terminal. The callers are left to fend for themselves.

Even with the new BBS software that's been released (and will no doubt continue to be released), there are very few variations on the BBS theme that warrant inclusion in this book. I'm sticking with four of the five I explained in the first edition of *The Computer Phone Book.* (RCP/M is omitted because it's explained in the previous chapter, under MicroShare.)

ABBS

ABBS is the first system we'll look at. ABBS stands for Apple Bulletin-Board System. Don't be confused by its name, though. It's not just for people who own or use Apple computers. It's named after the kind of computer it runs on.

When you call an ABBS, press **Return** several times when you get the carrier signal. This allows the system to figure out at what bps you're calling and set itself to that speed. On most ABBSs, you'll see this on your screen (although it depends on the version of the software the system is using):

```
TYPE <C/R>
TYPE <C/R>
```

This might confuse you. Although it looks as if the system is asking you to type the characters <C/R>, it really means to press your **Return** key two more times. Then you'll be asked

```
WHAT IS YOUR FIRST NAME?
WHAT IS YOUR LAST NAME?
```

These questions appear one at a time, not together as shown here. Just type the information you're being asked for. Remember, your name isn't being circulated or placed on some sort of devious list. As you've already seen on CIS (see Chapter 7, Using the CompuServe Information Service), your name is required so you can use all parts of the system. On CIS, you have to type your name to become a member of a Forum. This is the same principle as calling a BBS: The sysop would like to know how many individuals are calling and if they're male or female. It's not surprising that a sysop would be curious; you'd be, too. Don't use a pseudonym. You'll only embarrass yourself. After this, the system will ask

```
WHERE ARE YOU CALLING FROM
(CITY, STATE)?
```

It's standard practice to type the full name of your city and the two-letter postal service abbreviated form of your state; for example, CA for California and NY for New York. If you try to type the full state name, the system will probably reject it and ask you to try again.

Next, you'll be asked

```
WHAT IS YOUR PHONE NUMBER?
(XXX-XXX-XXXX)
```

The format for typing your phone number is area code-exchange-number, for example, 800-555-5555. Even if you're in the same area code as the system, you'll still have to type the area code. Again, your phone number will *not* appear in the system's userlog, so don't be concerned about getting calls from strangers in the dead of night. The reason sysops ask for a phone number are many, including the following:

- The sysop wants to know that a real person is calling the system.
- The sysop wants to discourage people who would try to vandalize the system.

- The sysop has had problems in the past with harassment from callers and wants to be able to hand over such offenders to the authorities if they return.
- The system is not for the general public, and the sysop would like to be able to phone new callers to let them know that.
- If the system crashes while you're on it, the sysop will want to know what happened so it can be fixed and not occur again.

Some systems won't let you go any further if you don't type your phone number. If you have any qualms about giving out your home phone number, type your work number.

When you're done entering this information, the system will repeat it so you can verify that everything is OK.

```
HELLO MIKE CANE FROM NEW YORK,NY
HAVE I MISSPELLED ANYTHING (Y/N)?
```

If something isn't correct, type **Y** and the process will start again. If everything is A-OK, type **N** to see

```
IS THIS YOUR FIRST TIME ON THIS SYSTEM
(Y/N)?
```

If it is, type **Y.** You'll probably see a brief explanation of the system's commands, as well as information about the system's hours, it's purpose, and how you're expected to conduct yourself as a caller.

On your second call, once you've been given this introduction, you can type **N** here. That's what I'll do in this illustration, which will display the next step of the signon process:

```
TIME IN:Ø1:46:16
YOU ARE CALLER 15775
LOGGING MIKE CANE TO THE DISC. . .
```

This means that your name, city, and state are being placed in the online userlog. It may also be printed out on paper on the sysop's end, along with your phone number.

Then you'll see

```
                WELCOME TO THE

          APPLE BULLETIN BOARD SYSTEM

                 VERSION 4.1
```

Next, you might see some system bulletins with notices about current events taking place on the BBS. After that, you'll see the main prompt of the system:

```
FUNCTION:
(A,B,C,D,E,G,H,K,L,N,Q,R,S,T,V,W,X,
DOWNLOAD, UPLOAD, NEWS, CONF?)?
```

Not every ABBS will have all of the features shown in this prompt. Download, upload, News, and Conf(erence) are options that sysops must add themselves. They aren't standard on every system.

Now that you have the system prompt, what do you do? On virtually all BBSs, just as you've seen on the National Systems in this book, you can type a ? (question mark) or an H. Either of these will bring an explanation or a full menu. Typing a **?** at this prompt will display the full system menu, which looks like this:

```
FUNCTIONS SUPPORTED:

A     =  APPLE 40 COLUMN
B     =  PRINT BULLETIN
C     =  CASE SWITCH
D     =  DUPLEX SWITCH (ECHO/NO ECHO)
E     =  ENTER MESSAGE INTO SYSTEM
G     =  GOOD-BYE (LEAVE SYSTEM)
H     =  HELP WITH FUNCTIONS
K     =  KILL (ERASE) A MESSAGE
L     =  LINE FEED (ON/OFF)
N     =  NULLS (SET AS REQ'D)
Q     =  QUICK SUMMARY OF MSG'S
R     =  RETRIEVE MSG
S     =  SUMMARY OF MSG'S
T     =  TIME OF DAY
V     =  TOGGLE VIDEO/PRINTER TERMINAL MODE
W     =  PRINT WELCOME MESSAGE
?     =  PRINTS FUNCTIONS SUPPORTED
DOWNLOAD  =  DOWNLOAD SOFTWARE TO YOUR APPLE
UPLOAD  =  UPLOAD FILES/SOFTWARE TO THIS SYSTEM

NEWS  =  INFO OF INTEREST TO SYSTEM USERS
CONF  =  SWITCH CONFERENCES

FUNCTION:
(A,B,C,D,E,G,H,K,L,N,Q,R,S,T,V,W,X,
DOWNLOAD, UPLOAD, NEWS, CONF?)?
```

Typing H at this menu will give you an explanation of each function. These explanations are reprinted in the Appendix.

Now that you've seen the full complement of commands available on an ABBS, where do you go from here? It depends on you. Some people go directly into reading the messages. Others get a list of subject headers and then choose the individual messages that have an interesting subject.

Here, I'll show you the fastest way to go through an ABBS's message base. This will keep your connect-time to a minimum and still allow you to get in some interesting reading.

First, type **X** at the long prompt to shorten it:

```
FUNCTION:
(A,B,C,D,E,G,H,K,L,N,Q,R,S,T,V,W,X,
DOWNLOAD, UPLOAD, NEWS, CONF?)? X

FUNCTION:
```

Now, type **Q** for a quick summary and you'll see this:

```
FUNCTION: Q

STARTING MSG # (25ØØ/26ØØ)?
```

This means that the system has 100 messages on it, starting with number 2500 and ending with number 2600. You can start with the earliest message (2500) or the latest (2600) or even somewhere in the middle. Let's start with the earliest. You don't have to type 2500, though, when you start with the earliest message. Just type **1**, and the system will understand what you mean. At that point, you'll see the abbreviated message headers. Have a piece of paper and a pen nearby so you can jot down the numbers of the messages that you'd like to read after the scan.

```
STARTING MSG # (25ØØ/26ØØ)? 1

MSG #25ØØ SUBJ: DOCTOR WHO
DATE: 1Ø/Ø1/85
MSG #25Ø1 SUBJ: CAPTAIN HARLOCK
DATE: 1Ø/Ø1/85
MSG #25Ø5 SUBJ: HAWKNEST <PRIVATE>
DATE: 1Ø/Ø1/85
MSG #25Ø6 SUBJ: GALAXY EXPRESS 999
DATE: 1Ø/Ø1/85
MSG #25Ø7 SUBJ: RAIDEEN
DATE: 1Ø/Ø1/85
```

This list continues until you reach message number 2600 or interrupt the scan by issuing a Control-K. You won't be able to read any message that's marked <PRIVATE> as number 2501 is.

After you've scanned as many messages as you care to, you can retrieve them individually like so:

FUNCTION: **R;2500**

This will display message number 2500:

MSG #2500
SUBJ: DOCTOR WHO
TO: ALL
FROM: JIM CRAWFORD
DATE:10/01/85

Does anyone know when the PBS station
here is going to start showing the
Colin Baker episodes? The Davison ones
ended two months ago and all we've been
seeing now are the Pertwee ones. Does
anyone know anything about this? Will
we all have to build a TARDIS to see
the Colin Baker series?

After the message, you'll be prompted with

MSG# TO RETRIEVE (2500/2600)?

You can now type the number of the next message to retrieve. You can also retrieve a group of messages by separating the numbers with semicolons, like this:

MSG# TO RETRIEVE (2500/2600)?**2510;2511;2537**

or like this:

FUNCTION?**R;2510;2511;2537**

Experiment with the various ways you can retrieve messages after you've read the appendix that details all of the ABBS functions.

If you want to leave a message on the system, type **E** for Enter a Message. You'll see this:

FUNCTION?**E**

```
THIS WILL BE MESSAGE #2601
SUBJECT?
```

Type a subject:

```
SUBJECT?WHO IS COLIN BAKER?
TO?
```

Type ALL if the message is for everyone to read or a name if the message is for a specific caller:

```
SUBJECT?WHO IS COLIN BAKER?
TO?JIM CRAWFORD
LOCK (Y/N)?
```

If you don't want the message to be erased from the system by anyone except yourself and the sysop, type **Y** in response to this prompt:

```
LOCK (Y/N)?Y
PASSWORD FOR ERASE (4 CHARS. MAX.)?
```

Type any four letters that you wish, but make sure that you write them down somewhere so you'll be able to erase the message later if you want to.

```
PASSWORD FOR ERASE (4 CHARS. MAX.)?DWHO
MARK AS PRIVATE MAIL?
```

When you make a message private, the recipient has to know the password of the message in order to read it. In this example, I'll type **N**:

```
MARK AS PRIVATE MAIL?N
YOU MAY NOW ENTER UP TO 20 LINES OF
UP TO 64 CHARACTERS OF TEXT PER LINE
1?
```

"1" is the prompt for you to start typing the text of the message. The reason there is a question mark following the number is so you can upload the message, using a terminal program that'll send a line of text each time it sees that question mark. When that question mark appears, it lets the terminal program know it's okay to transmit a line of text. This is known as prompted uploading and is available in some form or another on most National, Local, and BBS online systems. If you're not uploading your message text, you should type it online, like this:

```
1?Jim: I've ben a Dr. Who fan for
2?some time, too. I think the Baker
3?episodes will be on it the Fall.
4?[RETURN]
```

When you're finished typing the message, press **Return,** as shown, on a blank line to go to the next step in the process, which looks like this:

```
4?[RETURN]

(A,C,D,E,L,R,S,?)?
```

Typing a **?** will display the full menu of options:

```
(A,C,D,E,L,R.S,?)??

ENTRY FUNCTIONS:

A   =   ABORT
C   =   CONTINUE ENTRY
D   =   DELETE A LINE
E   =   EDIT A LINE
L   =   LIST LINE(S)
R   =   RESTART FROM BEGINNING
S   =   SAVE MESSAGE TO DISC

(A,C,D,E,L,R,S,?)?
```

There's a mistake on line number 1. "Ben" should be "been." To correct it, type **E** for Edit a Line:

```
(A,C,D,E,L,R,S,?)?E
EDIT WHICH LINE?
```

Type the line number, which is **1:**

```
EDIT WHICH LINE?1
LINE 1 CURRENTLY IS:

Jim: I've ben a Dr. Who fan for

NEW LINE? (C/R TO LEAVE THE SAME)
```

On some BBSs, you have to retype the entire line just to correct a simple mistake. This is not so with ABBS and BBSs of its caliber. ABBS has a line editor similar to the ones you've seen on CIS (see Chapter 7, Using the CompuServe Consumer Information Service) and The Source (see Chapter 15, Using The Source).

Carrying out an edit looks like this:

LINE 1 CURRENTLY IS:

Jim: I've ben a Dr. Who fan for

NEW LINE? (C/R TO LEAVE THE SAME)

/ben/been
LINE 1 CURRENTLY IS:

Jim: I've been a Dr. Who fan for

NEW LINE? (C/R TO LEAVE THE SAME)**[RETURN]**
(A,C,D,E,L,R,S,?)?

Type **S**, for Save to Disc, in order to place the message on the system for others to read and respond to. You'll see

(A,C,D,E,L,R,S,?)?**S**
SAVING TO DISC. . .

FUNCTION?

If you wish, you can read the message to make sure it's there, using the methods for message retrieval you've already read about.

Once you're done using the system, type **G** to log off. Remember, hanging up on a system can cause it to lock up and prevent others from using it. Sysops don't need that kind of aggravation and added work. Even if you don't agree with the content of a system or like a system, you don't have a right to harass the system, its sysop, and its callers. No one is forcing you to call a system. Sysops would rather have friends online, not enemies. Be a friend.

Of all of the BBSs you can call, none are as easy for a first-time caller as is ABBS. If there's an ABBS in your area and you've never called a BBS before, do yourself a favor and give it a try. Not only will you meet new people and see what's happening in your area, you'll gain confidence in using a BBS. That'll help you to move onto other systems.

Conference Tree

One such system that you could move onto is Conference Tree, which is a wonderful tree-structured conferencing system. Always imitated yet never bettered, this is the model for computer conferencing systems, offering a handful of commands that allow you to maneuver through a large textual database with ease. Developed by the CommuniTree Group, a firm dedicated to demystifying computers for the general public, Conference Trees usually provide a lively forum for all sorts of topics. Nuclear disarmament, software piracy, hardware clones, music, television, and movies are just a few of the topics that've brought people together in heated debate and discussion. Signing onto a C-Tree (as it's also called) looks like this:

```
WELCOME TO THE CONFERENCE TREE
TERMINAL LINE LENGTH (2Ø-8Ø,
OR CARRIAGE RETURN FOR 8Ø?)[RETURN]
LOWER CASE OK? (C/R = YES)?[RETURN]

TYPE "READ HELP" ANY TIME
OR "READ CONFERENCES" TO START
"S" KEY TO PAUSE OR RESUME PRINTING

COMMAND?
```

In this example, I've pressed Return to accept an 80-character per line display with uppercase and lowercase letters. The system prompt is "COMMAND?" and this signon notice has given you just enough information to start using the system. Typing **READ CONFERENCES** (without the surrounding quotes shown in the signon message) will start the display of conferences on the system, which will look something like this:

```
COMMAND? READ CONFERENCES

***CONFERENCES              Ø-JAN-83

    PARENT = NONE            USAGE 15ØØ

CURRENT CONFERENCES ON THIS CONFERENCE TREE SYSTEM ARE:

    + + + SUBMESSAGES + + +
HELP                       16-JUL-83
ANNOUNCEMENTS              2Ø-JUL-83
FLAGSHIP                   2Ø-JUL-83
```

```
SYSOP                    20-JUL-83
USERS                    21-JUL-83
SOFTWARE-REVIEWS         23-JUL-83
HARDWARE                 25-JUL-83

COMMAND?
```

This is the list of conferences on this system. To read any of them, type **READ** and the conference's name. For example, **READ SOFTWARE-REVIEWS** will read that conference. When you're on a C-Tree, you'll see conferences that may have several words separated by hyphens or periods or other nonalphabetical characters. You must type the conference name exactly as it appears in order to read it. When you read a conference, you'll see the first message that was posted; replies to that original message will be listed as submessages below, like this:

```
COMMAND? READ SOFTWARE-REVIEWS

***SOFTWARE-REVIEWS               23-JUL-83

    PARENT = CONFERENCES                USAGE 1300

This is where you are to place your personal reviews of
software for any type of machine. Please be as
detailed as possible in your reviews. -- Sysop.

     + + + SUBMESSAGES + + +
APPLE-SOFTWARE                 23-JUL-83
COMMODORE-SOFTWARE             23-JUL-83
IBM-PC-SOFTWARE                24-JUL-83
TRS-80-SOFTWARE                25-JUL-83
```

To read any of the submessages, which are really conferences, too, type **READ** followed by its name.

That's how a C-Tree works. The more you read, the deeper into the message system you go. Conferences are made up of one message and replies to that message and then replies to those messages, and so on, extending for as many levels as the system can support. How deep a conference will be depends on the contributions from the callers and the amount of disk space the sysop can spare for any one conference. Some C-Trees are nothing more than one large conference, covering a single topic that's broken into smaller chunks that each cover one aspect of the topic.

A very useful command to know is INDEX. It allows you to see just how much activity is going on in any single conference or portion of a conference. As an example, I'll illustrate the index for the SOFTWARE-

REVIEWS conference. To use this command, type **INDEX** and the conference name:

```
COMMAND? INDEX SOFTWARE-REVIEWS

SOFTWARE-REVIEWS                      2Ø-JUL-83
  APPLE-SOFTWARE                      23-JUL-83
    GAMES                             24-JUL-83
      ZORK-I                          25-JUL-83
        LOCKED-DOOR?                  26-JUL-81
      FROGGER                         27-JUL-83
        VIDEO.GAMES                   27-JUL-83
    VIDEO-GAMES                       25-JUL-83
    DATABASES                         24-JUL-83
      APPLEWORKS                      24-JUL-83
      DB-II                           24-JUL-83
  COMMODORE-SOFTWARE                  23-JUL-83
    TERMINAL-PGMS                     24-JUL-83
      VIDTEX-64                       24-JUL-83
        VIDTEX-WOES                   24-JUL-83
          V4.ØC                       25-JUL-83
      SKIWRITER                       26-JUL-83
        WHO-MAKES-IT?                 27-JUL-83
          PRENTICE-HALL               28-JUL-83
        ANY-GOOD-4-WP?                27-JUL-83
          YES!                        27-JUL-83
          IT-DEPENDS                  27-JUL-83
  IBM-PC-SOFTWARE                     24-JUL-83
    LOTUS                             21-JUL-83
      TOO-MUCH-$$$                    24-JUL-83
        WORTH-IT!                     24-JUL-83
        R-U-NUTZ?                     24-JUL-83
    SYMPHONY                          24-JUL-83
      FORT-KNOX-PRICES!               25-JUL-83
  TRS-8Ø-SOFTWARE                     25-JUL-83
```

It goes on.

As you can see, it looks like an index. And that's what it is. The INDEX command shows you the logical progression of all of the conferences, the original submessages, the submessages to the submessages, and the submessages to those submessages. In other words, the whole conference is mapped out for you.

You can also use INDEX at any point on just one part of a conference to see how long the conference is and how far you'd have to read to reach the end of a discussion. Typing **INDEX TERMINAL-PGMS,** for example, would show you how far this submessage of the COMMODORE-SOFTWARE discussion is carried:

```
COMMAND? INDEX TERMINAL-PGMS

  TERMINAL-PGMS               24-JUL-83
    VIDTEX-64                 24-JUL-83
      VIDTEX-WOES             24-JUL-83
        V4.OC                 25-JUL-83
    SKIWRITER                 26-JUL-83
      WHO-MAKES-IT?           27-JUL-83
        PRENTICE-HALL         28-JUL-83
      ANY-GOOD-4-WP?          27-JUL-83
        YES!                  27-JUL-83
        IT-DEPENDS            27-JUL-83
```

You can also abbreviate the READ and INDEX commands to their first letters, R and I, respectively. Knowing just these two commands will allow you to go through a C-Tree with little, if any, trouble the first time you call it. To get the most out of the system, though, be sure to read the complete list of instructions for all C-Trees that's reprinted in the appendix of this book.

A Conference Tree system is worth a long-distance call anytime to nearly any place. They're seldom dull, often very interesting, and always worth your time. This is a distinction and a blanket recommendation I can't give to any other type of BBS.

Dial-Your-Match

The next type of BBS you'll get a peek at is called Dial-Your-Match (commonly referred to as DYM). Its sole purpose is matchmaking. The sexual slant of a DYM depends on the individual sysop, so don't be surprised if you call a DYM without knowing its slant beforehand and finding out its orientation is not your cup of tea.

When you call a DYM, you'll see a signon message similar to this one:

```
=*  =*=*=*=*=*=*=*=*=*=*=*=*=*=*=*=*=*=*=*=*  =*
=*                                            =*
=*                                            =*
=*              WELCOME TO        TM          =*
=*                                            =*
=*                                            =*
=*                                            =*
```

```
=*                  DIAL-YOUR-MATCH #1                   =*
=*                                                       =*
=*                                                       =*
=*                THE ONLY WORLD-WIDE                    =*
=*                                                       =*
=*                                                       =*
=*             COMPUTER MATCHING SERVICE                 =*
=*                                                       =*
=*                                                       =*
=*         (C) 1982 MATCHMAKING ENTERPRISES              =*
=*                                                       =*
=*   =*=*=*=*=*=*=*=*=*=*=*=*=*=*=*=*=*=*=*=*            =*
```

```
—> DIAL-YOUR-MATCH WILL NOW ONLY ALLOW
—> YOU TO STAY ON FOR UP TO 25 MINUTES
```

This time limit, by the way, will vary from system to system. It depends on how many people use the system each day.

```
675 CALLERS NOW IN THE DATE-A-BASE!
YOU ARE CALLER #51345
LOGGED ON AT 02:45 on 10/10/85
HAVE YOU CALLED DIAL-YOUR-MATCH BEFORE?
=>
```

If you haven't called the individual DYM system before, type **N**. If you type **Y**, you'll have up to three chances to type your password before the system hangs up. As a first-time caller, you won't have a password and you'll have to go through the process of getting one if you want to gain entry to the system. Once you've typed **N**, you'll see a notice that reads something like the following one. It varies, of course, from system to system.

```
=*=*=*=*=*=*=*=*=*=*=*=*=*=*=*=*=*=*=*

BEFORE YOU CAN DIAL-YOUR-MATCH, YOU

MUST ANSWER A QUESTIONNAIRE GIVING THE

COMPUTER INFORMATION ABOUT YOURSELF.

THE COMPUTER WILL THEN BE ABLE TO

MATCH YOU TO OTHER COMPATIBLE CALLERS.


=*=*=*=*=*=*=*=*=*=*=*=*=*=*=*=*=*=*=*
```

WARNING!! ALL INFORMATION IN THE

FOLLOWING QUESTIONNAIRE MAY BE

RELEASED TO ANYONE CALLING THIS SYSTEM.

REMEMBER! NONE OF YOUR PERSONAL

INFORMATION IS CONFIDENTIAL AND

YOU MUST COMPLETE A QUESTIONNAIRE

TO BE ALLOWED ON THIS SYSTEM.

=> DO YOU WANT TO CONTINUE?

=> (YES/NO) =>

Typing **Y** in response will begin the questionnaire, which usually looks like this:

```
=*   =*=*=*=*=*=*=*=*=*=*=*=*=*=*=*=*=*=*=*=*   =*
=*                QUESTIONNAIRE                 =*
=*   =*=*=*=*=*=*=*=*=*=*=*=*=*=*=*=*=*=*=*=*   =*
```

WHAT IS YOUR FIRST NAME (OR HANDLE):
=> **MIKE**
WHAT CITY ARE YOU CALLING FROM:
=> **NEW YORK**
WHAT IS THE 2-LETTER POST OFFICE
ABBREVIATION OF THE STATE YOU ARE
CALLING FROM:
=> **NY**
YOUR FIRST NAME IS: MIKE
YOU'RE CALLING FROM: NEW YORK, NY
IS THAT CORRECT? =>

Confirming the correctness of the information by typing **Y** will start the actual questions:

WHAT IS YOUR SEX?
A. MALE
B. FEMALE
=> **A**
YOU PICKED: A —> MALE
CORRECT? —> **Y**

You'll be required to confirm the correctness of your reply to each question. This is to make sure that you don't make a mistake and that your questionnaire answers are the ones that you want everyone who calls the system to see.

A typical DYM questionnaire contains no more than 25 questions. Take your time filling them out making sure that you don't use up the system's time limit on just the questionnaire alone.

Once you've completed the questionnaire, you'll be assigned an Address Code. This is your User ID for the system and will consist of your first name (or part of it) and three numbers. This ID will be your system address to receive private mail from other callers. You'll also receive a password that'll allow you to gain access to the system without having to fill out the questionnaire each time you call. *Make sure that you write down your Address Code and password immediately after you get them!* The system will ask you if you've written down both of them. If you type **Y** in response, your screen will go blank and you'll be asked to type each of them for the system to check that you noted them correctly.

Next, you'll see the following menu:

```
—> DIAL-YOUR-MATCH COMMANDS <—

B     —> BROWSE QUESTIONNAIRES
C     —> CHAT WITH THE MATCHMAKER
G     —> GOODBYE
M     —> MATCHMAKER, MAKE ME A MATCH
N     —> SET NULLS
O       > OTHER DIAL-YOUR-MATCH SYSTEMS
P     —> PUBLIC MESSAGE BOARD
R     —> READ PRIVATE MAIL
S     —> SEND PRIVATE MAIL
?     —> HELP WITH COMMANDS

MIKE, WHAT NOW?
—> ?,B,C,G,M,N,O,P,R,S =>
```

The above menu is pretty much self-explanatory. I'll illustrate choice **M** here:

```
MIKE, WHAT NOW?
—> ?,B,C,G,M,N,O,P,R,S =>M

MATCHMAKER, MAKE ME A MATCH
=> COMPLETE SEARCH TAKES 7 MINUTES
```

```
*NOW SEARCHING FOR YOUR PERFECT MATCH*
     P TO PAUSE, S TO STOP
```

Actually, the search time will vary from system to system. It depends on how many callers are in the "Date-A-Base." DYMs with few callers will take only 2–3 minutes to complete a match.

Eventually, you'll see something like this on your screen:

```
ADDRESS CODE        %       AGE      ST      PREF
==========        ====    ======     ==      ===

ALICEØØØ           64%     18-2Ø     CA     HETERO
BRATØØØ            57%     26-3Ø     PA     HETERO
CATHYØØØ           53%     13-17     CA     BI
DEBSKIØØØ          51%     31-4Ø     PA     HETERO
```

It shows you the Address Code of the people in the system, the percentage of matches between their questionnaire answers and yours, their age range, the state they live in, and their sexual preference. HETERO means heterosexual, BI means bisexual.

The next step you take depends on you. You can either immediately send private mail to those you've been matched with, or you can look at the answers they gave in their questionnaires to see if you're really compatible and to what degree. To look at the questionnaires, type **B,** for Browse Questionnaires. You'll be given the option of only reading each person's answers or of reading the questions with the answers. When you use the B command, you'll also get some statistics on the person, such as how many times that person has called the system, how many days ago the last call was, and if the person has any open mail slots to receive a private message from you.

In the 1960s, there was a flurry of hype about the arrival of computerized dating services. Most of it was bunk. The "computers" were clerks who did the tabulations themselves. Dial-Your-Match is a true computerized dating service. The best part is that it's only the price of a phone call.

PMS

The final BBS we'll look at is PMS. PMS stands for People's Message Service, and it's my personal favorite of all types of BBS software. I'll illustrate a feature you'll find on other systems, too—marking messages.

I've chosen PMS to illustrate this feature because on PMS it's easier and faster than on any other online system, including National Systems.

Once you've established contact with a PMS, you'll see

```
PMS - SANTEE, CA
USERID (N=NONE):
```

If you don't have a User ID, type **N.** You may request a User ID from the sysop before you log off. (Don't be disappointed if he or she can't give you one; they're sometimes limited to only 100 callers.) After you've typed **N**, you'll see this series of questions, which I've already replied to in this illustration:

YOUR FULL NAME?**MIKE CANE**
City, St.?**New York, NY**
Phone number ?**212-555-5555**
You are Mike Cane from New York,NY
Is that right?**Y**
Logging caller #75655 at 16:32 Pacific

Notice how PMS switched from sending all uppercase to uppercase and lowercase when I typed uppercase and lowercase. After the system has logged your name onto the disk, you'll get a brief command reminder and the system prompt:

```
Type "N" for system news.
Type "?" for commands.
Command ?
```

Remember that virtually any online system will give you a menu or a help file when you type a **?** (question mark). In this case, typing a **?** will display the full menu of PMS commands. It'll look like this:

```
——>> System Commands

E    =   Enter a message into system.
F    =   Features, articles, excerpts.
G    =   Goodbye. Leave system. (Hangup)
H    =   Help with various system functions.
I    =   Information about system.
K    =   Kill a message from the file.
M    =   Message alert. Messages for you?
N    =   News -- System news.
O    =   Other systems current summary.
Q    =   Quickscan of all message headers.
```

```
QP          =  Quickscan of private msg headers.
R           =  Retrieve a message from the files.
S           =  Scan of all message headers.
SP          =  Scan of private message headers.
SR          =  Selective message retrieval.
T           =  Time, date and connect time.
U           =  User modifiable system functions.
X           =  eXpert user mode. (On/Off toggle)
Z           =  Continue message entry after abort.
?           =  Prints this list of commands.
*           =  Flagged message memory retrieval.
TALK        =  Lets you talk to the Sysop.
TEST        =  Modem continuous test loop.
NEWCALL     =  Information for new callers.
ALT         =  Switch message bases.
GENERAL14   =  File transfer - Download files.
GENERAL15   =  File transfer - Upload files.

Command ?
```

The PMS help file, reprinted in the appendix, details all of the above commands. Familiarize yourself with all of the commands that you can use on a PMS before you call one. This is especially important if you're calling long distance.

Two tricks that'll save you time online are illustrated here—the SR and Q commands. SR stands for Selective Retrieval. As it implies, it's a way to search the Subject fields of messages for any keyword that you supply. It's almost like using a search service, the CIS Forum message base, or POST on The Source. (See appropriate chapters.)

Using the SR command to look for all messages that contain the word "BBS" in their Subject field looks like this:

Command ?**SR;BBS**

Notice that I combined the two elements by separating them with a semi-colon, just like on ABBS.

The actual search will look like this:

```
Command ?SR;BBS

Msg #45Ø on 1Ø/Ø9/85 @ 23:28 (2)
Subj: BBS???, To: All
From: Akira Fitton, New York,NY

Has anyone found a BBS devoted to
filmmaking or video???
```

```
Msg #490 on 10/10/85 @ 16:55 (4)
Subj: Resistance BBS, To: All
From: Mike Donovan, Los Angeles,CA

Announcing the Freedom BBS!
Join the *real* Freedom Network! Help exterminate the lizards!
This is a 9600 bps system only, since we have to work fast!
Call now!—> 555-5555. V!
```

The search continues.

As you can see, PMS retrieved messages that had the letters "BBS" in the Subject field, regardless of any other words or characters present. It's a great time-saver, allowing you to zip through the messages without having to scan or quickscan all of the headers.

In the two message headers illustrated above, you'll notice there are numbers within parentheses in their first lines—(2) and (4). These are the numbers of lines of text in the message. This information is helpful in determining how long you'll be online reading messages when you've done a quickscan of the messages.

I'll now illustrate a quickscan:

```
Command ?Q
Msg# (240/490) ?490
```

PMS asked me which message the quickscan should start at, and I specified the highest number in the system. This will cause PMS to run through the messages from the most recent to the earliest. I could've done a command string such as Q;999 to accomplish the same thing. Not all PMSs have that ability, though, and some will prompt you for a starting message number. The quickscan will look like this:

```
Command ?Q
Msg# (240/490) ?490

Msg #490 on 10/10/85 @ 17:05 (4)
Subj: Hello America!, To: All
Msg #489 on 10/10/85 @ 16:55 (4)
Subj: Resistance BBS, To: All
Msg #488 on 10/10/85 @ 16:15 (10)
Subj: HawkNet, To: All
Msg #484 on 10/10/85 @ 16:05 (6)
Subj: Macintosh, To: All
Msg #483 on 10/10/85 @ 15:55 (3)
Subj: CBM Amiga, To: All
```

It goes on until you interrupt the process by pressing **K** key. Doing a quickscan alone won't save you much time, though, if you have to scramble to write down the message numbers you want to read.

When you're doing a quickscan on PMS, you can use a powerful subcommand while the message headers are scrolling up your screen. This subcommand is to press your R key after the display of a header for which you want to read the text. This will mark the message so you can display it in full later just by pressing one key. To mark a message, you have to press the R key during the display of the *next* message header to mark the *previous* header. In other words, if you wanted to read message 490, above, you'd have to press R while the header of message number 489 was being displayed. It'd look like this:

```
Msg #49Ø on 1Ø/1Ø/85 @ 17:Ø5 (4)
Subj: Hello America!, To: All
Msg #489 on 1Ø/1Ø/85 @ 16:55 (4)
```

Press **R** now, as 489 is being displayed:

```
Subj: Resistance BBS, To: All
**OK** <49Ø>
```

The appearance of "**OK** <490>" on the screen verifies that PMS has marked that message for later retrieval.

When you're ready to retrieve the message, type an * (asterisk) at the system prompt, like so:

```
Command ?*

Subj: Hello America!, To: All
Msg #489 on 1Ø/1Ø/85 @ 16:55 (4)

From: Madeline Simon, Jersey City,NJ

Well, I'm back from my European Adventure, everyone!
Now you can start swamping me with messages and job
offers!
Arrividerci. MS
```

Combining a quickscan (Q) with the R-key message marking subcommand and following it with the * (asterisk) message retrieval command will help you to get in and out of any PMS system in a short period of time. If more PMS callers used this shortcut, there'd be less busy signals and more people could enjoy the systems.

The final part of using a PMS that I'll illustrate is the process creating, editing, and leaving a message. Type **E** to begin the process:

Command ?**E**
To: ?**Madeline Simon**
Subject: ?**Welcome home!**
C/r to end.

1
?**Madelene! Well, it's been long enough! We wondered**
2
?**if you had defected to the Reds or if the KGB**
3
?**had abducted you for some nefarious plot!**
4
?**We started to take up a collection to hire the A-Team**
5
?**to go and bring you back!**
6
?

Once the message is finished, you could press Return at the ? prompt for line 6 and get a list of editing options. If you already know the editing options, you can just enter the first letter of the editing command you need, preceded by a "." (period). This is like using the dot-commands in SMail on The Source (see Chapter 15, Using The Source).

In line 1 there's a mistake. Here's how to correct it using the dot-command and the PMS line editor:

6
?**.E1**
line #1:
Madelene! Well, it's been long enough! We wondered
edit:
?/**Madelene/Madeline**
line #1:
Madeline! Well, it's been long enough! We wondered
edit
?

Once line 1 has been edited and the rest of the message is correct, save it to the system. Since this message is for a particular person and would only hold limited interest, if any, for other callers, save it as a private message for the person it's addressed to. To do this, type **.S** (period S) at the edit prompt:

```
?.S
Password (4 Chrs. max) ?LOCK
```

"LOCK" isn't the password for the message. It's a command to the system that this message should be stored as private. After this, you'll be prompted for a password for the message:

```
Password (4 Chrs. max) ?LOCK
Password (4 Chrs. max) ?BACK
Msg# 491. . . .saved
```

"BACK" is the password given to this particular message. Placing a password on the message means that only you, the sysop, or the person receiving the message can delete it. It's a safeguard against abusive callers.

If you've read to this point in the book, you'll be able to use virtually any online system. BBSs all tend to work in the same way. Only the menu of commands and the letters assigned to the commands change from system to system.

18 One if by land, two if by sea...

In the TV series, *Hunter*, the lead character (of the same name) has a saying: It works for me.

Despite all that you've read in this book, this should be your *modus operandi* in choosing and using an online system.

If, for instance, you find Western Union's EasyLink to be a cost- and time-effective alternative to, say, AT&T WATS, that's all that should concern you. If you can put up with that system's patchwork design—if you're *satisfied*—that's all that should matter. It works for you.

As I stated at the beginning of this book, my purpose has been to make you more aware of how systems operate, so that you can be more discriminating in your use and selection. This does *not* mean:

- That you should switch from one system to another, based on what I've written. (You shouldn't.)
- That my comments should be construed to mean that one system is better than another. (That would be like saying an apple is better than an orange.)
- That one system alone can offer you everything that you'll ever conceivably need. (Nothing—online or offline—can ever hope to offer that.)

You should, however, come away from this book better informed. That has been my sole purpose.

Since I stated several times throughout this book that you should never take someone else's reviews as the final word, it is only fair that I exhort you to apply this rule to this book, too.

Explore, examine, criticize, and praise on your own. The bottom line is to find a system that works for you.

Remember that the online systems shown in this book could very well change drastically by the time you buy it. In the online world, nothing is more certain than change.

With that in mind, let's take a look in the proverbial crystal ball and see what lies in wait for online systems down the road. . .

The most important development will be CD-ROM. CD stands for Compact Disc. This is a 4¾″ plastic-coated disc that's being marketed as an alternative to (and possibly a replacement for) standard audio records. Standard 33s and 45s are analog products. The CD is a digital product. (This is leaving aside the actual studio recording process for music, which may be either analog or digital.)

Although the CD will enjoy a great success as a medium for delivering music, its biggest market will be data storage. In terms of information that could be accessed by a microcomputer, one CD can hold *550 megabytes* of data. That is approximately *100,000 pages of information.* Although this makes the CD sound as if it's just one large hard disk, it's not. CD technology is currently at the point where it's just a read-only medium. That's why it's called Compact Disc-Read Only Memory (CD-ROM).

CD-ROM will have a great impact on online information retrieval because it'll no longer be necessary for historical data to be stored on a remote computer for access over telephone lines. The information can be pressed onto a small CD that you can purchase and from which you can then retrieve the information *offline*, without worrying about connect-time charges upward of $100 an hour.

For example, encyclopedias could be placed on a CD. This would do away with using either the Kussmaul Encyclopedia (on Delphi) or the Academic American Encyclopedia (on several systems). An encyclopedia on a CD would also take up less space than a printed version and should be less expensive, too.

Historical data about companies, industries, stocks, and more could be placed onto a CD that a company or individual could purchase. This would do away with having to go online to get such material.

Plus, information that has never been online—and information that could never *be* online—will soon have a market, thanks to the CD. The CD can store digital images—full color photos, for instance—as well as audio and ASCII-encoded information. The encyclopedia on a CD, could not only let you read about a person, place, or thing, but could also let you see a high-resolution drawing or photograph. That's something that could never be done online without great expense.

All of this will not happen overnight. Within three to five years I expect we will be looking at an online industry that has been considerably altered by the existence of CD-ROM. The only online systems that will survive—that will have a reason to *exist*—will contain and offer:

- Perishable, timely information that can't be delivered—or delivered as well—on (conventional) radio, (conventional) TV or in print. This would include wire services such as AP, UPI, several of the databases offered by DJNRS, and OAG (Official Airline Guides). In short, late-breaking news and information that is better served by being delivered online or must be online as its sole delivery medium.
- Communications services that can't be offered as inexpensively or as effectively by (conventional) voice phone. This would include things such as delayed-time and real-time conferencing (such as PARTICIPATE, CB, or Conference Trees), message sending (offered by systems such as EasyLink and MCI Mail, among others), bulletin-boards (of most types and categories), and special interest groups (SIGs, Forums, Clubs, Groups).
- Services that are unique to online delivery. This would include software uploading and downloading as well as multiplayer games. In the category of unique online services, our imagination has yet to be let loose to discover and create new things.

Any online system, however, that is principally a remote depository for static information will, in a few years, discover its customer base evaporating. A per-hour connect-time fee is no competition for a one-time flat fee for unlimited use of a CD-ROM database. Online systems are already aware of the fact that many of their customers capture information for storage and retrieval in local, offline databases. CD-ROM will do away with that by offering more information for a small fraction of the cost.

Something else that will have an impact on the online world are Bulletin-Board Systems (BBSs) run by individuals. It's clear that both National and Local Systems aren't offering the variety of information or freedom of choice that can be found, in total, on BBSs today.

BBSs, as a medium, are maturing at rates faster than National and Local Systems and are beginning to offer them a level of competition that can no longer be brushed aside or ignored. A BBS that offers 35 megabytes of storage to its callers is approaching the storage capacities of some Local Systems. Plus, more BBSs than ever before are becoming multi-user systems, allowing more callers at one time—something that in the past only a National or Local System could do. When any BBS has these two features—and a low flat fee for access—there's no reason for someone to spend more on a National or Local System.

Early in 1985, the first professionally run news service for BBSs was created. Called INFO MAT™, it's published weekly on a subscription basis by the BBS Press Service (BPS). Subscribing BBS sysops download the latest issue from the BPS BBS, place it on their own system, and offer it to their callers for free or a small fee. Sysops have reported that it measurably increases the number of callers to their systems. INFO-MAT concentrates on consumer electronics, which makes it a perfect match for its intended high-tech audience. That such a service has found a ready market in BBSs further indicates that sysops don't intend to leave the online world in the hands of large organizations.

Another factor that could make a difference in the online world is not a sure bet but a dark horse. It's teletext, a medium that delivers text and graphics over TV (broadcast VHF/UHF and cable) by using the vertical blanking interval (VBI). The VBI can be seen on your TV by adjusting its vertical hold. Within the large black stripe that borders the screen, you'll be able to see a thin line of excess video signal. That's the VBI.

A complete teletext database is continually sent over the air on a TV station's VBI. A special decoder is used that contains a certain amount of RAM. When you press a specific button on the remote control of the decoder, you'll get the main menu of the teletext database. To get any teletext page that you want to see, you punch in its number and when that page is transmitted, the decoder will grab it and store it in RAM for you to display on your TV screen.

A complete teletext database can be transmitted anywhere from every 18 seconds to every 10 minutes (or even longer), depending on the number of pages in the database. For instance, a database of just 50 pages would take about 18 seconds to transmit. That means you'd have to wait up to 18 seconds for the page to appear on your TV screen. This is not the drawback that it seems to be. Even if it took 10 minutes to get a requested page, you could sit back and watch a TV program and then display the captured page during commercials. You could even route the signal to your VCR to record it.

What makes teletext a contender is that everyone already has a TV set. All that's needed to receive teletext is a decoder. There's no connect-time charges or any other costs involved; you just have to buy a decoder. If teletext decoders were available in the $50 range (instead of the current $200 range), we'd see an explosion of activity in this field.

The unfortunate thing about teletext is that it's mostly been in the hands of large corporations, and they really don't know how to make use of it. Time, Inc., for instance, bailed out of a teletext project after spending about $20 million to develop a database of several thousand pages. More recently, NBC discontinued its smaller teletext project as well. In the hands of local nonprofit groups and community activists, teletext could become a medium that would easily eclipse online systems in terms of information variety and boldness. In the NYC metro area, for instance, there are 15 broadcast TV channels. Cable TV delivers over 30 channels. If each channel had a local teletext magazine, online systems would have a harder time finding subscribers. Imagine an online system trying to convince someone to pay a per-hour fee for its single information delivery medium when 15 to 30 free ones are available via teletext.

Another medium that's being explored is radio subcarrier delivery. It's similar to teletext in that it's transmitted over an unused portion of the broadcast spectrum. In this case, it's radio (AM and FM), not TV. Radio subcarrier transmissions can be up to 9600 bps, a speed that cannot be used reliably on (conventional) voice phone lines. Radio subcarrier delivery requires the purchase of a special radio-receiving modem that can decode the analog broadcast signal and convert it into digital information. This medium is currently being used to transmit public domain software and real-time stock quotes. It's still too early to tell how else this medium will be used.

Of course, there is room enough for everything: National and Local Systems, CD-ROM, BBSs, teletext, and radio subcarrier. Ten years ago, very few people could even guess that such choices were being developed. The next year alone will offer yet more choices and more surprises.

An ancient Chinese blessing is: May you live in interesting times. We certainly do.

APPENDIX: Bulletin-board system help files

Although not every BBS software format is represented in this section, enough are to give you a solid understanding of all of the commands available to you on all of the software formats. You will be able to refer to this section for particular menu selections should you find yourself somehow stranded in Expert Mode.

ABBS: Apple Bulletin Board System

Main menu:

A = Apple 40 column
B = Print Bulletin
C = Case switch
D = Duplex switch (Echo/No Echo)
E = Enter message into system
G = Good-bye (leave system)
H = Help with functions
K = Kill (erase) a message
L = Line feed (on/off)
N = Nulls (set as req'd)
Q = Quick summary of msg's
R = Retrieve msg
S = Summary of msg's
T = Time of day

V = Toggle video/printer terminal mode
W = Print Welcome message
? = Prints Functions Supported
DOWNLOAD = Download software to your Apple
UPLOAD = Upload files/software to this system
NEWS = Info of interest to system users
CONF = Switch conferences

Main prompt:

FUNCTION:
(A,B,C,D,E,G,H,K,L,N,Q,R,S,T,V,W,X,
DOWNLOAD, UPLOADED, NEWS, CONF,?)

Message entry menu:

Entry Functions:
A = Abort
C = Continue Entry
D = Delete a line
E = Edit line
L = List line(s)
R = Restart from beginning
S = Save message to disk

Message entry prompt:

(A,C,D,E,L,R,S,?)?

Help file:

Ctrl C -- Cancels printing of the current line being output.

Ctrl H (Backspace) -- Allows you to backspace one character at a time and prints a '/' followed by the character you are backspacing over. This is the same routine that is used for Delete or Rubout instead of true Delete (for the benefit of printers).

Ctrl K -- Cancels current function.

Ctrl U (Forward Arrow) -- Starts you back at the beginning of the current line being typed (ie: start over).

A -- Toggle display mode between 64 and 40 column mode. When you sign on, you are allowed to put up to 64 characters/line. A bell will sound at 59 and on, up to 64 columns, at which point you would be forced onto the next line of text. In the Apple 40 column mode, the bell will ring at 35, then again at 38 and 39, dropping you to the next line at 39. 39 was used instead of 40 to avoid an extra blank line because of the 40th character.

B -- Print Bulletin. Reprints Bulletins that you see when you sign on.

C -- Case Switch. When you sign on, the system defaults to UPPER CASE input and output. The "C" command allows you to switch between UPPER CASE ONLY and UPPER/lower case mode.

D -- Duplex Switch. Alternately selects full or half duplex operation and informs you of current status.

E -- Enter Message. Allows you to enter a message into the system. Entry commands are basically self-explanatory. A carriage return (C/R) at this point will list out the command menu for entries. The "change" command allows you to change an entire line or just part of it. To change just part of a line, enter the following:

/string to change/replacement string

You will then be shown the new version of the line and you should hit Return to leave the change mode. You can exit the Enter mode entirely by entering the 'A' command. You should be sure to enter an 'S' to Save a message to disk.

G -- Good-bye. Exits system and hangs up the phone at the ABBS end of the connection.

H -- Help. Prints this documentation.

K -- Kill a message. Enter this to delete a message from the system. A password may be necessary if one was used at the time of message entry.

L -- Line Feed On/Off. Normally on. For terminals that need an extra line feed character to advance to the next line

N -- Nulls. Adds an extra delay after a carriage return, to allow printers time to move the printhead back to the starting position. This option only works with the line feed option on. Each null is equivalent to a 30-millisecond delay and is adjustable from 1 to 30 nulls. It defaults to 1.

Q -- Quick Scan. An abbreviated Scan, showing only a message's number, its subject, and date. See "S" for Scan.

R -- Retrieve Message. Allows you to retrieve a message from the system. You can specify a single message, multiple messages, or all of the messages from a given number on up. To specify a single message, enter R;N, where "N" is the number of the message you wish to read. To read multiple messages, separate each message number with a ";" (semicolon; ie : R;1;2;3;7;8). To retrieve all of the messages starting from a certain message number, enter 'R' followed by a ";" then the starting message number, followed by "^" (an up-arrow; ie : R;101;^). (In some cases you may replace an up-arrow with an at-sign, "@.")

S -- Scan Messages. Allows you to scan over messages starting at the message number that you specify. You will be able to see who the message is from, who it is addressed to, its subject, and the date it was posted.

T -- Time and Date. Gives you the current time and date. This is automatically used during login.

W -- Welcome. Prints Welcome message at the beginning of the system.

X -- Expert User. Does away with certain explanatory messages. It also allows certain C/R defaults. Example: a C/R in response to "FUNCTION:" will print functions supported by this system.

? -- Prints functions supported in that current mode of operation.

CONF -- Allows you to switch between sets of messages. This feature operates only if the optional Conference module has been installed.

NEWS -- Displays a list of text files that are available for reading. This feature operates only if the optional News module has been installed.

DOWNLOAD -- Gives you access to a library of software that can be downloaded to your system. This feature operates only if the optional Download module has been installed.

UPLOAD -- Allows you to transfer a file (text or program) to this system. This feature operates only if the optional Upload module has been installed.

In addition to the above documentation, an ABBS sysop provides this information:

- Please kill old messages that are addressed to you when you no longer need them. This will allow the general interest messages to stay on the system longer.
- There is a feature in this system that will not permit you to erase too many of your old messages at one time. If you have many old messages to erase, you may not be able to do so all at one time. This feature is to protect someone from erasing all of the messages on the system.
- When you enter a message, the system will ask you if you would like to "lock" it with a password, so that only you may erase the messages you have left, using your password. The password may be any four characters you wish. The system will then ask you if you would like the message marked as "private mail." If you reply "Yes" to this, the person the message is addressed to must also know the password in order to read the message and erase it. Although you may address your message to a particular person, it will not be treated as a private message -- anyone can read it -- unless you specify it as such.
- The upload function of this system will only accept one line at a time. You must wait for the "?" prompt before sending a line. The system is writing each line to the disk as it is received, and there may be a delay ranging from 1 to 20 seconds.

AMIS: Atari Message and Information System

Main menu (representative):
(^ = CTRL, ^S PAUSE, ^Q RESUME, ^X QUIT)
A = ASCII/ATASCII mode
B = Bulletin reprint
C = Callers listing
D = Download file
F = File listing for download
G = Good-bye (leave system)
H = Help with functions
I = Index of download programs
L = Line feed (ON/OFF) switch
M = Message base
N = New user information
O = Other BBS list
T = Time, day and date
U = Upload file
W = Welcome message reprint
X = eXpert user
Y = Yell for sysop (chat)
? = This list
^ = Control key
^S = Suspend display
^Q = Resume display
^X = Abort function

Main prompt (representative):
A,B,C,D,F,G,H,I,L,M,N,O,T,U,W,X,Y,
or ? >

Message base functions (representative):
E = Enter message
K = Kill message
M = Main menu
Q = Quick scan
R = Retrieve message
S = Summary

Message entry functions (representative):
A = Add line(s)
E = Edit message
L = List line(s)

Q = Quit entry (abort)
R = Read message entered
S = Save message on system

AMIS is similar to the other BBSs in format. Its differences arise when downloading files. You must use the ATASCII function in order to receive programs and run a communications program such as AMODEM, JMODEM or XMODEM. Also, Atari computers do not require line feeds.

Bullet-80

Main menu (version 8.0)

<A>utolog	<B>ulletins
<C>lub	<D>irections
<E>lec-Shopping	<F>ile-Transfer
<G>ames	<H>ow-Long
<I>nterests	<L>ine-test
<M>essage-Center	<O>ther-Systems
<R>equest-Chat	<S>ystem-Config
<T>erminate	<U>sers-Log
<V>iew-System	<X>pert-User

Message-Center menu:
<C>hange Section #
<H>elp With Functions
<L>eave Message
<R>ead Messages
<S>can Messages
<T>erminate Session
<A>bort to Bullet-80

Message entry commands:
<I> -- Insert a new line before the current line, or to begin to enter message
<D>+Line Number -- deletes that line (D3 will delete line 3)
<+> -- Step forward one line
<−> -- Step backward one line
<R> -- Replace word, ex: r/word1/word2
<RG> -- Global Replace
<B> -- Position to <B>eginning
<E> -- Position to <E>nd of text
<C> -- Continue message entry
<K> -- Kill Editing Session (Return to module menu)
<H> -- Prints this HELP screen

<L> -- Lists all lines in buffer
<L> + Line Number -- List That Line (L3 Will List Line 3)
<S> -- Send Message
<A> -- Abort, return to Bullet-80
<T> -- Terminate Session
<?> -- To read instructions.
End ALL Inserts With A Blank Line

Help file (<D>irections):

To use this system is simple, just press the FIRST letter of any command you care to execute. Entering a Carriage Return, <C/R>, or pressing <ENTER> at an abbreviated menu will display an expanded menu if you're not sure what to do.

Note ** You can also press <S> to stop or CONTROL-S or <P> to pause during the print out of module instructions, and MESSAGE-CENTER messages. Any input will restart the display.

Here is an explanation of the commands:

<A>utolog -- In the past, the sysop had to activate your logon password. Now it becomes active immediately. Please note that passwords must begin with a number from Ø to 9, followed by up to 8 characters. Passwords must be at least 6 characters long.

<B>ulletins -- This command will display the current system <B>ulletins. I try to update them periodically.

<C> -- This command will activate our <C>lub module. It's easy to join and fun to belong. To get more information, run <C>lub and read instructions.

<D>irections -- This command will print out these directions on how to use Bullet-80 Version 8.0.

<E>lectronic Shopping -- This module opens up for use a new use for your home or business computer. It offers you a selection of items that you could purchase and bill to your charge card. It's easy and fun!!

<F>ile-Transfer -- This command combines 2 functions into one. <D>ownloading and <U>ploading. Bullet-80 also supports 4 kinds of file transfer, Standard ASCII, DFT, XModem, and Modem. Be sure you know which method you support before selecting your option. Modem not available at 1200 baud.

<D>ownload: This module allows you to get programs from our database for free. I will only keep this section open as long as I get support from my users. If you care to donate programs to the database, you can use our <U>pload module or call our voice line to make arrangements.

<P>rogram Uploading: This module will allow you to upload programs to Bullet-80 so others can enjoy your ORIGINAL or PUBLIC DOMAIN programs. After review they will be placed in our downloading section.

<G>ames -- This module allows you to play assorted games online. These may change for variety from time to time. Please try to limit your game playing to 30 minutes or less, so Bullet-80 will be available to other users for their needs.

<H>ow-Long -- This function will tell you how long you've been on Bullet-80 for this session. It will also give you the current local time and date.

<I>nterests -- This module will allow you to enter any interests or hobbies you have, or things you like to do. This information will be made available to other Bullet-80 users to read and see if you have anything in common. This is a great way to get to know each other.

<M>essage-Center -- This module is where you gain access to the <M>essage Center on Bullet-80. Here you have the option of <R>eading, <S>canning, or <L>eaving mail for Bullet-80's other users. Each section of the message center has help menus for full instructions.

<O>ther Network Phone Numbers -- Prints out a list of many online systems. This option allows you to search for any BBS by city, state, area code, or network name. If you know of any not listed, leave me a message as you terminate and I will add it.

<R>equest-Chat -- This will allow you to chat with the sysop via the TRS-80. Generally available from 12PM on, for this particular system. If the sysop isn't available, leave him a private message as you terminate.

<S>ystem Configuration -- This function allows you to customize Bullet-80 to your terminal by letting you adjust screen width, line feeds, upper and lower case, nulls and your bell code.

<T>erminate -- Logs you off of Bullet-80. At this time you can leave a private message to the sysop or be placed on our mailing list. Always use this option so your information can be recorded.

<U>sers Log -- Will display Bullet-80 users for you. You can scan <F>orward or <R>everse or <S>earch for a certain user.

<V>iew System Configuration -- Will tell you about the hardware Bullet-80 uses and a bit about its development.

<X>pert User -- The first time you call Bullet-80, you will be considered a novice user and all menus will be printed out in full. On all future calls, you will be in expert mode with short menus. You can always have the option of toggling your <X>pert status with the <X> command.

Bullet-80 Message Center Instructions
Version 3.0

To leave mail for other users, enter <L> from the main menu. When in that section, at the EDIT prompt, enter <?> for help.

To read mail, you have several new options. You now have the ability to read selectively by sections. When you enter the message center, Section Ø is activated. This means that all open mail in all the public sections is available for you to read. If you would like to read mail for a certain section, use the <C>hange Section # option. At that time, you can view the available sections by entering a C/R at the section # question. Club members with Level 2 clearance will need to enter the <C>lub module to establish their identity, and then will be able to select Section 8, which is the private club mail call. Bullet-80 sysops need to enter the Bullet-80 sysop section for the same reason, and then can select Section 9, which is the sysop mail section.

The message center offers you many ways to read the mail:

Full messages forward and reverse
Scan headers forward and reverse without passes
Scan headers forward and reverse with marking option
Individually by message number

The message center is fully menu-driven. At short menus, pressing <ENTER> will display the expanded menu. Please leave any questions or suggestions you may have addressed to the SYSOP of this system.

Bullet-80 Download Instructions

Bullet-80 version 8.0 supports 4 different kinds of downloading.
Here are the download protocols we support:

Standard ASCII
DFT
Modem (300 baud only)
XModem

Most terminal programs will support ASCII file transfers. They are the most common type available.

DFT (Direct File Transfer) requires that you purchase the DFT package if you want to transfer files a sector at a time with error-checking. The advantage of DFT is that the program re-sends each sector until it's told by your computer that it's been received and has been verified. DFT works with tape and disk. It is available for purchase in the shopping section.

Modem file transfer is a disk-based program and is one in the public domain. It is also a sector-by-sector file transfer program that writes to your disk automatically after its buffer is full. Has some error-checking. 300 baud only.

XModem file transfer is similar to Modem, except it works at both 300 and 1200 baud.

WARNING!!!

DON'T ATTEMPT TO USE ANY STYLE YOU DON'T HAVE THE PROPER SOFTWARE FOR. YOU WILL HAVE A LONG WAIT BEFORE THE SYSTEM REALIZES YOU HAVE SELECTED IT IN ERROR!!

Modem and XModem, along with their documentation, should be in the download section in this system. If not, please leave a message for the SYSOP asking him to place it there.

If you experience any problems with any form of download, please notify the SYSOP. His goal is to keep this Bullet-80 system running as smoothly as possible.

CBBS: Computerized Bulletin-Board System

Main menu (Version 3.6):

MAJOR FUNCTIONS:

(E)nter message	(H)elp <= =	(Q)uick summary
(G)ood bye	(R)etrieve msg	(S)ummarize msgs (see also (O) below)

MINOR FUNCTIONS:

# Print caller # etc.	(P)rompt bell off	(U)ser update (password, etc.)
(A)lter Baud rate	(K)ill message	(V)ideo backspace
(B)ulletin reprint	(N)ulls: How many?	(W)elcome reprint
(C)ase upper/lower	(O)ne line summary	e(X)pert user mode
(D)uplex echo off	(T)ime/date/E.T.	

] >> For details, type H, press return, then type the letter. << CHAT See if Randy is available to talk via the keyboard.

(Please don't abuse this for for "Hi, how are you" -- it's meant to be used to report bugs, seek advice on CBBS usage, etc.)

HELP New user help; (vs. H: keyword based help)
MINE find my messages
NEWS What's new on CBBS
SHORT Shorten output; no dup spaces, etc.

Main prompt:

Function:A,B,C,D,E,G,H,K,N,O,P,Q,R,S,T,U,V,W,X,#
(OR ? IF NOT KNOWN)?

Keyword help list:

HISTORY	KEYWORDS	MINE	STAT	CHAT
OTHER	PARITY	COMMANDS	MAIN	INFO
MENU	MESSAGES	SIGNON	USER	*
U	NULL	GAMES	-	LINEFEEDS
SALE	SELL	CLUB	CLUBS	CBBS
OVERVIEW	SHORT	LONG	BRIEF	NEXT
#	MARK	NEW	MAIL	FUNCTIONS
HELP	H	CTL CHARS	^C	^E
^H	^K	^L	^N	^R
^S	^W	^X	HEADLINES	NEWS
C	CASE	ENTER	MESSAGE	E
INPUT	ESUB	EDIT	LEAVE	PASSWORD
KILL	DELETE	ERASE	K	SUMMARY
O	S	Q	SR	QR
QUICK	SEARCH	FIND	SCAN	BOOLEAN
AND	OR	RETRIEVE	READ	R
FLAG	F	M	STOP	END
EXIT	OFF	QUIT	GOODBYE	G
BYE	COMMENTS	NULLS	N	PHONE
BULLETIN	B	WELCOME	W	DUPLEX
D	ECHO	DOUBLE	BELL	PROMPT
P	EXPERT	X	USE	NEWBAUD
ALTER	BAUD	1200 BAUD	SPEED	A
TIME	T	VIDEO	BACKSPACE	V
TABS	FILES	SOFTWARE	FLIP	OTHER
CPM	CP/M	CPMUG	HARDWARE	OPERATOR
OPERATORS	WHY			

Control Functions:

ASCII	CONTROL	
	DEL/BS	Character delete
C	C	Cancel output (*)
	I	Tab (Tabs set every 8)
K	K	Function abort (*)
N	N	Send 5 more nulls (*)
	R	Retype input line
S	S	Stop/start output (*)
ESC	U	Line delete
	W	Video word backspace
	X	Video line delete

(*): Use while CBBS types to you.

Conference Tree

A hierarchical conferencing system. No menus as such, although the trunk and branches are in this format:

```
*** CONFERENCES   Ø-JAN-8Ø
  PARENT= NONE       USAGE15ØØ
      + + + SUBMESSAGES + + +
HELP              Ø-JAN-8Ø
ANNOUNCEMENTS     Ø-JAN-8Ø
FLAGSHIP          Ø-JAN-8Ø
SYSOP             Ø-JAN-8Ø
USERS             Ø-JAN-8Ø
```

Retrieval commands:
Read Conference-name options
Browse Conference-name options
Index Conference-name options

Retrieval options:
Starting (date)
Find (string)
Beyond Conference-name
Exiled
Onlyexiled

Message entry command:
Addto Conference-name

Message edit commands:
List
Replace
Quit
Savepermanent

Help file (READ HELP COMPLETE):

```
*** HELP                            16-JUL-81
PARENT=CONFERENCES                USAGE175Ø
"READ CONFERENCES" for current subjects.
"READ <NAME>" where <NAME> is any message or submessage.
"BROWSE CONFERENCES COMPLETE" to skim.
"INDEX <NAME>" for index of subtree.
Commands and options may be abbreviated to their first letters.
Press "S" key to pause or resume printing.
Press "K" key to stop message listing.
```

Press "C" key to kill current command.
Control-H or DEL key for backspace.
To leave system, just hang up!
"READ HELP-COMMANDS" for more features.
"READ HELP COMPLETE" for all help documentation.
+ + + SUBMESSAGES + + +
*** HELP-COMMANDS 16-JUL-81

PARENT = HELP USAGE12ØØ
The commonly-used commands are:
READ <NAME> <OPTIONS>
BROWSE <NAME> <OPTIONS>
INDEX <NAME> <OPTIONS>
ADDTO <NAME> <OPTIONS
The other commands, used less often, are:
TERMINAL
EXILE <NAME>
UNEXILE <NAME>
+ADDTO <NAME>
SERIAL

The <NAME> above refers to any message name; for example, "CONFERENCES" or "HELP." <OPTIONS> are optional search techniques described later -- they can be ignored for now.

The "READ" command prints out the named message and then lists its submessages (children) if any -- i.e., all other messages directly attached to it. A message can have any number of submessages, limited only by the system's capacity, and each can have children of its own, to almost any depth. Therefore, the whole structure of messages forms a tree, which grows as users add new items to it.

The "READ" command also shows the message creation date, its parent, and the number of times it has been read (its usage count).

The "BROWSE" command is like "READ" except that it only prints the first line of the message. It is usually used with search options to skim sections of the message tree.

The "INDEX" command shows the name, creation date, and usage count of the message and its complete subtree (the names of all of its children and grandchildren), each properly indented on the printout. It gives a quick overview of what is going on in a section of the tree or the whole tree. For example, try "INDEX HELP" or "INDEX CONFERENCES" (you can abort the command by typing "C" or Control-C while it is printing).

"ADDTO" allows you to add a new message. It must always be added to a message which already exists in the system. "READ HELP-ADDTO" for more details.

The remaining commands are used less often:

"TERMINAL" lets you request special options -- half-duplex, carriage return nulls, and linefeed suppress -- which some terminals require.

"EXILE" and "UNEXILE" are used mainly by the system operator, to control outdated or inappropriate messages without deleting them. Messages that have been exiled are ignored by "READ," "BROWSE," and "INDEX" unless they are requested by name or unless special options (described later) are used. The system operator can avoid clutter such as unwelcome advertising messages, but the reader has the ultimate choice of what to see—a form of soft censorship.

*** HELP-COMMANDS-2 16-JULY-81
PARENT=HELP-COMMANDS USAGE=6ØØ

Eventually, the exiled messages, and any others attached to them, go away when the system operator "squeezes" the disk to reclaim the space they had used. Usually, "EXILE" and "UNEXILE" will require a password.

The "+ADDTO" command is also used mainly by the system operator. It works like "ADDTO" except that the last message read or browsed is retained for re-editing. Usually, a password is required for this command, also.

"SERIAL" prints out a Copyright notice and the serial number of the particular CommuniTree system. This is primarily a software protection feature, although it may be helpful in cases when one can't recall which system one is currently using.

All the commands, except for "+ADDTO" and "SERIAL" can be abbreviated to their first letters only: R, B, A, and I.

*** HELP-OPTIONS 16-JUL-81
PARENT=HELP USAGE=4ØØ

The following options can be used with the "READ," "BROWSE," and "INDEX" commands:

COMPLETE
STARTING <DATE>
FIND <STRING>
BEYOND <NAME>
EXILED
ONLYEXILED

These can be used in any combination and in any order. They are entirely optional, but if they are used, they must appear after the <NAME> argument of the command.

"COMPLETE" causes the entire subtree to be printed -- all submessages and their children, etc. -- not just the individual message named. It is automatic with the "INDEX" command, so it needn't be specified. It is also automatic with all other options, i.e., they cause "COMPLETE" to be assumed.

"STARTING" must be given a date in the exact form DD-MMM-YY or D-MMM-YY, where MMM is the first three letters of the month name. "READ CONFERENCES STARTING 6-JUL-81" will skip all messages created before that date. "STARTING" is commonly used in each session to check what's new since the last time you were on the system.

"FIND" must be given a search string. "READ GAMES FIND ROLE" will print any message in a game conference (subtree) with "role" in it: "role playing," etc.

A "FIND" search of the complete "CONFERENCES" can take a long time, up to 15 minutes or more for a large data base. All the other options are much faster because they use data which are always kept in the computer's memory and do not need to be read from the disk. To make "FIND" searches run faster, search only the subtrees of interest, not all of "CONFERENCES," and/or use "STARTING" or other options to limit the search. Or use "FIND" with the "INDEX" command, which is fast because only titles are searched, not the full text, and the disk is not involved. A search can be interrupted by typing "C" or Control-C.

To search for a string that includes spaces, enclose the string in double quotes: 'READ GAMES FIND "ROLE PAYING".' It is usually better to search for single words or parts of words instead, to get spelling and phrasing variations: "comput" gets "computer," "computing," etc.

The "BEYOND" option suppresses printing until the named message has been seen. It is used mainly to continue a printout which has been interrupted.

"EXILED" includes messages which the system operator or others have exiled for some reason. "ONLYEXILED" will display only those messages.

All options can be abbreviated to their first letters. "READ CONFERENCES STARTING 10-JUL-81 FIND GAME EXILED" could be written "R CONFERENCES S 10-JUL-81 F GAME E."

*** HELP-ADDTO 16-JUL-81
PARENT=HELP USAGE=375

ADDTO COMMAND

"ADDTO <NAME>" lets you enter your own message to the system.

You will be asked to confirm the date setting, and to give your message a name. Try to pick a name that is somewhat descriptive of content, and unlikely to be used elsewhere on the tree, to avoid confusion when searching by message name. You may "ADDTO" any message. On some systems, you may need a password to "ADDTO" messages; on others, you may need a password in order to "ADDTO PRIVATE" or "ADDTO CONFERENCES." These variations depend on the system operator and the application. You can experiment with the "ADDTO" command, as long as you don't use the "SAVEPERMANENT" word, which will save your experiment permanently.

*** EDITOR 16-JUL-81
PARENT=HELP-ADDTO USAGE=275
THE EDITOR

When you use the "ADDTO NAME" command, you are given a simple line-oriented editor with which to enter your text. You may enter up to 50 lines of text with up to 80 characters in each line. The editor prompts are self-descriptive. To help keep the text readable, you should avoid ending lines with parts of words or hyphenated words. You will be able to "LIST" and "REPLACE" lines that are erroneous before you save them permanently. When typing a line, you may type the entire 80 character line before hitting Return. If you go over, the system will give you a "bell" warning. To get out of the editor, simply type "QUIT" when the editor prompt line appears, and this will put you back into the main command mode.

*** MISC-HELP 16-JUL-81
PARENT=HELP USAGE=3ØØ

These tips will help you get the most out of the system, and will also prove beneficial to all if they are heeded.

1) Descriptive message names, preferably unique, are recommended. The use of hyphens is preferred over the use of periods to separate words in message titles.

2) Children of exiled messages will go away when the disk is squeezed, so be careful not to add valued messages to messages that are dated.

3) There is a limit of 321 messages that can be in the system at any given time, so one big message is preferred to several small ones.

4) "BROWSE" returns the first line of a message, so it is helpful to make that first line as descriptive as possible of the message's content.

*** SYSTEM-PASSWORD 16-JUL-81
PARENT=HELP USAGE=29Ø

The system operator can choose from seven levels of password protection—from none at all, to requiring a password just to log on. At any time, there is only one password, which is usually given to anyone who is a Fairwitness of a conference. The default is medium protection, with the password required for "+ADDTO," "EXILE," "UNEXILE" and starting a new private conference.

A higher password level allows the public to read only and not enter any new messages; this level might be used for a commercial movie guide or similar service. In this case you can still add messages to the "GUEST" message (if the system operator has provided one), to give feedback to the system operator on an otherwise read-only system.

The system operator does not see what you are writing or reading, but does see erroneous command names and erroneous passwords on a log. This can allow you to communicate with the system operator (say, to send a phone number to him or her privately . . . since the phone number is not a valid command name, it will show up on the log). But this channel is unreliable, as the information may be dropped off the screen before it is seen.

PMS (People's Message Service)

Main menu:
---->> System Commands
E = Enter a message into system.
F = Features, articles, excerpts.
G = Goodbye. Leave system. (Hangup)
H = Help with various functions.
I = Information about system.
K = Kill a message from the files.
M = Message alert. Messages for you?
N = News -- System news.
O = Other systems current summary.
Q = Quickscan of all message headers.
QP = Quickscan of private msg headers.
R = Retrieve a message from the files.
S = Scan of all message headers.
SP = Scan of private message headers.
SR = Selective message retrieval.
T = Time, date and connect-time.
U = User modifiable system functions.
X = eXpert user mode (On/Off toggle).
Z = Continue message entry after abort.
? = Prints this list of commands.
* = Flagged message memory retrieval.

TALK = Lets you talk to the sysop.
TEST = Modem continuous test loop.
NEWCALL = Information for new callers.
ALT = Switch message bases.
GENERAL14 = File Transfer -- Download files.
GENERAL15 = File Transfer -- Upload files.

Main prompt:
Command?

Message entry menu:
---->> Message entry commands
A = Abort message.
C = Continue entry.
D = Delete line (Dx).
E = Edit line (Ex).
H = Help with message entry functions.
I = Insert a line (Ix).
L = List lines from specified # (Lx).
S = Save completed message to disk.<<<
W = reWrite an old message.

Message entry prompt:
(A,C,D,E,H,I,L,S,W,?)?

Help file:

* * SYSTEM CONTROL FUNCTIONS AND CODES * *

There are certain characters which cause specific functions to occur while system is printing to you, NOT when waiting for input. These may be Control, lower or upper case characters.

-- C -- Stops printing the current line up to carriage return. Use this if you want to skip over several lines of text without aborting the function. Use one 'C' for each line you want to jump over.

-- K -- Causes a jump to the next logical operation. As an example, if you were retrieving several messages, it would cause a jump to the next message. During message entry listing, will return you to the message entry command level. The ONLY time this command will return to main COMMAND level is if there is no logical next function.

-- N -- Adds to nulls for each 'N' types. Use this when you have a printer online, which needs nulls (is dropping first characters of lines). May be used at any time in system operation. Up to 100 nulls can be added, but in practice no more than 20 should ever be needed, and even that is extreme.

-- P -- Cancels nulls to zero. Regardless of current null setting, resets nulls to zero. You can then add again with 'N' if you wish.

-- R -- Flags messages during a scan or quickscan to be later retrieved with the * command. Type an 'R' at the NEXT message header. It will always be one message behind. There is usually not time to comprehend a message header and type the 'R' before that header is done being printed. Just pause slightly and then type it. At the end of that next message header, you will see an "**OK** <xxxx> verification. The 'xxxx' will contain the number of the message actually flagged.

-- S -- Stops text output until any other character is sent.

-- X -- This guy causes an unconditional abort of whatever function you're in, and an immediate jump to main COMMAND level.

In addition, there are three other Control characters that are used during text entry. They are:

-- ^I -- Tab to next column (mod eight)

-- ^R -- Retype the line up to current position. Use this to verify what you have typed so far.

-- ^X -- Abort and start current line over.

* * SYSTEM COMMANDS * *

All system commands are input to the main COMMAND level. Certain commands (H, K, O, R, S, SR, and others) may also have extenders describing or anticipating the next question asked. As an example: Since H is for help, if you wanted help on everything, you could type H;ALL. Using R as another example, if you wanted to retrieve message #1937, you could type R;1937. More examples of various multiple parameters are explained for each individual command.

-- E -- Enter a message into the system. Pretty self-explanatory, just follow the prompting. You must enter a password when asked. This is the password used to kill the message. There are also two levels of security messages available. If you type LOCK as your password (you will be asked again for the password for killing), the message will be marked as private, and will automatically open for the person to whom it's addressed or who wrote it. Others will be asked for a password which will be the same as the password for killing it. If you enter LOCX instead of LOCK, the message can be read ONLY with the password unless the caller has signed in with a USERID. If you decide you're not done with the message and want to continue instead of saving, just type R in response to password.

-- F -- Features. Articles on interest. To read an article, type the name of the article as a command. Do not use F.

-- G -- Goodbye. Exit the system and hang up the phone. Files will be updated at this time. System will also respond to: END, OFF, BYE, and a few others. Comments can be left or type R to return to program.

-- H -- System help files. Typing an H by itself will print out all the possible areas you can obtain help for. Typing H; (character) will print help on a specific function.

-- K -- Kill a message. This will remove a message from the system files. You must have the password (entered during message entry) to use it. You also have the option of automatically killing messages that are addressed to you at the time you read them. See more details in 'R' command.

-- M -- Message alert. This command is issued directly after you're logged on. It allows you to automatically retrieve all messages addressed to you. You may use it at any time in the program. One word of caution: If you have flagged messages for retrieval and use this command, all the flagged messages will be lost. If you do use it, and don't retrieve all the messages to you, you can continue with the * command (same as flagged retrieval).

-- N -- News. Display system news, highlights.

-- O -- Other systems list. Updated regularly, is the nationally distributed P.A.M.S. list, a summary of all known Public Access Message Systems of all types, in alphabetical order. It can also be printer formatted by following the prompting. When asked to format, and your printer is not the standard 66 lines per page default of PMS but you still want to format to your printer, type the effective number of lines per page for your printer INSTEAD of a 'Y' response. You can also specify a string to look for within this file by typing O;search, where 'search' is the area code, or system name in question. All lines containing appropriate information will be displayed.

-- Q -- Quickscan of message headers. Not that much quicker. See also, 'S.'

--R -- Retrieve messages from the files. There are several modes here. You can select messages singly or in multiples. Examples of entries: R;381 or R381; R560;etc. To retrieve all messages starting from a certain point, type: R;555^ or R;1010+ (for example). See also the * command for flagged messages.

When you retrieve a message that is addressed to you, at the end of it, you'll drop to a secondary level with the option "Kill this message (y/n/a/u)." 'Y' means, yes, kill the message. 'N' means, no, don't kill it. 'A' means read it again. 'U' means to Unmark it. Unmarking a message removes it from your message alert section, but leaves it for others to read. You would use this if you wanted to leave a message containing useful information for others to read. You cannot, however, Unmark a private message, as others couldn't read it anyway.

You'll then be asked if you have a reply. If you do, answer yes, otherwise answer no. The automatic reply does some of the busywork for you (To: From: etc) and upon completion of the reply and saving the message, will continue with retrieving other messages you may have specified. During auto-reply, if you just type carriage return in response to 'Subject?', it will take the subject of the message that was to you and add a 'r/' to it, meaning reply to the previous message.

-- S -- Scan message headers. Here you specify a starting message number to start the scan. S;500 would start scanning at message 500 or the next highest if there is no message 500. You can also scan in reverse order by either specifying a number greater than or equal to the highest message number, or by adding a '–' (minus sign) directly AFTER the message number to start. Examples: S;500 S1200 S;1040– etc. As you are scanning you use 'R' to flag messages you want to read later with the * command. (See *.)

-- SR -- Selective retrieval. Use this command to retrieve all messages whose headers contain data you are looking for. As an example, if you enter FOR SALE, it would automatically retrieve all messages with FOR SALE in the header. This will work for ALL aspects of the header. FROM, TO, DATE, SUBJECT and LOCATION. All messages that meet these parameters are put in flagged memory and automatically retrieved. If there are no matches, it will tell you.

-- T -- Prints current local time and date, and the length of time since you logged on.

-- U -- User modifiable functions. These are parameters which affect certain default conditions of the system. You modify them to your current needs.

A) Apple 40 mode. Toggles between Apple 40 and 64 column message entry mode. Does not affect text output.

C) Case switch. Toggles between UPPER ONLY and UPPER/lower case text output. Lower case text is accepted during message entry and comments in either mode.

CS) Clear screen. Allows setting the character or sequence of characters that will cause the local terminal to clear its screen. In this mode, after each message has been displayed, the string 'more--' will display. The system will sit there and wait for a response from you. This is to keep the screen from clearing before you are ready to move on to the next message. Should you want to temporarily remove this option for the retrieval of a particular string of messages (say for printing them), you can type the letter 'N' at 'more--'. If you wish to abort the string of messages altogether, you can type 'K' or 'X.' You can then continue with *.

D) Duplex switch. Toggles between full (echo) and half (no echo) duplex modes.

L) Line feed switch. Turns linefeeds on or off. System default when your call is on.

N) Nulls. Displays the current number of nulls in effect, and allows you to modify them directly.

P) Prompt. Allows you to change the current system prompt, which is usually a '?' (a question mark). Here you can enter either the character you want the prompt to be or the ASCII value of it. The prompt will stay defined as such through all system functions, until you change it again, or log off. This feature can be used to good advantage with automatic upload or download programs (automatic message entry, etc).

T) Term - video/printer mode toggle. In the video mode, recognizes Control-H (backspace), delete (underscore) and rubout (ASCII Ø8, 95 and 127, respectively) as backspace characters and echoes backspace-space-backspace as destructive backspace. In the printer mode, the same characters are recognized, but during the backspacing additional reverse slashes and the characters being backspaced over will appear in reverse order.

PAR) Parity. Allows you to modify the word length, parity, and number of stop bits employed. Displays a little chart with 8 positions. One of them will have a circumflex (^) under it, indicating the current system default at that time. Examples of numbers could be: 7E1 or 8N2, etc. 7E1 means 7 bit word, even parity, and 1 stop bit. 8N2 would mean 8 bit word, no parity, and 2 stop bits, etc. Enter the position number 1-8 of the mode you need to use.

STAT) Displays current system status of all the modes covered by the 'U' function, so you can see your current setup.

-- X -- eXpert user mode. System default is on. Does away with the additional prompting at command level, the pausing between messages during a multiple retrieval and allows certain other privileges. However, when clear screen option is in effect (U;CS), the pausing between messages will return.

-- Z -- Allows you to resume entering a message after you have aborted it. Let's say you were entering a message and realized you had forgotten something relevant to that message and needed to reread an earlier message or article. You can abort the message, reread the other messages or articles and then re-enter your message with all data intact, and continue. Should you be disconnected while entering a message, and you are the very next caller calling back, the system will ask if you want to continue the message. Answering 'yes' will list the message so far and allow you to pick up from there. If you were in abort when carrier was lost and call right back, the system will not ask about continuing the message, but you can with the 'Z' command. Also your flagged messages will be preserved if losing carrier occurs during flagged retrieval. Just continue with*.

-- ? -- Prints a list of all commands available at your current level of operation.

-- * -- Retrieve messages in flagged memory. This can be messages flagged during a scan or using the 'M' or 'SR' function. You may pick up where you left off with this command, if you ended your retrieval for any reason. Using this command with scanning messages (such as S;1000*) will clear the flagged memory completely for starting fresh.

Those calling with USERIDs will be able to retain various parameters of their last visit to the system automatically. All parameters set by U;STAT except nulls are retained in the USERID system plus the highest message number of each visit. After logging in, if you would like to scan messages starting from the highest of the last visit, type 'S;!'. If you would rather just retrieve all those messages, type 'R;!'. If you do not access S;! or R;!, your message marker will not be updated.

* * MESSAGE ENTRY COMMANDS * *

Note: All the following commands can be issued as DOT commands. A dot command may be entered as '.A' or '.E' or whatever the desired command is, as long as the dot is the first character throughout message entry.

-- A -- Abort message and return to command level. You may continue your message with the 'Z' command.

-- C -- Continue with message entry. Allows you to continue your message at whatever the next line in succession would be.

-- D -- Delete a line. Specify the number of the line you wish to delete. D;x and Dx are legal here. (x = line number.)

-- E -- Edit or retype a mesage line (Ex or E;x also legal). To replace the line, just enter the new line. Editing a line is accomplished by specifying a string you want to replace with what you want to replace it with, in this form: OLD/NEW with old and new string separated by a slash. You can also use three slashes as in the old editing routine: /OLD/NEW/. To remove a section of text, type: OLD// or /OLD//.

To insert text at the beginning of a line, type: <this is new text. The

left arrow means insert at the beginning. To append text at the end of a line, type: >this is new text. The right arrow means append at the end. If you type a Control-S (Control-S only) as the first character of the line, the contents of the line will be automatically centered. If you are modifying an existing line and just type a Control-S by itself, whatever is already on that line will be centered. Control-S as the first character of a line will also work during regular line entry (not just during edit).

One eccentricity of this type of editing is that the '/' (slash) character cannot be contained within the text you are actually editing. It would be necessary to retype the new line up to the '/' and then append ('>') at the end of that section.

Should the line you are editing get mangled beyond recognition, you can type '!' (exclamation point) on the line by itself, and the original line will be reinstated as it was when you first started the edit.

-- I -- Insert a line (Ix or I;x also legal). Allows you to insert a line directly BEFORE whatever line # you specify.

-- S -- Save the completed masterpiece to disk. You MUST use this command for your message to be saved!

-- W -- reWrite an old message. Using this command, you can kill an older message (with the correct password, of course) with the contents of it appearing in the message you are currently entering. The old message lines will be appended to your current position in the message. As an example, if you were at line 10 of a message, and wanted some data that was in an old message, use 'W.' The contents of the message you killed will start at line 10. You can then edit or modify as required, then save it.

General Index

System/Command Index

COLLECTORS DATA SERVICE (CDS), 56–99

COMPUSERVE INFORMATION SERVICE (CIS) 100–222

DELPHI, 221–228

DOW JONES NEWS/RETRIEVAL SERVICE (DJNRS) 229–262

EASYLINK, 263–287

KNOWLEDGE INDEX 288–304

MCI MAIL, 305–324

NEWSNET, 325–348

PLAYNET, 349–356

THE SOURCE, 357–397

GAMEMASTER, 398–405

MICROSHARE, 406–409

STARTEXT, 409–416

ABBS, 428–436

Cross-Reference Index

To order use coupon on next page.